Taxing Corporate Income in the 21st Century

Most countries levy taxes on corporations, but the impact – and therefore the wisdom – of such taxes is highly controversial among economists. Does the burden of these taxes fall on wealthy shareowners, or is it passed along to those who work for, or buy the products of, corporations? Can a country with high corporate taxes remain competitive in the global economy? This book features state-of-the-art research by leading economists and accountants that sheds light on these and related questions, including how taxes affect corporate dividend policy, stock market value, avoidance, and evasion. The studies promise to inform both future tax policy and regulatory policy, especially in light of the Sarbanes-Oxley Act and other actions by the Securities and Exchange Commission that are having profound effects on the market for tax planning and auditing in the wake of the well-publicized accounting scandals in Enron and WorldCom.

Alan J. Auerbach is the Robert D. Burch Professor of Economics and Law, Director of the Burch Center for Tax Policy and Public Finance, and former Chair of the Economics Department at the University of California, Berkeley. He taught at Harvard and the University of Pennsylvania before moving to California. Professor Auerbach is a Research Associate of the National Bureau of Economic Research and was Deputy Chief of Staff on the U.S. Congress's Joint Committee on Taxation in 1992. He has served as a member of the Executive Committee and as Vice President of the American Economic Association and is a Fellow of the Econometric Society and of the American Academy of Arts and Sciences. Professor Auerbach is a member of the Advisory Committee, Bureau of Economic Analysis, U.S. Department of Commerce; the Revenue Estimating Review Panel of the U.S. Congress's Joint Committee on Taxation; and the Board of Academic Advisors of the International Tax Policy Forum. He is the editor or co-editor of 10 books and the author or co-author of 3 books.

James R. Hines Jr. is the Richard A. Musgrave Collegiate Professor of Economics in the department of economics and Professor of Law in the law school at the University of Michigan. He also serves as Research Director of the business school's Office of Tax Policy Research. He taught at Princeton and Harvard prior to moving to Michigan in 1997 and has held visiting appointments at Columbia, the London School of Economics, and Harvard Law School. He is a research associate of the National Bureau of Economic Research, research director of the International Tax Policy Forum, and co-editor of the American Economic Association's *Journal of Economic Perspectives* and was an economist in the U.S. Department of Commerce.

Joel Slemrod is the Paul W. McCracken Collegiate Professor of Business Economics and Public Policy at the Stephen M. Ross School of Business at the University of Michigan and also serves as Director of the Office of Tax Policy Research, an interdisciplinary research center housed at the Ross School. Professor Slemrod was a National Fellow at the Hoover Institution and in 1984–1985 was the senior staff economist for tax policy at the President's Council of Economic Advisers. He has also been a consultant to the U.S. Department of Treasury, the Canadian Department of Finance, the New Zealand Department of Treasury, the South African Ministry of Finance, the World Bank, and the Organisation for Economic Co-Operation and Development (OECD). He is a member of the Joint Committee on Taxation Revenue Estimating Board and has testified before Congress on domestic and international taxation issues. From 1992 to 1998, Professor Slemrod was editor of the *National Tax Journal*. He is the editor or co-editor of 10 books and the co-author, with Jon Bakija, of *Taxing Ourselves: A Citizen's Guide to the Debate over Taxes*, now in its third edition.

Taxing Corporate Income in the 21st Century

ALAN J. AUERBACH

University of California, Berkeley

JAMES R. HINES JR.

University of Michigan

JOEL SLEMROD

University of Michigan

CAMBRIDGE
UNIVERSITY PRESS

CAMBRIDGE UNIVERSITY PRESS
Cambridge, New York, Melbourne, Madrid, Cape Town, Singapore, São Paulo

Cambridge University Press
32 Avenue of the Americas, New York, NY 10013-2473, USA

www.cambridge.org
Information on this title: www.cambridge.org/9780521870221

First published 2007

Printed in the United States of America

A catalog record for this publication is available from the British Library.

Library of Congress Cataloging in Publication Data
Auerbach, Alan J.
Taxing corporate income in the 21st century / Alan J. Auerbach, James R.
Hines Jr., Joel Slemrod.
p.   cm.
Includes bibliographical references and index.
ISBN-13: 978-0-521-87022-1 (hardback)
ISBN-10: 0-521-87022-4 (hardback)
1. Corporations–United States–Taxation.   I. Hines, James R.
II. Slemrod, Joel.   III. Title.
HD2753.U6A18   2006
336.2–dc22   2006015961

ISBN   978-0-521-87022-1 hardback

Contents

Contents

Contributors

Alan J. Auerbach
University of California, Berkeley, and NBER

Joseph Bankman
Stanford University

Stephen R. Bond
Institute for Fiscal Studies and Nuffield College, Oxford

Jeffrey R. Brown
University of Illinois at Urbana-Champaign and NBER

Donald Bruce
University of Tennessee

Raj Chetty
University of California, Berkeley, and NBER

Mihir A. Desai
Harvard University and NBER

John Deskins
Creighton University

Michael P. Devereux
University of Warwick and Institute for Fiscal Studies

Dhammika Dharmapala
University of Connecticut

Brian Erard
B. Erard and Associates

Contributors

William F. Fox
University of Tennessee

Winnie Fung
Harvard University

William G. Gale
The Brookings Institution

William M. Gentry
Williams College

Roger Gordon
University of California, San Diego, and NBER

Jane Gravelle
Congressional Research Service

Jonathan Gruber
Massachusetts Institute of Technology and NBER

Gustavo Grullon
Rice University

Michelle Hanlon
University of Michigan

Kevin A. Hassett
American Enterprise Institute

James R. Hines Jr.
University of Michigan and NBER

Steven N. Kaplan
Graduate School of Business, University of Chicago

Alexander Klemm
Institute for Fiscal Studies and University College, London

Edward L. Maydew
University of North Carolina

Charles E. McLure Jr.
Hoover Institution, Stanford University

Lillian Mills
University of Texas

Contributors

Jack M. Mintz
University of Toronto

Casey B. Mulligan
University of Chicago

James Poterba
Massachusetts Institute of Technology and NBER

Joshua Rauh
University of Chicago and NBER

Joseph Rosenberg
University of California, Berkeley

Emmanuel Saez
University of California, Berkeley, and NBER

Richard Sansing
Tuck School of Business at Dartmouth and Tilburg University

Douglas A. Shackelford
University of North Carolina and NBER

Douglas J. Skinner
Graduate School of Business, University of Chicago

Joel Slemrod
University of Michigan

Jeff Strnad
Stanford University

John Douglas Wilson
Michigan State University

George R. Zodrow
Rice University

Preface

Modern governments have taxed income earned by corporations for as long as they have taxed income earned by individuals, yet the economic effects of corporate income taxation remain shrouded in mystery, and the appropriate role of corporate income taxation in generating significant government revenue is as unclear now as it ever was. At the onset of the 21st century, governments continue to rely on corporate income taxes as important revenue sources, the product of uneasy compromises between some forces that would reduce, and others that would increase, the tax burden on corporations.

The ability, and evident willingness, of corporations to locate and structure their activities to avoid corporate income taxes is always an important consideration in the design of corporate tax policy. Governments in an increasingly competitive world face pressures to reduce their tax rates, lest corporations relocate their activities elsewhere in search of more hospitable tax climates. Quite apart from their relocation incentives, high corporate tax rates encourage firms to undertake transactions designed to reduce taxes rather than stimulate productivity and may also have the undesired effect of discouraging business formation and expansion. In most countries, corporate income may be taxed twice – first when earned by corporations and second when received as dividends by taxable individual shareholders – which, in the eyes of some, is unfair, inefficient, and just cause for significant reduction of either corporate- or shareholder-level taxation. These considerations must be weighed against the ability of corporate taxation to provide revenues for cash-strapped treasuries and the largely unappetizing features of many alternative revenue sources.

With the appropriate taxation of corporations an unsettled issue, it is not surprising that recent events involving the corporate sector have significantly affected tax policy. The accounting scandals that engulfed major corporations in the United States and around the world, together with press attention to the use of questionable tax shelters, sparked a reexamination of the corporation income tax and, indeed, the very governance of corporations. The tax shelter publicity led in 2002 to the Sarbanes-Oxley bill in the United States, requiring taxpayers to disclose potentially questionable transactions on their tax returns and requiring promoters to maintain customer lists for the same transactions. Most significantly, the Jobs and Growth Tax Relief Reconciliation Act of 2003 contained the most fundamental change since the inception of the income tax in how corporate-source income is taxed, by limiting the personal tax rate on dividends and capital gains to 15 percent.

Although the public discussion of corporate accounting problems was quite separate from those about corporate governance and corporate tax changes, several connections link these debates. At a political level, the weakened public image of corporate America may explain why the 2003 legislation did not include a reduction in the corporation tax rate. Through its reduction of the shareholder level tax on dividends, advocates argued that the 2003 bill would induce companies to increase dividends paid, thereby reducing the power of corporate directors and officers to make decisions at variance with shareholder interests. These legislative developments have proceeded in the absence of much theoretical or empirical study of the interaction among corporations' accounting, financial, and operating decisions on the one hand and the tax, accounting, and governance rules on the other hand. As an example, whereas it is clear that some corporations are willing to incur higher tax liabilities as the cost of reporting higher earnings to shareholders, the magnitude of this practice, and its implications for tax policy, remain open questions. Even the effect of a dividend tax reduction on total dividend payouts in the economy is not known for certain.

In an effort to contribute to this ongoing rethinking of the corporate income tax, the Office of Tax Policy Research at the Stephen M. Ross School of Business at the University of Michigan, in partnership with the Robert D. Burch Center for Tax Policy and Public Finance at the University of California, Berkeley, commissioned nine studies on the issues surrounding the corporation income tax. These papers were presented at a conference held at the Stephen M. Ross School of Business on May 5–6, 2005. This volume presents the nine commissioned papers, each followed by the remarks delivered at the conference by two formal commentators.

Preface

The editors thank the Lynde and Harry Bradley Foundation and Mr. Frank Gray for providing financial support for this conference, and Mary Ceccanese for her leading role in organizing the conference and coordinating the preparation of this volume.

Alan J. Auerbach
James R. Hines Jr.
Joel Slemrod

The Effects of Taxes on Market Responses to Dividend Announcements and Payments: What Can We Learn from the 2003 Dividend Tax Cut?*

Raj Chetty

University of California, Berkeley and NBER

Joseph Rosenberg

University of California, Berkeley

Emmanuel Saez

University of California, Berkeley and NBER

1. Introduction

There is a long-standing debate in the finance and public economics literatures about the role of taxation in corporate dividend payout policies. Starting with Elton and Gruber (1970), researchers have investigated whether
the tax-favored treatment of capital gains relative to dividends affects excess
returns on ex-dividend and announcement dates.[1] The answers to these
questions can potentially shed light on the efficiency consequences of dividend taxation as well as the reasons why corporations pay dividends despite
their tax disadvantage, as explained in greater detail below.[2] Despite substantial research, the empirical literature on this topic remains controversial
(see Allen and Michaely, 2003 for a recent survey).

---

[1] The ex-day is the date at which the dividend leaves the share.
[2] Note, however, that ex-dividend day price behavior does not allow us to distinguish the old
view from the new view of dividend payout policies (see Auerbach, 1983).

* Raj Chetty, chetty@econ.Berkeley.edu; Joseph Rosenberg, jwr@econ.berkeley.edu; and
Emmanuel Saez, saez@econ.berkeley.edu; University of California, Department of Economics,
549 Evans Hall, Room 3880, Berkeley, CA 94720. We thank Alan Auerbach, Douglas Bernheim,
Gustavo Grullon, Francisco Perez-Gonzalez, James Poterba, Douglas Skinner, and Joel Slemrod for helpful comments and discussions. Financial support from NSF Grant SES-0134946
and the Sloan Foundation is gratefully acknowledged.

This paper proposes to use the 2003 dividend tax cut in the United States to cast light on these issues. The 2003 tax cut, part of the Jobs and Growth Tax Relief Reconciliation Act of 2003, eliminated most of the tax disadvantage of dividends relative to capital gains. Blouin et al. (2004) and Chetty and Saez (2005) have shown that the reform indeed raised dividend payments significantly and in particular induced many firms to initiate dividend payments. Here, we aim to investigate whether this reform had a significant effect on the ex-day and announcement-day price behavior as well. Consistent with the no-arbitrage conditions in standard models, we find that the ex-dividend day premium increased from 2002 to 2004, when the dividend tax rate was cut. Consistent with the signaling theory of dividends (and in contradiction with the agency models of dividends), we find that the excess return for dividend increase announcements went down from 2002 to 2004.

In order to have a broader perspective and assess with greater confidence whether there was a sharp change after 2003, we construct a time series of ex-day price changes and excess returns around dividend increase announcements at an annual level since 1962 (the first year daily price data became available) for all companies in the Center for Research in Security Prices (CRSP) data. To the best of our knowledge, despite the large number of studies on these issues, such a time series had not been constructed and examined in prior work. A number of useful findings emerge from this long-run analysis.

First, we find that there is substantial year-to-year volatility in the annual time series of excess returns around both the ex-day and announcement day that is unrelated to tax changes. The annual variation in the time series is not simply due to idiosyncratic firm level noise, because this variation should be averaged out given the very large samples we are using. Powerful year effects (aggregate shocks) unrelated to taxes are responsible for this pattern. Unfortunately, the time-series pattern is non-monotonic and therefore is unlikely to be explained by a single change (such as the elimination of discrete pricing in the U.S. stock market) or by a gradual trend (such as the rise of the share of corporate stocks owned by pension funds). Moreover, we are unable to find a set of covariates that had much explanatory power in smoothing the aggregate fluctuations. A simple power analysis shows that even the effects of large tax reforms would be difficult to detect given the aggregate volatility of the series. We conclude that one should be careful when comparing individual years (e.g., around a reform) to detect a tax effect. The 2003 tax change illustrates this point well. As mentioned above, the ex-day premium pattern suggests a strong tax effect if one compares

2002 to 2004, but a placebo test comparing 2002 to 2000 would produce a false positive.

Second, the long-run time pattern of the ex-day price behavior does not follow the long-run reduction in the advantage of capital gains versus dividends. Therefore, overall it is difficult to detect any robust pattern that one could attribute with confidence to a tax effect along the lines that Elton and Gruber (1970) originally proposed. More work is needed to test the various theories of ex-day price changes using the full time-series evidence rather than a focus on particular years, as has been the tradition in the literature.

Third, consistent with the empirical results of the influential study by Bernheim and Wantz (1995), we find that the overall effect of dividend increase announcements on prices has declined over time while the tax disadvantage of dividends has fallen. This finding supports the signaling theory of dividend payments, which argues that firms pay dividends despite their tax disadvantage in order to send a signal to the market about their profitability. However, again because of the large year-to-year variation in the time series of price effects, it is impossible to detect systematic effects around the major tax reforms in the United States since 1962, including the 2003 dividend tax cut. Therefore, the conclusion supporting the signaling theory rests on the strong assumption that no other long-term trend has driven the price effects down. However, it is quite plausible that factors other than tax changes (such as the increased availability of information about corporate activities) could have caused the secular decline in announcement premiums.

Our general assessment is therefore that little knowledge about tax effects can be gained even from large reforms such as the 2003 tax cut because of the extreme aggregate volatility in the time series of the data. The estimates of prior studies – which obtain significant results by making strong assumptions about the functional form or statistical properties of the error terms in regressions or by focusing on particular windows around tax changes – should therefore be viewed with caution. To be clear, we are not advocating time-series analysis instead of focusing on sharp tax experiments. Rather, we argue that credible empirical analysis requires examination of whether the changes in excess returns around a tax experiment are exceptional relative to the fluctuations in a long time series.

The remainder of the paper is organized as follows. Section 2 presents the conceptual framework and discusses previous work. Section 3 describes the data and our methodology. Sections 4 and 5 present the empirical results on ex-dividend premiums and dividend increase announcements, respectively. Section 6 describes the main methodological conclusions that we draw from this analysis.

2. Conceptual Framework and Previous Work

Dividend payments affect short-term stock price behavior in two ways. First, firms announce dividend payments about four to six weeks before the actual payment is made. Announcements of dividend initiations (by a firm starting to pay dividends) or dividend increases (by a firm already paying dividends) are generally viewed as good news and generate, on average, a positive excess return around the announcement date (see Allen and Michaely, 2003 for a survey). This is because increases in regular dividend payments are perceived by the market as a strong commitment to pay more dividends in the future. Historically, regular dividend payments (in general, quarterly, but sometimes annual or semi-annual) tend to be very smooth: Firms do not increase their dividend payments very often, and they are extremely reluctant to decrease or terminate dividend payments.

Second, when the dividend is paid, the book value of the corporation is reduced by the amount paid out, which generates a negative excess return around the payment event. More precisely, when a corporation announces a dividend payment, it sets two key dates: the ex-dividend date and the payment date. The payment date is the date when the corporation effectively pays out the dividend and is in general about two weeks after the ex-dividend date. Dividends, however, are paid out to stockholders according to stock ownership just before the ex-dividend date (and not according to stock ownership at the time of payment). In other words, a stockholder is entitled to the dividend payment if and only if he or she owns the stock just before the start of the ex-dividend day.[3] Therefore, we should expect a drop in price between the end of day preceding the ex-day (sometimes called the "cum-day" to mean that the stock is trading *with* the dividend on that day) and the beginning of the ex-day because those buying the stock after the beginning of the ex-day are no longer entitled to the dividend payment.

The effects of dividend announcements and ex-dates on stock prices can be nicely illustrated with the extremely large special dividend payment of $3 per share made by Microsoft at the end of 2004. This special dividend (along with a doubling of the regular dividend) was announced on July 20, 2004.[4] One can clearly see in Figure 1 that the share price rose quickly in the days surrounding the announcement (illustrated with vertical lines in

---

[3] An individual purchasing the stock between the ex-day and payment day would not receive the dividend, but the former owner would.

[4] On the same day, Microsoft announced an increase in its regular dividend payment. Microsoft had previously paid an annual dividend of 16 cents per share and announced that it was switching to quarterly payments of 8 cents per share, effectively doubling its regular dividend payments.

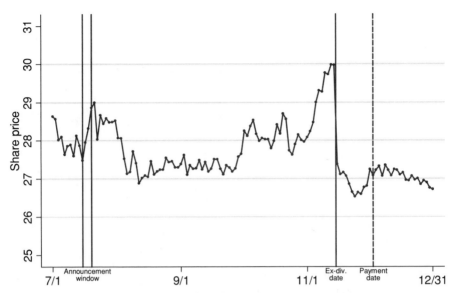

Figure 1. Microsoft Dividend Announcement and Ex-Day Price Effects

The Figure reports the daily closing prices of Microsoft shares from July 1, 2005 to December 31, 2005 from CRSP data. On July 20, Microsoft announced a doubling of its regular dividend payment as well as the payment of a very large one-time special dividend of $3 per share. The three-day window around the announcement date, which is used to estimate abnormal returns, is depicted by the first two vertical lines. The ex-day for the $3 special dividend is November 15. The drop in price from the cum-day (November 14) to the ex-day (November 15) is depicted by the third vertical line. The payment date, December 2, is also depicted by a dashed line.

Figure 1). This jump represents the "excess return" around the announcement date, which we define formally below. The ex-dividend day for the special dividend was set as November 15, 2004. Hence, all individuals and institutions owning Microsoft shares before the start of November 15, 2004 were entitled to a $3 dividend per share. The sharp drop in the price at this time is consistent with the negative excess return that we expect around the ex-date. Finally, dividend payments were made by Microsoft to those shareholders on December 2, 2004 (irrespective of whether they had sold their stock after November 15).

Our analysis roughly seeks to answer the question "How would the excess returns around the announcement and ex-dates in the Microsoft figure have differed if these events had occurred prior to the 2003 tax cut?" We answer this question essentially by averaging excess returns around the ex-day and announcement dates for many firms and comparing the means during different tax regimes. Because the timing of the tax change is quite important for our analysis, it will be helpful to review the details of the reform here. The Jobs and Growth Tax Relief Reconciliation Act of 2003 introduced favorable treatment for individual dividend income whereby dividends are taxed at a rate of 15 percent instead of facing the regular progressive individual income tax schedule with a top rate of 35 percent.[5] The reform was officially signed into law on May 28, 2003, but was first proposed by the Bush administration on January 7, 2003.[6] The tax cut on dividend income was made retroactive to the beginning of 2003. Therefore, during the first two quarters of 2003, corporations knew that dividends would face lower taxes with some probability. President Bush initially proposed a full exemption of dividend taxation at the individual level, potentially biasing pre-enactment expectations toward a larger tax reduction than what actually occurred. The tax rate on long-term realized capital gains was also reduced by the Jobs and Growth Tax Relief Reconciliation Act of 2003, but the reduction was smaller, from 20 percent to 15 percent, and applied only to capital gains realized after May 28, 2003. Thus, this change reduced significantly the tax disadvantage of dividends relative to capital gains. The tax cut is scheduled to expire by 2009, but it could be made permanent during the second Bush administration.

2.1. Ex-Dividend Day Returns and Taxes

The profit from selling at the end of cum-day (just preceding the ex-day) should equal the profit from selling at the beginning of the ex-day in order to eliminate arbitrage opportunities. In a world without taxes, this would mean that the drop in share price around the ex-day should equal the dividend per share. However, as first recognized by Elton and Gruber (1970), dividend and capital gains taxation can prevent this equality from holding. Ignoring overnight interest, the no-arbitrage condition with taxes is:

$$P_B - t_g(P_B - P_0) = P_A - t_g(P_A - P_0) + D(1 - t_d), \qquad (1)$$

[5] More precisely, taxpayers in the bottom two income tax brackets (facing a regular marginal tax rate of 10 or 15 percent) face a new dividend tax rate of 5 percent, while taxpayers in the top four brackets (facing marginal tax rates of 25, 28, 33, or 35 percent) face a new dividend tax rate of 15 percent. Taxpayers on the Alternative Minimum Tax schedule (flat rate of 28 percent) benefit from the reduced 15 percent tax rate on their dividend income as well. Individual dividend income earned through tax-favored accounts such as 401(k)s and dividend income earned by government agencies, non-profit organizations, and corporations are not affected by the tax change.

[6] Auerbach and Hassett (2007) discuss the timing of the tax reform legislative process in detail. They find that the reduction of dividend taxation was not discussed seriously before the end of 2002. It was not mentioned in the Bush 2000 campaign platform either, suggesting that there was no anticipation that such a tax change would take place before the very end of 2002.

where

P_A is the stock price cum-dividend (just before the ex-dividend day starts),
P_B is the expected stock price on the ex-day,
P_0 is the stock price at initial purchase (tax base),
D is dividend amount per share,
t_g is the tax rate on realized capital gains, and
t_d is the tax rate on dividend income.
Rearranging equation (1), we obtain:

$$\frac{P_A - P_B}{D} = \frac{1 - t_d}{1 - t_g} \equiv \rho. \tag{2}$$

The left-hand side of this expression is called the *ex-day premium*. The right-hand side variable captures the differential tax treatment of dividends versus realized capital gains and is called the *ex-day tax preference ratio*, which we denote by ρ. Without taxes, the premium is expected to be equal to one: The price falls by the exact amount of the dividend premium.[7]

Figure 1 depicts the case of the large $3 special dividend payment from Microsoft. This special payment represented about 10 percent of the share price value and thus was large relative to day-to-day variation in stock prices, making the ex-dividend day drop in price clearly visible on the graph.[8] The drop in price is $2.58, generating a premium of 0.86. This value is fairly close to the value of one predicted by equation (2) in 2004, when the statutory rates for dividends and long-term realized capital gains were equal.[9]

There is a controversial debate in the literature about whether taxes actually affect the premium as in equation (2). Traditionally, the individual tax rate of dividend income has been substantially higher than the individual tax rate on (long-term) realized capital gains. Elton and Gruber (1970) estimated premiums for U.S. corporations in 1966–7 lower than one and argued that the differential tax could explain those results. Consistent with this claim, Barclay (1987) showed that the premium was not significantly

---

[7] This simple derivation hides complexities that can arise if the marginal investor considers *buying* (instead of selling) just before or after the ex-day. If the resulting capital loss incurred at the ex-day can be offset against capital gains, the same premium formula applies. The premium formula would be different, however, if the capital loss could not be offset or was offset against ordinary income.

[8] Most dividend payments are small relative to day-to-day price variations, making the drop in price impossible to detect looking at a single firm price series.

[9] More precisely, the rates were 15 percent for taxable individuals who had owned the stock at least one year. Hence, we would observe a premium equal to one if only taxable individuals had been trading.

different from one in the United States before the individual income tax was introduced in 1913, but it was significantly below one in 1962–5, when the tax differential was large. However, Michaely (1991) found no significant increase in the premium around the Tax Reform Act of 1986 (TRA86), which eliminated the favorable tax treatment of realized capital gains and thereby raised ρ sharply.[10]

One limitation of equation (2), which could explain why it fails to explain observed premiums well, is that it assumes that all agents face the same tax rates. In practice, however, there is substantial heterogeneity in the tax preferences of shareholders, as pointed out by Michaely (1991). Table 1 reports the overall ex-day tax preference ratio weighted by share of stock ownership in the U.S. economy. The estimates are based on Poterba (2004) as well as an unpublished appendix series kindly made available to us by the author.[11] Long-term individual owners in high-income tax brackets have typically faced a tax preference less than one. The tax ratio was equal to one briefly after TRA86 and again after the 2003 dividend tax cut. All non-taxable institutions – such as pension funds and individual pension accounts (IRAs and 401(k)s), nonprofit organizations, and government agencies, as well as individuals holding stock for the short term – have faced a tax ratio equal to one. In contrast, corporations have typically faced a ratio above one because only a fraction of dividend income received by a corporation is taxable and realized capital gains made by a corporation are fully taxable at normal rates.

A number of studies (see, e.g., Auerbach, 1983 in the public economics literature or, more recently, Michaely and Villa, 1995 in the finance literature) have developed models with heterogeneous risk-averse investors. Those studies show that equation (2) can be generalized. In that case, the premium equals the average of the tax ratios weighted by risk tolerance. Kalay (1982) and Eades, Hess, and Kim (1984) point out that discreteness in prices may cause a bias in measuring the ex-day price drop relative to the dividend (until recently, the minimum tick size was one-eighth in the United States). This bias may cause the average price drop to be less than

---

[10] Similarly, Lakonishok and Vermaelen (1983) did not find that the premium moved in the expected direction following a tax change in Canada. Poterba and Summers (1984), however, did find evidence consistent with the predicted tax effect in the case of the United Kingdom.

[11] Poterba (2004) includes only 25 percent of the statutory realized capital gains tax rate because he wants to estimate the effective burden on accrued capital gains. For the ex-dividend date tax ratio, however, the statutory tax rate on realized capital gains is the relevant one, and this is what we use for our analysis of ex-day premiums.

Table 1. *Ex-Dividend Day Statistics and Results*

Year	(1) Tax Preference (ρ)	(2) Number of Events	(3) Median Premium	(4) Weighted-Mean Premium	(5) Trimmed-Mean Premium
1963	0.80	4,089	0.95	0.95	0.95
1964	0.81	4,418	0.95	0.98	0.97
1965	0.81	4,767	0.91	0.89	0.85
1966	0.82	5,029	0.89	0.95	0.90
1967	0.82	5,259	0.85	0.81	0.84
1968	0.80	4,697	0.88	0.74	0.69
1969	0.81	5,074	0.74	0.71	0.67
1970	0.82	4,910	0.71	0.69	0.66
1971	0.84	4,851	0.81	0.78	0.76
1972	0.83	4,974	0.85	0.81	0.85
1973	0.84	5,232	0.84	0.90	0.90
1974	0.85	5,317	0.87	0.89	0.89
1975	0.86	5,451	0.96	0.93	0.91
1976	0.83	5,782	0.97	0.97	0.98
1977	0.84	6,234	1.02	1.03	1.02
1978	0.84	6,347	1.03	1.05	1.08
1979	0.84	6,034	1.00	0.97	0.96
1980	0.84	6,035	1.05	0.99	0.99
1981	0.86	5,712	0.94	0.89	0.88
1982	0.90	5,239	0.85	0.84	0.82
1983	0.91	5,404	0.83	0.80	0.76
1984	0.91	5,977	0.76	0.76	0.75
1985	0.92	6,813	0.67	0.67	0.64
1986	0.92	7,345	0.79	0.80	0.70
1987	1.00	7,498	0.83	0.83	0.75
1988	1.02	7,432	0.81	0.76	0.67
1989	1.02	7,334	0.76	0.77	0.69
1990	1.01	6,882	0.75	0.69	0.67
1991	1.01	6,484	0.88	0.80	0.79
1992	1.01	6,807	0.80	0.80	0.79
1993	0.99	7,231	0.87	0.85	0.76
1994	0.99	7,594	0.83	0.81	0.76
1995	0.99	8,030	0.69	0.61	0.56
1996	0.99	8,022	0.74	0.67	0.61
1997	0.96	7,764	0.68	0.63	0.62
1998	0.93	6,984	0.66	0.56	0.55
1999	0.93	7,190	0.70	0.61	0.64

(*continued*)

Table 1 *(continued)*

	(1)	(2)	(3)	(4)	(5)
Year	Tax Preference (ρ)	Number of Events	Median Premium	Weighted-Mean Premium	Trimmed-Mean Premium
2000	0.94	6,058	0.46	0.39	0.32
2001	0.95	5,661	0.47	0.43	0.39
2002	0.95	5,905	0.61	0.60	0.45
2003	1.02	6,147	0.69	0.64	0.57
2004	1.02	6,347	0.74	0.81	0.77
Std deviation	*0.08*		*0.14*	*0.15*	*0.17*
Total	0.90	256,360	0.81	0.79	0.76

Column (1) reports the tax preference ratio $\rho = (1 - t_d)/(1 - t_g)$ measuring the tax preference of realized capital gains over dividends for U.S. corporate stock (weighted by ownership) from 1963 to 2004. This ratio is constructed based on the data appendix from Poterba (2004).

Column (2) reports the annual number of ex-dividend days in the sample for all taxable regular and special dividends.

Columns (3), (4), and (5) report the corresponding time-series measures of the (market-adjusted) dividend premium $\Delta P/D$. Column (3) reports the median. Column (4) reports the dividend-yield weighted mean. Column (5) reports the mean (trimmed for the smallest 25 percent dividend yield events).

the dividend amount. In principle, these other effects should not eliminate the tax effects, but rather describe other channels that can potentially affect ex-day premiums.

2.2. Dividend Increase Announcement-Day Returns and Taxes

Corporations distribute profits to shareholders in two main forms: dividends and share repurchases. In a world without taxes and with perfect information, share repurchases and dividends are equivalent. However, the market appears to treat these two forms of payout very differently in practice. Reducing or terminating regular dividend payments carries a very negative signal and is heavily penalized by investors. In contrast, share repurchases (or one-time special dividend payments) are not seen as a commitment to continue paying in the future, and accordingly announcements of repurchases generate far lower excess returns than announcements of dividends.

   One reason that these two forms of payout may not be equivalent in the current equilibrium is that their tax treatment differs. Under U.S. tax law, realized capital gains have traditionally been taxed more lightly than dividend income, making share repurchases a more tax efficient way of distributing profits. The relative tax disadvantage of dividends relative to capital gains (repurchases) can be measured using the tax preference parameter constructed by Poterba (2004). This tax ratio is estimated as the average across all types of shareholders in the U.S. economy and weighted by ownership of $(1 - t_d)/(1 - t_{ac})$ where t_d is the *marginal* tax rate on dividend income and t_{ac} is the *effective* tax rate on capital gains. This effective rate measures the real tax rate on capital gains on an accrual equivalent basis. It should not be confused with the actual rate on realized capital gains that we used above. Because of tax deferral (or no tax at all if capital gains are not realized before death), the effective rate is much lower than the statutory rate. We denote this deferral-adjusted tax preference parameter by θ and report its time series in Table 2.

Share repurchases became more common following an SEC ruling in 1982 that clarified the rules under which corporations could legally make share repurchases without being subject to dividend taxation (Grullon and Michaely, 2002). Despite the rise in share repurchases, dividends remain an important conduit for distributing profits. That dividends have not been entirely replaced by share repurchases has been termed the "dividend puzzle." The literature has proposed two main theories to resolve this puzzle: the signaling theory and the agency theory. Bernheim and Wantz (1995) pointed out that the effect of taxes on announcement premiums could be used to test theories of dividend payment. Allen and Michaely (2003) provide an extensive survey of this literature, which we summarize below.

Under the signaling theory (see Bernheim and Wantz, 1995) for a clear exposition), dividends serve as a costly signal of a firm's profits prospects. Firms effectively burn money in the form of dividend payments (because they incur a higher tax burden than if they repurchased shares) to signal to the market their profitability. Higher-profits firms are able to burn more money and therefore in equilibrium dividends indeed signal profitability. If the relative tax of dividends versus realized capital gains increases, it is more costly to pay dividends. Therefore, the market reaction to dividend increases should be stronger when θ is low.

Under the agency theory (see, e.g., Jensen and Meckling, 1976), there is a conflict of interest between management and stockholders. In this context, dividends can be seen as a device to prevent managers from spending the earnings of the corporation in inefficient projects (e.g., pet projects or empire building). Increasing the dividend tax rate relative to realized capital gains

Table 2. *Dividend Increase Announcements Statistics and Results*

Year	(1) Tax Preference (θ)	(2) Number of Events	(3) Median Premium	(4) Weighted-Mean Premium	(5) Trimmed-Mean Premium
1963	0.68	307	6.05	7.59	6.78
1964	0.69	531	5.78	5.45	7.47
1965	0.70	679	6.18	5.83	8.26
1966	0.71	667	8.31	8.98	11.00
1967	0.71	490	7.25	8.07	11.25
1968	0.68	390	6.80	8.11	10.78
1969	0.70	368	11.71	10.65	15.93
1970	0.72	293	10.48	7.37	9.04
1971	0.74	245	5.36	5.95	8.40
1972	0.74	491	11.84	10.73	13.82
1973	0.74	1,119	3.98	6.13	9.53
1974	0.75	932	5.91	7.07	10.51
1975	0.76	707	5.18	6.43	9.80
1976	0.73	1,264	6.98	7.53	9.44
1977	0.74	1,397	6.83	7.21	8.13
1978	0.74	1,388	6.14	6.68	7.54
1979	0.73	1,270	5.98	7.27	7.03
1980	0.73	1,077	5.40	6.17	5.51
1981	0.75	902	5.57	6.70	7.94
1982	0.80	645	4.70	7.09	6.51
1983	0.81	707	6.89	9.61	13.01
1984	0.82	868	4.24	4.28	5.92
1985	0.82	1,045	3.16	3.65	4.36
1986	0.83	1,066	1.64	2.46	8.53
1987	0.86	1,099	4.17	6.12	7.58
1988	0.87	1,261	3.83	4.41	6.69
1989	0.87	1,311	2.06	3.68	4.83
1990	0.88	1,047	4.61	5.44	7.52
1991	0.87	825	4.68	6.13	6.99
1992	0.87	963	4.35	6.56	9.94
1993	0.86	1,139	5.61	8.10	11.13
1994	0.86	1,230	3.63	4.75	6.52
1995	0.86	1,371	3.25	4.23	7.85
1996	0.86	1,342	5.20	7.82	6.69
1997	0.85	1,267	5.09	8.91	10.28
1998	0.84	1,123	2.40	4.45	8.81
1999	0.83	1,092	1.65	2.08	7.42
2000	0.85	939	2.35	5.08	8.19

Table 2 *(continued)*

Year	(1) Tax Preference (θ)	(2) Number of Events	(3) Median Premium	(4) Weighted-Mean Premium	(5) Trimmed-Mean Premium
2001	0.85	801	4.46	5.24	9.36
2002	0.86	878	8.53	9.46	12.07
2003	0.93	1,222	4.06	5.04	4.89
2004	0.93	1,193	4.37	5.63	6.52
Std Dev	*0.07*		*2.34*	*1.99*	*2.46*
Total	0.80	38,951	5.40	6.43	8.57

Column (1) reports the tax preference ratio $\theta = (1 - t_\text{d})/(1 - t_\text{ac})$ measuring the tax preference of accrued capital gains over dividends for U.S. corporate stock (weighted by ownership) from 1963 to 2004. This ratio is from Poterba (2004).

Column (2) reports the annual number of regular taxable dividend nominal increases or initiations in the sample.

Columns (3), (4), and (5) report the corresponding time-series measures of the (market-adjusted) dividend increase premium $\Delta P/\Delta D$. Column (3) reports the median. Column (4) reports the weighted mean (weight is $\Delta D/P$). Column (5) reports the mean (trimmed for the smallest 25 percent dividend increase to price ratio events).

increases the costs of dividends without affecting benefits. Therefore, the market should react less favorably to dividend increases when θ is low. Thus, the signaling theory and the agency theory generate opposite predictions on the effect of changing the relative tax of dividends and capital gains on the excess stock price return around announcement dates of dividend increases.

Bernheim and Wantz (1995), using U.S. data from 1962 to 1988, show that the market premium for increasing or initiating dividends is larger when the relative tax rate on dividends is higher. This result supports the signaling theory. However, Bernhardt, Robertson, and Farrow (1994), using Canadian data, and Grullon and Michaely (2001), using U.S. data around the TRA86, investigated the same issue and found that higher tax rates were actually associated with lower dividend announcement premiums, supporting the agency theory. Much of the dispute in both the ex-date and announcement date literatures stems from the lack of sharp, credible variation in tax rates. In this chapter we investigate the broader time series and examine in detail the 2003 dividend tax cut episode to assess whether robust results on the effects of taxes can be obtained.

3. Data and Methods

We use data from the CRSP, which reports all dividend events (announcements, ex-dividend date, dividends per share) as well as price series at the daily level since 1962 for all companies listed on the major U.S. exchanges: NYSE, AMEX, and NASDAQ.[12] Specifically, we take all ordinary dividends paid in U.S. dollars (CRSP distribution codes beginning with 12) on ordinary common shares (CRSP share codes 10, 11, and 12) trading on either the NYSE, AMEX, or NASDAQ (CRSP exchange codes 1, 2, and 3). We focus our analysis exclusively on taxable dividend events (CRSP distribution codes ending in 2) and discard all non-taxable events.[13]

For our ex-dividend day analysis, we consider all events whose ex-date is between 1963 and 2004 and for which the stock was traded on the ex-dividend day and the business day preceding the ex-dividend day. We also discard events for which CRSP does not report actual closing prices for either the ex-day or cum-day. As noted by Elton and Gruber (1970), it is important to discard events during which there was no trading of the stock because in those cases regulations require to adjust the stock price mechanically downward by the full value of the nominal dividend. This mechanical adjustment would produce a premium equal to one. In addition, we discard a very small number of events with dividend yields of less than 0.1 percent (roughly 1 percent of the total sample) or ex-day price changes of more than 80 percent (seven events). The annual number of events in the sample is reported in Table 1, column (2). Annual times series are always reported according to *payment date*, which is the relevant date for tax purposes.

For each of the 256,360 ex-day events in our sample, we compute the ex-day premium as the beta-adjusted difference between the cum-day closing price and the ex-day closing price divided by the nominal dividend payment per share. Specifically, the premium for firm i is:

$$Prem_i = \frac{P_i^{cum} - P_i^{ex}/(1 + \hat{\alpha}_i + \hat{\beta}_i r^m)}{D_i},$$

where r^m is the value-weighted return on the CRSP NYSE/AMEX/NASDAQ market index, and $\hat{\alpha}_i$ and $\hat{\beta}_i$ are estimated using a firm-level regression of

---

[12] The NASDAQ was introduced in 1972.

[13] Non-taxable dividends are very rare, making it difficult to use such dividends as a control. See Eades, Hess, and Kim (1984) for such an attempt.

the firm return on the market return and a constant over a 91-day window centered on the ex-dividend date.[14]

Columns (3), (4), and (5) in Table 1 report various annual statistics for the premiums: the median, the weighted (by dividend yield) average, and the trimmed unweighted average (events with dividend yields less than 0.45 percent, roughly 25 percent of events, are discarded).[15]

For our announcement analysis, we consider all regular dividend events (CRSP distribution codes 1222, 1232, 1242, and 1252) that were higher (in nominal terms) than the previous regular dividend payment of the same firm. We also include all dividend initiations, defined as a firm paying a regular dividend payment for the first time over the last six quarters. A firm making its first dividend payment will only be classified as an initiator if the firm existed in the CRSP database for at least six quarters prior to announcing the dividend. We exclude a dividend event if its periodicity (annual, semiannual, or quarterly) is different from the previous payment. Similar to the ex-day analysis, we discard a very small number of events with change in dividend yield of less than 0.001 percent (less than 1 percent of the total sample) or three-day excess returns of more than 80 percent in absolute value (one event). Column (3) in Table 2 reports the annual number of such dividend increase events.[16]

For each of the 38,951 dividend increase announcements in our sample, we compute the announcement premium as the beta-adjusted excess return between the closing price on the day after announcement and the closing price two days before announcement divided by the nominal change in the dividend payment per share (adjusted for splits). The beta adjustment is estimated using a firm level regression of the firm return on the market return and a constant over the 91 days centered on the announcement date. Presumably, an annual dividend increase of x cents should be equivalent to a quarterly dividend increase of $x/4$ cents. Therefore, in order to normalize our estimate of $\Delta P/\Delta D$ to quarterly dividend increases (by far the most common form of regular dividend payments), we divide the premium by four for annual payments and by two for semi-annual payments.

---

[14] Our premium equation considers P^{cum} as the base price and deflates P^{ex} by the market-adjusted return. Alternatively, we could have considered P^{ex} as the base price and inflate P^{cum} by the market-adjusted return. As the time window between the cum- and ex-days is very short, these two definitions produce extremely similar results.

[15] It is necessary to trim the unweighted average because for that series very small dividend payments will drive the results and generate substantial noise in the series.

[16] Again, announcements are classified in the time series according to *payment date*, which is the relevant date for tax purposes.

Columns (4), (5), and (6) in Table 2 report various annual statistics for the dividend announcement ratio: the median, the weighted (by the ratio of the change in the nominal dividend per share to the closing share price two days before announcement) average, and trimmed unweighted averages (in that case dividend events in which the change in the dividend per share divided by the preannouncement share price is less than 0.045 percent, roughly the bottom 25 percent, are discarded).

For our regression analysis, we merge the CRSP data with the annual Compustat database, losing some firms because not all firms listed in CRSP are covered by Compustat.

4. Empirical Results for Ex-Dividend Days

4.1. The 2003 Tax Cut Experiment

We start by analyzing the 2003 dividend tax cut. Table 3 shows that the 2003 tax cut increased the ex-day tax ratio ρ significantly from 0.95 (in 2002) to 1.02 (in 2003 and after). Because the 2003 tax change was enacted only in late May 2003, there was considerable uncertainty in the first half of 2003 about the tax rates for dividends and capital gains that would apply then. Therefore, we compare 2002 and 2004, years for which the tax rates were unambiguously defined throughout.

Table 3a reports the trimmed mean, median, and dividend-weighted mean of the ex-day premium $(\Delta P / D)$ in the pre-reform (2002) and post-reform (2004) periods, as well as the change in these three measures between the two periods.[17] All three measures increase from 2002 to 2004, consistent with the tax theory described above. All the increases are statistically significant at the 5 percent level. Those standard errors are computed assuming i.i.d. errors and in particular no year-specific aggregate shocks.[18] However, the magnitudes of the changes are generally far larger than the change in the premium of 0.07, contradicting the 1–1 response predicted by the simple Elton-Gruber framework described above.[19] To assess the robustness of these findings from a broader perspective, we now analyze the full 1962–2004 period and examine whether the behavior of ex-day premiums around the 2003 tax cut is unusual.

---

[17] All those premiums are regression-adjusted for market returns as described in the data section.

[18] Obviously, with only two years of data, it is impossible to estimate standard errors if year-specific aggregate shocks are not assumed away.

[19] In addition, the premium measures are lower than the tax ratio ρ in each period.

Table 3a. *2003 Tax Episode Analysis: Ex-Dividend Day Premiums*

	(1)	(2)	(3)
	Pre-reform	Post-reform	Change
Ex-day tax preference ratio (ρ)	0.95	1.02	0.07
Median premium	0.61	0.74	0.13
	(0.04)	(0.03)	(0.05)
Weighted-mean premium	0.60	0.81	0.20
	(0.06)	(0.05)	(0.08)
Trimmed-mean premium	0.45	0.77	0.32
	(0.06)	(0.05)	(0.08)

Notes: Pre-reform refers to dividends paid out in 2002, while post-reform refers to dividends paid out in 2004. The standard errors in column (3) are estimated from a median, weighted OLS, and simple OLS regressions, respectively.

Table 3b. *2003 Tax Episode Analysis: Dividend Increase Announcements*

	(1)	(2)	(3)
	Pre-reform	Post-reform	Change
Poterba tax preference ratio (θ)	0.86	0.93	0.07
Median premium	8.53	4.37	−4.16
	(1.83)	(1.11)	(2.01)
Weighted-mean premium	9.46	5.63	−3.83
	(2.37)	(1.29)	(2.56)
Trimmed-mean premium	12.07	6.52	−5.54
	(2.94)	(1.76)	(3.22)

Notes: Pre-reform refers to dividends paid out in 2002, while post-reform refers to dividends paid out in 2004. The standard errors in column (3) are estimated from a median, weighted OLS, and simple OLS regressions, respectively.

4.2. Time-Series Perspective

Figure 2 displays the time series of the trimmed mean, median, and dividend-weighted mean of the ex-day premium along with the average tax preference ratio ρ. All of these series are taken directly from Table 1. The three measures of the ex-day premiums are relatively close in levels and highly correlated. The mean/median premium is almost always below 1, consistent with the original Elton-Gruber prediction. However, there is substantial time variation in the premium: It declines from 1 to 0.7 in the 1960s, then goes back up to 1 in the 1970s. It then drops again in the 1980s to 0.7. Since 1990, the ratios have generally remained below 0.8, but year-to-year variations are even larger. Most notably, the three premium measures dropped

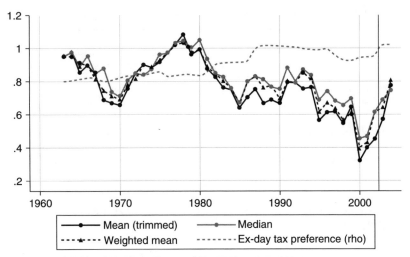

Figure 2. Ex-Dividend Day Premium and Tax Ratio, 1963–2004

This figure depicts the tax preference ratio $\rho = (1 - t_d)/(1 - t_g)$ measuring the tax preference of realized capital gains over dividends for U.S. corporate stock (weighted by ownership) from 1963 to 2004. The figure also depicts three annual time-series measures of the (market-adjusted) dividend premium $\Delta P/D$ for all taxable regular and special dividend payments from 1963 to 2004: (1) the mean (trimmed for the smallest 25 percent dividend yield events), (2) the dividend-yield weighted mean, and (3) the median. All four time series are displayed in Table 1.

dramatically from about 0.7 in the mid 1990s to less than 0.4 from 1999 to 2000. The premiums increased consistently from their low in 2000 and quickly returned to 0.8 in 2004.

Parametric Regression Estimates

To assess the relationship between taxes and the premium following methods used in the existing literature, we run dividend-yield weighted regressions of the following form:

$$\frac{\Delta P_{it}}{D_{it}} = \alpha + \delta\rho_t + \gamma X_{it} + \varepsilon_{it},$$

where X is a set of covariates. Specifications 1–3 of Table 4 run this regression, restricting the sample to particular years around tax events. The covariate set in these and all subsequent regressions reported in the tables is each firm's lagged (prior-year) cash, assets, liabilities, earnings, and investment and the level and square of the 10-year U.S. Treasury yield. The main results are very similar when the covariates are dropped or the set of covariates

Table 4a. *Ex-Dividend Day Regression Results: Dependent Variable* $= \Delta P / D$

	(1)	(2)	(3)
	1980–1985	1985–1989	2000–2004
Tax preference (ρ)	−2.742	0.666	1.323
	(0.550)	(0.611)	(1.477)
R-squared	0.001	0.001	0.001

Notes: All regressions are weighted by dividend yield. Interest rate controls include the level and square of the 10-year U.S. Treasury yield. Firm controls include lagged levels of cash, assets, liabilities, earnings, and investment.

Table 4b. *Ex-Dividend Day Regression Results: Dependent Variable* $= \Delta P / P$

	(1)	(2)	(3)
	1980–1985	1985–1989	2000–2004
Tax preference (ρ)	0.006	−0.001	0.006
	(0.009)	(0.005)	(0.009)
Dividend yield	3.627	0.382	0.454
	(0.619)	(0.432)	(0.453)
Dividend yield* ρ	−3.097	0.578	0.460
	(0.703)	(0.437)	(0.461)
R-squared	0.064	0.317	0.346

Notes: Interest rate controls include the level and square of the 10-year U.S. Treasury yield. Firm controls include lagged levels of cash, assets, liabilities, earnings, and investment.

is changed. Table 4 shows that results are very fragile when one examines specific "natural experiments" using windows around sharp changes in tax rates. Specification 1 examines the period from 1980 to 1985. The premium fell significantly from 1980 to 1985, while ρ increased, yielding a negative and highly significant estimate of δ in this specification. But as Michaely (1991) found, specification 2 shows that the premium during 1985–9 is relatively stable while ρ increases sharply because of TRA86 (note that the levels we estimate are different from Michaely mainly because of differences in sample), yielding an estimate of zero. Finally, as discussed above, the ex-day premium increases sharply (and significantly) from 2002 to 2004, coincident with the 2003 tax cut, which increased ρ by 0.07. This yields a positive estimate of δ (specification 3). Hence, depending on which short-run tax episode one picks, one can obtain a negative, zero, or positive association between ρ and the ex-day premium.

Moreover, "placebo tests" suggest violations of the identification assumptions that there are no other short-run trends. For instance, the ex-day premium also rose at a significant rate from 1999 to 2002, a time when ρ was virtually flat. This suggests that it would not be credible to attribute the increase in the premium around the 2003 dividend tax cut solely to the tax change. Hence, our initial results using the 2003 tax cut are not robust when examined in the context of the longer time series. The changes around the 2003 reform, though large and significant in short-window regressions, are hardly unusual relative to other non-tax-related time-series fluctuations.

Power Analysis

The fragility of these estimates arises fundamentally from the very large aggregate volatility in the excess returns. This point can be seen with a simple power analysis. First, note that the standard deviation of the trimmed *mean premium* in the time series is $\sigma = 0.13$. Now suppose there is a one-time, discrete change in ρ of 10 percentage points, a value larger than any single tax change in our sample. Assume that the true mean change in $\Delta P/D$ caused by this tax change is 10 percentage points (consistent with the Elton-Gruber model). To see how much data are needed to detect this effect, note that the standard error interval for the mean premium over n years is $\frac{\sigma}{\sqrt{n}} = \frac{0.13}{\sqrt{n}}$. If observations are independent across years, the standard error for the change in the premium with n years each of pre-reform and post-reform data is $se = \sqrt{2}\frac{\sigma}{\sqrt{n}}$. Note that increasing the sample size within any given year is unlikely to reduce σ drastically because idiosyncratic firm-level shocks are essentially washed out in the large samples used for each year (see Table 1). Therefore, the primary way to increase the precision of the estimates is to increase the number of years in the data.

To detect a change in $\Delta P/D$ of 0.1 at conventional significance levels, we would need an $se = 0.05$, which would require $n = 14$ years of pre-reform data and 14 years of post-reform data! Even if there were a sharp change in ρ and $\Delta P/D$ of 20 percentage points (which equals the change in ρ from 1964 to 2004), we would need eight years of data (four pre-reform and four post-reform) to pick up the effect. Given the volatility in the data, one needs both a very large tax change and also a long pre-reform and post-reform period to have a chance of detecting even large tax effects.[20] Of course, these conditions guarantee precision but not necessarily consistency.

---

[20] The pattern of the time series on Figure 2 suggests that the year-to-year fluctuations are actually positively serially correlated. In that situation, our power calculation is too optimistic, and even more years of data would be required to detect an effect.

Consistency of estimates using this identification strategy requires that there be no unobservable contemporaneous trends that may make the average premiums in the pre-reform and post-reform periods differ. Unfortunately, this assumption is quite tenuous when one is comparing premiums over long horizons, especially given the apparently non-tax-related aggregate fluctuations and short-term trends (such as the one from 2000 to 2004) evident in the data. The power analysis therefore indicates that the ability to make credible inferences about tax effects is quite limited using raw data on ex-dividend returns.

Attempted Solutions

One way to try to increase power is to control for other factors that may be contributing to the aggregate volatility. Intuitively, if one can pin down the factors that are driving the fluctuations, the residuals after controlling for these factors will be much smoother, permitting more reliable inferences about tax effects. To investigate this approach, we run a dividend-weighted regression of the ex-day premium on year dummies, the 10-year nominal interest rate, and a set of observable variables from Compustat data: cash, assets, liabilities, earnings, and investment. Figure 3 plots the coefficients on the year dummies in this regression, which correspond to the ex-day premiums adjusting for controls, alongside the weighted mean shown in Figure 2. The main lesson is that adding controls hardly affects the pattern of the ex-dividend day premiums, indicating that the main observables are poor predictors of the aggregate fluctuations. In addition, the lack of monotonicity in the excess premiums suggests that it is impossible to explain the evolution of the premium with variables such as reductions in trading transaction costs, the elimination of discrete pricing rules, or the development of tax-sophisticated arbitrage techniques.

Given our inability to smooth cross-year fluctuations, we now turn to a slightly different test that exploits the within-year variation in the size of dividend payments. Specifically, we examine whether larger dividend payments are associated with larger ex-day returns particularly in years with high ρ. The following dividend-weighted regression is estimated for each year t:

$$r_{it} = \alpha_t + \delta_t \frac{D_{it}}{P_{it}} + \gamma X_{it} + \varepsilon_t,$$

where r_{it} denotes the ex-day excess return ($\Delta P / P$), $\frac{D_{it}}{P_{it}}$ is the dividend yield, and δ_t is the slope coefficient in year t. We then investigate the link between the estimated $\{\delta_t\}$ time series and the time series of ρ graphically

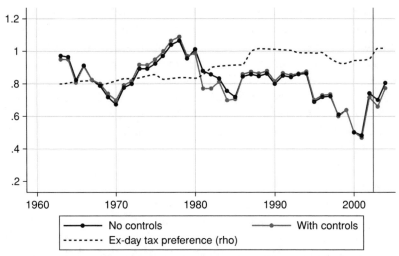

Figure 3. Ex-Dividend Day Premium, with and without Controls, 1963–2004

This figure depicts the ex-dividend tax preference ratio ρ. The figure also depicts the dividend-yield weighted mean of the premium (as in Figure 2) along with dividend-yield weighted mean of the premium, controlling for the 10-year nominal interest rate and observable firm-level variables (cash, assets, liabilities, earnings, and investment) from Compustat. The latter series is obtained from a regression of the adjusted premium on a full set of year dummies and the control variables.

(to permit a semi-parametric analysis as above). A tax effect would imply that δ_t should be larger when ρ_t is large because larger dividend payments should generate especially large (negative) excess returns on the ex-date if the dividend payment is very valuable to investors, that is, if dividend taxation is low and ρ_t is high. Figure 4 shows the evolution of δ_t from a specification that includes the standard control set described above. The δ_t coefficients are consistently positive, confirming that larger dividend payments generate larger ex-day price reductions. However, the δ_t coefficients also vary tremendously from year to year, suggesting that this approach will not help in our ultimate goal of raising power so that we can detect tax effects.

Panel B of Table 4 examines whether regression analysis can uncover significant effects in this within-year test. This panel reports estimates of the following specification:

$$r_{it} = \alpha + \delta_0 \rho_t + \delta_1 \frac{D_{it}}{P_{it}} + \delta_2 \rho_t \frac{D_{it}}{P_{it}} + \gamma X_{it} + \varepsilon_{it}.$$

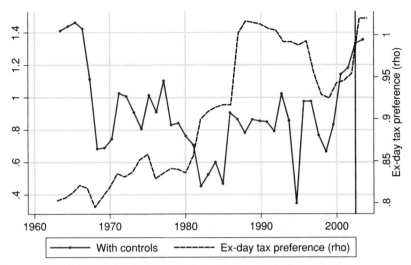

Figure 4. Ex-Dividend Day Premium Slopes, with Controls, 1963–2004

This figure depicts the ex-dividend day tax preference ratio ρ (on the right scale). The figure also depicts the year dummy coefficients interacted with the dividend yield D/P of the regression equation in the text (with controls). The (adjusted) excess return around the ex-day is regressed on a full set of year dummies and year dummies interacted with the dividend yield D/P. The additional control variables are the same as in Figure 3.

The key coefficient of interest for this test is the interaction term, δ_2. The same three specifications in Panel A of Table 4 are repeated here, and the results are insignificant and of varied signs in all short-window regressions. Given the lack of power suggested by Figure 4, it should not be surprising that the parametric (linear) regression counterparts to this graph yield little information.

Finally, we explore whether the pattern of premiums becomes smoother when one constructs the sample of firms differently to control for potential changes in the sample over time. First, we limit the sample to large firms (ranked by market capitalization), for which trading costs are lower and whose dividends are perhaps more visible to traders. As shown in Figure 5, Panel A, the resulting series is even noisier than that depicted in Figure 2 and is not any more closely related to the tax parameter ρ. Second, to control for potential noise from entry and exit effects, we also estimate average premiums for a stable set of firms over time (those alive since 1990). This series also remains as noisy as the original one (Figure 5, Panel B).

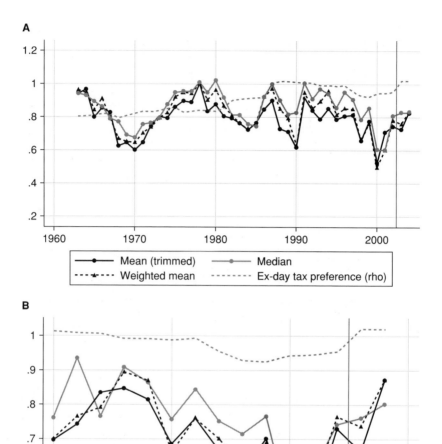

Figure 5. A. Largest 1,000 Firms by Year; B. Consistent Sample of Firms, 1990–2004

This figure depicts the tax preference ratio ρ and the three annual time-series measures of the (market-adjusted) dividend premium $\Delta P/D$ (mean trimmed, weighted mean, and median), as in Figure 2, for alternative samples. In Panel A, the sample is restricted to the largest 1,000 firms (ranked by market capitalization) in each year. In Panel B, the sample consists of all firms present in the CRSP data in every year from 1990 to 2004. The number of such firms is 1,402.

Summary
A graphical (semi-parametric) analysis of the full time series of ex-day premiums helps reconcile the various ex-day tax effects estimated using regressions that make parametric assumptions (e.g., linearity) in the literature. Each of the estimates is significant within the specific event window analyzed in the study but is not robust to a broader examination that takes into account the tremendous aggregate volatility in the premiums. This point also applies to the 2003 tax cut analyzed above. The lack of a robust relationship between taxes and the ex-day premium in the data should not be interpreted as evidence that taxes are not relevant. Rather, it reveals that one cannot place a reasonable confidence interval on the size of the tax effect with the methods employed in the existing literature.

5. Empirical Results for Dividend Announcements

We now investigate the relationship between taxes and excess returns on announcement days. As the methods and basic conclusions are very similar to those in the ex-day analysis, the discussion below is much briefer.

5.1. The 2003 Tax Cut Experiment

Table 3, Panel B, shows that the 2003 tax cut increased the deferred-capital taxation adjusted-tax preference ratio θ from 0.86 (in 2002) to 0.93 (in 2003 and after). As above, we compare 2002 and 2004, years for which the tax rates were unambiguously defined throughout. Panel B reports the trimmed mean, median, and ΔD-weighted mean of the premium $\frac{\Delta P}{\Delta D}$ associated with a dividend increase of ΔD. All three of these measures decrease from 2002 to 2004. The first decline is statistically significant (at the 5 percent level), while the last two are only marginally significant. These results are consistent with Bernheim and Wantz (1995). They support the signaling theory of dividend payments while rejecting the agency theory. To assess the robustness of this result, we now analyze this event in the context of the full 1963–2004 sample period.

5.2. Time-Series Perspective

Figure 6 shows the time series of the trimmed mean, median, and weighted-mean premium. It also shows the average tax preference ratio θ taken from Poterba (2004) on a separate (right-hand side) scale. All of these series are taken directly from Table 2. The three measures of the premiums are

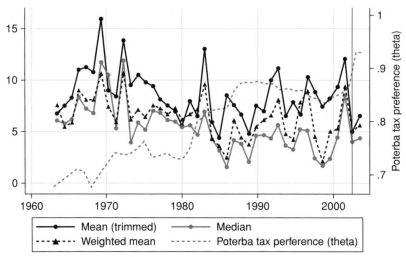

Figure 6. Dividend Increase Announcement Premium and Tax Ratio, 1963–2004

This figure depicts (on the right-hand scale) the tax preference ratio $\theta = (1 - t_d)/(1 - t_{ac})$ from Poterba (2004), which measures the tax preference of accrued capital gains over dividends for U.S. corporate stock (weighted by ownership) from 1963 to 2004. The figure also depicts three annual time-series measures of the (market-adjusted) dividend increase premium $\Delta P/\Delta D$ for all regular dividend increases and initiations from 1963 to 2004: (1) the mean (trimmed of the smallest 25 percent dividend increase to price ratio events), (2) the weighted mean (weight is $\Delta D/P$), and (3) the median. All four time series are displayed in Table 2.

reasonably similar for most years. They are consistently positive, confirming the well-known result that dividend increase announcements generate a positive market reaction on average. There is a clear decline in the announcement premiums over time, although there is substantial year-to-year variation as well. The median and weighted-mean series are smoother than the trimmed-mean series. This is to be expected given that the signal-to-noise ratio in small ΔD announcements is presumably much lower.

Parametric Regression Estimates

To investigate the effect of taxes on the announcement premium using traditional linear regression methods, we fit models of the following form:

$$\frac{\Delta P_{it}}{\Delta D_{it}} = \alpha + \delta\theta_t + \gamma X_{it} + \varepsilon_{it}.$$

Table 5, Panel A, reports a set of estimates of this equation, with a control set X identical to that used in Table 4. The regressions are weighted by $\Delta D/P$. Examination of the key tax reform episodes using "natural experiment"

Table 5a. *Dividend Increase Announcements Regression Results: Dependent Variable* $= \Delta P/\Delta D$

	(1)	(2)	(3)
	1980–1985	1985–1989	2000–2004
Tax preference (θ)	−16.954	36.993	−61.576
	(14.515)	(27.106)	(51.408)
R-squared	0.001	0.003	0.002

Notes: All regressions are weighted by the change in the nominal dividend amount divided by the pre-announcement share price. Interest rate controls include the level and square of the 10-year U.S. Treasury yield. Firm controls include lagged levels of cash, assets, liabilities, earnings, and investment.

Table 5b. *Dividend Increase Announcements Regression Results: Dependent Variable* $= \Delta P/P$

	(1)	(2)	(3)
	1980–1985	1985–1989	2000–2004
Tax preference (θ)	0.002	−0.081	−0.050
	(0.022)	(0.037)	(0.046)
Δ Dividend yield	26.231	31.405	3.225
	(6.565)	(8.052)	(10.557)
Δ Dividend yield* θ	−30.754	37.631	−2.376
	(8.277)	(9.529)	(11.712)
R-squared	0.020	0.008	0.032

Notes: Interest rate controls include the level and square of the 10-year U.S. Treasury yield. Firm controls include lagged levels of cash, assets, liabilities, earnings, and investment.

methods is equally problematic here. As shown in columns (1) to (3) of Table 5, the three tax episodes each yield very different estimates with very large standard errors. Placebo tests also suggest problems. The premium is indeed lower in 2004 than in 2002, after the tax ratio increases. But this negative relation is not robust, for example, to choosing the year 2000 instead of year 2002 as the pre-reform comparison. Hence, as with the ex-dividend case, we conclude that our initial results using the 2003 reform are far from compelling when viewed from the longer time-series perspective.

Power Analysis
The fragility of these estimates can again be traced to the aggregate volatility in the excess returns around announcement days. An analysis identical to that for the ex-dividend days suggests that detecting even a very large change

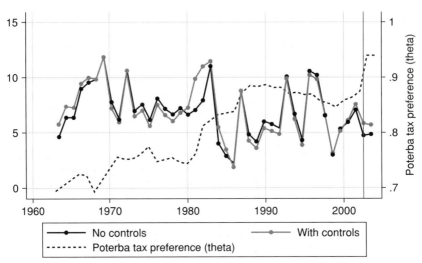

Figure 7. Dividend Increase Announcement Premium, with and without Controls, 1963–2004

This figure depicts the Poterba (2004) tax preference ratio θ (on the right-hand scale). The figure also depicts the weighted mean of the announcement premium (as in Figure 6), along with weighted mean of the announcement premium controlling for the 10-year nominal interest rate and observable firm-level variables (cash, assets, liabilities, earnings, and investment) from Compustat. The latter series is obtained from a regression of the adjusted premium on a full set of year dummies and the control variables.

in the premium of $\Delta P / \Delta D = 3$ (a 50 percent increase relative to the mean $\Delta P / \Delta D$) would require eight years of pre-reform and eight years of post-reform data given the observed degree of aggregate volatility. Examining such a long horizon raises the same identification problem related to other trends that were discussed in the context of the ex-day analysis. Hence, there the power to make inferences about announcement premiums appears equally limited.

Attempted Solutions

We consider the same three approaches to resolving this aggregate noise problem as we did in the ex-dividend case. First, we investigate whether controls can smooth aggregate fluctuations. We run a ΔD-weighted regression of the announcement premium $\Delta P / \Delta D$ on year dummies, the 10-year interest rate, and the following set of observables from Compustat: cash, assets, liabilities, earnings, and investment. Figure 7 plots the coefficients on the year dummies in this regression alongside the weighted mean shown in

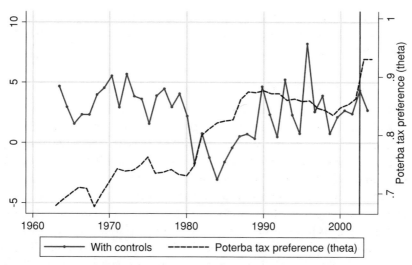

Figure 8. Bang-for-the-Buck for Announcement Premium, with Controls, 1963–2004

This figure depicts the Poterba (2004) tax preference ratio θ (on the right-hand scale). The figure also depicts the year dummy coefficients interacted with the dividend yield increase $\Delta D/P$ of the regression equation in the text (with controls). The (adjusted) excess return around the announcement date is regressed on a full set of year dummies and year dummies interacted with the change in dividend yield $\Delta D/P$. The additional control variables are the same as in Figure 7.

Figure 6. It is clear that the addition of controls does little to mitigate the aggregate fluctuations.

Second, we examine whether larger dividend payments are associated with larger announcement returns, particularly in years with high or low θ_t. Specifically, we run the following $\Delta D/P$-weighted regression:

$$r_{it} = \alpha_t + \delta_t \frac{\Delta D_{it}}{P_{it}} + \gamma X_{it} + \varepsilon_{it},$$

where r_{it} denotes the ex-day excess return ($\Delta P/P$), $\frac{D_{it}}{P_{it}}$ is the dividend yield, and δ_t is the slope coefficient in year t. We then investigate the link between the estimated $\{\delta_{it}\}$ time series and the time series of θ graphically, as in the ex-day analysis. Figure 8 shows the evolution of δ_t from a specification that includes the standard controls. The δ_t coefficients are consistently positive, confirming that larger dividend payments generate larger announcement premiums. However, the δ_t coefficients also vary tremendously from year to year, suggesting that power is not any greater for this type of test.

Panel B of Table 5 examines whether regression analysis can uncover significant effects in this within-year test. This panel reports estimates of the following specification:

$$r_{it} = \alpha + \delta_0 \theta_t + \delta_1 \frac{\Delta D_{it}}{P_{it}} + \delta_2 \theta_t \frac{\Delta D_{it}}{P_{it}} + \gamma X_{it} + \varepsilon_{it}.$$

Note that this is precisely the "bang-for-the-buck" specification implemented by Bernheim and Wantz (1995). The key coefficient of interest for this test is the interaction term, δ_2. The results are insignificant and of varied signs in the short-window regressions that are perhaps most credible from an identification perspective. Unfortunately, it appears that little is gained from examining the within-year variation in the size of dividend increase announcements because of the instability of the relationship over time.

Finally, we explore whether changes in the sample construction affect the smoothness of the series. The results (not reported) suggest little difference between constant-firm samples or large-firm samples and the full sample we initially examined.

Summary
Our conclusions for the announcement-day tax effects mirror those for the ex-dividend day analysis. Both time-series and event-study methods yield very unstable results with wide confidence intervals for the effects of taxation on announcement premiums.

The problem again is aggregate volatility and the resulting lack of power. Some obvious attempts to smooth the series fail. The source of the aggregate fluctuations must therefore be understood before real progress can be made on estimating the tax effects.

6. Conclusion

The original goal of our analysis was to use the sharp change in the tax treatment of dividend income in 2003 to examine the effect of taxes on dividend announcement and ex-day premiums. The 2003 tax cut is unique in its size and relatively unanticipated nature and thereby provides one of the best "natural experiments" to study these issues. Unfortunately, we found that few robust inferences can be drawn about the effects of taxation on excess returns even using this large experiment. Analysis of the full time series of excess returns around announcement and ex-dates reveals a high degree of aggregate volatility that cannot be smoothed using covariates such as assets or interest rates or by changes in sample construction. Our main conclusions are therefore methodological:

1. Existing methods, which generally involve parametric (often linear) regressions or examination of short windows around tax changes, yield unstable and sometimes misleading results. Looking at the time series from 1962 to 2004, we found that the results are extremely sensitive to the window of analysis and the specification used. The contradictory estimates of prior studies can be explained by the particular event windows and specifications that were chosen in each study.
2. Obtaining credible estimates of tax effects requires the use of a long time series of data. The objective is *not* to do a time-series analysis, but rather to check whether the changes in the series around a tax experiment are unusual relative to historical non-tax-related aggregate fluctuations. Semi-parametric tests showing that changes around a particular reform are very different from other fluctuations could give the most robust evidence of tax effects.
3. In the context of ex-day and announcement premiums for dividends, the aggregate series is so volatile that even large tax changes yield very wide confidence intervals on the tax effects. The statistical power to pick up even large tax effects is limited. Credible estimates of the effects of dividend taxation on equity returns are likely to remain elusive until we have better models that explain the non-tax-driven fluctuations in the aggregate time series. We view the search for such models as the most promising direction for future research in this area.

Another promising avenue for more research would be to look directly at trading data (as opposed to only prices, as done here) to uncover the mechanisms of tax arbitrage around the ex-day dates. Indeed, several studies (see Allen and Michaely, 2003 for a survey) have started to explore trading volume data around ex-dividend dates. A natural extension of this work would be to explore whether trading volume and the nature of traders around ex-days correlate with the size of premium over time.

References

Allen, Franklin, and Roni Michaely. 2003. "Payout Policy." In George Constantinides, Milton Harris, and Rene Stulz, eds., *Handbook of the Economics of Finance* (Amsterdam: North-Holland), pp. 337–429.

Auerbach, Alan. 1983. "Stockholder Tax Rates and Firm Attributes." *Journal of Public Economics* 21(2): 107–127.

Auerbach, Alan J., and Kevin Hassett. 2007. "The 2003 Dividend Tax Cuts and the Value of the Firm: An Event Study." In Alan J. Auerbach, James R. Hines Jr., and Joel Slemrod, eds., *Taxing Corporate Income in the 21st Century.* (Cambridge: Cambridge University Press).

Barclay, Michael. 1987. "Dividends, Taxes, and Common Stock Prices: The Ex-Dividend Day Behavior of Common Stock Prices Before the Income Tax." *Journal of Financial Economics* 19: 31–44.

Bernhardt, Dan, J. Fiona Robertson, and Ray Farrow. 1994. "Testing Dividend Signaling Models." Working paper. (Kingston, ON: Queen's University).

Bernheim, Douglas, and Adam Wantz. 1995. "A Tax-Based Test of the Dividend Signalling Hypothesis." *American Economic Review* 85(3): 532–551.

Blouin, Jennifer, Jana Raedy, and Douglas Shackelford. 2004. "The Initial Impact of the 2003 Reduction in the Dividend Tax Rate." Working paper. (Chapel Hill: University of North Carolina).

Chetty, Raj, and Emmanuel Saez. 2005. "Dividend Taxes and Corporate Behavior: Evidence from the 2003 Dividend Tax Cut." *Quarterly Journal of Economics* 120(3): 791–833.

Eades, Ken, Pat Hess, and E. Han Kim. 1984. "On Interpreting Security Returns During the Ex-Dividend Period." *Journal of Financial Economics* 13(1): 3–34.

Elton, Edwin, and Martin Gruber. 1970. "Marginal Stockholder Tax Rates and the Clientele Effect." *Review of Economics and Statistics* 52(1): 68–74.

Grullon, Gustavo, and Roni Michaely. 2001. "Asymmetric Information, Agency Conflicts and the Impact of Taxation on the Market Reaction to Dividend Changes." Working paper. (Ithaca, NY: Cornell University).

Grullon, Gustavo, and Roni Michaely. 2002. "Dividends, Share Repurchases, and the Substitution Hypothesis." *Journal of Finance* 57(4): 1649–1684.

Jensen, Michael C., and William H. Meckling. 1976. "Theory of the Firm: Managerial Behavior, Agency Costs and Ownership Structure." *Journal of Financial Economics* 3(4): 305–360.

Kalay, Avner. 1982. "The Ex-Dividend Day Behavior of Stock Prices: A Re-Examination of the Clientele Effect." *Journal of Finance* 37(1): 1059–1070.

Lakonishok, Josef, and Theo Vermaelen. 1983. "Tax Reform and Ex-Dividend Day Behavior." *Journal of Finance* 38(4): 1157–1179.

Michaely, Roni. 1991. "Ex-Dividend Day Stock Price Behavior: The Case of the 1986 Tax Reform Act." *Journal of Finance* 46(3): 845–859.

Michaely, Roni, and Jean-Luc Vila. 1995. "Investors' Heterogeneity, Prices and Volume Around the Ex-Dividend Day." *Journal of Financial and Quantitative Analysis* 30(2): 171–198.

Poterba, James. 2004. "Corporate Payout Policy." *American Economic Review* 94(2): 171–175.

Poterba, James, and Lawrence Summers. 1984. "New Evidence That Taxes Affect the Valuation of Dividends." *Journal of Finance* 39(5): 1397–1415.

Comments

Gustavo Grullon
Rice University

This chapter tries to improve our understanding of how taxes affect both the ex-dividend day premium and the market reaction surrounding dividend changes. Although previous studies have examined these issues, this chapter uses the 2003 dividend tax cut as a natural experiment to investigate these important questions. Consistent with the tax argument, the chapter documents that the ex-dividend day premium significantly increased after the 2003 dividend tax cut. Further, consistent with the signaling hypothesis, the chapter shows that the market reaction surrounding dividend increases significantly declined after 2003.

To check the robustness of their primary empirical results, Chetty, Rosenberg, and Saez examine the long-run relation between tax changes, the ex-dividend day premium, and the market reaction surrounding dividend changes over the period 1963–2004. Three interesting findings emerge from this analysis. First, there is a large variation in the time series of the ex-dividend day premium and the market reaction surrounding dividend increases that cannot be explained by changes in taxes. Second, there is no time-series correlation between the ex-dividend day premium and tax changes. Finally, consistent with the signaling hypothesis, there is a positive time-series correlation between the market reaction surrounding dividend increases and tax changes. However, the authors acknowledge that this last empirical finding may be spurious because they do not control for other factors that could potentially affect the time-series behavior of the market reaction surrounding dividend increases.

Overall, this chapter examines an important and interesting issue. Its main contribution is that it shows that the time series of the ex-dividend day premium and the market reaction surrounding dividend changes are so volatile that few reliable inferences can be drawn about the effects of taxes on these variables even when examining large tax reforms, such as the one in

2003. This is an important result because it suggests that the changes in the behavior of dividend variables around tax changes documented in previous studies could be just noise.

Given the findings in this chapter, I agree with the authors that researchers need to control for the long-run time series volatility of the ex-dividend day premium and the market reaction surrounding dividend changes before making inferences about the behavior of these variables around tax reforms. One potential way to solve this issue is to examine the cross-sectional behavior of the dividend variables rather than the time-series behavior. For example, a recent paper by Elton, Gruber, and Blake (2005) indirectly addresses this issue by examining the ex-dividend effects on a sample of taxable and non-taxable closed-end funds. This is an excellent "natural" cross-sectional experiment because for the taxable (non-taxable) funds, the ex-day premium should be less (greater) than one. Consistent with the tax story, these authors find evidence supporting these predictions.

My only concern about this chapter is regarding the evidence on the signaling hypothesis. It is important to note that finding a positive correlation between taxes and the market reaction surrounding dividend increases is a necessary but not sufficient condition to validate the signaling hypothesis. Another necessary condition is finding improvements in operating performance after dividend increases. However, the evidence in recent studies does not support this important empirical prediction (see, e.g., DeAngelo, DeAngelo, and Skinner, 1996; Grullon, Michaely, Benartzi, and Thaler, 2005; Grullon, Michaely, and Swaminathan, 2002; and Lie, 2005). Further, if firms are using dividends as a signaling device, one would expect dividend payers to be firms with high levels of uncertainty about their future probability (e.g., small young firms). However, most of the dividend payers in the United States are very large mature firms (DeAngelo, DeAngelo, and Skinner, 2004). In general, I think that the results from the tests on the signaling hypothesis should be taken with a grain of salt because other important predictions from this hypothesis are not supported by the data.

References

DeAngelo, Harry, Linda DeAngelo, and Douglas J. Skinner. 1996. "Reversal of Fortune: Dividend Policy and the Disappearance of Sustained Earnings Growth." *Journal of Financial Economics* 40(3): 341–371.

DeAngelo, Harry, Linda DeAngelo, and Douglas J. Skinner. 2004. "Are Dividends Disappearing? Dividend Concentration and the Consolidation of Earnings." *Journal of Financial Economics* 72(3): 425–456.

Elton, Edwin J., Martin J. Gruber, and Christopher R. Blake. 2005. "Marginal Stockholder Tax Effects and Ex-Dividend Day Price Behavior: Evidence from Taxable versus Nontaxable Closed-End Funds." *Review of Economics and Statistics* 87(3): 579–586.

Grullon, Gustavo, Roni Michaely, Shlomo Benartzi, and Richard H. Thaler. 2005. "Dividend Changes Do Not Signal Changes in Future Profitability." *Journal of Business* 78(5): 1659–1682.

Grullon, Gustavo, Roni Michaely, and Bhaskaran Swaminathan. 2002. "Are Dividend Changes a Sign of Firm Maturity?" *Journal of Business* 75(3): 387–424.

Lie, Erik. 2005. "Financial Flexibility, Performance, and the Corporate Payout Choice." *Journal of Business* 78(6): 2179–2201.

Comments

Douglas J. Skinner

Graduate School of Business University of Chicago

1. Introduction

As someone who is not a tax economist but who has written a number of papers on dividend policy, I was most interested in the findings of Chetty, Rosenberg, and Saez (2007; hereinafter, CRS). The authors are to be congratulated for documenting an interesting result: that the evidence from ex-date price changes before and after the 2003 tax cut is consistent with dividends being tax disadvantaged. Perhaps more important, however, is the authors' determination to probe further and look at the full time-series of data, in this case going back to 1962. When they do this, they find two things: that the evidence is much less clear-cut than the evidence they document around the 2003 tax cut and that there is a lot of unexplained variation in the time series of returns around both ex-dates and announcement dates. In the end, they are left with the conclusion that the evidence does not clearly support the tax explanation for dividends.

CRS also address the idea of dividend signaling, which has also been in the literature for a long time. CRS do find some support for this argument. Dividend signaling is an area of some interest to me, and so my comments largely address this aspect of the paper. In short, my view is that the typical version of the dividend signaling argument is not likely to be of much help in explaining dividend policy, especially in recent years. As part of this discussion, I also discuss some recent changes in the nature of dividend policy. These regularities may be useful to the authors and others who seek to explain some of the variation in time series related to dividends. In particular, I argue that there are probably good reasons why we see a decline in the information content of dividends over time, as the authors' evidence on declining announcement effects of dividends suggests.

2. The Signaling Argument and Recent Evidence on Dividend Policy

The authors investigate a tax-based version of the signaling argument attributable to Bernheim and Wantz (1995). Under this view, as the tax disadvantage of dividends increases, the cost of using dividends as a signal also increases, increasing their information content. This argument implies that, other things held constant, we should observe a positive relation between the informativeness of dividends and the extent to which they are tax disadvantaged. This is what the authors find – while the Poterba (2004) tax preference ratio tends to increase over the sample period (indicating a decrease in the relative tax disadvantage of dividends), the announcement effect associated with dividend increases and initiations declines. As the authors point out, however, this interpretation rests on the rather strong assumption that nothing else has changed. Let me offer some thoughts on what else might have changed over this period that also could explain the declining announcement effect of dividends.

Fama and French (2001) show that there has been a substantial decrease in the propensity of listed U.S. industrial firms to pay dividends over the last 25 years or so. They find that the fraction of these firms paying dividends declines from a peak of 67 percent in 1978 to only 21 percent in 1999. Fama and French attribute this decline to two factors. First, there has been a change in the nature of publicly listed firms over this period, with a shift toward younger, newly listed firms that both are less profitable and have more investment opportunities than other firms, which makes them less likely to pay dividends. Second, after controlling for other factors known to affect dividend policy (investment opportunities, etc.), they find that firms' general propensity to pay dividends declines over time – firms are simply less likely to pay dividends now than they once were.

DeAngelo, DeAngelo, and Skinner (2004) follow up on the Fama and French findings and report that, in spite of the marked decline in the number of dividend payers, aggregate (real and nominal) dividend payments increase over the same period. This finding implies that there has been a substantial increase in the concentration of dividend payments over this period, and DeAngelo et al. find evidence consistent with this. For example, they report that in 2000 the top 25 dividend payers accounted for just over half of aggregate dividends for U.S. industrials.

So how is all of this evidence related to the CRS results on signaling? At least in my view, these regularities make the signaling argument less plausible. As DeAngelo et al. (2004) point out, it is hard to reconcile the fact that most dividends are paid by large, well-known firms, such as General Electric and Exxon Mobil, with the dividend signaling story. If signaling is important, one would expect it to be most prominent for relatively small firms that are not closely followed by Wall Street analysts. In contrast, there are numerous ways for investors to obtain information about the earnings prospects of firms such as GE that dominate the supply of dividend payments, so signaling is likely to be relatively unimportant for these firms. In addition, it is well-known in the disclosure literature that larger firms are more likely to hold conference calls, provide earnings guidance (issue earnings forecasts), have a large analyst following, and so forth (e.g., Skinner, 2003), all of which seem like reasonably good substitutes for dividend signaling.

Moreover, for those firms that still pay dividends, dividend policy seems to have become increasingly conservative. While we have known since at least the time of Lintner's (1956) survey that managers are reluctant to reduce dividends, managers' tendency to increase dividends in small increments so as to avoid the possibility of subsequent decreases seems especially pronounced in the last decade or so (Brav et al., 2005). For instance, GE paid a quarterly dividend of 16 cents per share for the first three quarters of 2001. In the fourth quarter of that year, GE increased the dividend to 18 cents per share, followed by increases to 19 cents in the fourth quarter of 2002, 20 cents in the fourth quarter of 2003, and 22 cents in the fourth quarter of 2004. During this same interval, GE quarterly earnings per share (EPS) fluctuated between 25 cents and 50 cents, with approximately as many quarter-to-quarter decreases as increases. It is hard to see how such a smooth and predictable dividend policy tells us much about GE management's views about its future EPS prospects.

3. Recent Changes

As the authors describe, some of these trends have reversed in the last three years or so, roughly contemporaneous with the 2003 tax law change. As documented in papers by Blouin, Raedy, and Shackelford (2004) and Chetty and Saez (2005), there has been an increase in the number of firms that initiate and increase dividends since the 2003 Act. It is hard to see how this evidence is *not* at least partly attributable to the more favorable tax treatment of dividends. There is, however, another potentially important factor that may have affected dividend policy over roughly the same period. Specifically, in the wake of the recent accounting scandals at companies like Enron, WorldCom, Global Crossing, etc., there has been increasing investor skepticism about the quality of reported earnings. Some commentators have advanced the idea that a way of convincing investors about the veracity of firms' reported earnings is for the firm to pay an economically significant dividend.[1] As yet, however, it is not clear whether this argument has much explanatory power, although it would also predict an increase in the propensity of firms to pay dividends, especially those firms with low perceived earnings quality.

4. Conclusion

In my view, the CRS paper does a good job of using the recent change in U.S. tax law, as well as a longer time series of evidence, to help answer the long-standing question of whether taxes have an important effect on dividend policy. What is interesting about the paper is the fact that the authors find little convincing overall support for the story, in spite of the apparently convincing evidence around the time of the 2003 Act. In the end, then, dividends remain as much of a puzzle as always, perhaps increasingly so in the wake of the careful and thorough job that these authors, among others, have done in analyzing dividend policy.

References

Bernheim, Douglas, and Adam Wantz. 1995. A Tax-Based Test of the Dividend Signalling Hypothesis. *American Economic Review* 85(3): 532–551.

Blouin, Jennifer, Jana Raedy, and Douglas Shackelford. 2004. The Initial Impact of the 2003 Tax Reduction in the Dividend Tax Rate. Working paper. (Chapel Hill: University of North Carolina).

Brav, Alon, John R. Graham, Campbell R. Harvey, and Roni Michaely. 2005. "Payout Policy in the 21st Century." *Journal of Financial Economics* 77(3): 483–527.

Breeden, Richard. 2003. "Restoring Trust: Report to The Hon. Jed S. Rakoff, The United States District Court for the Southern District of New York, on Corporate Governance for the Future of MCI, Inc." http://news.findlaw.com/hdocs/docs/worldcom/corpgov82603rpt.pdf.

Chetty, Raj, and Emmanuel Saez. 2005. "Dividend Taxes and Corporate Behavior: Evidence from the 2003 Dividend Tax Cut." *Quarterly Journal of Economics* 120(3): 791–833.

Chetty, Raj, Joseph Rosenberg, and Emmanuel Saez. 2007. "The Effect of Taxes on Market Responses to Dividend Announcements and Payments: What Can We Learn from the 2003 Dividend Tax Cut?" In Alan J. Auerbach, James R. Hines Jr.,

---

[1] One of the recommendations contained in Richard Breeden's (2003) report on the accounting and corporate governance problems at WorldCom is for the company to pay out at least 25 percent of net income each year as a regular cash dividend. The report says in this regard that "dividends are another method of gauging the reality of reported earnings" and that "significant differences between the levels of reported earnings and the availability of cash for dividends would eventually be a red flag of potential problems" (pp. 127–129).

and Joel Slemrod, eds., *Taxing Corporate Income in the 21st Century.* (Cambridge: Cambridge University Press).

DeAngelo, Harry, Linda E. DeAngelo, and Douglas J. Skinner. 2004. "Are Dividends Disappearing? Dividend Concentration and the Consolidation of Earnings." *Journal of Financial Economics* 72(3): 425–456.

Fama, Eugene F., and Kenneth R. French. 2001. "Disappearing Dividends: Changing Firm Characteristics or Lower Propensity to Pay?" *Journal of Financial Economics* 60: 3–43.

Lintner, John. 1956. "Distribution of Incomes of Corporations among Dividends, Retained Earnings, and Taxes." *American Economic Review* 46(2): 97–113.

Poterba, James. 2004. "Corporate Payout Policy." *American Economic Review* 94(2): 171–175.

Skinner, Douglas. 2003. "Should Firms Disclose Everything to Everybody? A Discussion of 'Open Versus Closed Conference Calls: The Determinants and Effects of Broadening Access to Disclosure.'" *Journal of Accounting and Economics* 34(1–3): 181–187.

TWO

Dissecting Dividend Decisions: Some Clues about the Effects of Dividend Taxation from Recent UK Reforms*

Stephen R. Bond

Institute for Fiscal Studies and Nuffield College, Oxford

Michael P. Devereux

University of Warwick and Institute for Fiscal Studies

Alexander Klemm

Institute for Fiscal Studies and University College, London

1. Introduction

Recent changes to the taxation of company dividends in the UK provide an opportunity to investigate empirically how dividend taxes affect firms' dividend policies, cost of capital, and investment. Prior to July 1997, the UK tax system was unusual in that a major class of shareholders – UK pension funds and insurance companies managing pension-related assets – had a more favorable tax treatment of dividend income than capital gains. Tax credits, which reduced personal income tax on dividends for tax-paying shareholders, were repaid to these tax-exempt funds. This position changed sharply in July 1997. Although dividend tax credits remained for taxpayers, they were no longer refundable to UK pension funds and insurance companies. After July 1997, these institutional investors had an equal tax treatment of dividend income and capital gains. This chapter studies the effects of this

---

* This paper is part of the research of the Large Business Tax Programme at the Institute for Fiscal Studies, supported by the Hundred Group, the Inland Revenue, and the Economic & Social Research Council Centre for the Microeconomic Analysis of Public Policy. We thank Alan Auerbach, Tim Besley, Roger Gordon, Jim Hines, Stephen Matthews, Jim Poterba, Joel Slemrod, David Ulph, and participants in seminars at the ESRC Public Economics Working Group, Institute for Fiscal Studies, International Monetary Fund, Inland Revenue, University of Manchester, University of Michigan, University College London, and University of Warwick for helpful comments.

tax reform on the dividend payments and investment spending of quoted nonfinancial UK companies.

In a companion paper, we argue that domestic dividend taxation has little or no effect on the stock market valuation of UK companies. This reconciles the fact that pension funds and insurance companies owned around half the equity in quoted UK firms before July 1997, with the fact that there was no sharp fall in the UK stock market around the time when these repayable tax credits were abolished. The theoretical argument is straightforward and consistent with standard asset pricing models when investors have heterogeneous tax rates.[1] All investors holding some, but not all, of their wealth in an asset must agree on the value of their marginal holding. When a small group of investors has a more favorable tax treatment for a particular risky asset, they will hold more of that asset, up to the point where the additional risk that they bear just balances the tax advantage. This will have a significant effect on the price of the asset only if the wealth controlled by this group of investors is large relative to the international capital market. Essentially, this says that UK equities are priced at their value to foreign investors, which was largely unchanged by the July 1997 tax reform. After July 1997, UK pension funds diversified out of UK equities, and foreign investors increased their holdings, with little or no impact on prices. Bond, Devereux, and Klemm (2007) provide more detail and empirical evidence consistent with these predictions.

If all firms chose their dividend policies simply to maximise their stock market valuations, that would be the end of the story. However, we document that there were significant changes to the form in which UK companies chose to pay dividends immediately after the tax change in July 1997. At that time, UK multinationals with profits earned outside the UK could elect to pay dividends in a special form, known as Foreign Income Dividends (FIDs), which could permit a tax saving for the firm. Before July 1997, FIDs were less attractive than ordinary dividends for UK pension funds, because they did not provide a refundable tax credit. After July 1997, this relative disadvantage was eliminated by the abolition of refundable tax credits on ordinary dividends. Importantly, the tax treatment of both FIDs and ordinary dividends was unchanged for all other shareholders. However, both the number of firms paying FIDs and the proportion of total dividends paid in the form of FIDs increased sharply after July 1997. This is consistent with some influence of UK pension funds over at least this aspect of dividend policies for a group of UK firms.

---

[1] See, for example, Brennan (1970).

Given this, we investigate whether this tax reform had further effects on either the level of dividend payments or the level of investment. We identify a group of quoted nonfinancial UK companies that could have paid FIDs in the period before July 1997 but who chose not to do so, consistent with the tax preference of UK pension funds prior to the abolition of refundable tax credits on ordinary dividends. We then ask whether dividend payments or investment changed for this group, relative to a "control group" of all other quoted nonfinancial UK firms. In making these comparisons, we distinguish between those firms that switched to paying FIDs after July 1997 and those firms that continued not to pay FIDs. This distinction is important because the group that switched to paying FIDs enjoyed a tax saving at the corporate level, whereas other firms did not. We find evidence that this group increased its dividend payments after July 1997, suggesting that some or all of this corporate tax saving was paid out to shareholders as higher dividends. We find no clear evidence of any change in dividend payments for other firms whose reluctance to pay FIDs before July 1997 indicates that they may have been subject to influence from UK pension funds. We also find no evidence of changes in investment spending for either of these groups.

These results are consistent with a version of the "new view" or "trapped equity" model of dividend taxation, developed by King (1974) and Auerbach (1979). We present a simple model in the Appendix that predicts that a reduction in dividend taxes paid by firms will increase dividends paid to shareholders, while an increase in dividend taxes paid by shareholders will have no effect on dividends or investment. However, we acknowledge that our tests may have low power to reject these predictions of the "new view" against reasonable alternatives. We rely partly on an assumption that all firms that could have paid FIDs before July 1997 and chose not to do so were more likely to be influenced by UK pension funds than firms that did not have the option to pay FIDs. This test would have no power if UK pension funds were equally likely to influence both groups of firms.

Perhaps the most interesting aspect of our results is the identification of a group of UK companies that switched from not paying FIDs to paying FIDs immediately after the tax reform in July 1997. This implies a saving in tax at the corporate level, which can account for the observed increase in their dividend payments. Almost certainly, many of these firms could have enjoyed the same tax saving in the period before July 1997, but they chose not to take advantage of this, presumably in the interest of UK pension funds. Yet if the tax treatment of UK pension funds has little or no impact on firms' share prices, this would imply that these firms were not maximizing their stock market valuations in the period before July 1997. To test this, we consider how the share prices of this group of firms reacted to the abolition of refundable dividend tax credits in July 1997. After a small initial fall, we find a significant increase in their share prices relative to those of other quoted nonfinancial UK companies, around one month after the tax reform. While not conclusive, this is consistent with the suggestion that large institutional shareholders can influence at least the financial behaviour of large corporations, even when this is clearly disadvantageous for other shareholders, and even when this results in a lower valuation of the company on the stock market.

The remainder of the paper is organized as follows. Section 2 describes relevant aspects of UK dividend taxation over the period of our study and presents evidence on the increased use of Foreign Income Dividends after July 1997. Section 3 summarizes theoretical predictions about the possible effects of these tax changes, with a formal model presented in the Appendix. Section 4 presents our main empirical evidence on the levels of dividends and investment, while Section 5 presents a simple event study analysis of how this tax reform affected share prices for different groups of firms. Section 6 concludes.

2. UK Dividend Taxation, Before and After July 1997

The tax treatment of UK dividends in the 1990s was complex and changed significantly in July 1994, July 1997, and April 1999. Our review in this section focuses on the features that are particularly important for the empirical analysis in this paper.

Between April 1973 and July 1997, the UK operated a standard form of partial imputation system, with dividend tax credits for domestic shareholders providing tax relief against personal income tax in recognition of part of the corporate income tax paid by UK firms.[2] The rate of these credits fell in line with the basic rate of UK income tax, from 33 percent in 1979 to 25 percent in 1989, and was further cut to 20 percent (below the basic rate of income tax) in 1993.[3] Still, these credits implied that each £1 in cash dividends had a value of £1.25 to tax-exempt shareholders, before they were made nonrefundable in July 1997.[4] This tax reform reduced the value of a

---

[2] Depending on bilateral tax treaties, foreign shareholders may have benefited to a small extent from these tax credits on dividends paid by UK firms. Importantly, this benefit was not reduced by the July 1997 tax reform that we study here, although it may have been reduced by the later reform in April 1999.

[3] The income tax rate on dividends for basic-rate taxpayers was cut to 20 percent at the same time, so the main effect of this change was to reduce the value of dividend tax credits paid out to tax-exempt shareholders.

[4] The credit was expressed as 20 percent of the "grossed-up" value of the dividend (i.e., the cash dividend plus the tax credit).

given cash dividend payment to UK pension funds by 20 percent and was estimated to save the UK government around £5 billion annually, close to 20 percent of total corporate income tax receipts.

These dividend tax credits were at least nominally financed by Advance Corporation Tax (ACT), a tax paid by firms at the time that dividends were paid to their shareholders. For most firms, this was simply a prepayment of the corporate income tax and could be reclaimed in full a few months later, when the annual payment of (mainstream) Corporation Tax was made. However, there was an asymmetry in this system that affected firms whose dividend payments were high relative to their UK taxable profits. Such firms could find themselves in a position where recovery of their ACT payments was deferred, so that ACT acted at least in part as an additional tax.

This asymmetry, known as unrelieved or surplus ACT, particularly affected UK-based multinational firms. These firms earn profits and pay corporate income taxes abroad, so that their UK taxable profits could appear to be low relative to their worldwide operations and dividend payments. Following lobbying from these firms, a special class of dividend payments with a different tax treatment was introduced in July 1994. Firms with foreign profits could opt to pay FIDs.[5] Advance Corporation Tax paid on FIDs could be reclaimed in the same year, regardless of the level of UK taxable profits. This could represent a significant tax saving for firms where recovery of ACT payments on ordinary dividends could not be anticipated in the foreseeable future.

At the shareholder level, the tax treatment of FIDs was equivalent to that of ordinary dividends for taxpaying shareholders, but not for tax-exempt shareholders. Although there were no tax credits on FIDs, they were taxed more favourably under the personal income tax, so that in effect there was the same tax treatment for taxpaying shareholders. However, for tax-exempt shareholders, there was a significant disadvantage: As there were no tax credits on FIDs, there was nothing to be repaid to tax-exempt shareholders. Each £1 received as a FID was thus worth £1 to tax-exempt shareholders. This meant that, prior to July 1997, £1 received as a FID was worth substantially less to these shareholders than £1 received as an ordinary dividend with a repayable tax credit attached.

Considering both corporate and shareholder level taxes, this implied that for firms with unrelieved ACT and foreign income, who could save tax by

---

[5] Firms with foreign income could choose to pay ordinary dividends, FIDs, or both. If FIDs were paid, they had to be paid to all shareholders.

Table 1. *Tax Treatment of Ordinary Dividends and Foreign Income Dividends*

	Type of Shareholder	
	UK Pension Fund	UK Basic Rate Taxpayer
Before July 1997		
Ordinary dividend	$1.25 - 0.25\alpha$	$1 - 0.25\alpha$
Foreign Income Dividend	$1 - \beta$	$1 - \beta$
After July 1997		
Ordinary dividend	$1 - 0.25\alpha$	$1 - 0.25\alpha$
Foreign Income Dividend	$1 - \beta$	$1 - \beta$

Entries show the dividend received if the firm issues £1 of new equity and pays out the proceeds immediately as either an ordinary dividend or a Foreign Income Dividend, to either a UK pension fund or a UK basic rate taxpayer.

$0 \leq \alpha \leq 1$ reflects the tax cost of surplus Advance Corporation Tax, with $\alpha = 0$ indicating no surplus ACT and $\alpha = 1$ indicating extreme irrecoverable ACT.

$\beta \geq 0$ reflects the tax cost of repatriating foreign profits in order to pay a Foreign Income Dividend.

paying FIDs rather than ordinary dividends,[6] the payment of FIDs rather than ordinary dividends was strictly tax-efficient for taxpaying shareholders. The firm saved tax because all ACT paid on FIDs could be recovered without delay, and there was no disadvantage at the personal level for taxpaying shareholders. However, except in an extreme position, the payment of FIDs rather than ordinary dividends was strictly tax-inefficient for UK pension funds in the period from July 1994 to July 1997. The value of the tax credit foregone by these shareholders if the firm paid FIDs was at least as high as the tax saved by the firm, and they could only be equal if there was no prospect of ever recovering any part of the ACT payment.

Table 1 summarises the tax treatment of ordinary dividends and FIDs for two different types of shareholders. In each case, the table shows the net dividend received after all taxes when the firm raises £1 by issuing new shares and pays out the proceeds, either as an ordinary dividend or as a FID. Because a FID can only be paid out of foreign income, we consider the case in which the £1 raised is used to purchase £1 of new shares in a foreign subsidiary, with £1 of this subsidiary's profits being paid back to the parent, before being distributed to the shareholders. We ignore transactions costs.

---

[6] Not all firms with unrelieved ACT and foreign income could make a net tax saving by choosing to pay FIDs, as there may have been offsetting effects on their UK corporation tax charge. We discuss this further below.

Before July 1997, if the shareholder is a UK pension fund, the net value of an ordinary dividend financed in this way can be expressed as $1.25 - 0.25\alpha$, where α is a parameter that varies between 0 and 1 depending on the firm's surplus ACT position. For a firm that is unaffected by surplus ACT, $\alpha = 0$, while for a firm that is in the extreme position with no chance of ever recovering any additional payment of ACT, $\alpha = 1$.[7] After July 1997, the abolition of refundable dividend tax credits on ordinary dividends for UK pension providers reduces this value to $1 - 0.25\alpha$. In both periods, the dividend received by a UK pension fund if the firm instead pays out the proceeds in the form of a Foreign Income Dividend is $1 - \beta$, where $\beta \geq 0$ is a parameter that reflects any UK corporation tax incurred through the additional repatriation of profits from the subsidiary.[8] Similarly, if the shareholder is a basic rate UK taxpayer, the value of the dividend received both before and after this tax reform would be $1 - 0.25\alpha$ if the firm pays an ordinary dividend and $1 - \beta$ if the firm pays a FID.

It is clear from Table 1 that, prior to the reform, a UK pension fund would have strictly preferred to receive income in the form of a FID rather than an ordinary dividend only if $\alpha > 1 + 4\beta$. However, because $\alpha \leq 1$ and $\beta \geq 0$, this could not be the case. Only at the extreme of $\alpha = 1$ and $\beta = 0$ would the pension fund have been indifferent between the two types of dividend. After July 1997, however, the UK pension fund would strictly prefer income in the form of a FID if $\alpha > 4\beta$, a condition that may or may not hold, depending on the firm's surplus ACT position and the cost of repatriating foreign income. Indeed, this is exactly the same condition that determined the tax preference of basic rate taxpayers throughout this period.

It follows that the only change directly brought about by the 1997 reform is in the preferences of UK pension funds. They would have preferred ordinary dividends to FIDs prior to 1997, but – depending on α and β – may have preferred FIDs to ordinary dividends after 1997. Basic rate taxpayers and other shareholders may have preferred FIDs prior to 1997; importantly, there was no change in their preferences as a result of the 1997 reform. Changes in the form in which dividends were paid after this tax reform would therefore be consistent with UK pension funds influencing the dividend behaviour of

---

[7] Abstracting from uncertainty about the delay before an additional ACT payment could be recovered against the firm's corporation tax liability, this parameter can be expressed as $\alpha = 1 - \left(\frac{1}{1+r}\right)^n$, where n is the number of periods before ACT payments are recovered, and r is a discount rate.

[8] This could be significant – for example, if the foreign profits were earned by a subsidiary located in a jurisdiction with a much lower corporate income tax rate than that in the UK. The value of β is thus likely to vary considerably across firms.

Table 2. *UK Firms Paying Foreign Income Dividends*

Year	Number of Firms That Paid FIDs (%)	Proportion of Firms That Paid FIDs (%)	Proportion of Firms with Foreign Activities That Paid FIDs (%)
July 94–June 95	5	0.4	0.6
July 95–June 96	33	2.4	3.8
July 96–June 97	46	3.2	5.1
July 97–June 98	130	8.9	14.5
July 98–March 99	108	8.2	13.4

Notes. This is based on a sample of 1,788 quoted UK companies.

Presence of foreign activities is inferred from reported payment of foreign corporate taxes.

Data is from Thomson Financial Datastream.

UK companies. Note also that, assuming pension funds received ordinary dividends before the tax reform, the net income they received from each £1 of dividends paid must fall after the reform. This is true whether or not the firm switches the form of its dividend payment. In other words, there is an effective increase in dividend taxation for UK pension funds, but not for other shareholders.

Table 2 reports how many quoted UK companies paid FIDs in the period from July 1994 until their abolition in April 1999.[9] Prior to July 1997, fewer than 50 firms were opting to pay FIDs. We cannot be certain how many firms were entitled to do so, but based on information in company accounts about payment of foreign corporate taxes, we estimate that only around 5 percent of quoted UK firms with foreign income were choosing to pay FIDs. Immediately after the abolition of repayable tax credits on ordinary dividends for UK pension funds, however, the number of firms paying FIDs almost trebled, as did the proportion of firms with foreign income that chose to pay FIDs. We stress that the only shareholders who were affected by the abolition of repayable tax credits in July 1997 were UK pension funds and UK insurance companies managing pension assets.

Figures 1 and 2 present quarterly data on the number of FID payments as a fraction of all dividend payments and on the value of FID payments relative to the value of all dividend payments. The proportion of dividend payments taking the form of FIDs was increasing a little before July 1997,

---

[9] Both Advance Corporation Tax (ACT) and Foreign Income Dividends (FIDs) were abolished in April 1999. Further technical changes were made to dividend tax credits at that time, but domestic shareholders were largely unaffected by these changes.

Figure 1. Number of FIDs Relative to Number of Dividend Payments

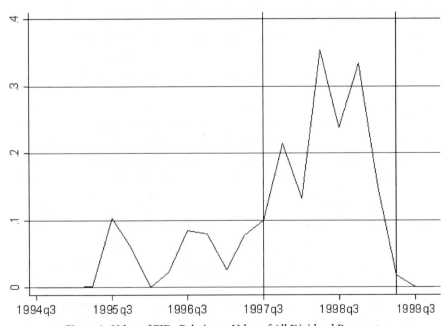

Figure 2. Value of FIDs Relative to Value of All Dividend Payments

but it jumped to a new, higher level immediately after the tax reform. The share of dividends paid as FIDs was more stable at under 10 percent before July 1997 and increased to around 30 percent in 1998.

There are other possible reasons why the use of FIDs may have increased after July 1997. The abolition of FIDs with effect from April 1999 was announced in the July 1997 Budget, at the same time as the abolition of repayable dividend tax credits for UK pension funds. Some firms that had planned to pay FIDs at a later date may have brought forward FID payments as a result. In general, it is not clear why firms that would save tax by paying FIDs rather than ordinary dividends should delay doing so, although expectations of how dividends would be taxed after April 1999 could provide some explanation.[10] Another possibility is that some firms had delayed paying FIDs in the period from July 1994 to July 1997, correctly anticipating that changes to the tax treatment of ordinary dividends would reduce the opposition of UK pension funds to income in the form of FIDs in the near future.

We do not observe the ideal comparison between dividend behaviour in two worlds, one where dividend taxation is fixed forever under the pre-July 1997 regime, and one where dividend taxation is fixed forever under the post-July 1997 regime. Hence, we can only conclude that the sharp increase in the use of FIDs immediately after July 1997 is consistent with some influence of UK pension funds over the dividend behaviour of UK companies, at least in the period before the abolition of repayable dividend tax credits in July 1997.

Nevertheless we regard this as prima facie evidence that the form in which some UK companies chose to pay dividends may have been affected by the tax preference of UK pension funds. This, in turn, suggests the possibility that their dividend policies may have been influenced more generally by the tax treatment of this class of shareholders. To test this, we can investigate whether the abolition of repayable dividend tax credits in July 1997 – which represented a significant increase in the taxation of dividends for these shareholders – affected the level of dividends paid by these firms.

More precisely, we consider a group of firms that could have paid FIDs in the pre-reform period but chose not to do so. These are firms that, in

---

[10] How dividends were to be taxed after April 1999 did not become clear until the Pre-Budget Report of November 1998. The abolition of Advance Corporation Tax and details of the "shadow ACT" regime proposed in November 1998 gave firms that could do so an incentive to pay FIDs rather than ordinary dividends in the short period between November 1998 and April 1999, although in fact the share of dividends paid in the form of FIDs began to decline during this period (see Figure 2).

the period between July 1994 and July 1997: (a) reported paying foreign corporate taxes; (b) paid dividends; and (c) did not pay Foreign Income Dividends. These criteria select a group of firms whose dividend policies were particularly tax-efficient for UK pension funds. In Section 4, we investigate changes in these firms' dividend and investment behaviour, before and after the July 1997 tax reform, relative to other UK companies. In doing this, we distinguish between the subset that switched to paying FIDs in the period between July 1997 and April 1999 and those that did not. The former group is likely to have made a net tax saving at the corporate level, which the latter group clearly did not. As we explain in the next section, this corporate tax saving may also have affected their dividend and investment decisions. First, we review theoretical arguments for why an increase in dividend taxation for a relevant group of shareholders may or may not affect firms' dividend choices or their cost of capital.

3. Alternative Views of Dividend Taxation

The "new view" or "trapped equity" model of dividend taxation, developed by King (1974) and Auerbach (1979), predicts that a change in the level of dividend taxation[11] paid by shareholders has no effect on either dividends or the cost of capital, at least for firms that are paying dividends and whose marginal source of finance for investment is retained earnings (i.e., lower dividend payments). This assumes that shareholders face a higher tax rate on dividend income than on capital gains. A "round trip" that involves issuing one additional unit of new equity and paying out one additional unit of dividends therefore imposes an unnecessary tax charge on shareholders.

Abstracting from factors other than taxation, this makes retained earnings a cheaper source of finance than new share issues. The tax-efficient financial policy is to fund investment by reducing dividends, issuing equity only if attractive investment opportunities exceed the firm's current cash flow. Dividends are paid if cash flow exceeds attractive investment opportunities, but they are determined as the residual. For investment financed by retained earnings, the shareholder gives up dividends today in return for higher dividends in the future. Provided the tax rate on dividends is constant, this lowers both the cost of the investment and the return on the investment in the same way and has no effect on the cost of capital (i.e., the required rate of return from the marginal investment project). Thus, neither

---

[11] Throughout this section, our analysis relates to a change in dividend taxation that is both unanticipated and assumed to be permanent.

investment nor dividends (the difference between cash flow and investment) depend on the rate of dividend taxation paid by shareholders. In effect, dividends are minimised at any tax rate higher than the effective rate on capital gains and are insensitive to the level of dividend taxation within this region.

Applying this analysis to a case where the relevant shareholder faces a lower tax rate on dividends than on capital gains produces uncomfortable predictions. The round trip of issuing equity to pay out dividends becomes a one-way bet. UK pension funds do not pay income tax on dividends or capital gains, but prior to July 1997 they received a repayable tax credit on dividends from UK firms. By issuing £1 of new equity, a firm could pay a cash dividend of £1, which, as explained in the previous section, was worth £1.25 to UK pension funds.[12] A firm choosing dividend policy in the interest of UK pension funds thus had a strong incentive to issue new equity to pay out high dividends. Abstracting from the additional tax cost at the corporate level imposed by surplus Advance Corporation Tax, the optimal levels of both new issues and dividends would appear to be infinite. Even recognising the presence of surplus ACT, the optimal policy would appear to involve issuing equity to pay dividends up to the point where the probability of ever recovering the ACT payment on the last unit of dividends was driven down to zero.[13]

These incentives changed sharply after July 1997. UK pension funds now had no strict tax preference for dividend income rather than capital gains. Indeed, for firms that had previously accumulated a stock of surplus ACT, the payment of ordinary dividends became strictly tax-inefficient. By minimising ordinary dividends, such firms could maximise the rate at which past ACT payments could be recovered against their current corporate income tax liabilities.

This analysis thus predicts that at least some firms whose dividend policies had previously been influenced by the tax treatment of UK pension funds would choose lower dividend payments, at least temporarily, in the period after the abolition of repayable tax credits in July 1997. However, we are skeptical about the extreme financial policies that are predicted. While many UK firms did accumulate surplus Advance Corporation Tax, this was

---

[12] The value of each unit of cash dividends D can be expressed as γD, where $\gamma = 1/(1 - c) > 1$ and $c = 0.2$ is the rate of the tax credit.

[13] Only in this extreme case did the additional tax cost imposed by surplus ACT fully offset the tax credit on dividends paid to tax-exempt shareholders. Devereux, Keen, and Schiantarelli (1994) provide a rigorous analysis of optimal financial policies for firms in this context.

typically due to earning profits outside the UK, rather than to excessive new equity issues. We are also doubtful about the implication that financial policies would be indeterminate in the absence of distortionary taxes.

In the Appendix, we outline a simple formal model in which there are also non-tax costs and benefits associated with the payment of dividends.[14] More specifically, in the spirit of Rozeff (1982), we assume that the use of new equity finance may increase the efficiency with which investment projects are managed by subjecting investment decisions to scrutiny and monitoring from the external capital market. This can explain why firms may choose to issue new equity and pay out dividends at the same time.[15] At the same time, we assume that transaction costs are incurred when firms issue new shares.[16] This can explain why retained earnings may remain the cheapest source of finance, even if relevant shareholders have a tax preference for dividend income over capital gains, as was the case for UK pension funds prior to July 1997.

Provided these transaction costs are high enough, this model can generate similar predictions about the effects of dividend taxes as those associated with the standard version of the "new view" or "trapped equity" model. If small changes in the level of new share issues generate no additional efficiency benefits, an increase in dividend taxes levied on shareholders will have no effect on either the level of new issues or the level of investment chosen by dividend-paying firms and consequently will have no effect on the level of dividend payments.

However, this model also suggests mechanisms through which such dividend taxes could affect dividends or investment, even for dividend-paying firms. For example, an increase in dividend taxation raises the cost of using new equity finance. If small changes in the level of new issues do generate additional efficiency benefits, the firm will trade off these gains against the cost of issuing equity. A higher cost of issuing equity will thus induce the firm to choose a lower level of new issues. If this has no implications for investment, this results in a lower level of dividend payments, as the firm relies less on new issues and more on retained profits to finance its investment spending. If reduced reliance on external finance also reduces the marginal

---

[14] Earlier papers that present interesting extensions to the basic "new view" model include Poterba and Summers (1985) and Auerbach and Hassett (2002).

[15] In the sample of quoted nonfinancial UK companies that we analyse in Section 4, dividends are paid in 96 percent of the accounting periods in which firms issue new shares.

[16] More loosely, we can think of these transaction costs as representing any costs associated with issuing outside equity, such as the signaling cost emphasised by Myers and Majluf (1984) in an asymmetric information context.

profitability of additional investment spending, this increase in the cost of issuing new equity may also result in a lower level of investment.

As in the standard "new view" model, there is also a regime in which dividends are zero and firms rely exclusively on new share issues to finance additional investment spending. For investment financed by new share issues, an increase in dividend taxation lowers the return to shareholders in the form of future post-tax dividend income, with no offsetting effect on the cost to shareholders of financing this investment. In this case, we get the standard result that an increase in dividend taxation raises the cost of capital and results in a lower level of investment.

This more general model thus suggests that an increase in dividend taxation for a relevant group of shareholders could reduce both dividends and investment. Dividends would fall for dividend-paying firms if the higher tax cost of paying dividends induces firms to reduce their reliance on new share issues. Investment would fall for dividend-paying firms if the more limited use of finance from the external capital market reduces the marginal profitability of investment. Alternatively, as predicted by the standard "new view" model in the case where dividends are taxed more heavily than capital gains, an increase in dividend taxation for a relevant group of shareholders could have no effect on either dividends or investment, at least for dividend-paying firms, if neither of these mechanisms is important.

It is also important in the context of UK dividend taxation in the 1990s to consider the effects of dividend taxes levied on firms. Surplus Advance Corporation Tax acted, at least in part, as a corporate tax charged on the payment of ordinary dividends. Firms that switched from paying ordinary dividends to paying Foreign Income Dividends following the abolition of repayable dividend tax credits for UK pension funds thus saved tax at the corporate level.[17] In both the standard "new view" and the corresponding special case of our more general model, it is relatively straightforward to derive the implications of a reduction in dividend taxes levied on firms. The residual left when desired investment has been financed from earnings plus desired new share issues (if any) is now not paid out entirely as cash dividends to shareholders, but is paid out partly as cash dividends to shareholders and partly in the tax on these dividends to the government. A reduction in this tax

---

[17] There are two reasons why we cannot be sure how much tax was saved by individual firms. First, only part of their ACT payments on ordinary dividends may have been irrecoverable. Second, payment of FIDs may have triggered an increase in UK corporate income tax. We can, however, be reasonably confident that these firms enjoyed some net tax saving, as they could have chosen not to pay FIDs otherwise.

implies a straightforward transfer from tax payments to dividend payments. Thus, a saving in corporate tax on dividend payments is expected to result in an increase in cash dividends paid to shareholders. In richer versions of our model, this effect could be reinforced by an increase in the level of new equity issues induced by the lower tax cost of paying dividends.

We have been careful in this section to discuss the tax treatment of "relevant" shareholders, without being specific about the identity of these shareholders in cases where different types of shareholders face different tax rates. We have argued in the introduction that the tax treatment of UK pension funds has little or no effect on the stock market valuation of quoted UK companies, so that if dividend policies are chosen to maximise share prices, we would not expect the taxation of pension funds to be relevant. However, we have presented evidence in the previous section that suggests that at least the form in which UK companies paid dividends may have been influenced by the tax treatment of UK pension funds. We do not attempt to resolve here how firms should behave when different shareholders have conflicting tax preferences. In the next section, we investigate how UK firms did behave in response to the abolition of repayable dividend tax credits for UK pension funds.

4. Evidence on Dividend Payments and Investment

We study the dividend and investment behavior of a sample of 696 quoted nonfinancial UK companies in the period 1994–2001. More precisely, our sample includes accounting periods that end between January 1994 and December 2001, and we require at least one observation on each firm to fall within the pre-reform and post-reform periods. Data on these firms are obtained from Thomson Financial Datastream.

4.1. Dividends

We estimate simple econometric models to explain the level of these firms' dividend payments, controlling for their reported profits and sales. Our main objective is to investigate whether there was any change in dividend behaviour after the July 1997 tax reform, particularly for firms whose prior dividend choices suggest that they may have been influenced by the tax treatment of UK pension funds. Our regression models thus have the general form

$$Div_{it} = Controls_{it}\beta + Dummies_{it}\delta + \varepsilon_{it}, \tag{1}$$

where Div_{it} is the level of dividends paid by firm i in period t, $Controls_{it}$ is a vector of current or lagged control variables including profits and sales,[18] and $Dummies_{it}$ is a vector of dummy variables indicating whether the period is before or after the tax reform and whether we classify the firm as belonging to a group that was more or less likely to be influenced by the tax treatment of UK pension funds.

Quoted UK companies typically pay dividends twice a year, with a relatively small interim dividend being paid during the accounting period and a relatively large final dividend being paid when profits are reported. Our measure of dividends includes both these payments or, more generally, includes all cash dividend payments that are declared to be paid out of the profits reported for accounting period t.[19] This includes any payment of Foreign Income Dividends. Our measure of profits ($Profits_{it}$) is net of depreciation, interest, taxes, exceptional items, and preference dividends.[20] Our measure of firm size is total sales ($Sales_{it}$).[21]

Datastream provides the exact dates on which all dividend payments are made. We use this information to classify company accounts to the post-reform period only if all dividend payments occurred after the tax change on 2 July 1997. All other accounts are classified to the pre-reform period, even if some of the related dividend payments fell after this date.[22] The dummy variable $Post97_t$ takes the value one for accounts classified to the post-reform period and zero otherwise.

As explained in Section 2, we use the choice of not paying FIDs in the period between July 1994 and July 1997 as indicating a group of firms whose dividend behavior may have been influenced by the tax preference of UK pension funds. More precisely, we first define the dummy variable $NoFID_i$ to be equal to one if firm i paid no FIDs between July 1994 and July 1997 and if in the pre-reform period we observe that the firm paid ordinary dividends and reported paying foreign corporate taxes (suggesting that it had foreign activities and could have chosen to pay dividends in the form of FIDs). We then divide the group of firms with $NoFID_i$ equal to one into those firms that continued not to pay FIDs in the post-reform period ($NeverFID_i = 1$)

---

[18] We also consider controlling for unobserved time-invariant, firm-specific "fixed" effects.

[19] This corresponds to item 187 in Datastream's classification of the profit-and-loss account.

[20] This corresponds to item 625 (earned for ordinary) in Datastream's classification of the profit-and-loss account.

[21] Item 104 (total sales) in Datastream's classification of the profit-and-loss account.

[22] Broadly similar results are obtained if we classify to the pre-reform period only those accounts for which all dividend payments occurred before 2 July 1997. Typically, this results in one additional year being allocated to the post-reform period for each firm.

and those that switched to paying FIDs after the abolition of repayable dividend tax credits for UK pension funds ($FIDswitch_i = 1$).

Notice that these dummy variables are time-invariant, so that we use choices made by the firm in the pre-reform period to indicate possible influence from UK pension funds at that time. This is sufficient for the purpose of our test. That is, if these firms change their dividend behavior after July 1997, we are not concerned whether this is because they are still influenced by UK pension funds and the tax preference of UK pension funds has changed or because they are no longer influenced by UK pension funds after July 1997.[23]

Our interest centers on the interaction terms $Post97_t * NeverFID_i$, and $Post97_t * FIDswitch_i$. These dummy variables pick out observations in the post-reform period on the groups of firms whose dividend behavior, at least prior to the reform, may have been influenced by the tax treatment of UK pension funds. Given that we include both these interaction terms and a basic post-reform dummy ($Post97_t$) in our specifications, the coefficient on $Post97_t * NeverFID_i$ tests whether or not there was any differential change in dividend payment behavior after the tax reform for firms that chose not to pay FIDs both before and after the reform; and the coefficient on $Post97_t * FIDswitch_i$ tests whether or not there was any differential change in dividend payment behavior after the tax reform for firms that chose not to pay FIDs before the reform and switched to paying FIDs after the reform.

The null hypothesis that the coefficients on both these interaction terms are zero corresponds to the case in which any change in dividend behavior after July 1997 is common to all quoted nonfinancial UK firms. A significant negative coefficient on $Post97_t * NeverFID_i$ would indicate that, given profits and sales, dividend payments fell on average for the firms that chose never to pay FIDs, relative to firms that could not pay FIDs because they had no foreign income. A significant positive coefficient on $Post97_t * FIDswitch_i$ would indicate that, given profits and sales, dividend payments increased on average for the firms that chose not to pay FIDs in the pre-reform period and switched to paying FIDs in the post-reform period, relative to the same group of other quoted nonfinancial UK companies.

Formally, these can be interpreted as "difference-in-differences" tests, in which those firms that chose never to pay FIDs and those firms that switched

[23] As discussed in more detail in Bond, Devereux, and Klemm (2007), ownership of quoted UK equity by UK pension funds fell sharply after July 1997. The Office for National Statistics estimates that the fraction of quoted UK equity owned by UK pension funds fell from 28 percent in December 1994 to 18 percent in December 2000.

after July 1997 are classed as "treatment groups" and the remaining firms are classed as the "control group." We note that there may be substantial classification errors in our assignment of firms to these groups, in the sense that not all the firms who chose not to pay FIDs in the pre-reform period will have done so because they were influenced by UK pension funds, and UK pension funds may have influenced the dividend behavior of some firms that had no foreign profits and so were not eligible to pay FIDs.

This will certainly weaken the power of our tests, but our tests remain consistent provided that any firms who were influenced by the tax treatment of UK pension funds are more likely to be in one of our treatment groups than in our control group. This assumption is probably more reasonable in the case of firms that switched behavior after the tax reform, because the change in the tax treatment of UK pension funds is likely to have been one of the main reasons why the popularity of FID payments increased after July 1997. It is possibly more debatable in the case of firms that continued not paying FIDs after July 1997. At first sight, the fact that these firms did not switch to paying FIDs after this tax reform might suggest that there were other reasons why these firms had not paid FIDs in the pre-reform period. However, firms that were influenced by UK pension funds, paid high ordinary dividends, and encountered surplus ACT in the period before July 1997 could respond in one of two ways after July 1997. They could avoid the additional tax cost imposed by surplus ACT by switching from ordinary dividends to FIDs, or they could just reduce payments of ordinary dividends. In the former case, they would be in our group with $FIDswitch_i = 1$, but in the latter case they would be in our group with $NeverFID_i = 1$.

It should also be noted that the assignment of firms to these groups is far from random. To be eligible to pay FIDs, firms must have foreign activities and therefore tend to be large. Table 3 reports some basic descriptive statistics for the 690 firms that we observe with accounting periods ending in 1997. The median firm in our treatment group that chose never to pay FIDs has sales that are twice as high as the median firm in our control group, whilst the median firm in our treatment group that switched to paying FIDs has sales that are 18 times higher than the median firm in our control group. These differences in size are even greater when we consider profits and dividends. This illustrates the importance of controlling for differences in size and profitability before inferring that any differential changes in dividend payments after the 1997 tax reform are attributable to changes in the tax treatment of dividends introduced by that reform.

The residuals (ε_{it}) in specifications like equation (1) were found to be severely heteroskedastic. We report weighted least squares estimates, in

Table 3. *Descriptive Statistics*

	Mean	Standard Deviation	Median
FIDswitch firms			
Dividends	68,132	172,180	26,899
Profits	123,480	257,309	51,500
Sales	2,281,408	5,558,159	1,048,100
Investment	109,128	175,311	40,870
NeverFID firms			
Dividends	32,261	216,987	2,685
Profits	41,589	157,930	5,997
Sales	756,946	1,943,478	120,622
Investment	47,912	195,194	4,794
Other firms			
Dividends	11,004	57,625	956
Profits	29,280	200,095	2,245
Sales	396,658	2,077,500	56,729
Investment	28,458	149,267	2,102
All firms			
Dividends	24,453	152,977	1,897
Profits	42,110	191,328	4,040
Sales	702,977	2,566,452	98,755
Investment	43,258	172,662	3,546

Notes: This is a sample of 690 firms in 1997 – 59 of these are classified to the *FIDswitch* group and 278 are classified to the *NeverFID* group.

All figures are in thousands of UK pounds.

which the variance of these residuals is assumed to be proportional to the square of current sales.[24] Ordinary least squares coefficients were generally of the same sign, but estimated much less precisely. Very similar results were obtained using a weighted Tobit maximum likelihood estimator to account formally for the presence of firms paying zero dividends.[25]

Table 4 reports estimates of two basic models, with and without controlling for unobserved firm-specific effects. Columns (1) and (2) include

[24] Noting that these weighted least squares estimates of model equation (1) can also be interpreted as ordinary least squares estimates of the scaled model

$$\frac{Div_{it}}{Sales_{it}} = \left(\frac{Controls_{it}}{Sales_{it}}\right)\beta + \left(\frac{Dummies_{it}}{Sales_{it}}\right)\delta + \frac{\varepsilon_{it}}{Sales_{it}},$$

this estimator will also be less sensitive to the presence of outliers in the highly skewed distributions of profits and sales (see Table 3 for our sample, and the related discussion in Chetty and Saez (2005)).

[25] This is not surprising, as zero dividends are observed for only 8 percent of our sample.

Table 4. *Dividend Models Dependent variable: Total dividends (Div_{it})*

	(1)	(2)	(3)	(4)
Firm Fixed Effects	No	Yes	No	Yes
$Sales_{it}$	0.017	0.020	0.016	0.018
	(0.002)***	(0.002)***	(0.001)***	(0.002)***
$Profits_{it}$	0.149	0.045	0.116	0.047
	(0.024)***	(0.017)***	(0.017)***	(0.016)***
$Lagged\ profits_{it}$			0.080	0.024
			(0.012)***	(0.006)***
$FIDswitch_i$	−379.199		−67.651	
	(393.205)		(379.640)	
$NeverFID_i$	14.362		46.525	
	(42.143)		(54.635)	
$Post97_t$	40.015	−5.687	25.407	−6.578
	(22.818)*	(8.729)	(18.215)	(8.100)
$Post97_t$ * $FIDswitch_i$	866.821	727.184	613.339	682.462
	(390.297)**	(324.477)**	(342.275)*	(290.172)**
$Post97_t$ * $NeverFID_i$	−104.404	6.075	−103.041	−8.819
	(61.157)*	(27.762)	(66.695)	(36.134)
Constant	31.324	66.743	32.300	67.044
	(24.218)	(5.629)***	(20.027)	(5.441)***
Observations	4219	4219	4219	4219
R-squared	0.57	0.87	0.63	0.88

Robust standard errors in parentheses.
* significant at 10 percent; ** significant at 5 percent; *** significant at 1 percent

only current levels of our profits and sales variables. Columns (3) and (4) also allow current dividends to be influenced by profits from the previous period.

As expected, higher profits are associated with higher dividends, and larger firms tend to have higher dividend payout ratios. Other results are quite sensitive to whether or not we control for unobserved firm-specific effects, which in turn affects the estimated coefficients on our observed control variables, particularly those on current and lagged profits. In the specifications that do not control for unobserved heterogeneity, we find evidence of both a significantly higher increase in cash dividends for the firms that switched to paying FIDs after July 1997 and some indication of a relative reduction in cash dividends after July 1997 for the group of firms that could have paid FIDs but chose not to in both periods.[26] However, only the former of these effects is found in the specifications that control for unobserved firm-specific effects. It is also worth noting that in these more general specifications there is no indication of a significant increase in dividend payments, given profits and sales, for our control group.

An increase in cash dividend payments for the firms that saved corporate tax by switching from ordinary dividends to FIDs is consistent both with the predictions of the basic "new view" model and with reasonable alternatives. We do not find robust evidence of an effect on dividend payments for the group of firms that chose not to pay FIDs, both before and after July 1997. This is also consistent with the basic "new view" prediction, although we acknowledge that this test may have low power to reject reasonable alternatives. In particular, we rely here on the assumption that UK pension funds were more likely to have influenced the dividend behavior of this group of firms than that of firms that could not pay FIDs because they had no foreign income.

4.2. Investment

We use a similar approach to investigate differential changes in investment behavior after the 1997 tax reform for these groups of firms. Our investment models have the general form

$$(I/K)_{it} = Controls_{it}\beta + Dummies_{it}\delta + \varepsilon_{it}, \tag{2}$$

where $(I/K)_{it}$ is the rate of gross investment for firm i in period t,[27] the controls include current and lagged values of real sales growth and profitability,[28] and the dummies are those defined in the previous section. Because both investment rates and these control variables do not vary in proportion

---

[26] The p-values of the coefficients on *Post97t* * *NeverFIDi* are 0.093 and 0.080 in columns (1) and (3), respectively.

[27] Gross investment is measured as purchases minus sales of fixed capital assets (Datastream item 1026) plus any net change in fixed capital assets due to the acquisition or disposal of subsidiaries (Datastream item 479). This is scaled by an estimate of the replacement cost value of the net capital stock at the start of the period, constructed using a simple perpetual inventory formula with an assumed depreciation rate of 8 percent (see Bond et al. (2004) for details).

[28] Profitability is measured as reported net profits (earned for ordinary, Datastream item 625) scaled by total sales (Datastream item 104). Very similar results were obtained in alternative specifications in which net profits were scaled by our estimate of the net capital stock at the start of the period.

Table 5. *Investment Models Dependent variable: Investment rate $(I/K)_{it}$*

	(1)	(2)	(3)	(4)
Firm Fixed Effects	No	Yes	No	Yes
Real Sales Growth$_{it}$	0.391 (0.036)***	0.317 (0.042)***	0.382 (0.038)***	0.303 (0.045)***
Lagged Real Sales Growth$_{it}$	0.066 (0.029)**	0.002 (0.035)	0.058 (0.027)**	−0.011 (0.033)
Profitability$_{it}$			0.026 (0.045)	0.040 (0.064)
Lagged Profitability$_{it}$			0.125 (0.070)*	0.167 (0.085)**
FIDswitch$_i$	0.000 (0.051)		0.001 (0.051)	
NeverFID$_i$	−0.003 (0.020)		−0.003 (0.020)	
Post97$_t$	−0.029 (0.017)*	−0.032 (0.019)*	−0.031 (0.017)*	−0.033 (0.018)*
Post97$_t$ * FIDswitch$_i$	0.013 (0.055)	0.010 (0.062)	0.012 (0.055)	0.007 (0.061)
Post97$_t$ * NeverFID$_i$	0.016 (0.021)	0.007 (0.024)	0.017 (0.021)	0.006 (0.024)
Constant	0.170 (0.017)***	0.180 (0.008)***	0.164 (0.018)***	0.173 (0.010)***
Observations	3988	3988	3988	3988
R-squared	0.08	0.31	0.08	0.32

Robust standard errors in parentheses

* significant at 10 percent; ** significant at 5 percent; *** significant at 1 percent

to firm size, we here report ordinary least squares rather than weighted least squares estimates of our investment specifications.

Table 5 reports estimates of two basic models, with and without controlling for unobserved firm-specific effects. Columns (1) and (2) include only current and lagged real sales growth controls, as suggested by a basic accelerator model. Columns (3) and (4) add current and lagged profitability controls, which could proxy for expectations of future profitability or reflect a "financial accelerator" mechanism.[29]

---

[29] See Bond et al. (2004) for further discussion.

As expected, investment rates are related to both sales growth and profitability. Whether or not we control for unobserved firm-specific effects, there is also a significant fall in investment rates on average for this sample of quoted, nonfinancial UK firms after 1997. However, this pattern is common to all groups of firms. There is no evidence of any differential changes in investment behavior after the abolition of repayable dividend tax credits for UK pension funds, either for the firms that chose not to pay FIDs in the pre-reform period and switched to paying FIDs in the post-reform period or for the group of firms that chose not to pay FIDs in either period.

These findings are again consistent with a version of the "new view" model of dividend taxation. In particular, firms that saved tax at the corporate level by switching to pay FIDs may have used some of this tax saving to increase dividend payments, but do not appear to have increased their investment.[30] Given that we do not detect significant changes in dividend behavior for the group that chose not to pay FIDs in both periods, it is perhaps not surprising that we also find no change in their investment behavior.

5. Stock Market Valuations

The behavior of the firms that switched from paying ordinary dividends to paying FIDs after the abolition of repayable dividend tax credits for UK pension funds appears to be particularly interesting. The switch from ordinary dividends to FIDs suggests that these firms were in a surplus ACT position and reduced the extent to which their ACT payments were irrecoverable by switching to FIDs. This saving in tax at the corporate level can account for the increase in their cash dividend payments, relative to other UK companies.

However, it seems very likely that these firms could have enjoyed the same corporate tax saving if they had switched to paying FIDs in the period before July 1997. Our interpretation is that their reluctance to pay FIDs in the earlier period reflected the influence of UK pension funds, which would have lost out on the refundable tax credits on ordinary dividends if these firms had paid FIDs before July 1997. UK pension funds became indifferent between ordinary dividends and FIDs only after the abolition of these refundable credits in July 1997.

---

[30] One implication is that the investment of this group of firms did not appear to be "financially constrained." As we discuss further in the Appendix, this is perhaps not surprising given that there are almost no observations on firms with zero dividends in this group. Also, as we noted above, this group comprises very large multinational corporations.

The choice of paying ordinary dividends rather than FIDs in the period before July 1997 was tax-inefficient for other types of shareholders if these firms were indeed in a surplus ACT position. But only when it also became tax-inefficient for UK pension funds, after July 1997, did we see these firms switching to paying FIDs rather than ordinary dividends.

In Bond, Devereux, and Klemm (2007), we argue that the tax treatment of UK pension funds had little or no impact on the stock market's valuation of dividend income paid by UK firms. If this is right, then the dividend choices made by this group of firms would also have been tax-inefficient from the perspective of their stock market valuations. When it became clear that they could save tax, and hence pay higher cash dividends, by switching from ordinary dividends to FIDs, we would expect to see an increase in their share prices. This is expected not because the stock market valuation of a given pound paid in cash dividends changed, but because by adopting a more tax-efficient form of dividend payments, these firms were able to pay higher cash dividends.[31]

It is difficult to test this hypothesis directly because it is not clear how quickly after the tax reform in July 1997 the market would learn that this group of firms was able to make this tax saving. In Figure 3, we plot the difference in cumulative stock returns between the portfolio of firms that switched to paying FIDs after July 1997 and the portfolio of all other quoted nonfinancial UK companies, for a period of 45 trading days following the Budget statement of 2 July 1997. We present results both for cumulative total returns and for cumulative abnormal returns, where we adjust for movements in the FTSE All Share index.[32] This shows that there was an initial fall in the relative value of the firms that subsequently switched to paying FIDs, which peaked around one week after the Budget. However this fall was quickly reversed, and subsequently there was a substantial increase in the value of these firms, relative to other quoted nonfinancial companies. This rise in their stock market valuation became statistically significant around five weeks after the Budget and then persisted.

---

[31] For the analysis in this section, it is not essential that the tax saving was paid out immediately in higher cash dividends. It would be sufficient for the market to be aware of the tax saving and to anticipate that this would eventually be reflected in higher dividends or lower new issues.

[32] To implement this adjustment, we estimate a beta coefficient for each firm in the sample using data on daily stock returns for a one-year period ending on 1 July 1997. The abnormal return is the actual return minus the firm's beta coefficient times the return on the FTSE All Share index for the same period. All data are obtained from Thomson Financial Datastream.

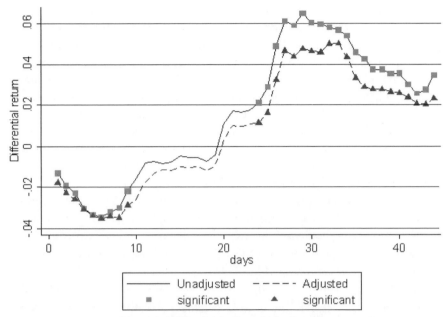

Figure 3. Difference in Cumulative Returns

This increase in the stock market valuation of these firms is consistent with the suggestion that they were previously making dividend choices in the interest of UK pension funds that were costly not only to shareholders with different tax preferences but also having an adverse impact on their share prices. Of course, this evidence is not conclusive. If the stock market had understood immediately that firms would subsequently save tax as a result of these dividend tax changes, we would have expected their share prices to increase immediately. There may have been quite different reasons why the stock market valuation of these large, multinational corporations rose relative to smaller UK companies during August 1997. Nevertheless, it is interesting that for those UK firms whose dividend choices before July 1997 appeared in theory to be inconsistent with stock market value maximization, there is some evidence that this may indeed have been reflected in lower stock market valuations than they could have achieved.

6. Conclusions

We have analysed the implications of the abolition of repayable dividend tax credits for UK pension funds in July 1997 for the dividend policies and investment spending of UK companies. UK dividend taxation was complex in this period, and it is important to consider the form in which dividends were paid, as well as the level of total dividend payments. We identify a group of firms that saved tax at the corporate level by switching to a particular form of dividend payments, following the equalization of the tax treatment of these and ordinary dividends at the shareholder level for UK pension funds. For this group, we report evidence that at least part of this corporate tax saving may have been paid out as higher cash dividends. We find no evidence of any change in their investment behavior. For other firms whose dividend choices may also have been influenced by the tax preference of UK pension funds in the period before July 1997, we find no clear evidence of any changes in dividend payments or investment.

These findings are consistent with a version of the "new view" of dividend taxation. However, we acknowledge that our empirical tests may have low power to reject predictions of the "new view" against reasonable alternatives. This reflects the fundamental difficulty of identifying subsamples whose dividend behavior was particularly likely to have been influenced by UK pension funds in the pre-reform period; with the possible exception of those firms that switched from paying ordinary dividends to paying Foreign Income Dividends (FIDs) in the post-reform period. The level of dividends paid by this group was affected by the associated tax saving at the corporate level, as well as by the change in the tax treatment of UK pension funds.

The behavior of this group of firms is particularly interesting and difficult to reconcile with the objective of (stock market) value maximization. By choosing not to pay FIDs in the pre-reform period, these firms declined an opportunity to save tax at the corporate level. This may have been tax-efficient from the perspective of UK pension funds, but it was tax-inefficient from the perspective of most other shareholders. Asset pricing theory suggests that the tax treatment of UK pension funds is unlikely to be significant for the stock market valuation of UK firms, whose shares are traded internationally. Consistent with this, we observe that the stock market valuation of this group of firms rose significantly around one month after this tax reform. While not conclusive, this is consistent with the suggestion that large institutional shareholders can influence the dividend behavior of large corporations, even when this is disadvantageous for other shareholders and even when this results in a lower stock market valuation.

References

Auerbach, Alan J. 1979. "Wealth Maximization and the Cost of Capital." *Quarterly Journal of Economics* 93(3): 433–446.

Auerbach, Alan J., and Kevin A. Hassett. 2002. "On the Marginal Source of Investment Funds." *Journal of Public Economics* 87(1): 205–232.

Bond, Stephen R., and Jason G. Cummins. 2001. "Noisy Share Prices and the Q Model of Investment." Working paper W01/22. (London: Institute for Fiscal Studies).

Bond, Stephen R., Michael P. Devereux, and Alexander Klemm. 2007. "The Effects of Dividend Taxes on Equity Prices: A Re-examination of the 1997 UK Tax Reform." Working paper 07/01. (Oxford: Oxford University Centre for Business Taxation).

Bond, Stephen R., Alexander Klemm, R. Newton-Smith, M. Syed, and G. Vlieghe. 2004. "The Roles of Expected Profitability, Tobin's Q and Cash Flow in Econometric Models of Company Investment." Working paper 222. (London: Bank of England).

Brennan, Michael J. 1970. "Taxes, Market Valuation and Corporate Financial Policy." *National Tax Journal* 23(4): 417–427.

Chetty, Raj, and Emmanuel Saez. 2005. "Dividend Taxes and Corporate Behavior: Evidence from the 2003 Dividend Tax Cut." *Quarterly Journal of Economics* 120(3): 791–833.

Devereux, Michael P., Michael J. Keen, and Fabio Schiantarelli. 1994. "Corporation Tax Asymmetries and Investment: Evidence from U.K. Panel Data." *Journal of Public Economics* 53(3): 395–418.

Fazzari, Steven M., R. Glenn Hubbard, and Bruce C. Petersen. 1988. "Financing Constraints and Corporate Investment." *Brookings Papers on Economic Activity* 1: 141–195.

Hayashi, Fumio. 1985. "Corporate Finance Side of the Q Theory of Investment." *Journal of Public Economics* 27(3): 261–280.

King, Mervyn A. 1974. "Taxation and the Cost of Capital." *Review of Economic Studies* 41(125): 21–35.

Myers, Stewart C., and Nicholas S. Majluf. 1984. "Corporate Financing and Investment Decisions When Firms Have Information That Investors Do Not Have." *Journal of Financial Economics* 13(2): 187–221.

Poterba, James M., and Lawrence H. Summers. 1985. "The Economic Effects of Dividend Taxation." In Edward Altman and Marti Subrahmanyam, eds., *Recent Advances in Corporate Finance* (Homewood, IL: Richard D. Irwin), pp. 227–284.

Rozeff, Michael S. 1982. "Growth, Beta, and Agency Costs as Determinants of Dividend Payout Ratios." *Journal of Financial Research* 5(3): 249–259.

APPENDIX

A Simple Formal Model of Dividends and Investment

We consider a stylised model in which the firm invests in the first period and pays out the proceeds in the form of dividends in the second period. To focus on the implications of dividend taxation for dividend payments and new share issues, we assume the firm issues no debt. We first consider a dividend tax paid by shareholders.

In the first period, the firm has a predetermined level of cash flow, denoted C. It invests an amount I and issues new shares with a value $N \geq 0$. If shares are issued, a transaction cost f per unit is paid to a third party. The firm pays a dividend of $D = C - I + (1 - f)N \geq 0$. This dividend is valued by the relevant shareholder at γD, where $\gamma \neq 1$ reflects the presence of distortionary taxes. For example, if the relevant shareholder pays income tax on dividends at rate m and no tax on capital gains, we would have $\gamma = 1 - m < 1$. If the relevant shareholder is a tax-exempt institution that receives a repayable tax credit on dividends at rate c, we would have $\gamma = \frac{1}{1-c} > 1$.[33]

At a given level of investment, paying a higher dividend requires the firm to issue more shares, so the transaction cost on new share issues represents a nontax cost of paying dividends. Whilst we model this formally as a transaction cost, we could think more loosely of this representing other costs associated with issuing outside equity, such as the signaling cost emphasized by Myers and Majluf (1984).

In the second period, the investment generates a payoff $\Pi(I, N)$, with $\Pi_I \geq 0$, $\Pi_{II} \leq 0$, $\Pi_N \geq 0$, $\Pi_{NN} \leq 0$, and $\Pi_{IN} \geq 0$. In the spirit of Rozeff (1982), the positive dependence of this payoff on the level of new equity reflects possible "control benefits" of subjecting the investment decision to scrutiny and monitoring from the external capital market, rather than relying on internal finance. This effect on future profits represents a nontax benefit of paying dividends. For simplicity, this payoff in the second period is assumed to be paid out in full as a dividend, and each unit of dividends is valued by the relevant shareholder at the same value of γ in the second period as in the first.

The firm is assumed to choose I and N to maximize the present value of net distributions

$$\gamma D - N + \gamma \beta \Pi,$$

where $\beta < 1$ is a discount factor, subject to nonnegativity constraints on dividend payments and new share issues. Because there is no uncertainty in the model, we have $\beta = \frac{1}{1+r}$, where r is the risk-free interest rate between the two periods. The firm thus maximizes

$$V = \gamma(C - I + (1 - f)N) - N + \lambda^D(C - I + (1 - f)N)$$
$$+ \lambda^N N + \gamma \beta \Pi(I, N),$$

---

[33] This treatment of shareholder taxes is standard in the "new view" literature. See, for example, King (1974) and Auerbach (1979).

where λ^D and λ^N are shadow values associated with the nonnegativity constraints. The first-order conditions for investment and new issues are, respectively:

$$V_I = -(\gamma + \lambda^D) + \gamma\beta\Pi_I = 0$$
$$\Rightarrow \Pi_I = (1+r)\left(\frac{\gamma + \lambda^D}{\gamma}\right) \tag{3}$$

and

$$V_N = \gamma(1-f) - 1 + \lambda^D(1-f) + \lambda^N + \gamma\beta\Pi_N = 0$$
$$\Rightarrow \lambda^D(1-f) + \lambda^N = 1 - \gamma(1-f) - \gamma\beta\Pi_N \tag{4}$$

We first consider an internal solution with strictly positive levels of both dividends and new share issues, so that $\lambda^D = \lambda^N = 0$. In this case, the first-order conditions simplify to

$$\Pi_I = (1+r) \tag{5}$$

and

$$\Pi_N = (1+r)\left(\frac{1}{\gamma} - (1-f)\right). \tag{6}$$

Notice that this requires $(\frac{1}{\gamma} - (1-f)) \geq 0$, or the standard "pecking order" in which external finance is not less expensive than internal finance. This is satisfied automatically if $\gamma < 1$, so that dividends are taxed more heavily than capital gains, but otherwise requires transactions costs to be high enough to outweigh the tax advantage of dividends. However, firms facing a tax (or tax plus transaction cost) disadvantage of paying dividends do not reduce new share issues to zero here, because exposure to the external capital market is assumed to result in better corporate control.

In general, the levels of investment and new share issues are jointly determined by the interest rate (r), the tax discrimination parameter (γ), and the transaction cost (f). An increase in dividend taxation implies a reduction in γ. Provided we remain at an internal solution, the first-order condition for new share issues, equation (6), shows that this requires an increase in the marginal benefit of issuing new shares (Π_N), which in turn requires a reduction in the level of new shares issued. In turn, a lower level of new equity will reduce the marginal productivity of investment (Π_I) if the cross-derivative Π_{IN} is strictly positive, thus implying a lower level of investment from equation (5). This is one channel through which higher dividend taxes can affect investment in this model. A higher level of dividend taxes will also result in a lower level of dividends, provided the reduction in investment is less than the reduction in new share issues.

The model also has a corner solution in which dividend payments are zero. This occurs when the inherited cash flow (C) is so low relative to investment opportunities that, if the firm issues the optimal level of new shares (N^*) suggested by the analysis above, it cannot finance the optimal level of investment (I^*) and pay positive dividends in the current period. This results in a corner solution with $N > 0$ so that $\lambda^N = 0$, but with $D = 0$ so that $\lambda^D > 0$. In this case, the first-order conditions are

$$\Pi_I = (1+r)\left(1+\frac{\lambda^D}{\gamma}\right) \tag{7}$$

and

$$\Pi_N = (1+r)\left(\frac{1}{\gamma} - (1-f)\left(1+\frac{\lambda^D}{\gamma}\right)\right). \tag{8}$$

Because $\lambda^D > 0$, this requires Π_N to be lower and Π_I to be higher than they would be (for the same values of r, γ, and f) in the internal solution. Assuming that the own-partial derivatives dominate the cross-partial derivative, this implies that new share issues will be higher and investment will be lower than they would be if the same firm had inherited a level of cash flow that was high enough, given its investment opportunities, to enable it to pay strictly positive dividends.

We note that the firm is "financially constrained" in this regime. A windfall increase in cash flow (C) would reduce the shadow value of internal funds (λ^D), reducing new share issues and increasing investment. Thus, "control benefits" of issuing new equity can rationalize why many firms simultaneously pay dividends and issue new shares (in the internal solution),[34] without ruling out the possibility of some firms being subject to financial constraints. However, the firms in this constrained regime are identified by having strictly zero dividends.[35]

The presence of this constrained regime provides a second channel through which dividend taxes can affect investment. As we noted above,

[34] In the sample of quoted nonfinancial UK companies that we analyse in Section 4, dividends are paid in 96 percent of the accounting periods in which firms issue new shares.

[35] As noted by Hayashi (1985) and emphasized by Fazzari, Hubbard, and Petersen (1988), investment also displays "excess sensitivity" to cash flow in a constrained regime of the standard "new view" or "pecking order" model. See Bond and Cummins (2001) and Bond et al. (2004) for recent evidence on investment cash flow sensitivity in samples of quoted U. S. and UK companies.

for firms at an internal solution, a higher level of dividend taxes will tend to reduce both new share issues and investment. Assuming that the reduction in new issues exceeds the reduction in investment (i.e., that a higher level of dividend taxes results in lower dividends), this may shift a previously dividend-paying firm into the constrained regime. In this case, the required return on investment increases from $(1 + r)$ as in equation (5) to the higher value in equation (7), and the chosen level of investment is lower.

A higher level of dividend taxation also reduces investment for firms that are within the constrained regime. To illustrate this, suppose that the marginal benefit Π_N falls to zero beyond some level of new issues. In this case, the first-order condition for new issues equation (8) gives

$$\left(1 + \frac{\lambda^D}{\gamma}\right) = \frac{1}{\gamma(1 - f)} > 1,$$

and the first-order condition for investment becomes

$$\Pi_I = \frac{1 + r}{\gamma(1 - f)} > 1 + r.$$

In this limiting case, the required rate of return on investment is increasing in dividend taxes, which lower the valuation parameter γ. This corresponds to the standard result in the "new view" model that dividend taxes raise the cost of capital for firms that pay zero dividends and whose marginal source of finance is new equity.[36]

The general model is illustrated in Figure 4. A firm with inherited cash flow C chooses to issue new shares N^* from equation (6) provided it is at an internal solution for dividends. A firm with investment opportunities described by the marginal profitability schedule Π_I^A chooses to invest I^* and pays dividends $(C + (1 - f)N^* - I^*)$. An otherwise similar firm with more attractive investment opportunities described by the schedule Π_I^B would be at a corner solution with zero dividends.[37] This firm invests I^B and issues new shares to the value $\frac{I^B - C}{1 - f}$.

Figure 5 illustrates the effects of an increase in dividend taxation for a firm that remains within the dividend-paying regime. The optimal level of new

---

[36] Strictly, this holds when at least part of the return on the investment will be paid out in the form of dividends. In this case, higher dividend taxes reduce the return on the investment to shareholders, with no corresponding reduction in the cost borne by shareholders when the investment is financed by new equity.

[37] In Figure 1, we assume for simplicity that these two firms would have the same level of new issues N^* in the unconstrained regime.

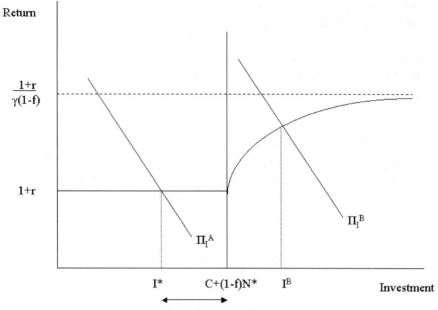

Figure 4. Dividends and Investment

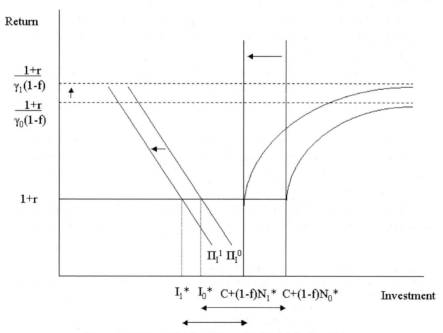

Figure 5. Higher Dividend Taxes; Dividend-Paying Firms

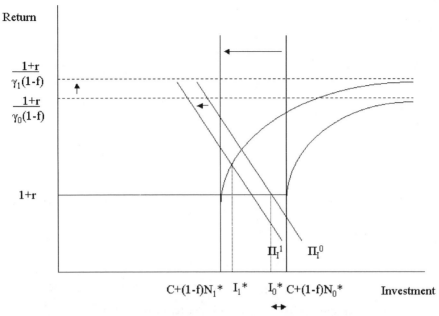

Figure 6. Higher Dividend Taxes; Regime-Switching Firms

shares falls from N_0^* to N_1^*, and the optimal level of investment falls from I_0^* to I_1^*. Dividend payments fall by the amount $(1 - f)(N_0^* - N_1^*) - (I_0^* - I_1^*)$. Notice that the cost of capital does not depend on the level of dividend taxation in this regime, but investment may nevertheless fall if the more limited use of finance from the external capital market reduces the marginal profitability of investment.

Figure 6 illustrates the effects for a firm that shifts from the dividend-paying regime to the zero dividend regime. This results from the reduction in N^*. In this case, the cost of capital is affected, and investment falls even if the marginal profitability of investment does not depend on the level of new share issues. Investment falls for two reasons in the general case illustrated. Dividends obviously fall to zero for firms in this position.

Figure 7 illustrates the effects for a firm that remains within the zero dividends regime. For such firms, the cost of capital increases and investment falls, whether or not marginal profitability depends on new share issues. Clearly, dividends are unchanged in this case.

A special case of the model that is of some interest is the case where $\Pi_{IN} = 0$, so that the payoff is additively separable in the levels of investment and new share issues. In this case, for firms at an internal solution, the first-order condition equation (5) determines investment and the first-order condition equation (6) determines new issues. Firms may simultaneously

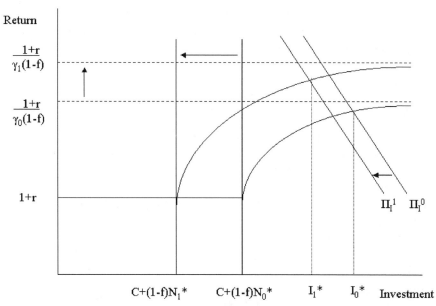

Figure 7. Higher Dividend Taxes; Zero-Dividend Firms

issue new shares and pay dividends, and dividend taxation will influence the level of dividends, but – as in the standard "new view" – investment does not depend on the level of dividend taxation for firms that pay positive dividends. There is still a corner solution with zero dividends, and an increase in the level of dividend taxes reduces investment for firms that are in (or sufficiently close to) this regime.

Another special case of the model has $\Pi_N = \Pi_{NN} = \Pi_{IN} = 0$. In this case, we have a version of the standard new view model with transactions costs for new equity issues incorporated to ensure that retained earnings remain the preferred source of finance even if the relevant shareholder has a tax preference for dividend income over capital gains. Firms should not simultaneously pay dividends and issue new shares, and an increase in the level of dividend taxation has no effect on either dividends or investment for dividend-paying firms.

Finally, the Modigliani-Miller separation between real and financial decisions emerges in the special case with $\Pi_N = \Pi_{NN} = \Pi_{IN} = 0, \gamma = 1$, and $f = 0.$[38] In this case, investment is determined by the first-order condition equation (5) for all firms and financial policy is indeterminate.

To summarize: The key prediction of our general model is that an increase in dividend taxation for relevant shareholders will reduce dividend payments

[38] Or, more generally, with $\gamma^{-1} = 1 - f$.

for dividend-paying firms, if the higher tax cost of paying dividends induces firms to reduce their reliance on new share issues. This may also reduce investment for these firms, if the more limited use of finance from the external capital market reduces the marginal profitability of investment.

A Dividend Tax Paid by Firms

We now extend this model to include a tax on dividends paid by the firm. This provides a stylised representation of the tax cost associated with unrelieved Advance Corporation Tax in the UK and in particular allows us to consider the implications for dividends of the corporate tax saving achieved by firms that switched from paying ordinary dividends to paying Foreign Income Dividends.

If the firm pays tax T on its dividend payments, the full cost of paying a cash dividend D to its shareholders becomes $D^F = D + T$. If this tax is expressed as a rate s charged on D^F, we obtain $D^F = D + sD^F = D/(1 - s)$. The firm thus pays a dividend of $D = (1 - s)(C - I + (1 - f)N) \geq 0$ in the first period and $(1 - s)\Pi$ in the second period. The firm now maximizes

$$V = \gamma(1 - s)(C - I + (1 - f)N) - N + \lambda^D(1 - s)(C - I + (1 - f)N)$$
$$+ \lambda^N N + \gamma(1 - s)\beta\Pi(I, N).$$

In general, the first-order condition for investment is still given by equation (3) above, whilst the first-order condition for new issues becomes

$$\lambda^D(1 - s)(1 - f) + \lambda^N = 1 - \gamma(1 - s)(1 - f) - \gamma(1 - s)\beta\Pi_N.$$

For dividend-paying firms, we obtain

$$\Pi_N = (1 + r)\left(\frac{1}{\gamma(1 - s)} - (1 - f)\right).$$

If the optimal level of new share issues does not depend on the level of dividend taxation, we obtain the "new view" result that for dividend-paying firms a reduction in the rate of a dividend tax (s) levied on firms will leave investment and hence the full cost of paying dividends (D^F) unchanged. In this case, the cash dividend (D) paid to shareholders increases, to keep $D^F = D/(1 - s)$ constant. The tax saved by the firm is simply paid out to its shareholders. If this reduction in dividend taxation induces the firm to increase the level of new issues, this will imply a further increase in both D^F and D; and if $\Pi_{IN} > 0$, then there could also be an increase in investment.

Comments

Roger Gordon

University of California, San Diego and NBER

The objective of this chapter is to analyse how firms responded to a tax reform in the UK in July 1997 that altered the tax treatment of dividends. The behavioral responses were dramatic, making the analysis of particular importance.

In order to understand the nature of the tax reform, it helps to describe first the nature of the UK tax law prior to the tax reform. During this time period, dividends could take either of two forms: ordinary dividends or foreign-income dividends (FIDs). There had been three key differences in the tax treatment of these two types of dividends:

1. Domestic recipients of ordinary dividends received a refundable credit for corporate taxes paid on the underlying income. Domestic recipients of FIDs did not receive such a credit, but *taxable* domestic recipients received the equivalent of the credit through reduced tax rates. Tax-exempt domestic recipients did not receive a credit for FIDs, though they did for ordinary dividends.
2. Ordinary dividends were subject to a minimum corporate tax, set to ensure that corporate tax payments per pound of ordinary dividends at least equaled the credit per pound of dividends received by a domestic recipient. FIDs were not subject to this minimum corporate tax.
3. To pay FIDs, firms had to repatriate profits from abroad sufficient to finance these dividends. Repatriations were subject to domestic corporate taxes, though with a credit for corporate taxes paid abroad on this income.

The tax reform act of July 1997 changed these tax provisions in two key ways. First, domestic tax-exempt recipients of ordinary dividends were no longer eligible for a credit, eliminating one advantage of ordinary dividends compared with FIDs. Second, as of April 1999, FIDs would no longer be available as an alternative form of dividends – all dividends would be classified as ordinary dividends.

In response to the tax reform, payments of FIDs and the number of firms paying FIDs tripled! It seems obvious just from the time-series variation that the act had a huge effect on behavior. Even with this tripling, however, only about 15 percent of firms with foreign operations paid FIDs, so that most firms continued to use ordinary dividends instead. In addition, the paper mentions briefly that the portfolios of domestic tax-exempt investors also changed dramatically following the tax reform, shifting out of domestic equity as would have been expected given the nature of the tax change.

The objective of the chapter is not, however, to analyse which firms changed behavior. This is disappointing, because such a dramatic change in behavior justifies close analysis. Instead, the chapter uses the decision by a firm to initiate payments of FIDs after the reform as an indicator that it faces different incentives. The chapter then investigates the extent to which the total dividend payout rate, investment rate, and share values responded differently to the tax reform for these firms compared with other firms that had foreign operations but did not initiate FIDs after the reform.

The key question, given this research strategy, is then to assess how we would expect firms that chose to initiate payments of FIDs following the tax reform to differ from firms that chose not to initiate payments of FIDs. The presumption in this chapter is that firms that initiated FID payments must have a particularly large fraction of their shares owned by domestic tax-exempt investors. The basis for this presumption is that these investors strictly preferred ordinary dividends prior to the tax reform, because only ordinary dividends were eligible for the credit, yet other investors could well prefer FIDs in order to avoid any risk of extra corporate tax payments arising from ordinary dividends due to the minimum corporate tax on such dividends. After the tax reform, tax-exempt investors are no longer affected by the form of dividend, so that other considerations dominate. If these firms are responding primarily to domestic tax-exempt investors for one decision, then the presumption is that they will be responding primarily to these investors on other decisions as well, and their share price would also reflect the preferences of tax-exempt investors.

Yet no evidence is provided in the paper to support this presumption that the firms that initiate FIDs are in fact more heavily owned by domestic tax-exempt investors. Even if they were, it is still not obvious that their incentives differ from those of other firms.

Why such skepticism? Standard models of portfolio choice, ignoring taxes, forecast that the equity portfolios of all domestic investors should have the same composition. More risk-averse investors will put a smaller share of their assets into equity, but the composition of their equity portfolio will still be the same as that for other investors. Taxes of course do affect portfolio choices, so that tax-exempt investors will find shares with a high dividend payout rate to be more attractive than would be the case for taxable investors. There is no evidence provided that firms that initiate FIDs have high dividend payout rates, though such a pattern is not implausible.

However, even if portfolios differ by investor due to such tax differences, existing models of asset pricing (e.g., Brennan (1970) or Gordon and Bradford (1980)) indicate that the relative values assigned by the market to ordinary dividends, FIDs, or capital gains generated by retentions should be the same across all firms. There is no "marginal" investor, because all investors according to the models should own at least some of each firm's shares. The influence of investors on equity prices is greater if their wealth is greater or if they are less risk averse. But their influence does not depend on the size of their holdings in the share, per se.

Why, then, do some firms initiate FIDs and others do not? Clearly, something systematic must differ among these firms.

To assess this, let me lay out the overall tax implications for both the firm and its investors of paying ordinary dividends versus FIDs. The presumption is that the firm will choose the *form* of payout to minimize its overall tax liabilities.

If the firm currently pays ordinary dividends of D, the resulting tax costs prior to the 1997 tax reform would have consisted first of minimum corporate tax payments of $\tau_d D/(1 - \tau_d)$,[1] resulting in extra corporate taxes to the extent that this exceeds regular corporate tax liabilities of $\tau_d \pi_d$. In addition, domestic investors receive a credit of $\tau_d/(1 - \tau_d)$ per pound of dividends they receive. Let β denote the fraction of ordinary dividends going to domestic investors. Finally, domestic taxable investors owe personal tax on the underlying corporate income used to finance the dividends. Let β^* denote the fraction of dividends going to taxable domestic investors and denote their average marginal tax rate by $\bar{m}$.[2] Overall tax liabilities on ordinary dividends are therefore

$$\max\left(\frac{\tau_d}{1 - \tau_d} D - \tau_d \pi_d, 0\right) - \beta \frac{\tau_d}{1 - \tau_d} D + \beta^* \bar{m} \frac{D}{1 - \tau_d}. \tag{1}$$

[1] Here, the corporate income that must have been earned to finance D in dividends should have been $D/(1 - \tau_d)$, so that minimum corporate taxes are $\tau_d D/(1 - \tau_d)$.

[2] For simplicity, I ignore here any tax liabilities incurred by foreign investors. These liabilities will cancel out in the following derivation.

Similarly, the tax liabilities incurred when the firm pays an amount F in FIDs equal

$$\max\left(\frac{\tau_d - \tau_f}{1 - \tau_f}F, 0\right) - \beta^*\frac{\tau_d}{1 - \tau_d}F + \beta^*\bar{m}\frac{F}{1 - \tau_d}. \tag{2}$$

Here, the first term measures the domestic corporate taxes due when dividends of F are received from abroad, as needed in order to finance FIDs.[3] By statute, only taxable domestic investors in effect receive a credit when they receive FIDs, offset by any personal taxes they owe on the underlying corporate income.

The firm should then choose D and F to minimize the sum of the expressions (1) and (2), for any given overall payout rate $P \equiv D + F$. Increasing F by a pound and simultaneously cutting D by a pound to maintain the same overall payout rate, the change in overall tax liabilities equals

$$\max\left(\frac{\tau_d - \tau_f}{1 - \tau_f}, 0\right) + (\beta - \beta^*)\frac{\tau_d}{1 - \tau_d} - \delta\frac{\tau_d}{1 - \tau_d}, \tag{3}$$

where $\delta = 1$ if $D > \pi_d(1 - \tau_d)$, and $\delta = 0$ otherwise. By paying F, some taxes may be due on the repatriated profits needed to finance an extra FID. Payments of F were not eligible for a credit for domestic tax-exempt recipients, though payments of D would have been eligible. Finally, payments of F were not subject to a minimum corporate tax, while payments of D were. This matters only if the existing minimum corporate tax payments exceed what would have been owed anyway under the regular corporate tax.

The firm would find shifting from F to D to be attractive if expression (3) is negative, and conversely. What can we say about the sign of expression (3)? First, the evidence in Hines and Hubbard (1990), admittedly just for the United States, suggests that firms are largely able to avoid repatriation taxes, perhaps by selectively repatriating profits from locations with high corporate tax liabilities. If this same pattern exists for the UK, then the first term in expression (3) should be small.[4]

Given this assumption, we can then conclude that the composition of dividends will be chosen such that only D is paid as long as total payouts are less than $\pi_d(1 - \tau_d)$. As emphasized in the paper, ordinary dividends provide a credit for domestic tax-exempt investors, while FIDs do not. If total payouts are larger than $\pi_d(1 - \tau_d)$, then $D = \pi_d(1 - \tau_d)$ and all further

---

[3] The foreign profits needed to finance these dividends equal $F/(1 - \tau_f)$, where τ_f is the foreign corporate tax rate. This income is taxable in the UK, but with a credit for corporate taxes paid abroad.

[4] This is also the presumption in the chapter by Bond, Devereux, and Klemm.

dividends take the form of FIDs. When the minimum corporate tax due on extra ordinary dividends implies increased overall corporate tax payments, this liability is large enough to dominate all other considerations. Ordinary dividends will never be increased to the point that extra corporate taxes arise due to this minimum corporate tax.

We then conclude that firms with $P > \pi_d(1 - \tau_d)$ pay FIDs, and conversely. Which firms would likely have an overall desired payout rate larger than $\pi_d(1 - \tau_d)$? The presumption in the past literature is that overall dividend payouts are proportional to "expected" after-tax profits: $P \approx \alpha(\pi_d(1 - \tau_d) + \pi_f(1 - \tau_f))$ for some α.[5] Then $P > \pi_d(1 - \tau_d)$ whenever

$$\pi_f(1 - \tau_f) > \frac{1 - \alpha}{\alpha}\pi_d(1 - \tau_d).$$

Firms paying FIDs should therefore be firms that have an unusually large fraction of their profits coming from foreign operations. This certainly seems to be the case on the basis of the statistics reported in the chapter.

Given this model for payment of FIDs versus ordinary dividends, though, how would forecasted behavior change with the 1997 tax reform? This reform consisted of two pieces. The chapter by Bond, Devereux, and Klemm focuses on the first piece, which eliminated the availability of the dividend tax credit for domestic tax-exempt investors. Specifically, this reform implies that β is replaced by $\beta^* < \beta$ in expression (1).

However, forecasted behavior based on expression (3) does not change as a result. Whether or not minimum corporate taxes result in extra corporate tax liabilities remains a dominant consideration.

The other piece of the 1997 tax reform could well explain the jump in the number of firms paying FIDs, however. This other piece of the legislation announced that FIDs would no longer be available as an option after April 1999. How would this announcement change current behavior?

If a firm expects that $P < \pi_d(1 - \tau_d)$ for the indefinite future, then the above model forecasts that all payouts will take the form of ordinary dividends: $F = 0$.

What if the firm expects that $P > \pi_d(1 - \tau_d)$ sometime after 1999? Until July 1997, the firm would have planned to make any payouts above $\pi_d(1 - \tau_d)$ after 1999 in the form of FIDs, in order to avoid owing any extra corporate taxes due to the minimum corporate tax. With the reform, this

---

[5] While originally attributed to Lintner (1956) as a behavioral description of firm behavior, this pattern is also consistent with a signaling model (more profitable firms are able to signal more aggressively) and with an agency model (more profitable firms have greater worthwhile investment projects, so that shareholders are willing to leave more money within the firms).

will no longer be feasible after 1999. But it remains feasible until then – the firm can still avoid these extra minimum corporate tax liabilities by shifting payouts to dates before April 1999.

The above model then forecasts that firms whose desired payout now is less than $\pi_d(1 - \tau_d)$ but whose desired payout in the future is above $\pi_d(1 - \tau_d)$ may well respond to the tax reform by prepaying future dividends at an earlier date (prior to April 1999) in order to save on corporate taxes. Total payouts should go up, and the increase will largely take the form of FIDs.[6]

Firms responding this way will be firms with a substantial share of their profits coming from abroad, but not *so* large a share that they would already like to have an overall payout rate above $\pi_d(1 - \tau_d)$, inducing them to pay FIDs before the 1997 tax reform.

If this is the explanation for the jump in the number of firms paying FIDs after the 1997 tax reform, what does this model imply for the questions focused on in this paper?

Let's begin with the overall payout rate. For firms with $P < \pi_d(1 - \tau_d)$, only the first part of the tax reform matters. For these firms, the effective tax rate on dividends increases slightly, because the dividend credit is no longer available for domestic tax-exempt investors. Facing a higher tax rate on dividends, all of the past literature would lead us to expect a fall in the dividend payout rate.[7] The data reported in this paper do in fact indicate a slight fall in the overall dividend payout rate, though it is not statistically significant.

For firms that initiate FIDs after the tax reform, however, the above model suggests that they are prepaying dividends that normally would have been paid out after April 1999 but are being paid earlier in order to avoid minimum corporate tax liabilities. This suggests a potentially substantial increase in the current payout rate, even if there were no change in the present value of payouts. The empirical work focuses on the immediate response only and does find a large increase in the payout rate for these firms, consistent with the above model.

How would the investment behavior of firms respond to this tax reform? Consider first the behavior of firms with $P < \pi_d(1 - \tau_d)$. For these firms, the reform consists of a tax increase on dividend payouts. Under the "new

---

[6] The firm may previously have been willing to pay F after 1999, even though it could have paid more D prior to 1999 without incurring extra corporate tax, due to a higher rate of return being earned abroad than in the UK. In this case, the extra dividends induced by the tax reform could take the form of extra D as well as extra F.

[7] While the "new view" forecasts no change in the overall payout rate from a *permanent* increase in the dividend tax rate, it still forecasts a drop if the tax increase may turn out to be transitory.

view" of dividends, investment should increase slightly for firms already paying dividends, due to the fall in dividends induced by a transitory increase in the dividend tax rate. Investments financed out of new share issues should fall, however. Forecasts under an agency model of dividends are similar. Under an agency cost model, a higher tax rate on dividends implies a lower dividend payout rate and therefore larger retentions and a higher current investment rate. Investments financed with outside funds should fall, however. Under a signaling model of dividends, a more expensive signal could be good or bad, depending on the tax cost of the current signal compared with the tax cost that minimizes the overall cost of signaling.[8] If the tax increase raises the overall cost of signaling, then new investment becomes more costly and should fall, and conversely. All three models therefore have ambiguous forecasts for investment rates.

Yet for these firms, the chapter documents a large and statistically significant fall in investment. This fall is far too large to be attributed to the increase in the tax rate on dividends. To my mind, a likely explanation is overall macro conditions in the UK during this time period. What happened, for example, to investment in noncorporate firms, firms not affected by the 1997 tax reform? My guess is that investment fell substantially as well in these firms.

How should the response of investment differ for firms with substantial foreign operations? These firms also are affected by the same overall macro conditions, so to that extent the change in their investment should be the same as for other domestic firms. However, they also now face potentially large extra costs for dividend payments greater than $\pi_d(1 - \tau_d)$ after 1999. As emphasized above, one way to avoid these costs is to pay out the dividends before 1999. Another way, though, is to increase domestic profits or reduce foreign profits after 1999. This could be done by domestic acquisitions and foreign divestitures. If neither solves the problem, then investment abroad should fall and investment in the UK should increase. The chapter finds no evidence for an increase in investment in the UK, but it would be interesting to see if any of the other reactions show up in the data.

What do we expect to happen to firm values due to the tax reform? Due to the tax reform, firms that expected to have $P > \pi_d(1 - \tau_d)$ should be harder hit than other firms and so suffer a relative fall in their share values. The chapter does, in fact, document a small but statistically significant fall in

---

[8] The overall cost is minimized when the tax plus nontax (presumably liquidity) costs are minimized at the resulting equilibrium payout rate. Higher tax costs imply a lower payout rate, so they have ambiguous effects on total signaling costs.

share prices for firms initiating FIDs compared with other firms, consistent with this forecast.

The authors also note, however, that the share prices for these firms recover and then continue to grow relative to those for other firms during the rest of the month after the tax reform. Based on the normal logic of an event study, the expected effects of the tax reform on share prices should show up immediately. Investors can certainly revise their estimates of these effects subsequently. However, there should be no systematic sign to these revisions, and these revisions will likely be lost in the normal variability of the market, whereas the effects of the tax reform could have loomed large on the day when investors first learned of it.

What might then explain this subsequent drift in the prices of shares for firms initiating FIDs? According to the above model, the key difference between firms initiating FIDs and other firms is that firms initiating FIDs receive a large share of their profits from abroad. The natural explanation for this drift in their share prices compared with those for other firms is that investors were receiving more favorable news about foreign profits than about domestic profits.[9] This was certainly just the time of the sharp run-up in equity prices in the United States, and the United States presumably represents an important share of the foreign operations of UK firms. One way to test for this would be to include in the regression a weighted average of the equity price indices in other countries, weighting by their importance as locations for UK multinationals.

In sum, this chapter documents a dramatic change in firm behavior following the tax reform act of 1997. Such dramatic changes clearly make this chapter of broad interest to tax economists. My own instincts are that the chapter does not focus on the provision of this tax reform that should matter most for firm behavior. However, on the basis of the reasoning described above, I very much expect that many of the behavioral responses documented in the paper do arise from the 1997 tax reform.

References

Brennan, Michael J. 1970. "Taxes, Market Valuation and Corporate Financial Policy." *National Tax Journal* 23(4): 417–427.

Gordon, Roger H., and David F. Bradford. 1980. "Taxation and the Stock Market Valuation of Capital Gains and Dividends: Theory and Empirical Results." *Journal of Public Economics* 14(2): 109–136.

[9] Note that such favorable news about foreign profits would also lead to a jump in dividend payouts for firms with large foreign operations, providing another explanation for the results on dividend payout rates.

Hines, James R., Jr., and R. Glenn Hubbard. 1990. "Coming Home to America: Dividend Repatriations by U. S. Multinationals." In Assaf Razin and Joel Slemrod, eds., *Taxation in the Global Economy*. (Chicago: University of Chicago Press), pp. 161–200.

Lintner, John. 1956. "Distribution of Incomes of Corporations Among Dividends, Retained Earnings, and Taxes." *American Economic Review* 46(2): 97–113.

Comments

James Poterba

Massachusetts Institute of Technology and NBER

Prior to the UK tax reform of 1997, dividends paid by UK firms were taxed under a standard imputation regime. British investors and some foreign investors who received dividends paid by UK firms could claim a credit for the distributing firm's corporate taxes. This credit offset income tax liability for taxable investors, and it was refundable for tax-exempt investors such as pension funds and charitable endowments. A dividend payment of 1£ was effectively worth 1.33£ to such institutions. The 1997 reform eliminated the refundable imputation credit for pension funds and life insurance companies, reducing the value of corporate dividends for these investors. This paper investigates how this tax reform affected dividend payments by UK firms. The data do not reject the null hypothesis that the reform did not affect the level of dividend payments. There is no evidence that this tax reform affected corporate investment decisions, either.

The paper uncovers one change in corporate behavior in the aftermath of the 1997 reform: a shift in the composition of dividends. The fraction of large UK multinational companies paying FIDs, dividends attributable to repatriated foreign earnings, increased after the reform. The change in FID payout occurs immediately after the 1997 tax reform, and it is a discrete change in corporate behavior. The chapter argues that this change in behavior is attributable to the changing tax treatment of tax-exempt investors. Prior to 1997, pension funds and life insurance companies could not claim refundable imputation credits on FIDs, which made such dividends less valuable than ordinary dividends. While tax-exempt investors were penalized prior to 1997 when they received FIDs, corporations could reduce their tax burden by paying such dividends both before and after the 1997 reform. The authors attribute the rise in FIDs after 1997 to the increased willingness of tax-exempt investors to receive such income.

In a related study, "The Effects of Dividend Taxes on Equity Prices: A Re-Examination of the 1997 U.K. Tax Reform,"[1] the authors explore how the tax reform affected the share prices of UK companies and the market's relative valuation of dividends and capital gains. The authors do not find any substantial effect on the market value of UK companies. Moreover, in contrast to Bell and Jenkinson's (2002) finding of a change in the ex-dividend day valuation of dividends paid by high-yield firms, the authors find no systematic evidence of a change in ex-dividend day pricing patterns. While the average ex-dividend valuation of dividends relative to capital gains declined after 1997, the pattern of dividend valuation across quintiles of the dividend payout distribution is inconsistent with a standard dividend clientele analysis. The decline in this ratio for firms in the highest payout quintile is smaller than that for some of the lower payout firms, which is inconsistent with the prediction that the highest payout firms should attract an investor clientele composed of nontaxed institutions.

Taken together, this chapter and its counterpart offer important new evidence on the relationship between dividend taxes and firm behavior. Yet the analysis could do more to focus on the specific mechanism linking the change in the tax treatment of FIDs to the change in firm behavior. Neither this study nor the study of dividend valuation considers whether the reduction in the tax disadvantage of FIDs for tax-exempt investors affected the market's relative valuation of FIDs and capital gains. This is an important component of understanding firm response to the tax reform. If market valuations of FIDs did not change in the aftermath of the tax reform, then it is difficult to understand why firms changed their payout policy. Focusing on aggregate ex-dividend day pricing patterns or on patterns across payout quintiles cannot address this question, because FIDs represent only a fraction of total dividends, particularly before the reform. It is even possible that different fractions of FID firms in the various payout quintiles confounds the link between payout rate and ex-dividend valuation, thereby offering a potential explanation for the difference between the authors' ex-dividend day findings and those in Bell and Jenkinson (2002). Finding that FIDs were valued more highly after reform than before would be consistent with the growing use of FIDs after the reform. This is a natural topic for further research.

One of the most intriguing empirical findings in the chapter is the evidence that UK pension funds sold shares in UK companies after the 1997 reform. Because their net return from dividends from UK firms had declined,

---

[1] See Bond, Devereux, and Klemm (2005).

this is a natural prediction of dynamic models of investor clienteles. One issue that the authors do not address, but that represents an important challenge to dynamic clientele models, is whether the growth of corporate FIDs was due to greater valuation of such dividends by tax-exempt investors, or whether it was due to changing investor clienteles at the firms that increased their FIDs.

The chapter does not consider alternative explanations for the observed change in payout policy in the aftermath of the 1997 tax reform. The reader is left to speculate about other potential factors that might have induced a rise in FIDs immediately after the 1997 tax reform. One alternative explanation for the findings might focus on the changing UK corporate income tax, rather than the changing treatment of tax-exempt investors. Two years after the tax reform studied in this chapter, in 1999, the corporate tax credit for foreign taxes was changed, thereby eliminating the corporate income tax saving associated with the payment of FIDs. If managers were aware of this possibility when the 1997 tax reform was enacted, they may have accelerated their repatriation of earnings to take advantage of the potentially limited window for tax saving. Because repatriated earnings generate FIDs, any change in repatriation policy would translate to a change in the fraction of firms paying FIDs.

The authors describe their findings in terms of heterogeneous investor clienteles holding the shares in different firms. Their results on dynamic clientele formation support the view that different investors hold shares in different firms. Yet they sidestep a difficult set of conceptual issues about the theoretical foundation for the market equilibrium that emerges in the presence of heterogeneous investor taxation. The 1997 UK tax reform affected only a subset of taxpayers, so the empirical findings are a joint test of whether investor-level taxes affect corporate payout policy *and* of whether the investors who were affected by the tax reform affect market equilibrium. One of the unresolved issues in the literature on taxation and corporate financial policy is how heterogeneous investors choose which securities to hold and how these holdings in turn affect the prices of financial assets. Previous research offers two alternative approaches to securities market equilibrium in this setting.

The first approach, suggested by Miller and Scholes (1978), argues that there are "marginal investors" whose tax treatment sets the equity market's relative valuation of dividends and capital gains. Miller and Scholes suggested that large securities firms that trade on their own account, and that face very low marginal trading costs, were likely to be marginal traders. They hypothesized that the tax rules affecting these institutional traders would be reflected in the market-wide valuation of taxable income streams, in particular in the relative valuation of dividends and capital gains. They argued that if the tax preferences of these marginal investors were not reflected in market prices, they would be able to earn "tax arbitrage profits" by trading at the prevailing prices. While an equilibrium in which the tax preferences of these marginal traders were reflected in prices might leave analogous tax arbitrage opportunities for other investors, the trading costs facing other investors would make it uneconomic for them to trade at these prices. One of the difficulties with this approach is that it yields strong predictions about when investors whose tax rates are different from those of the marginal investors, and who plan to buy or sell a particular stock, should trade around ex-dividend days. While the round-trip transaction cost associated with trading for investors who are not marginal may exceed the net-of-tax profit associated with such trading, investors who can time their purchases or sales would have incentives to do so. For example, an individual investor who was planning to purchase a stock, and whose tax burden on dividends relative to capital gains was greater than that of a "marginal investor," would delay purchase until after an ex-dividend day. Whether such delayed or accelerated trading could affect prices is unclear.

The marginal investor view of market equilibrium implies that changes in the tax treatment of investors who are not the marginal investors, such as individual investors or pension funds, should neither affect the market valuation of firms nor alter the incentive for firms to pay dividends or to retain earnings. The voluminous literature on the ex-dividend day price movements of common stocks, reviewed by Allen and Michaely (2003), provides conflicting evidence on the role of income taxes on various investor classes in affecting market-wide dividend valuation. On balance, the evidence points toward the view that changes in the tax treatment of individual investors, typically with no change in the tax treatment of trading institutions and tax-exempt investors, affects dividend valuation.

A second approach to market equilibrium in the presence of heterogeneous investor taxes, the "after-tax capital asset pricing model," is derived in Brennan (1970), Gordon and Bradford (1980), and many other papers. In this model, the tax rules facing all investors affect the market-wide valuation of dividend payouts relative to capital gains. In the absence of short-selling constraints, the relative price of dividends and capital gains that faces *all firms* is

$$\theta_{mkt} = \Sigma w_i * \sigma_i * (1 - m_i)/(1 - z_i) \tag{1}$$

In this expression, $w_i = W_i / \Sigma W_j$ and $\sigma_i = (1/\gamma_i)/\Sigma(1/\gamma_j)$, where W_i denotes the total wealth of the i-th investor and $(1/\gamma_i)$ is the reciprocal of the i-th investor's coefficient of relative risk aversion. In this setting, the market equilibrium valuation of dividends and capital gains is a weighted average of each investor's relative after-tax income from 1£ of dividends $(1 - m_i)$ and 1£ of capital gains $(1 - z_i)$. An investor who is very wealthy and nearly risk neutral will have a substantial impact on the equilibrium market valuation of dividends and capital gains. A very risk-averse investor with very little wealth will have very little impact. In this equilibrium, changes in the tax rate on any investor will affect the market's equilibrium valuation of dividends and capital gains to some degree. In the marginal investor view, however, many investors could experience changes in tax rates without any associated change in the market valuation of dividends and capital gains.

While the marginal investor and after-tax CAPM approaches offer different perspectives on what determines market equilibrium, both predict that the relative valuation of dividend income and capital gains is the same for all stocks. This precludes the formation of investor clienteles that invest in particular firms. Yet a substantial body of empirical research, summarized in Allen and Michaely (2003) and including the current study, suggests that different firms attract different investor clienteles. This is reflected in their ex-dividend day price movements, and it is also evident in studies that directly evaluate the composition of the investor population.

While the theoretical basis for heterogeneous investor clienteles is not well developed, a number of empirical studies have built on the insight that different firms attract different sets of investors. Auerbach (1983) estimates firm-specific clientele parameters based on ex-dividend day price changes for corporate stock. He finds substantial differences across firms and then uses these estimates of the marginal tax preference of the investors who own each firm to try to explain the firm's financial policy. More recent work has tried to assemble data on the identity of investors in different firms. Pérez-González (2003) uses direct information on the ownership of company stock to develop an indicator of the firm's investor clientele and then shows that the effect of dividend tax changes on firm behavior depends in part on the firm's ownership structure. Desai and Jin (2005) find related evidence of a link between ownership structure and firm responsiveness to changes in dividend taxation.

A number of studies now suggest that taxes affect the formation of investor clienteles, but the evidence remains mixed on the causal links between ownership clienteles and firm behavior. Grinstein and Michaely (2005) suggest that a firm's dividend policy affects the likelihood that institutional investors will hold the stock. They find little evidence, however, that the presence of institutional investors in the firm's ownership base influences the firm's payout behavior. This is an important challenge to the current study, which argues that the presence of tax-exempt UK pension funds in the firm's shareholder base can explain the firm's dividend policy. As data on the ownership composition of different firms become increasingly available for the United States and elsewhere, there is likely to be growing evidence on the dynamics of shareowner clienteles and the effects of taxes and other factors on clientele formation.

The growing body of evidence suggesting that clienteles differ across firms, and that investors do not hold identical portfolios, makes it important to determine *why* ownership structure differs across firms. The formation of clienteles might be the result of transactions costs associated with the purchase of diversified portfolios. It might be the result of limits on short selling or of the near redundancy of different securities. It might reflect regulatory restrictions or other institutional constraints that prevent some types of investors from holding the quantities of some stocks that they would choose to hold in an unconstrained setting. Explaining why clienteles emerge is important because the efficiency cost of taxes that distort the set of investors holding different firms is likely to depend on the source of clientele formation. The lack of a convincing theory of clientele formation limits our ability to make welfare statements about tax changes or other factors that might alter clientele composition.

The present study offers interesting evidence that firms that did not pay FIDs prior to the 1997 tax reform and that were arguably affected by the tax preferences of UK pension funds were more likely to initiate such dividends after the reform. The central empirical challenge is identifying firms that were strongly influenced by UK pension funds in the pre-1997 period. The authors select firms with foreign income before 1997 and assume that all such firms could have paid FIDs. They further assume that the firms with foreign source income that chose *not* to pay FIDs had influential pension fund investors and infer that these firms were most likely to be affected when the tax treatment of pension funds changed in 1997. This prediction is supported by the empirical findings.

There may, however, be other explanations for the differences in behavior between multinational firms that did, and that did not, pay FIDs in the years prior to 1997. One possibility is that firms have heterogeneous opportunities to reinvest their earnings abroad. Firms with attractive reinvestment opportunities are less inclined to repatriate earnings, and thereby trigger FIDs, than firms with better reinvestment options. If the 1997

tax reform altered managers' perceptions of the long-term rewards of investing abroad relative to repatriating earnings, that could have led to changes in
FIDs even in the absence of improved investor acceptance of such payouts.
The termination of the favorable corporate tax treatment of FIDs in 1999,
and in particular the possibility that such a change was anticipated, adds to
the concern that firms may have altered their repatriation policy for reasons
unrelated to investor taxes. A firm that had been deferring repatriation of its
foreign source income prior to 1997, while planning to repatriate earnings
at a later date, faced a strong incentive to repatriate earnings between 1997
and 1999. After that date, it lost the corporate tax benefit associated with
repatriation. For firms that had limited long-term investment opportunities
abroad, repatriation between 1997 and 1999 was attractive. This illustrates
the problem of disentangling shareholder preferences from other factors
that affect repatriation decisions and the payment of FIDs.

This is not the only other factor that might be related to whether a firm
paid, or did not pay, FIDs before 1997. The repatriation decision pre-1997
could be a signal of managerial awareness of the corporate tax benefits of
FIDs. It is possible that firms with "less aware" managers did not repatriate
before 1997, but when faced with the prospect of tax benefits of repatriation expiring after 1999, they chose to repatriate. The 1997 tax reform may
have served as a wake-up call, alerting managers to the benefits of paying
FIDs and therefore resulting in new payout patterns. This explanation for
the empirical findings, as well as the earlier concern about heterogeneous
foreign investment prospects, underscores the need to consider alternative
hypotheses that might explain the statistical findings.

One way to try to control for such alternative hypotheses would be to
expand the set of firm-specific covariates that are included in the dividend
and investment models. The empirical models both for dividend payout
and for investment use lagged sales and lagged profits as key explanatory
variables, along with a measure of the firm's FID payout policy pre-1997 and
the availability of foreign source income. The investment specifications omit
variables such as firm-specific measures of Tobin's q that might be correlated
with investment prospects and that might improve the explanatory power of
the econometric models. The models for dividends exclude lagged dividends,
even though previous statistical analysis suggests that lagged dividends have
important predictive power for current dividends.

The present study makes an important first step in tracing the impact of
the 1997 UK tax reform on firm behavior. It could be expanded along the
lines of several recent U. S. studies of investor clienteles to provide even more
convincing evidence on the links between taxes, portfolio holdings, and firm

behavior. If data could be assembled on pension fund holdings of stock in each UK company, it would then be possible to test the clientele hypothesis directly rather than by relying on the firm's potentially-endogenous pre-1997 FID behavior as an indicator variable for investor clienteles. Such an empirical strategy would offer a more robust test of the hypotheses advanced in the current study.

References

Allen, Franklin, and Roni Michaely. 2003. "Payout Policy." In George Constantinides, Milton Harris, and Rene Stulz, eds., *Handbook of the Economics of Finance: Vol. 1A, Corporate Finance*. (Amsterdam: North-Holland), pp. 337–429.

Auerbach, Alan. 1983. "Shareholder Tax Rates and Firm Attributes." *Journal of Public Economics* 21(2): 107–127.

Bell, Leonie, and Tim Jenkinson. 2002. "New Evidence on the Impact of Dividend Taxation and the Identity of the Marginal Investor." *Journal of Finance* 57(3): 1321–1346.

Bond, Stephen, Michael Devereux, and Alexander Klemm. 2005. "*The Effects of Dividend Taxes on Equity Prices: A Re-examination of the 1997 U. K. Tax Reform.*" Mimeo. (London: Institute for Fiscal Studies).

Brennan, Michael. 1970. "Taxes, Market Valuation, and Financial Policy." *National Tax Journal* 23(4): 417–419.

Desai, Mihir, and Li Jin. 2005. "*Institutional Tax Clienteles and Payout Policy.*" Mimeo. (Cambridge, MA: Harvard Business School).

Gordon, Roger, and David Bradford. 1980. "Taxation and the Stock Market Valuation of Capital Gains and Dividends." *Journal of Public Economics* 14(2): 109–136.

Grinstein, Yaniv, and Roni Michaely. 2005. "Institutional Holdings and Payout Policy." *Journal of Finance* 60(3): 1389–1426.

Miller, Merton, and Myron Scholes. 1978. "Dividends and Taxes." *Journal of Financial Economics* 6(4): 333–364.

Pérez-González, Francisco. 2003. "*Large Shareholders and Dividends: Evidence from U. S. Tax Reforms.*" Mimeo. (New York: Columbia Business School).

THREE

The 2003 Dividend Tax Cuts and the Value of the Firm: An Event Study

Alan J. Auerbach

University of California, Berkeley, and NBER

Kevin A. Hassett

American Enterprise Institute

1. Introduction

On June 20th, 2003, President Bush signed the JGTRA03 into law. This act contained a number of significant tax provisions, but the most noteworthy may have been the changes in the dividend and capital gains tax rates. The top capital gains rate of 20 percent was reduced to 15 percent. The top rate on dividend income was reduced from the highest statutory income tax rate of 35 percent to 15 percent. Capital gains and dividend tax rates for low-income individuals were reduced to 5 percent, dropping to 0 in 2008.

The likely impact of these tax changes on economic activity has been explored in some detail.[1] A key consideration in this analysis is the marginal source of finance for firms that pay dividends. Under the "new view" of dividend taxation developed in Auerbach (1979), Bradford (1981), and King (1977), the marginal source of finance for new investment projects is retained earnings. In this case, the tax advantage of retentions precisely offsets the double taxation of subsequent dividends: Taxes on dividends have no impact on the investment incentives of firms using retentions as a marginal source of funds and paying dividends with residual cash flows. Alternatively, the dividend tax affects the marginal source of finance under the "traditional view," where firms rely on new share issuance as the marginal source of funds.

---

[1] See Carroll, Hassett, and Mackie (2003).

We thank Gordon Gray, Anne Moore, and Joe Rosenberg for excellent research assistance, Alex Brill for help in the identification of event dates, and conference participants, particularly our discussants Bill Gale and George Zordrow, for comments on an earlier draft.

To date, there has been a significant debate concerning the relative importance of the new and traditional views of dividend taxation. Poterba and Summers (1985) found evidence suggesting that the traditional view might best characterize the investment behavior of U.K. firms. Auerbach and Hassett (2003) analyzed dividend payout behavior and found support for both views in different subsamples of U.S. firms. Desai and Goolsbee (2004), on the other hand, reported evidence that suggests that investment behavior in the United States may be most consistent with the new view.

The political debate over the dividend tax reductions of 2003 took a number of surprising twists and turns. The original proposal put forward by President Bush was eventually dropped and replaced with a simpler version. There were times when the dividend tax reduction seemed almost dead, only to be revived by clever legislative gamesmanship. Accordingly, it is likely that the views of market participants concerning the probability of significant dividend tax reduction fluctuated significantly during 2003. In this chapter, we use this fact to estimate the effects of dividend tax policy on firm value. One of our aims in doing so is to shed new light on the academic debate concerning the economic impact of dividend tax policy and relevance of the two competing views of the impact of dividend taxation.

Specifically, embedded in the two views of dividend tax policy are different implications concerning the likely pattern of share price responses to news about lower dividend tax rates. These different implications allow us to use standard event-study methodology from the empirical finance literature to investigate whether observed share prices responses are more consistent with the predictions of the new view or with those of the traditional view. We also consider the effects of the dividend tax cut on the values of firms that pay no dividends, an important segment of the overall firm population. Such firms are not well characterized either by the new view, which presumes the availability of internal funds adequate to finance investment, or the traditional view, which presumes the need for firms to distribute dividends, even as they may be issuing shares. A simplistic, static perspective might see these firms as gaining little from a reduction in dividend taxes, for there are no immediate tax consequences for them, but we argue not only that these firms, too, would benefit from dividend tax cuts, but also that they might benefit even more than dividend-paying firms.

Briefly, we find that firms with higher dividend yields benefited more than other dividend-paying firms, a result that, in itself, is consistent with both new and traditional views. But further evidence points toward the new view and away from the traditional view. We also find that non-dividend-paying firms experienced *larger* abnormal returns than other firms as the result of the dividend tax cut and that a similar bonus accrued to firms likely to issue new shares, two results that may appear surprising at first but are consistent with the theory developed below.

The next section develops our predictions concerning the likely share price response to news concerning the tax rate on dividends.[2] Section 3 discusses the methodology that we employ to evaluate whether these effects are visible in the data. Section 4 presents our basic results regarding changes in firm valuation during the legislative window, roughly the first half of 2003. To help interpret and extend our basic findings, Section 5 extends our empirical investigation by considering changes in firm valuation during the months leading up to the 2004 presidential election, a close race in which the two candidates differed markedly in their attitudes toward the 2003 legislation. Section 6 considers alternative specifications to check the robustness of our results, and Section 7 concludes.

2. Theory

To consider the potential effects on market value of changes in the rate of dividend taxation, one must confront the alternative views of how dividend taxes affect market value. We follow the presentation in Auerbach (2002), to which the reader is referred for a more complete discussion.

We start with the expression derived there for the valuation at date t of a firm with a representative shareholder facing a tax rate θ on dividends and a tax rate c on accrued capital gains that reflects both the favorable capital gains rate and the deferral advantage conferred by the fact that gains are actually taxed only upon realization:

$$
V_t = \int_t^\infty e^{-\frac{\rho}{1-c_s}(s-t)} \left[D_s \left(\frac{1 - \theta_s}{1 - c_s} \right) - S_s \right] ds, \tag{1}
$$

where ρ is the shareholder's after-tax discount rate, D_s is the flow of dividends at date s, and S_s is the flow of proceeds from new share issues at date s.

---

[2] We focus here on the change in dividend taxation, as this should have been by far the most important change affecting firm value. The top capital gains tax rate was also reduced to 15 percent, but this represented a much smaller change from the previous top marginal rate of 20 percent. The "bonus depreciation" provision (discussed and analyzed by House and Shapiro 2005) provided immediate expensing of 50 percent of qualifying investment. But the provision applied only through the end of 2004, and represented a minor change in the law passed in 2002, which had provided 30 percent bonus depreciation for investment through September 2004.

Equation (1) is valid for any path of dividends and share issues, but there are a variety of constraints on the choice of these two variables. Dividends cannot be negative ($D_t \geq 0$), but there may be further restrictions on the payment of dividends, which is often summarized by a minimum distribution constraint, such as a requirement that dividends be at least some fraction total returns to the firm, or:

$$D_t \geq p\left(D_t + \dot{V}_t - S_t\right). \tag{2}$$

To represent the potential difficulties of engaging in share repurchases, we impose the simple constraint that rules them out[3]:

$$S_t \geq 0. \tag{3}$$

Associating the Lagrange multipliers λ_t and μ_t with the Equations (2) and (3), we obtain the following expression for the value of the firm under optimal equity policy:

$$V_t = \int_t^{\infty} e^{-\int_t^s \frac{p}{(1-c_s)(1-\lambda_v p)} dv} \left(1 - \frac{\mu_s}{1 - \lambda_s p}\right) G_s ds, \tag{4}$$

where $G_t \equiv D_t - S_t$ is the net cash flow at date s from the firm's operations before the determination of dividends and new share issues, and the two multipliers satisfy the relationship:

$$\lambda_t + \mu_t = 1 - \frac{1 - \theta_t}{1 - c_t}. \tag{5}$$

Assuming that $\theta > c$, at least one of the multipliers in (5) must be nonzero. At the margin, issuing new shares to pay dividends increases taxes (the increase in dividend taxes exceeding the reduction in capital gains taxes) and reduces the value of shares. To maximize value, firms will wish to decrease both new shares and dividends until at least one of the constraints binds.

---

[3] Imposing an absolute restriction on share repurchases, in condition (3), simplifies the analysis, but the key requirement is that share repurchases and dividends not be perfect substitutes except for their tax consequences. Were purchases and dividends perfect substitutes, then condition (2) would make little sense either, because then firms would prefer to make their required distributions in the form of repurchases, and neither the "traditional view" nor the "new view" discussed below would be particularly applicable to analysis of the effects of dividend taxation. However, the form of repurchases most similar to payment of a dividend – a proportional redemption of shares – is treated as a dividend for tax purposes, and other types of repurchases are subject to problems of asymmetric information. As a result, dividends and repurchases are not perfect substitutes, and their empirical patterns reflect this. See Auerbach (2002) and Auerbach and Hassett (2003) for further discussion.

We may distinguish three regimes, according to whether λ, μ, or both are positive, and firms may make transitions among these regimes over time.

When only the minimum-dividend constraint, Equation (2), binds at all dates (i.e., $\mu \equiv 0$), Equation (4) reduces to:

$$V_t = \int_t^\infty e^{-\frac{\rho}{[1-(1-p)c_s - p\theta_s]}(s-t)} G_s ds,\qquad(6)$$

which is the traditional view of the effects of dividend taxation. According to this expression, the value of the firm equals the present value of its cash flows net of new share issues and dividends, discounted with a before-personal-tax discount rate based on an individual tax rate that is a weighted average of the tax rates on dividends and capital gains, with weights based on the payout rate p, $\frac{\rho}{[1-(1-p)c-p\theta]}$. On the other hand, if only the repurchase constraint, Equation (3), binds at all dates (i.e., $\lambda \equiv 0$), Equation (4) simplifies to:

$$V_t = \int_t^\infty e^{-\frac{\rho}{1-c_s}(s-t)} \left(\frac{1-\theta_s}{1-c_s}\right) G_s ds,\qquad(7)$$

which is the new view of dividend taxation, under which the appropriate discount rate, $\frac{\rho}{(1-c)}$, is unaffected by the tax rate on dividends, and the net cash flows of the firm are multiplied by the ratio $\left(\frac{1-\theta}{1-c}\right) \leq 1$ in determining the firm's value.

How would a reduction in the tax rate on dividends affect the firm's value? We consider first the firm in isolation and then discuss how the responses of other firms may modify our initial conclusions.

2.1. Announcement Effects under the New View

Under the new view, a reduction in θ would directly increase the firm's value, with no further direct behavioral responses. As a pure lump-sum transfer to the owners of the firm, its only additional impact on firm value would come indirectly through potential effects on other firms' behavior or through wealth effects on consumption.

Note that, for a *permanent* reduction in θ, the firm's payout rate should not play a role in the impact on firm value, because the size of the lump-sum transfer to shareholders is independent of when dividends are distributed – the tax term is constant and factors out of the integral. That is, new-view firms with the same present value of cash flows, G_s, in Equation (7) should experience the same percentage change in value, even if the time pattern of these flows, and hence the share of earnings retained, differs across firms; the present value of dividend taxes on these flows is invariant to their timing, and so is any associated tax reduction.

If the tax cut is perceived to be temporary, though, the payout rate could matter, for a larger share of distributions would be subject to reduced taxes for the firm with a higher payout rate.

2.2. Announcement Effects under the Traditional View

Under the traditional view, dividend tax cuts should also increase firm value, but through a different mechanism. Rather than providing a lump-sum transfer to shareholders, the dividend tax cut would reduce the firm's discount rate. The larger the payout rate, p, the larger the decline in the discount rate and, for a given trajectory of cash flows, G_s (assuming all flows are positive), the higher the percentage increase in value.

Because of the decline in the discount rate, the firm's optimal investment policy will also be affected, with an increase in investment now desirable. For the firm in isolation (i.e., ignoring the behavioral responses of other firms), though, shifting to the new optimal investment policy will simply reinforce the initial increase in market value – the first-order effect on value is a lower bound for the individual firm.

These predictions contrast with those in the simple model of several identical firms. There, the tax shock raises the market value of the representative firm temporarily, and then investment drives the marginal product of capital back down to its eternal resting place of $q = 1$. In our regressions, we would expect the path of the marginal product of capital for a firm to depend on the behavior of other firms, with profits (and hence market value responses) accruing to firms that occupy industries with relatively unresponsive competitors.

2.3. Announcement Effects with Transitions in Regime

There are some firms for which neither the new view nor the traditional view provides an adequate characterization. The most important case, empirically, is firms that have yet to pay dividends. The new view clearly does not apply, for these firms are retaining all of their earnings and not paying dividends as a residual. On the other hand, they do not pay any positive share of their earnings as dividends, and so a reduction in dividend taxation would have no immediate impact on their cost of capital. This has led some observers to argue that such "immature" firms would not benefit from a reduction in dividend taxation.

But, as markets are forward-looking, we should expect these firms to experience an increase in value on the basis of expected future dividend policy, not simply current policy. Firms that are projected to follow a life cycle over which they eventually mature and commence paying dividends might gain from a dividend tax cut of sufficient duration.[4] Indeed, such firms might gain *more*, as a share of current market value.

To explain this point, consider a firm in the model described above, facing the constraints in Equations (2) and (3) on dividends and repurchases, but with the minimum payout rate in (2), p, set equal to 0. Suppose that the constraint in Equation (2) initially binds, as the firm is in a high-growth stage and devotes all its earnings to investment, but that, over time, investment opportunities diminish and the firm makes a transition to paying dividends each year, in which case only the constraint in Equation (3) binds. During this transition from being a traditional-view firm (with $p = 0$) to being a new-view firm, the firm may spend some time in the intermediate regime when both constraints bind, in which case no dividends are paid and no shares are issued. In this intermediate regime, additional investment is profitable if financed through after-tax retentions, but not profitable if financed through before-tax new share issues, so the firm is at a kink point.

On the basis of Equation (4) and the definition of G_s, we may write the value at date t for this firm as:

$$V_t = \int_t^T e^{-\frac{\rho}{1-c_s}(s-t)}(-S_s)\,ds + e^{-\frac{\rho}{1-c_{T'}}T'}\int_{T'}^{\infty} e^{-\frac{\rho}{1-c_s}(s-T')}\left(\frac{1-\theta_s}{1-c_s}\right)D_s\,ds,$$

$$(8)$$

where the firm exits the traditional-view regime at date T and enters the new-view regime at date $T' \geq T$. Recall that the interval between T and T' does not show up in the value formula because dividends and issuance have stopped. Consider the impact of a reduction in the dividend tax rate θ on the firm's market value. If we compare Equation (8) to Equation (7) and note that $G_s = D_s$ in Equation (7), we observe that the present value of dividends in Equation (7), multiplied by $(1-\theta)/(1-c)$, equals the value of the firm. But, in Equation (8), the present value of dividends multiplied by $(1-\theta)/(1-c)$ – the second integral in the expression – *exceeds* the value of the firm, because the first integral is negative. Because the firm will first issue additional shares before it begins paying dividends, the present value of its future dividends must equal the value of its current equity *plus* the value of the equity that will be issued in the future. In a competitive market

---

[4] Sinn (1991) analyzes the dynamics of such firms in making the transition from "traditional view" firms to "new view" firms.

for shares, any increases in the future after-tax value of dividends due to a tax cut will increase the amount for which shares can be sold, thus increasing the value of *current* equity.

The immature firm described in Equation (8) will wish to invest more *before* entering the new-view regime at date T', because during the *transition* between regimes it will face a lower cost of capital. Absent adjustment costs, this extra investment would occur immediately before the transition begins, beginning at date T; but with adjustment costs, the investment may begin much earlier than date T, because of the desire to smooth investment. Note, also, that the firm's response will likely change the dates T and T'. As under the traditional view, the firm's individual investment response will simply enhance the first-order increase in its market value.

To illustrate this scenario and confirm the predicted impacts on valuation and investment behavior, we consider an explicit model that can give rise to the discrete-time version of the life-cycle transition described by Equation (8). We suppose the firm has a production technology in one factor, capital, $F(K)$; invests subject to quadratic adjustment costs, $C(I) = qI + \frac{1}{2}\alpha I^2$; and starts with an initial capital stock, K_0. For simplicity, we assume that capital does not depreciate, that the capital gains tax and the corporate tax are both zero, and that the production function, too, is quadratic, $F(K) = \gamma K - \frac{1}{2}\delta K^2$. Clearly, this is a model in which the firm stops investing when it reaches its optimal capital stock and thus ends up in the new-view regime. If its capital stock starts close enough to this value, $K_\infty = (\gamma - q\rho)/\delta$, it will start off as a new-view firm; but if its initial capital stock is sufficiently low, it will wish to invest rapidly at first, pushing it into the zero-dividend, traditional-view regime. For the particular parameterization chosen, $\rho = .5, q = \alpha = 1, \gamma = .2, \delta = .03$, and θ initially equal to .3, for which $K_\infty = 5$, the firm pays dividends from the start if, for example, $K_0 = 3$, and initially issues shares and pays no dividends if, for example, $K_0 = .5$. In the latter case, the trajectory of investment and the timing of transitions among regimes also changes if θ changes.

These changes are shown in Figure 1 for a reduction in θ from .3 to .1, with the left axis measuring investment and the right axis measuring the capitalization factor q^*, which equals 1 in the traditional-view regime, $(1 - \theta)/(1 - c)$ in the new-view regime, and lies between these values in the intermediate regime. Under the initial trajectory, the firm transits out of the traditional-view regime after three periods and into the new-view regime after seven periods. As predicted, the dividend tax reduction speeds up investment from the start, and this delays by one period the cessation of

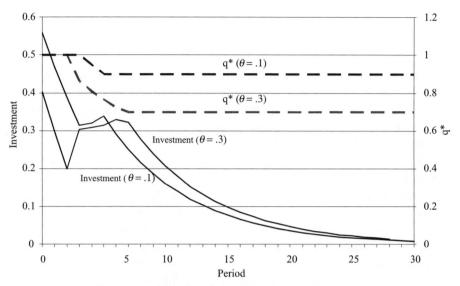

Figure 1. Investment and Transition for Immature Firms

new share issues and the departure from the traditional-view regime. However, with this faster capital accumulation, the firm also enters the new-view regime faster, after just five periods. And what of the impact on market value? For the firm with $K_0 = 3$, or for any new-view firm, value increases by 28.57 percent, equal to $[(1 - .1) - (1 - .3)]/[1 - .3]$. For $K_0 = .5$, the change depicted in Figure 1, the firm's value increases by 30.40 percent, higher as predicted.

The reasoning in this example carries over for firms experiencing more general shifts among regimes, such as mature firms that typically do not issue shares but may occasionally find it desirable to do so because of unusually strong investment opportunities. These firms, like the transitional immature firm just analyzed, will have a present value of dividends that exceeds their current equity value and hence will stand to gain more, as a fraction of that value, from a permanent reduction in dividend taxes.

For immature firms, as under the new view, one must qualify one's conclusions if tax cuts are perceived to be temporary. While the present value of dividends is higher as a share of equity value than for mature firms, these dividends are also likely to occur further in the future than for mature firms. Thus, a tax cut that is expected to expire would reduce the valuation impact more for immature firms, leaving the net effect for immature relative to mature firms uncertain.

2.4. The Impact of Collective Behavioral Responses

The analysis so far applies to firms in isolation, ignoring the behavioral responses of other firms. But it is still relevant in comparing the relative impacts on the values of different firms, as long as the responses among competing firms are held constant. Thus, if all firms are new-view firms, we would expect no behavioral responses at all, and so the above analysis applies.

If, on the other hand, all firms were traditional-view firms, we would expect that, in the long-run, increased investment would drive down before-tax rates of return. With adjustment costs, as in the standard q-theory of investment, firm values would jump temporarily as investment increases, with the temporary gain then eroding over time. But firms with a higher reduction in their costs of capital would still experience greater increases in value, both in the long run and in the short run.[5]

If, however, the responses of competitive firms differ, then our predictions might require modification. For example, suppose that there are two industries populated by traditional-view firms: In industry A, the typical payout ratio p is high, whereas in industry B the ratio is low. Then, a dividend tax cut might spur industry-wide investment more in A than in B, depressing values in A more than B. Thus, a firm with a given value of p in industry A would be predicted to have a smaller net increase in value than a firm with the same value of p in industry B.

2.5. Summary

Based on the preceding discussion, we would expect the effects on market value of a dividend tax reduction to interact with characteristics of firms as follows:

> *dividend yield*: positive under the traditional view; neutral under the new view, but positive if the tax cut is not perceived as permanent
> *propensity to issue new shares*: positive
> *"immaturity"* (firms not paying dividends): positive if the tax cut is perceived as permanent; unclear if the tax cut is perceived as temporary
> *competitive firms' payout ratios*: irrelevant under the new view; negative under the traditional view.

---

[5] Modeling the coexistence of firms with different costs of capital in the same market is beyond the scope of this paper, but it would be straightforward to do so using a standard model of monopolistic competition, under which each firm would face a downward-sloping demand curve.

Our approach is to explore whether these predictions are confirmed in the data. We now turn to a discussion of our methods.

3. Methodology and Data

3.1. Event Study Methodology

The multivariate regression model has been used extensively to measure abnormal returns (*ARs*) in stock market event studies. Although we must take into account how intertemporal and contemporaneous correlations affect the estimates of the variances of different measures of abnormal returns, these issues can mostly be easily overcome and have been extensively addressed in the literature.

The basic event-study methodology starts with the following regressions based on the capital asset pricing model (CAPM):

$$r_{it} = \alpha_i + \beta_i r_{mt} + \gamma_{it} D_t + \varepsilon_{it}, \tag{9}$$

where r_{it} is the return for firm i in period t and r_{mt} is the return on the market in period t.[6] D_t is a dummy variable that is equal to one if a given event occurs on date t and zero otherwise. The coefficient γ_{it} estimates the abnormal return caused by the event for firm i; as discussed below, we will parameterize γ_{it} as a function of variables associated with the theory of dividend taxation to distinguish the effects of events on firms with different attributes.

Cumulative abnormal returns (*CARs*) are estimated by summing estimated abnormal returns over an event window. However, the variance of the *CARs* is not the sum of the variances of the individual *ARs*. There is intertemporal correlation between the *ARs* because the same estimated market model parameters enter the calculation of all *ARs* for a firm.

It is easy, however, to estimate the variances of *CARs* (see Salinger, 1992, pp. 40–42, for a fuller discussion of the correlation between the *ARs* and how the following procedure corrects for it). Because $CAR_t = CAR_{t-1} + AR_t$, we can rewrite equation (9) as:

$$r_{i,t} = \alpha_i + \beta_i r_{mt} + \gamma_{it}^{CAR} D_t - \gamma_{i,t-1}^{CAR} D_{t-1} + \varepsilon_{it}, \tag{9'}$$

---

[6] A slightly different version of the CAPM would subtract the risk-free rate from the firm and market returns in (9). The results were not sensitive to the choice between these alternatives. Results based on a popular multifactor alternative to the basic CAPM are discussed in Section VI.

where γ_{it}^{CAR} is an estimate of the cumulative abnormal return at date t. The difference between this procedure and the standard dummy variable procedure is that, for t in the event window, the dummy for period t takes on the value of 1 and the dummy for period $t-1$ takes on the value of -1. Using the dummy variable procedure for estimating CARs and their standard errors simplifies things greatly, because the standard errors are reported directly by the regression package. To account for contemporaneous correlation of the abnormal returns of similar firms, though, we cluster standard errors by 3-digit industry.

Specifications in This Application

In order to investigate the relevance of the various theories of dividend taxation, we estimate the following extensions of the basic Equation (9) using daily stock price data:

$$r_{it} = \alpha_i + \beta_i r_t^m + \sum_{m=1}^{8} \sum_{n=1}^{5} \gamma_{n,m}^0 D_{n,m} + \varepsilon_{it} \tag{i}$$

$$r_{it} = \alpha_i + \beta_i r_t^m + \sum_{m=1}^{8} \sum_{n=1}^{5} \gamma_{n,m}^0 D_{n,m} + \sum_{m=1}^{8} \sum_{n=1}^{5} \gamma_{n,m}^1 D_{n,m} \times Div_i + \varepsilon_{it} \tag{ii}$$

$$r_{it} = \alpha_i + \beta_i r_t^m + \sum_{m=1}^{8} \sum_{n=1}^{5} \gamma_{n,m}^0 D_{n,m} + \sum_{m=1}^{8} \sum_{n=1}^{5} \gamma_{n,m}^1 D_{n,m} \times Div_i$$

$$+ \sum_{m=1}^{8} \sum_{n=1}^{5} \gamma_{n,m}^2 D_{n,m} \times ProbIss_i + \sum_{m=1}^{8} \sum_{n=1}^{5} \gamma_{n,m}^3 D_{n,m} \times ProbPurch_i + \varepsilon_{it} \tag{iii}$$

$$r_{it} = \alpha_i + \beta_i r_t^m + \sum_{m=1}^{8} \sum_{n=1}^{5} \gamma_{n,m}^0 D_{n,m} + \sum_{m=1}^{8} \sum_{n=1}^{5} \gamma_{n,m}^1 D_{n,m} \times Div_i$$

$$+ \sum_{m=1}^{8} \sum_{n=1}^{5} \gamma_{n,m}^4 D_{n,m} \times \overline{Div}_i + \varepsilon_{it}, \tag{iv}$$

where r_t^m equals the daily return on the CRSP total market value-weighted index, $D_{n,m}$ is a dummy equal to one for event m on day n of the 5-day event window, Div_i equals the 2002 dividend payout ratio for firm i, $ProbIss_i$ equals the 2002 new share issuance probability for firm i, $ProbPurch_i$ equals the 2002 repurchase probability for firm i, and $\overline{Div}_i$ equals the average 2002 dividend yield among mature firms in the same industry as firm i based on 3-digit SIC code and weighted by market capitalization. Construction of the probabilities is discussed in the data section below. We choose the 5-day window centered on the event in case news of the event leaks out early to the market or takes a while to be fully digested.

For "mature" firms – that is, firms that have already paid a dividend – we estimate specifications Equations (i)–(iv). For the full sample, we estimate a version that includes an interaction between our event dummies and a dummy variable for whether a firm is mature or not:

$$r_{it} = \alpha_i + \beta_i r_t^m + \sum_{m=1}^{8}\sum_{n=1}^{5} \gamma_{n,m}^0 D_{n,m} + \sum_{m=1}^{8}\sum_{n=1}^{5} \gamma_{n,m}^5 D_{n,m} \times Mature_i + \varepsilon_{it},$$

$$(v)$$

where $Mature_i$ is a dummy variable equal to one if firm i was a mature firm in 2002 (i.e., had paid a dividend in 2002 or any prior year).

In all of these regressions, the *cumulative* abnormal returns (*CARs*) were estimated, not the *ARs* (i.e., we use the versions of (i)–(v) based on (9′), not (9)). Each specification was estimated both unweighted and weighted by market capitalization. Similar regressions were run cumulating the abnormal returns across all eight events. Also, as mentioned above, the standard errors reported are clustered by 3-digit SIC code in all specifications.

3.2. Using the 2004 Election as an Alternative Experiment

As an alternative to our event study, we also consider identifying the effect of dividend tax changes using futures prices from the 2004 presidential election. Because the dividend tax reduction is currently scheduled to expire and because Senator Kerry expressed no desire to extend it, the probability that George Bush would win should have been positively associated with the probability of continued low dividend taxes in the future. Accordingly, we estimate the following regressions:

$$r_{it} = \alpha_i + \beta_i r_t^m + \gamma^6 \Delta Bush_t + \gamma^7 \Delta Bush_t \times Div_i + \varepsilon_{it} \qquad (vi)$$

$$r_{it} = \alpha_i + \beta_i r_t^m + \gamma^6 \Delta Bush_t + \gamma^7 \Delta Bush_t \times Div_i$$
$$+ \gamma^8 \Delta Bush_t \times ProbIss_i + \gamma^9 \Delta Bush_t \times ProbPurch_i + \varepsilon_{it} \qquad (vii)$$

$$r_{it} = \alpha_i + \beta_i r_t^m + \gamma^6 \Delta Bush_t + \gamma^{10} \Delta Bush_t \times Mature_i + \varepsilon_{it}, \qquad (viii)$$

where r_t^m equals the daily return on the CRSP total market value-weighted index, $\Delta Bush_t$ is the change in the probability of a George W. Bush victory on date t, and the remaining variables are defined as before: Div_i equals the 2002 dividend payout ratio for firm i, $ProbIss_i$ equals the 2002 new share issuance probability for firm i, $ProbPurch_i$ equals the 2002 repurchase

Table 1. *Key Event Dates for JGTRA03*

Event #	Event Date	Event Window	Description	S&P 500 (% Change)
1	12/25/2002	12/23–12/30	*NY Times* Article	−0.31
2	1/7/2003	1/3–1/9	Bush announces plan	−0.65
3	2/27/2003	2/27–3/5	Introduced into House	1.18
	3/4/2003		First hearing in House	−1.54
4	3/27/2003	3/25–3/31	Thomas floats 8/18 plan	−0.16
5	4/30/2003	4/28–5/2	Thomas floats 5/15 plan	−0.10
6	5/6/2003	5/6–5/12	Ways and Means passes	0.85
	5/9/2003		House passes	1.43
7	5/15/2003	5/13–5/19	Senate passes	0.79
8	5/23/2003	5/21–5/28	Conference version passes	0.14

probability for firm *i*, and *Mature_i* indicates whether firm *i* has ever paid a dividend. In principle, and as discussed further below, the interaction terms from this regression should provide evidence that is consistent with that provided by our event-study coefficients. Moreover, to the extent that the election specifically contains information concerning the permanence, or lack thereof, of the dividend taxes, it may allow us to distinguish the effects of permanent dividend tax cuts from the effects of temporary ones.

3.3. Data

Event Dates

An event study is only as good as the events chosen, and there is always the risk that poorly chosen event days will cloud any empirical analysis. In order to acquire event days for this study, we asked the senior economist for the House Ways and Means Committee, Alex Brill, to review his notes from that time and construct a list of dates on which important news concerning the dividend tax was released to the public. We then used the list he provided to us as our event list and did not alter the list after our research began. The events are contained in Table 1. While our focus here is on formal statistical analysis, we include in Table 1 the percent change in the Standard & Poor's (S&P 500) index on the day of each event. While some of the events were associated with a positive swing in equity prices, some were not.

The list contains eight 5-day event windows within which significant news concerning the likelihood of passage of the dividend tax cut was made public. The first event was a story by Edmund Andrews in the *New York Times* that first revealed that the White House would push for a 50 percent decrease in the tax rate on dividends.[7] Then, on January 7, 2003, President Bush formally announced his plan. On February 27, the plan was introduced in the House, and on March 4 hearings began. Because we use a window around each event of five days, these two events are grouped together.

After the president's plan appeared to lose steam, the dividend tax debate reignited on March 27, when Chairman Bill Thomas (R-CA) of the House Ways and Means Committee floated a plan that would reduce the tax rates on dividends and capital gains to 8 and 18 percent, a simpler plan than that initially proposed by President Bush. On April 30, Thomas announced a modified version of his initial plan that moved the rates to 5 and 15 percent. On May 6, this plan passed the Ways and Means Committee, and on May 9 it passed the House. These two events also ran together, given our event window rules. On May 15, the Senate passed an alternative bill that would have brought the tax rate on dividends to zero, but only for one year before its sunset. On May 23, the Thomas version of the bill, with a sunset date of December 31, 2008, emerged from the conference and passed both houses, passing in the Senate only with Vice President Cheney casting the tie-breaking vote. While different versions of a dividend tax cut were debated during this 5-month period, all shared the property of cutting dividend tax rates substantially more than capital gains tax rates.

Firm Data

The data sources, variable definitions, and procedures for excluding outlying observations follow Auerbach and Hassett (2003) very closely.

Balance sheet data come from the Compustat annual database for the period 1980–2002. Variables include:

Dividends = cash dividends paid on common stock
Investment = capital expenditures
Cash flow = after-tax income (net of preferred dividends) plus depreciation
Value = end-of-year market value
Debt = short-term plus long-term debt
Bond rating = the long-term credit rating assigned by S&P.

---

[7] Although unrelated to our choice of event dates, this article contained a quote by one of us voicing skepticism about the policy: "'One wouldn't think of this as the first or second or even third measure to stimulate consumption or investment,' said Alan Auerbach, an economist at the University of California at Berkeley who has studied the issue for years." There was (and is) disagreement between the authors concerning the advisability of this proposal. In any case, our views have not colored our analysis in this paper.

Financial firms (SIC codes 6000–6900) and firms that underwent a major merger during the period were eliminated. Questionable observations were dropped if any of the following conditions were met: (1) investment-assets ratio less than 0 or greater than 1, (2) cash flow-assets ratio less than –1 or greater than 1, (3) dividends-assets ratio above 0.5, (4) debt-assets ratio greater than 1, or (5) equity value-assets ratio greater than 20.

A variable measuring the number of analysts following the firm and providing earnings-per-share estimates in a given year comes from I/B/E/S. The daily price and stock-return data come from CRSP, for the period January 2, 2002–September 30, 2003.

New issues and share repurchase probabilities were estimated from the marginal probability distributions from a bivariate probit model, using the same specification as that in Auerbach and Hassett (2003). The dependent variables are indicator variables for whether a firm issued new shares (net new share issues above 2 percent of outstanding shares) or repurchased shares (net new share issues below –2 percent of outstanding shares) in a given year. The dependent variables include two lags of the investment, cash flow, value, and debt, as defined above. The estimation also includes year dummies, size dummies (four quartiles based on total assets), industry dummies (based on 3-digit SIC code), and categorical dummies for bond rating and number of analysts. The estimation was run only on the mature sample for the years 1985–2002.

Political Data

Daily closing prices from the Iowa Electronic Markets 2004 U.S. Presidential Winner Takes All Market were used to calculate implied probabilities of a George W. Bush win in the November election. The market opened on June 1, 2004 and closed on November 5, 2004. The Bush contract was structured to pay $1 in the event George Bush received the most popular votes. On September 22, the contract spun off into two separate contracts (one that paid if Bush won the most popular votes with less than 52 percent of the total two-party vote and one that paid if Bush won the most popular votes with more than 52 percent of the total two-party vote), and therefore we calculate the probability as the sum of the prices on the two Bush contracts.

4. Basic Results

Table 2 presents the first set of regression results based on the methodology just described. The sample consists of all mature firms defined, as described

Table 2. *Mature Sample: Dividend Interactions Only*
(t-statistics in parentheses)

	Unweighted	Weighted
Dividend yield 1	0.120	0.107
	(2.58)	(1.05)
Dividend yield 2	0.049	0.414
	(0.55)	(2.26)
Dividend yield 3	0.225	0.283
	(2.02)	(1.70)
Dividend yield 4	−0.116	0.157
	(−0.92)	(0.91)
Dividend yield 5	−0.251	−0.038
	(−3.56)	(−0.17)
Dividend yield 6	0.100	−0.217
	(0.62)	(−3.20)
Dividend yield 7	0.265	0.358
	(2.37)	(1.71)
Dividend yield 8	0.164	0.419
	(1.27)	(2.62)
Dividend yield (Cumulative)	**0.556**	**1.484**
	(1.42)	**(2.20)**
R^2	0.0014	0.0018
N	512,073	512,073

above, as firms that have paid dividends in the past. The table presents two sets of results, one in which observations are weighted by firm value, the other in which observations are not weighted. Standard errors of these least squares estimates are adjusted by clustering by 3-digit industries, to account for the likely correlation of return shocks within industries. All subsequent tables follow this same format of presenting both weighted and unweighted estimates and clustering standard errors by 3-digit industry.[8] Although the estimation procedure requires simultaneous estimation of

---

[8] In our 2003 paper, we found that the likelihood that a firm fell under either view was related to firm size but not monotonically. Very large firms and very small firms appeared to have dividend patterns consistent with the new view, whereas firms in between exhibited payout behavior consistent with the traditional view. Accordingly, weighting will likely have an important impact on the results, although the nonmonotonic relationship makes it difficult to predict ex ante what that impact might be. We also found that very large firms appeared to rely more on debt finance, which might make weighted regressions less likely to discern between the two views that work off of different marginal sources of finance.

event-date parameters and market-model parameters for every firm, we present only the former parameters in the tables.

The first eight rows of Table 2 present the coefficients for each of the eight event windows described above. For each event, the coefficient represents the cumulative abnormal return for a 5-day window centered on the event date. The ninth row, in boldface, presents the cumulative abnormal return for the eight events taken together, calculated by re-running the regression with the eight event windows treated as a single, noncontiguous 40-day episode. The cumulative effect is positive in both unweighted and weighted samples, but significant only in the latter, for which the point estimate is three times higher than that estimated using the unweighted sample. This coefficient of about 1.5 indicates a positive abnormal return of 1.5 percent for each percentage-point increase in the firm's dividend yield.[9]

The abnormal returns estimated for individual events are noisier, although at least one of the columns shows a significant positive abnormal return for five of the eight events. The three events for which this does not occur are events 4, 5, and 6. Each of these dates involved activity by the House Ways and Means Committee. Events 4 and 5, in particular, involved modifications to the original Bush plan that could potentially have indicated that a reduction in dividend taxes faced legislative hurdles. The last two events, associated with Senate passage and the conference agreement, eliminated any doubt of the tax cut's ultimate success, and each event is associated with large, positive abnormal returns.

Table 3 extends the analysis of Table 2 by adding further variables to explain the event-window abnormal returns. As discussed above, future issuance of new shares increases the present value of future dividends, relative to current market value, thereby increasing the potential gain as a share of current value from a permanent dividend tax cut. We include firm-specific estimated probabilities of new issues and repurchases, interacted with event-date dummies, as explanatory variables in the models presented in Table 3. Our logic suggests that the new issue propensity should increase abnormal returns. We have no equally clear intuition regarding the probability of repurchases, but include it for the sake of completeness.

---

[9] This is of the same order of magnitude as the aggregate gain as a share of market value of 6 percent suggested by Poterba (2004), but it is difficult to compare the two numbers because of the differences in methodology. Poterba's calculation is based on an infinite-horizon valuation model that assumes no behavioral changes, while our results are based on cross-section differences among firms.

Table 3. *Mature Sample: All Interactions (t-statistics in parentheses)*

	Unweighted	Weighted
Dividend yield 1	0.123	0.114
	(2.69)	(1.14)
Dividend yield 2	0.033	0.410
	(0.43)	(2.37)
Dividend yield 3	0.225	0.255
	(2.07)	(1.51)
Dividend yield 4	−0.124	0.150
	(−1.08)	(0.85)
Dividend yield 5	−0.256	−0.013
	(−3.46)	(−0.06)
Dividend yield 6	0.094	−0.224
	(0.58)	(−3.36)
Dividend yield 7	0.247	0.361
	(2.49)	(2.05)
Dividend yield 8	0.166	0.442
	(1.34)	(3.02)
Dividend yield (Cumulative)	**0.507**	**1.495**
	(1.52)	**(2.48)**
Probability of issuance 1	0.015	0.001
	(1.34)	(0.06)
Probability of issuance 2	0.029	0.045
	(1.89)	(1.58)
Probability of issuance 3	0.020	−0.015
	(1.42)	(−0.81)
Probability of issuance 4	0.050	0.006
	(3.86)	(0.35)
Probability of issuance 5	0.004	0.007
	(0.23)	(0.38)
Probability of issuance 6	−0.006	0.005
	(−0.52)	(0.45)
Probability of issuance 7	0.035	0.068
	(1.88)	(3.05)
Probability of issuance 8	0.039	0.043
	(3.11)	(2.60)
Probability of issuance (Cumulative)	**0.187**	**0.160**
	(4.42)	**(2.30)**
Probability of purchase 1	0.020	0.014
	(1.13)	(0.43)
Probability of purchase 2	−0.059	0.009
	(−2.86)	(0.26)

(continued)

Table 3 *(continued)*

	Unweighted	Weighted
Probability of purchase 3	0.007	−0.066
	(0.31)	(−2.36)
Probability of purchase 4	−0.012	−0.012
	(−0.58)	(−0.38)
Probability of purchase 5	−0.019	0.058
	(−0.58)	(1.58)
Probability of purchase 6	−0.028	−0.014
	(−1.27)	(−0.50)
Probability of purchase 7	−0.055	0.030
	(−2.44)	(1.00)
Probability of purchase 8	0.026	0.070
	(1.30)	(2.88)
Probability of purchase (Cumulative)	**−0.121**	**0.087**
	(−1.85)	**(0.73)**
R^2	0.0018	0.0027
N	512,073	512,073

Adding these new explanatory variables has little impact on the estimated effect of the dividend yield – its cumulative point estimates are very similar to those in Table 2 for both weighted and unweighted samples, and the precision of these estimates is slightly higher than before. As hypothesized, the probability of issuing shares has a positive impact on the cumulative abnormal return, indicating that a 1 percent increase in the probability of issuing shares in a given year leads to an abnormal return of just under 0.2 percent. As to the individual event dates, the largest positive effects for the new share probability tend to occur on the same dates as those for the dividend yield. For the weighted sample, for example, the three largest coefficients for new share issues (the last two of which are significant) are for events 2 (when President Bush first announced his plan), 7, and 8; these events also have the three largest coefficients for the dividend yield, all significant. This concentration of the new-issue and dividend-yield effects within the same event windows suggests that these variables are, indeed, picking up the effects of expected changes in dividend tax policy, rather than other contemporaneous news. Finally, the probability of repurchasing, for which we do not have a clearly predicted impact, also has no clear impact in the regressions, its cumulative effect being negative and insignificant for the unweighted model and positive and insignificant for the weighted model.

Table 4. *Full Sample (t-statistics in parentheses)*

	Unweighted	Weighted
Mature dummy 1	0.006	0.001
	(2.97)	(0.09)
Mature dummy 2	−0.011	−0.024
	(−2.23)	(−3.80)
Mature dummy 3	0.002	−0.004
	(0.89)	(−0.69)
Mature dummy 4	−0.017	−0.003
	(−4.82)	(−0.63)
Mature dummy 5	−0.010	0.000
	(−3.84)	(−0.05)
Mature dummy 6	−0.006	0.008
	(−1.86)	(1.17)
Mature dummy 7	−0.031	−0.010
	(−6.13)	(−0.90)
Mature dummy 8	−0.020	−0.004
	(−3.42)	(−0.47)
Mature dummy (Cumulative)	**−0.086**	**−0.037**
	(−7.14)	**(−2.29)**
R^2	0.0007	0.0011
N	1,855,535	1,855,535

Table 4 presents estimates for the entire sample of firms, including both mature and immature firms. As previously discussed, we should expect immature firms to gain more from a permanent tax cut, following the same logic that explains the positive impact of future new issues among mature firms. Of course, this reasoning depends on the tax cut being permanent, or at least of sufficient duration for the future dividends from new share issues to qualify for the tax cut. In Table 4, we interact the event-date dummies with a dummy variable for whether the firm is mature, to test this prediction.[10]

The results, for both unweighted and weighted estimates, confirm the prediction of higher abnormal returns for immature firms. Being immature generates an abnormal return of between 3.7 percent and 8.6 percent of value – a very large impact, relative to the impact of dividend yield among mature firms. The estimated effects in this case are larger for the unweighted

---

[10] We do not include the mature firm explanatory variables from Table 3, as these would have the same coefficients as before in a model for which they are set to zero for the immature firms added to the sample.

sample, but note that, again, the windows around dates 2, 7, and 8 are among the most important.

5. Further Results

Our theoretical predictions of various effects hinge on the expected permanence of the tax cut that eventually passed in 2003. In particular, if our theory underlies the empirical results presented so far, it should also be the case that increases in the expected duration of the tax cut should further enhance the relative returns to immature firms, as well as the returns to mature firms predicted to issue new shares in the future. Thus, increases in the tax cut's expected duration should reinforce the empirical results already found.

A different story applies for the estimated positive effect of the firm's dividend yield. Recall that, under the new view of dividend taxation, the positive impact of the dividend yield is attributable solely to the timing of the path of future dividends, with higher yields corresponding to a higher share of the firm's future dividends being paid out before the tax cut expires. Thus, an increase in the expected duration of the tax cut should *reduce* the importance of the dividend yield, mitigating the positive effect already found. Under the traditional view, on the other hand, a tax cut of longer duration should *increase* the bonus from a high dividend yield, for it would lower the discount rates applied to future cash flows. Thus, an event that affected the tax cut's expected permanence would provide an opportunity to confirm the theoretical model presented above and to distinguish between the new and traditional views with respect to the effects of dividend taxation.

Such an event – indeed, a series of such events – we argue, occurred during the 2004 presidential campaign, which pitted the dividend tax cut's sponsor, George W. Bush, against an opponent, John Kerry, who had included in his campaign platform a plan to eliminate all of the Bush tax cuts, including those enacted in 2003, for individuals earning over $200,000, a group that accounts for a significant fraction of taxable dividends. With the dividend tax cut already subject to a sunset after 2008, Kerry, even without a consenting Congress, could have shepherded the dividend tax cut into oblivion before the end of his first term. Thus, changes in the predicted election outcome should have changed the forecast of the tax cut's permanence among market participants. Daily trading in futures markets tied to the presidential election's outcome provide us with a record of the fluctuations in expectations during the 2004 campaign.

Table 5. *Mature Sample, Iowa Futures: Dividend Interactions Only (t-statistics in parentheses)*

	Unweighted	Weighted
ΔBush	0.035	-0.008
	(4.77)	(-0.68)
ΔBush $\times$ Dividend yield	-0.413	-0.106
	(-2.46)	(-0.47)
R^2	0.0007	0.0002
N	93,981	93,981

Table 6. *Mature Sample, Iowa Futures: All Interactions (t-statistics in parentheses)*

	Unweighted	Weighted
ΔBush	0.023	-0.046
	(1.91)	(-1.63)
ΔBush $\times$ Dividend yield	-0.419	-0.079
	(-2.62)	(-0.37)
ΔBush $\times$ Probability of issuance	0.052	0.152
	(1.68)	(3.04)
ΔBush $\times$ Probability of purchase	0.005	0.106
	(0.08)	(1.06)
R^2	0.0007	0.0011
N	93,981	93,981

For the period during which the Iowa Electronic Futures Presidential Winner Takes All market was open, June 1–November 5, 2004, we simultaneously estimate market model parameters for all firms and coefficients on the daily change in the price of a Bush contract, which we interpret as Bush's reelection probability.[11] We also interact this change in probability with other firm attributes of interest, including the firm's dividend yield, its new issue and repurchase probabilities, and whether it is a mature firm. Tables 5, 6, and 7 present the results, which can be compared to Tables 2, 3, and 4 to determine how the effects found during the 2003 event windows were altered by the changing election probabilities in 2004.

In Tables 5 and 6, the effect of an increase in the Bush reelection probability is to reduce the premium associated with a high dividend yield, consistent

---

[11] Very similar results were found using contract prices from intrade.com.

Table 7. *Full Sample, Iowa Futures (t-statistics in parentheses)*

	Unweighted	Weighted
ΔBush	0.023	0.031
	(3.86)	(3.94)
ΔBush × Mature dummy	0.005	−0.039
	(0.84)	(−3.15)
R^2	0.0002	0.0004
N	333,158	333,158

with the new view and inconsistent with the traditional view. This effect, though, is significant only in the unweighted version. In Table 6, we see that the impact of being likely to issue shares is reinforced by a higher Bush election probability as our theory would predict, but again with only one of the specifications (this time, the weighted version) having a significant coefficient. Once again, the repurchase probability is not significant. In Table 7, the impact of being mature is significantly reduced by an increase in the Bush election probability (in the weighted specification). That is, as predicted, the bonus to being an immature firm was enhanced by the prospect of a more permanent dividend tax cut. Taken together, the results in Tables 5–7, though noisy, reinforce our basic results regarding the bonuses received by immature firms and mature firms issuing shares and provide some new evidence as to why firms with high dividend yields experienced higher abnormal returns. In particular, the source of these gains appears to be connected to the timing of dividend payments, as hypothesized under the new view, rather than to a cost-of-capital reduction, as hypothesized under the traditional view.

One final piece of evidence concerning the new and traditional views comes from Table 8, which augments Table 2 by including not only the firm's own 2002 dividend yield, but also the value-weighted dividend yield from that year in the firm's own 3-digit industry. Recall that, under the traditional view, larger reductions in the cost of capital should induce more investment and a sharper drop in the before-tax rate of return. Thus, *ceteris paribus*, firms in an industry experiencing a larger reduction in the cost of capital – arguably an industry with a high dividend yield – should experience lower abnormal returns. If the industry is populated by new-view firms, though, the industry dividend yield should have no impact whatsoever, because the dividend tax cut has no impact on investment behavior. Contrary to either of these predictions, though, the industry dividend yield has a *positive* impact

Table 8. *Mature Sample: Dividend and Industry Average Dividend Interactions*
(t-statistics in parentheses)

	Unweighted	Weighted
Dividend yield 1	0.028	−0.080
	(0.49)	(−0.71)
Dividend yield 2	0.024	0.565
	(0.30)	(3.37)
Dividend yield 3	0.118	0.252
	(1.18)	(1.63)
Dividend yield 4	−0.199	−0.191
	(−1.61)	(−1.03)
Dividend yield 5	−0.125	0.064
	(−1.66)	(0.18)
Dividend yield 6	0.221	−0.095
	(1.28)	(−1.10)
Dividend yield 7	0.094	−0.157
	(1.12)	(−0.79)
Dividend yield 8	0.050	0.323
	(0.40)	(1.28)
Dividend yield (Cumulative)	**0.211**	**0.682**
	(0.68)	**(0.77)**
Industry average dividend yield 1	0.254	0.274
	(4.26)	(1.87)
Industry average dividend yield 2	0.068	−0.222
	(0.58)	(−0.96)
Industry average dividend yield 3	0.294	0.045
	(2.29)	(0.23)
Industry average dividend yield 4	0.226	0.512
	(1.90)	(2.45)
Industry average dividend yield 5	−0.346	−0.150
	(−3.18)	(−0.49)
Industry average dividend yield 6	−0.330	−0.181
	(−2.26)	(−2.12)
Industry average dividend yield 7	0.466	0.766
	(3.60)	(3.29)
Industry average dividend yield 8	0.313	0.142
	(2.53)	(0.56)
Industry average dividend yield (Cumulative)	**0.946**	**1.187**
	(2.54)	**(1.70)**
R^2	0.0017	0.0023
N	512,073	512,073

on firm abnormal returns. This could occur under the traditional view if there were large positive technology spillovers within an industry associated with increased investment. However, the literature claiming to document such effects has been largely discredited (see Auerbach, Hassett, and Oliner, 1994). On the other hand, this result could be due to the noisiness of our measures of firm-specific yields. For example, if all firms were new-view firms, and we measured each firm's dividend yield with some noise, the coefficient of the firm's measured dividend yield, which should be positive (as already discussed, due to the tax cut's temporary nature), would be downward biased, and the coefficient of the industry dividend yield, a variable that would likely be positively correlated with the firm's "true" yield, would therefore be upward biased (from zero). Under a scenario in which all firms respond according to the traditional view, though, it is harder to explain the results in Table 8, even if the firm's own yield is measured with error.

6. Robustness and Sensitivity Analysis

How robust are the results presented thus far to changes in specification? To what extent are there alternative possible explanations to the ones we have offered? This section provides some additional results aimed at addressing both questions.

At the foundation of all of the results in Tables 2–8 is the standard CAPM, based on a single factor: the daily aggregate market return. In recent years, many empirical studies have adopted as an alternative the three-factor model of Fama and French (1993), whose two additional factors are based on the differences in returns between portfolios of high and low book-to-market-value firms and small- and large-capitalization firms.

While inclusion of these additional factors may lack theoretical grounding, it has been found to improve the model's predictive performance. Moreover, these factors are potentially related to the types of heterogeneity we have studied. For example, immature firms are likely to be smaller than mature firms, and high dividend yields are more common among the slow-growing firms with low values of Tobin's q – the ratio of market value to book value. Thus, there may be some suspicion that our findings relating to dividend yield and firm maturity are spurious, with these variables simply picking up the missing Fama-French factors. This turns out, however, not to be the case. Table 3' (the first two columns) and Table 4' repeat the estimates of Tables 3 and 4 for mature firms and all firms, using the three Fama-French factors rather than just the market return as control variables. As a comparison of

Table 3′. *Mature Sample: All Interactions (t-statistics in parentheses)*

	3-Factor Model		Institutional Ownership	
	Unweighted	Weighted	Unweighted	Weighted
Dividend yield 1	0.123	0.126	0.135	0.130
	(2.71)	(1.22)	(2.89)	(1.18)
Dividend yield 2	0.008	0.382	−0.033	0.364
	(0.11)	(2.17)	(−0.42)	(1.97)
Dividend yield 3	0.191	0.204	0.214	0.201
	(2.05)	(1.17)	(1.89)	(1.18)
Dividend yield 4	−0.099	0.183	−0.127	0.204
	(−0.77)	(1.03)	(−1.04)	(1.13)
Dividend yield 5	−0.161	0.174	−0.302	−0.001
	(−2.19)	(0.79)	(−3.61)	(−0.00)
Dividend yield 6	0.098	−0.240	0.070	−0.201
	(0.63)	(−3.73)	(0.40)	(−3.30)
Dividend yield 7	0.189	0.224	0.257	0.389
	(2.24)	(1.30)	(2.40)	(2.08)
Dividend yield 8	0.224	0.546	0.170	0.507
	(1.49)	(3.63)	(1.27)	(3.60)
Dividend yield (Cumulative)	**0.573**	**1.600**	**0.385**	**1.594**
	(1.58)	**(2.65)**	**(1.13)**	**(2.74)**
Probability of issuance 1	0.015	0.003	0.014	−3.47E−04
	(1.34)	(0.16)	(1.26)	(−0.02)
Probability of issuance 2	0.030	0.057	0.033	0.050
	(1.94)	(2.06)	(2.24)	(1.64)
Probability of issuance 3	0.020	−0.006	0.022	−0.010
	(1.48)	(−0.34)	(1.55)	(−0.54)
Probability of issuance 4	0.048	−0.007	0.053	0.002
	(3.71)	(−0.37)	(4.02)	(0.10)
Probability of issuance 5	0.007	−0.001	0.004	0.006
	(0.34)	(−0.06)	(0.21)	(0.34)
Probability of issuance 6	−0.009	−0.007	−0.004	0.003
	(−0.73)	(−0.62)	(−0.33)	(0.30)
Probability of issuance 7	0.031	0.058	0.038	0.066
	(1.60)	(2.41)	(1.96)	(3.05)
Probability of issuance 8	0.040	0.033	0.040	0.037
	(3.01)	(1.91)	(3.15)	(2.27)
Probability of issuance (Cumulative)	**0.182**	**0.130**	**0.200**	**0.153**
	(4.33)	**(1.82)**	**(4.69)**	**(2.16)**
Probability of purchase 1	0.020	0.016	0.022	0.011
	(1.12)	(0.48)	(1.21)	(0.31)

(*continued*)

Table 3' *(continued)*

	3-Factor Model		Institutional Ownership	
	Unweighted	Weighted	Unweighted	Weighted
Probability of purchase 2	−0.068	0.014	−0.030	0.019
	(−3.29)	(0.44)	(−1.51)	(0.53)
Probability of purchase 3	−0.001	−0.063	0.015	−0.054
	(−0.04)	(−2.25)	(0.67)	(−1.83)
Probability of purchase 4	−0.002	−0.018	−0.009	−0.023
	(−0.11)	(−0.53)	(−0.44)	(−0.72)
Probability of purchase 5	−0.003	0.060	−0.006	0.054
	(−0.09)	(1.65)	(−0.19)	(1.54)
Probability of purchase 6	−0.021	−0.023	−0.020	−0.021
	(−0.96)	(−0.75)	(−0.94)	(−0.70)
Probability of purchase 7	−0.057	0.018	−0.043	0.026
	(−2.53)	(0.59)	(−1.95)	(0.94)
Probability of purchase 8	0.039	0.068	0.025	0.057
	(1.92)	(2.89)	(1.31)	(2.38)
Probability of purchase	**−0.094**	**0.073**	**−0.047**	**0.069**
(Cumulative)	**(−1.41)**	**(0.60)**	**(−0.76)**	**(0.59)**
Institutional Ownership 1	—	—	−0.002	0.008
			(−0.35)	(0.60)
Institutional Ownership 2	—	—	−0.042	−0.025
			(−4.11)	(−1.25)
Institutional Ownership 3	—	—	−0.011	−0.028
			(−1.48)	(−2.38)
Institutional Ownership 4	—	—	−0.002	0.025
			(−0.29)	(2.00)
Institutional Ownership 5	—	—	−0.021	0.006
			(−2.03)	(0.59)
Institutional Ownership 6	—	—	−0.012	0.015
			(−1.41)	(1.70)
Institutional Ownership 7	—	—	−0.016	0.010
			(−2.05)	(0.61)
Institutional Ownership 8	—	—	0.006	0.033
			(0.75)	(3.40)
Institutional Ownership	—	—	**−0.100**	**0.045**
(Cumulative)			**(−4.20)**	**(1.08)**
R^2	0.0011	0.0026	0.0021	0.0031
N	512,073	512,073	503,792	503,792

Table 4'. *Full Sample: 3-Factor Model (t-statistics in parentheses)*

	Unweighted	Weighted
Mature dummy 1	0.006	0.001
	(2.94)	(0.09)
Mature dummy 2	−0.013	−0.028
	(−2.74)	(−4.77)
Mature dummy 3	−0.001	−0.009
	(−0.32)	(−1.56)
Mature dummy 4	−0.014	0.001
	(−4.08)	(0.27)
Mature dummy 5	−0.002	0.014
	(−0.66)	(2.47)
Mature dummy 6	−0.005	0.008
	(−1.60)	(1.20)
Mature dummy 7	−0.035	−0.019
	(−6.47)	(−1.75)
Mature dummy 8	−0.014	0.005
	(−2.61)	(0.59)
Mature dummy (Cumulative)	**−0.079**	**−0.028**
	(−6.59)	**(−1.77)**
R^2	0.0004	0.0010
N	1,855,535	1,855,535

the original and new tables shows, the cumulative effects are little changed. In Table 3', the cumulative coefficient of the dividend yield interaction is slightly larger than before in both weighted and unweighted samples, while the new share and repurchase coefficients are slightly smaller (in absolute value). In Table 4, the mature firm dummy variable's cumulative coefficient is only slightly smaller.

Another issue involves differences in corporate governance. Recent papers by Chetty and Saez (2005) and Brown et al. (2004) find that dividend payout policy responses to the 2003 legislation varied with respect to variables measuring managerial incentives and shareholder oversight. In general, firms with managers' incentives aligned with value maximization, and firms with large institutional shareholders were more responsive to the tax cut. One might argue that these factors leading to more responsive financial decisions might also lead to larger increases in market value.

To test this hypothesis, we considered three variables based on the methodology and data sources of Chetty and Saez: the ratio to firm value of unexercisable options among top five executives; the fraction of the firm's shares owned by the top five executives, and the fraction of the firm's shares held by institutional investors. The first two of these variables had little explanatory power when interacted with the event dates (not shown). The results with only the third variable added are shown in the last two columns of Table 3'.[12] While having little impact on the other key variables in the equation, the institutional ownership variable itself has an insignificant effect in the weighted version of the model and a significant *negative* effect in the unweighted version. Re-running this equation with holdings of clearly tax-exempt entities excluded from the institutional ownership calculation (not shown) has little impact on the other variables of interest but does improve the performance of the institutional ownership variable, making it more positive and significant in the weighted version and less negative, though still significant, in the unweighted version. This improvement is consistent with the evidence Chetty and Saez present that dividend policy in 2003 responded to ownership by taxable rather than all institutional investors.

The variables on which we have focused might also be acting as proxies in the results in Tables 5–7, which relate changes in President Bush's election probability to firm excess returns. For example, suppose that high-yield firms are also firms in industries that would have benefited from a Kerry presidency? Then the results in Tables 5 and 6 would simply be picking up these firms' underperformance on pro-Bush days. As for Table 7, perhaps immature firms liked Bush.

To control for these explanations, we designated some firms as pro-Bush and others as pro-Kerry and interacted the associated dummy variables with the change in the Bush election probability. Our categories of firms were those that Knight (2006, Tables 2a and 2b) identified as being either pro-Bush or pro-Gore in the 2000 elections. All other firms were assigned to neither category. The results are shown in Tables 6' and 7'. None of the new variables are significant, and there is little impact on the other coefficients of interest. It is somewhat puzzling that, although they are not significant, the coefficients for the Bush firms tend to be negative and those for the Kerry firms positive, both opposite the predicted sign. As a check to see whether these results were attributable to the assignment method, we tried an alternative in which no firms were assigned to Kerry and *all* firms in the following industries – evident from Knight's breakdown to be prevalently pro-Bush – were assigned to the pro-Bush camp: Pharmaceuticals (SIC 283), Defense (SIC 372, 376, and 381), Energy (SIC 130 and 291), and

---

[12] We consider the specifications using these corporate governance variables only for the mature firm sample, as their coverage is not as complete among immature firms.

Table 6'. *Mature Sample, Iowa Futures: All Interactions (t-statistics in parentheses)*

	Unweighted	Weighted
ΔBush	0.024	−0.040
	(2.01)	(−2.09)
ΔBush × Dividend yield	−0.413	0.054
	(−2.55)	(0.21)
ΔBush × Probability of issuance	0.051	0.135
	(1.68)	(4.26)
ΔBush × Probability of purchase	0.005	0.088
	(0.08)	(1.11)
ΔBush × Bush favor	−0.021	−0.030
	(−0.73)	(−0.88)
ΔBush × Dem favor	0.005	0.016
	(−0.08)	(0.23)
R^2	0.0008	0.0012
N	93,981	93,981

Table 7'. *Full Sample, Iowa Futures (t–statistics in parentheses)*

	Unweighted	Weighted
ΔBush	0.023	0.031
	(3.82)	(3.59)
ΔBush × Mature dummy	0.006	−0.036
	(0.89)	(−2.77)
ΔBush × Bush favor	−0.027	−0.024
	(−1.26)	(−0.81)
ΔBush × Dem favor	0.059	0.056
	(1.54)	(1.67)
R^2	0.0002	0.0001
N	333,158	333,158

Tobacco (SIC 211–214). The resulting pro-Bush dummy variable also had a negative sign (not shown) when added to the specifications in Tables 6 and 7.

Finally, there is the issue of how one chooses event dates. As discussed above, we used a list of event dates on the basis of information about the legislative process and did not modify the list once our empirical investigation began. These dates were intended to represent the important dates on which the process of legislative passage moved forward. On other dates, presumably, little was happening, so these dates *together* should provide a reasonable measure of the value of passage, even if the information on some of the dates was unfavorable for passage.

While we have strived to include all important dates within the legislative window that began in late December, 2002, we have also assumed that little of note took place before then. There was always some possibility that a dividend tax cut would be introduced and become law, but we judge this possibility to have been quite remote until our first event date. Some, though, trace the origin of Bush's commitment to a dividend tax cut to his "economic summit" in Waco, Texas on August 13, 2002, after an exchange with brokerage magnate Charles Schwab. However, while Bush indicated an interest in reducing dividend taxes, he also expressed interest in other proposals, and, according to *Tax Notes* (August 19, 2002), "offered no indication whether the administration would throw any weight behind the tax changes." We are skeptical of this date's relevance given the lack of activity and press coverage of potential dividend tax changes prior to our chosen event window. Nevertheless, we estimated an alternative version of our model with this date added as a ninth event. The results for this date (not shown) were generally insignificant and of the wrong sign. For example, the dividend interactions in the mature-sample regressions (e.g., Table 2) were negative and insignificant for this event window, while the mature firm interactions in the full-sample regressions (e.g., Table 4) were positive and insignificant.

7. Conclusions

We find strong evidence that the 2003 change in the dividend tax law had a significant impact on equity markets. First, looking only at firms that have previously paid a dividend, we find that firms with higher yields outperformed firms with lower yields. In one specification, a 1 percentage point increase in yields led to a 1.5 percent higher abnormal return. Within this same set of firms, we also found that firms that were likely to issue new shares also benefited abnormally from the tax cut, with a 1 percent increase in the probability of new share issuance associated with a 0.2 percent increase in abnormal return.

When we included all firms, even those not paying dividends (so-called "immature" firms), in our analysis, we found that immature firms significantly outperformed mature firms on our event dates. The range of higher returns was from 3.7 to 8.6 percent. We found evidence consistent with our event analysis relying on a second approach that used the Bush election probability as a proxy for expected future dividend policy. Here we found that a higher probability of Bush being elected was associated with a reduced importance of the dividend yield and also enhanced the excess return "bonus" to being immature.

While these results at times seem counterintuitive, for the most part they are consistent with the predictions of the model developed in Section 2, in particular with the predictions for mature firms of the new view of dividend taxation. However, the difference in point estimates between weighted and unweighted regressions suggests that significant heterogeneity (perhaps consistent with that found in our 2003 paper) may exist below the surface. While the new-view model best describes the aggregate share price responses we have seen, it may well be that significant traditional-view patterns would appear with careful splits of the data. But a full treatment of firm heterogeneity also requires further consideration of the competitive environment when firms differ in their financial policies and constraints.

References

Auerbach, Alan J. 1979. "Share Valuation and Corporate Equity Policy." *Journal of Public Economics* 11(3): 291–305.

Auerbach, Alan J. 2002. "Taxation and Corporate Financial Policy." In A. Auerbach and M. Feldstein, eds., *Handbook of Public Economics*, Vol. 3 (Amsterdam: North-Holland/Elsevier), pp. 1251–1292.

Auerbach, Alan J., and Kevin A. Hassett. 2003. "On the Marginal Source of Investment Funds." *Journal of Public Economics* 87(1): 205–232.

Auerbach, Alan J., Kevin A. Hassett, and Stephen D. Oliner. 1994. "Reassessing the Social Returns to Equipment Investment." *Quarterly Journal of Economics* 109(3): 789–802.

Bradford, David. 1981. "The Incidence and Allocation Effects of a Tax on Corporate Distributions." *Journal of Public Economics* 15(1): 1–22.

Brown, Jeffrey R., Nellie Liang, and Scott Weisbenner. 2004. "Executive Financial Incentives and Payout Policy: Firm Responses to the 2003 Dividend Tax Cut." NBER Working Paper 11002. (Cambridge, MA: National Bureau of Economic Research).

Carroll, Robert, Kevin A. Hassett, and James B. Mackie III. 2003. "The Effect of Dividend Tax Relief on Investment Incentives." *National Tax Journal* 56(3): 629–651.

Chetty, Raj, and Emmanuel Saez. 2005. "Dividend Taxes and Corporate Behavior: Evidence from the 2003 Dividend Tax Cut." *Quarterly Journal of Economics* 120(3): 791–833.

Desai, Mihir A., and Austan D. Goolsbee. 2004. "Investment, Overhang, and Tax Policy." *Brookings Papers on Economic Activity* 35(2): 285–338.

Fama, Eugene F., and Kenneth R. French. 1993. "Common Risk Factors in the Returns on Stocks and Bonds." *Journal of Financial Economics* 33(1): 3–56.

House, Christopher L., and Matthew Shapiro. 2005. "Temporary Investment Incentives: Theory and Evidence from Bonus Depreciation." Working paper. (Ann Arbor: University of Michigan).

King, Mervyn. 1977. *Public Policy and the Corporation.* (London: Chapman and Hall).

Knight, Brian. 2006. "Are Policy Platforms Capitalized into Equity Prices? Evidence from the Bush/Gore 2000 Presidential Election." *Journal of Public Economics* 90(4–5): 751–773.

Poterba, James M. 2004. "Taxation and Corporate Payout Policy." *American Economic Review* 94(2): 171–175.

Poterba, James M., and Lawrence H. Summers. 1985. "The Economic Effects of Dividend Taxation." In E. Altman and M. Subrahmanyam, eds., *Recent Advances in Corporate Finance* (Homewood, IL: Richard D. Irwin), pp. 227–284.

Salinger, Michael. 1992. "Standard Errors in Event Studies." *Journal of Financial and Quantitative Analysis* 27(1): 39–53.

Sinn, Hans-Werner. 1991. "The Vanishing Harberger Triangle." *Journal of Public Economics* 45(3): 271–300.

Comments

William G. Gale[1]

The Brookings Institution

Identifying the marginal source of finance for new investment projects for mature corporations – that is, for firms that pay dividends – has significant implications for the economic effects of taxation. Under the so-called "traditional" or "old" view, new share issues are an important marginal source of finance, with one set of implications being that dividend taxes are distortionary, raise the cost of capital, and reduce investment. Under the so-called "new" or "tax capitalization" view, retained earnings are the marginal source of finance, so that a time-constant rate of taxation of dividends has no impact on investment or stock market valuation.

This chapter uses information from events leading up to the enactment of the 2003 dividend and capital gains tax cut and the 2004 election to develop new tests and evidence concerning the new and old views. This is a very interesting paper on a topic that is central to both academics and policy makers. The dividend tax cut is, in principle at least, an ideal way to pit the old view against the new view. The authors make clever use of theory and data, and it is impressive that new implications of the old and new views can be derived, given the decades-long research effort that the profession has devoted to this question.

The authors interpret their results as supportive of the new view. Under the new view, of course, the dividend tax cuts have no effect on firm investment, so that the dividend tax cut enacted in 2003 would simply represent a windfall gain to shareholders, with either no or negative long-term economic effects.

My comments focus on two broad themes. First, I find less support for the new view in the results than the authors do. Second, I suggest a number of ways the results could be reinterpreted or extended.

[1] Arjay and Frances Fearing Miller Chair in Federal Economic Policy and Codirector, Tax Policy Center, Brookings Institution, Washington, DC.

127

1. Main Results

The first set of tests relates firms' excess market returns to eight specific events that conveyed news about the likelihood that a dividend tax cut would be enacted in 2003. The authors estimate firm-specific excess returns over 5-day periods that straddle the eight events, using information on firm characteristics and market returns, and combine the results into a single 40-day period.

The first major result is that firms with higher dividend payout ratios in 2002 generally did better in the market when news raising the likelihood of a dividend tax cut was released. This result is reassuring, because it is consistent with both the new and old views, but for the same reason it does not help distinguish between them.

The second major result is that the same events had more positive effects on immature firms (those that have not yet paid dividends) than mature firms and had more positive effects on firms that were likely to issue new shares than on those that were not. These results are interesting and are consistent with a model developed by the authors in this chapter. But as the authors note, these results do not relate directly to the new- versus old-view debate, and so do not help distinguish the two views.[2] These results are, however, among the most robust in the chapter, and they are discussed further below. One might think of them as consistent "in spirit" with the new view, but I argue that they are consistent with a model in which dividend taxes are distortionary and reduce investment.

The third important result using this framework occurs in the sensitivity analysis. The authors argue that events that raise the likelihood of a dividend tax cut should have a negative effect on the valuation of firms in industries with higher average dividend yield under the old view and no effect under the new view. The estimated effect, however, in Table 8, is actually positive. This is inconsistent with either view. The authors report some assumptions under which this result could be made consistent with the new view, but that is different from finding support in favor of a theory.

Thus, in my view, the three sets of results above imply that the regressions using the eight events leading to the passage of the dividend tax cut provide no basis for supporting either the new view or the old view.

---

[2] The results for immature firms do not relate to the old view-new view debate because that debate focuses on the marginal source of finance for firms that are currently paying dividends. Issuing new shares can be thought of as starting up a new part of the firm that has not yet paid dividends.

The next set of tests relates firms' excess returns to the probability that President Bush would be reelected. As of 2004, the dividend tax cut had already been enacted, but as a temporary measure. Given Senator Kerry's desire to repeal the tax cuts benefiting high-income households and President Bush's desire to make his tax cuts permanent, the authors reasonably claim that the president's reelection prospects should be correlated with the likelihood that the dividend tax cut would be made permanent.

As the authors show, changes in the prospect of converting a temporary dividend tax cut to a permanent one provide a way to distinguish between the new and old views. Under the old view, making a temporary dividend tax cut permanent raises the value of high-dividend-yield firms relative to low-dividend-yield firms. Under the new view, when the dividend tax rate is constant over time, the dividend yield does not affect firm valuation; because the present value of future dividend payments is not affected by the payout ratio, firm value is not affected either. For a temporary tax cut, however, higher dividend yields will raise firm value because more dividends are paid in the tax-cut window. Thus, under the new view, changing from a temporary dividend tax cut to a permanent one should *reduce* the value of high-dividend-yield firms relative to low-dividend-yield firms.

This is, in my view, an extremely clever and subtle test. Unfortunately, the results are inconclusive. In Tables 5 and 6, the relevant coefficient (on the variable capturing the dividend yield interacted with the likelihood of a Bush victory) is negative, consistent with the new view, but it is insignificant in the weighted equations. In table 6', which provides sensitivity analysis, the coefficient is positive, consistent with the old view, but it is still insignificant in the weighted equations. Thus, the weighted regressions provide no net support for either view.

In contrast, in all three tables the coefficient is negative and significant in the unweighted regression. The unweighted regressions are difficult to interpret, though. One reason is that firm size varies dramatically in the sample and can be correlated with dividend behavior and other factors. In addition, as the authors note, the relation between a firm's size and its tendency to behave like a new- or old-view firm is not monotonic. As a result, my own view is that the unweighted regressions are not very compelling. But even if one accepts the unweighted regressions, it is important to note that the unweighted regressions using the 2004 election results are the only set of findings in the chapter that actually support the new view over the old view.

2. The Model and the Interpretation of the Results

As noted above, two of the most robust findings are that immature firms and
those likely to issue new shares received bigger benefits from the dividend
tax cuts than other firms. This finding is consistent with the theory that
the authors develop, and it appears consistent with the new view because
it implies that investors are capitalizing future taxes into firm valuation.
The authors' theoretical model, however, is closely related to Sinn's (1991)
"nucleus theory" of the firm, which integrates the old and new views. In
Sinn's model, a firm issues shares in its beginning phase, then stops issuing
shares, and then eventually, when marginal returns on investment fall to the
market rate of return, it begins to pay dividends. In this framework, when
firms are immature, dividend taxes are distortionary. That is, when people
bring funds into the corporate sector to establish a firm, they know that
eventually dividend taxes will be owed on the future dividends paid. This
reduces the infusion of new equity into the corporate sector. By the time the
firm starts paying dividends, though, firms are financing investments out of
retained earnings, which implies that the new view holds and that dividend
taxes are no longer distortionary.

Notably, Sinn's model is consistent with the empirical results (and the
underlying model) in this chapter. Sinn's theoretical result is that dividend
taxes impose higher costs of capital on immature firms. Auerbach and Hassett find that cuts in dividend taxes generate larger increases in market value
for immature firms, which makes sense if the cuts are reducing the cost of
capital more for those firms.

The important issue here is not just the link between the Auerbach-
Hassett results and Sinn's model, but rather that in Sinn's model dividend
taxes are distortionary. That is, the results in the chapter – that dividend tax
cuts provide larger benefits to immature firms than to mature firms – are
consistent with a model where dividend taxes create distortions.

3. The Events

In the analysis of events leading up to the enactment of the dividend tax
cut, the authors use a list of eight dates. For the moment, I assume that (a)
the events convey information only about changes in prospects for dividend
taxes, and (b) the only link between changes in dividend taxes and firm value
are the issues raised by the new and old view.

The most natural event window would be from the December 25, 2002,
New York Times article to either the Senate passage of the bill or the

conference agreement. Over that time frame, I think it is fair to say that people's perceptions of the likelihood of a dividend tax cut rose from "small" to 1.

Likewise, the 5-day period around Bush's signing of the bill could be used as a placebo test. There should have been no effect on objective grounds, because the likelihood of his signing the bill was virtually 1.

Interestingly, the list of eight events does not include any "negative" events, any events that signaled a smaller likelihood of a dividend tax cut. There must be ways to identify "negative" events in light of the dividend tax cut. After all, as the authors note, the dividend tax cut was given up for dead at various points: How would market participants know this in the absence of at least some public information? For example, there might be statements by influential senators at some point that the prospects looked dim. Alternatively, if no such events can be found, the time periods between the "positive" events could be defined as negative events and used in a regression.

In the absence of any negative events, it is hard to get a sense of the power of the model. This is related to the finding in Chetty, Rosenberg, and Saez (2005) that measured responses can be volatile over time, with resulting "false positives."

4. Information Content of the Events

The previous discussion assumes that the events listed convey information about dividend tax cuts and *only* about dividend tax cuts. Besides the dividend tax rate, however, several other tax parameters that may affect corporate valuation were altered in the 2003 legislation, and the events listed in this chapter may have conveyed news about the likelihood of those events as well as dividend tax cuts. If so, the regressions will be picking up information about more than just the dividend tax cut, which muddies the interpretation of the reported results.

The authors note that the dividend tax cut was the dominant feature of the 2003 tax cuts. I believe that assessment is correct. That does not, however, justify omitting the considerations discussed later because those considerations, although they may have been small in overall impact, are likely to have had *differential* effects across firms, and those differential effects may be correlated with dividend policy. If so, then the results could be biased or subject to misinterpretation. In any case, given the ambiguity of the empirical findings, controlling for additional factors might help sharpen some of the results.

First, bonus depreciation was expanded from 30 percent to 50 percent of qualified investment (and the expiration date slightly extended) in the 2003 legislation. The expansion and extension of the bonus depreciation rules may have created a significant impression that the rules would be made permanent.[3] This could have had a significant effect on firm valuation, and would naturally favor high-investment firms. If so, and if there is a correlation across firms in qualified investments and dividend behavior, then the coefficients may be picking up this effect rather than just a dividend effect. A simple way to resolve this problem would be to interact firms' qualified investment with the event dummies.

Second, the original Bush administration dividend proposal contained provisions that would likely have reduced corporate sheltering somewhat – namely, the dividend would have been tax free for the individual only to the extent that corporate tax had been paid at the firm level. This provision was dropped at some point in the proceedings. That change would affect firms differentially, depending on the extent of their sheltering activity. To the extent that sheltering activity and dividend behavior are correlated, then, the coefficients may be picking up an effect from prospective changes in sheltering rules rather than just a dividend effect. A simple way to address the issue would be to interact the event dummy with some measure of sheltering activity, perhaps the difference between book and tax income.

Third, the 2003 legislation reduced the capital gains tax rate. Consideration of changes in capital gains taxes could alter some of the findings. For example, suppose that reductions in capital gains taxes raise firm values but that higher-dividend-paying firms would be hurt by lower capital gains taxes relative to lower-dividend-paying firms, because the former retain less of their earnings. If so, the coefficients on the dividend yield may be understating the true effect of dividend tax cuts (holding capital gains taxes constant) on firm value.

On the other hand, the prospect of a reduction in capital gains taxes would likely have the biggest effect on firm value for immature firms and those likely to issue new shares. So the positive effects for those two variables could be related to capital gains as well as dividend tax cuts. As with the other variables, the omission of a variable controlling for firm-specific unrealized capital gains implies that it is hard to interpret the events as showing the effects just of dividend taxes. A simple way to resolve the problem would

---

[3] In a survey of the National Association for Business Economics, released on January 20, 2004, 62 percent said they expected the bonus depreciation rules to be made permanent.

be to control for some measure of unrealized firm-specific capital gains, perhaps capital gains over the previous 1-, 3-, or 5-year period.

5. The Relation between Dividend Tax Cuts and Firm Value

The new view-old view debate typically ignores the role of agency or governance considerations. Other papers, however, suggest clear links between firm value, dividends, and governance issues. In the revised version of this chapter, the authors include analysis of several variables based on Chetty and Saez (2005) and Brown, Liang, and Weisbenner (2004).

The work could be extended further in directions motivated by Desai, Dyck, and Zingales (2004). The model in their paper shows that higher taxation of corporate income increases the incentive of insiders to divert funds because it reduces the opportunity costs of diverting funds. By similar reasoning, a lower dividend tax should reduce incentives to divert funds. This should lead to more funds payable to outside shareholders, which should raise the value of the firm. This could also be controlled for in this chapter, perhaps through use of the same sheltering variable discussed above.

References

Brown, Jeffrey R., Nellie Liang, and Scott Weisbenner. 2004. "Executive Financial Incentives and Payout Policy: Firm Responses to the 2003 Dividend Tax Cut." NBER Working Paper 11002. (Cambridge, MA: National Bureau of Economic Research).

Chetty, Raj, and Emmanuel Saez. 2005. "Dividend Taxes and Corporate Behavior: Evidence from the 2003 Dividend Tax Cut." *Quarterly Journal of Economics* 120(3): 791–833.

Chetty, Raj, Joe Rosenberg, and Emmanuel Saez. 2005. "Market Responses to Dividend Announcements and Payments: Evidence from the 2003 Dividend Tax Cut and the Time Series." Working Paper. (Berkeley: University of California). "The Effects of Taxes on Market Responses to Dividend Accouncements and Payments: What Can We Learn from the 2003 Dividend Tax Cut?" NBER Working Paper 11452. (Cambridge, MA: National Bureau of Economic Research).

Desai, Mihir A., I. J. Alexander Dyck, and Luigi Zingales. 2004. "Theft and Taxation." NBER Working Paper 10978. (Cambridge, MA: National Bureau of Economic Research).

National Association for Business Economics. 2004. "NABE Panel: Employment Finally Improves as the Economy Roars Ahead." (Washington, DC: NABE).

Sinn, Hans-Werner. 1991. "Taxation and the Cost of Capital: The 'Old' View, the 'New' View, and Another View." In David Bradford, ed., *Tax Policy and the Economy* 5. (Cambridge, MA: MIT Press), pp. 25–54.

Comments

George R. Zodrow
Rice University

The debate over the economic effects of the taxation of dividends at the individual level has been long and contentious, is still unresolved, and is as critical as ever to an understanding of the desirability on efficiency and equity grounds of tax reforms that involve reductions in dividend taxation. The debate centers on which of two views most accurately describes the effects of dividend taxation. The "traditional" view holds that (1) individual-level taxation of dividends distributed from taxed corporate earnings results in a second level of taxation that increases the cost of capital and thus reduces investment, (2) dividends have an inherent value to shareholders, such as signaling current or future profits or limiting managerial discretion, that offsets their tax cost, (3) future dividend taxes are not capitalized into share values, and (4) the marginal source of equity finance is new share issues. By comparison, the "new" or "trapped-equity" view holds that (1) for investment financed with retained earnings (the vast majority of equity-financed investments), dividend taxes at the individual level have no effect on the costs of capital or investment, and (2) future dividend taxes are capitalized into share values.

When I surveyed the literature on the old and new views of dividend taxation 15 years ago (Zodrow, 1991), I concluded that there were important theoretical issues raised by both views but that virtually all of the existing empirical work supported the traditional view. This was also the position taken by the U.S. Department of the Treasury (1992), as it argued that some form of corporate-individual tax integration was highly desirable. In some sense, the issue is even more clouded today, as most recent empirical work, especially Harris, Hubbard, and Kemsley (2001) and Desai and Goolsbee (2004), has been supportive of the new view. The authors of the current chapter have also been important contributors to this literature (Auerbach and Hassett, 2003), with a study that suggests that firms are split roughly

50–50 between those whose behavior is consistent with the new view and those whose behavior is consistent with the old view. Indeed, they conclude that there is "no reason to argue which "view" is correct" (Auerbach and Hassett, 2003, p. 229), as the most likely scenario is similar to that posited by Sinn (1991), who argues that firms evolve from being immature enterprises with little or no retained earnings whose behavior is best characterized by the old view, to firms in transition whose behavior falls somewhere between those implied by the two views, to mature firms with retained earnings significantly in excess of their investment opportunities whose behavior is best described by the new view. Apparently, however, the authors have changed their minds to some extent, as this event study focuses primarily on choosing between the two views. In any case, this chapter nicely complements their earlier work, as well as the recent spate of empirical studies that are generally supportive of the new view.

The analysis focuses on whether various events that are indicative of an increase in the likelihood of passage of the 2003 dividend tax cuts caused changes in firm values that would be consistent with one view but not the other. As a preliminary question, one might ask whether large changes in firm value might be expected in response to changes in the probability of a dividend tax cut. Under the traditional view, firm values would be expected to increase somewhat in response to a dividend tax cut, as reform-induced increases in investment in the presence of adjustment costs would earn temporary above-normal returns until a new equilibrium was reached. However, because recent empirical evidence suggests that the costs of adjusting the capital stock are much lower than earlier estimates, the period of above-normal returns would be relatively short, so that large increases in firm value would not be expected. By comparison, under the new view, considerably larger effects would be expected as the capitalized value of future dividend taxes would be reduced significantly, especially with full capitalization in the case where the marginal investor is an individual in the top income tax bracket, as suggested by some admittedly controversial new research (Harris, Hubbard, and Kemsley, 2001). This relatively large firm value effect would be attenuated by various factors, including the availability of share repurchases, which lower the effective tax rate on distributions and the possibility that the marginal investor is a tax-exempt institution or a foreigner (over 60 percent of dividends are received by investors who are not subject to U.S. dividend taxes). Nevertheless, one might expect that positive effects of a dividend tax cut on firm values would be larger under the new view. Poterba (discussed in Gravelle, 2003) estimates that under the new view stock values would increase by approximately 5–6 percent for a dividend tax cut that was about 50 percent larger than the actual 2003 cut, while Gravelle (2003) argues that the various attenuating factors noted above would limit the increase to 1–2 percent. In this light, the firm-value effects estimated by Auerbach and Hassett seem somewhat large, although in principle large variations in firm values about a relatively small average effect are certainly possible. One piece of useful information that could be provided by the authors is the range of payouts – and thus changes in firm values – among the dividend-paying firms in their sample.

In any event, the challenges faced by the authors in their task are many, as isolating the effects of changes in the probability of the dividend tax cut on highly variable stock market values is exceedingly difficult (as suggested by the extremely low R-squared values in their results – which are, however, quite typical of stock market event studies). Accordingly, it might be useful to attempt to control for other factors that would affect changes in firm value, especially factors that would help differentiate between new-view and old-view firms, such as differences in risk and leverage, as well as controlling for contaminating events and the associated outlying observations. A multi-year measure of which firms are "high yield" would also help avoid problems caused by any atypical firm behavior in the single year the authors analyze (2002). In addition, a critical factor in any event study is the choice of events, and the authors might consider, as an event that would potentially have a negative impact on firm values, passage of the Senate finance bill on May 8; this bill made clear that the ultimate overall tax cut would be roughly half of the original proposal ($350 billion vs. $670 billion over 10 years) and that the dividend tax cut was likely to be much smaller than the $276 billion originally envisioned (the Senate bill called for a dividend tax cut of $80 billion, and the final figure was $125 billion). Indeed, negative coefficients on some of the events immediately prior to this date suggest that this event may have had some effect on stock values.

Consider next the main question addressed in the chapter: Did the old view or the new view win out? Unfortunately, the model used by the authors cannot capture absolute firm-value effects, which would be a good test of the new view, as one would expect considerably larger firm-value effects for new-view firms than for old-view firms for the reasons outlined above. Auerbach and Hassett argue that their main result – that high-dividend-yield firms have relatively large positive firm-value effects – might occur under either view. It is important to note, however, that this result would be expected under the new view only if the tax cut were perceived to be temporary, as firms would face an incentive to distribute dividends while their shareholders were temporarily subject to relatively low tax rates. By comparison, if the tax cuts were perceived to be permanent, the timing of dividend payments is irrelevant under the new view. Although a perception that the tax cuts were temporary is certainly possible, it may be that further cuts were perceived to be as likely as tax increases. After all, the original Bush administration proposal called for complete elimination of individual-level dividend taxes on earnings that had paid corporate tax, and fundamental tax reform involving either full integration or consumption-based tax options might have been perceived to be looming on the horizon. Thus, it is not clear that the interpretation of the tax cuts as temporary is entirely appropriate. (Note that this argument is analogous to that often used by proponents of the new view to explain the observed strong positive relationship between dividend payouts and dividend tax rate cuts – most recently, Chetty and Saez (2005) provide such evidence for the 2003 tax cut – that would arise under the new view only if the tax cut were perceived to be temporary.) One possible alternative interpretation of the result that high-yield firms tend to experience higher increases in value is that such firms are more likely to be paying enough dividends to be significantly far away from any traditional-view dividend constraints (under which dividends serve as a signaling device or to limit managerial discretion) and are thus new-view firms that are more likely to experience large-firm value effects for the reasons described previously.

The primary means used by Auerbach and Hassett to distinguish between the two views in the empirical analysis in the chapter is fairly subtle. The authors find that an increase in the probability that the dividend tax cut would be of a longer duration, which they associate with an increase in the probability that President Bush would be reelected, reduces the value premium experienced by high-yield firms. Such a result would occur only under the new view, as it implies that low-yield firms would have more time to pay out dividends while tax rates were relatively low and thus would not experience smaller increases in value than high-yield firms. By comparison, under the traditional view, a tax cut of a longer duration results in a longer period over which the cost of capital is reduced, which would imply a larger increase in firm value for high-yield firms. Although this is a very clever way of distinguishing between the new and old views in this event study, it is not entirely obvious that a Kerry election would necessarily result in higher dividend taxes; a Republican Congress would almost inevitably strive to extend the tax cut beyond its current 2008 expiration date, and raising taxes on high-income potential political contributors by allowing the tax cuts to expire would be difficult in an election year for members of both parties. More importantly, the effect of increased probability of a Bush reelection is statistically significant only for the estimates that do not weight firms by value; however, as noted by the authors, the weighted results are most applicable for differentiating between the two views of dividend taxation. An interesting question is whether the authors could replicate this result for a weighted estimate by controlling for the level of firm debt and thus avoiding the estimation problems caused by the relatively high leverage of high-value firms.

Another very interesting result obtained in the analysis is that immature firms (those that have never paid a dividend) and firms that are likely to issue new shares experience larger tax-cut-induced increases in value. Auerbach and Hassett show that this result is to be expected under the new view, since such firms have a higher present value of future taxable dividends and thus benefit disproportionately from a dividend tax rate cut if it is of sufficient duration. This result is particularly striking because such firms might be especially likely to return paid-in equity capital as share repurchases or be subject to mergers, buyouts, or liquidations, so that their distributions would be less likely to be taxed at individual dividend tax rates. In addition to being supportive of the new view, this result reinforces the notion that the economy is composed of some traditional-view firms, some new-view firms, and some in transition between the two regimes. Note, however, that an alternative explanation for this result is that deficit-financed dividend tax rate cuts increase the likelihood of higher future interest rates, which would tend to have a bigger negative impact on mature, highly leveraged firms, who would thus experience smaller increases in value than immature firms or firms likely to issue new shares. Auerbach and Hassett also show that immature firms and firms likely to issue new shares benefit disproportionately from an increase in the probable duration of the tax cut, as captured by an increase in the probability of a Bush reelection. Again, this result is consistent only with the new view, as it gives such firms more time to distribute their dividends at relatively low rates, and not with the traditional view, which implies that all firms would benefit similarly from a reduction in the cost of capital of longer duration. As above, however, this result could be attributed to a longer period of relatively high interest rates associated with deficit-financed dividend tax cuts, which would have a disproportionately large negative impact on more mature, leveraged firms.

In summary, this chapter is a very thoughtful and useful analysis that will be an important contribution to the ongoing debate regarding the relevance of the old and new views of dividend taxation. In particular, it adds to a burgeoning literature that provides empirical support for the new view, or perhaps more accurately, for the idea that there are some traditional-view firms that use new share issues as the marginal source of equity finance, some new-view firms for which the marginal source of finance is retained earnings or reductions in dividends, and some transitional firms that neither issue new shares nor pay dividends. In this vein, note that in the current chapter the characterization of firms as either immature (never having paid dividends) or mature is quite limited. Thus, a very useful extension of the analysis in this chapter would be to segregate the firms much more finely, using techniques similar to those in Auerbach and Hassett (2003) and then test the new- versus old-view predictions on the resulting subsamples. Such an approach would provide extremely useful additional information on the prevalence of new-view, traditional-view, and transitional firms and thus, hopefully, help resolve this long-standing and critical debate.

References

Auerbach, Alan J., and Kevin A. Hassett. 2003. "On the Marginal Source of Investment Funds." *Journal of Public Economics* 87(1): 205–232.

Chetty, Raj, and Emmanuel Saez. 2005. "Dividend Taxes and Corporate Behavior: Evidence from the 2003 Dividend Tax Cut." *Quarterly Journal of Economics* 120(3): 791–833.

Desai, Mihir A., and Austan D. Goolsbee. 2004. "Investment, Overhang, and Tax Policy." *Brookings Papers on Economic Activity* 35(2): 285–338.

Gravelle, Jane G. 2003. "Effects of Dividend Relief on Economic Growth, the Stock Market, and Corporate Tax Preferences." *National Tax Journal* 56(3): 653–672.

Harris, Trevor S., R. Glenn Hubbard, and Deen Kemsley. 2001. "The Share Price Effects of Dividend Taxes and Tax Imputation Credits." *Journal of Public Economics* 79(3): 569–596.

Sinn, Hans-Werner. 1991. "Taxation and the Cost of Capital: The 'Old' View, the 'New' View, and Another View." In David Bradford, ed., *Tax Policy and the Economy* 5. (Cambridge, MA: MIT Press), pp. 25–54.

U.S. Department of the Treasury. 1992. *Integration of the Individual and Corporate Tax Systems.* (Washington, DC: U.S. Treasury).

Zodrow, George R. 1991. "On the 'Traditional' and 'New' Views of Dividend Taxation." *National Tax Journal* 44(4): 497–509.

FOUR

How Elastic Is the Corporate Income Tax Base?

Jonathan Gruber

Massachusetts Institute of Technology and NBER

Joshua Rauh

University of Chicago and NBER

The federal government of the United States primarily finances its expenditures from income taxation, at both the individual and corporate levels. Traditionally, corporate income taxation was about half as large as individual income taxation as a source of federal revenue; today, the ratio of corporate tax revenues to individual tax revenues is only about 15 percent. Nevertheless, a large economics literature continues to consider the corporate tax as a primary determinant of corporate behavior in the United States. Numerous articles have addressed the impact of the corporate tax on corporate investment and financing.

Oddly, this literature has not addressed directly the question of how sensitive the base of corporate income taxation is to the corporate tax rate. Past literature has addressed pieces of this question, but there is no clear estimate that emerges from past work. As emphasized by Saez (2004), what determines the ultimate efficiency of a tax system, absent external effects of taxation, is the elasticity of the base of taxable income with respect to the tax rate. Indeed, a large literature has arisen in public economics devoted to estimating this elasticity with respect to the individual income tax system. Yet there is no comparable work on corporate taxation.

In this chapter, we estimate the impact of the corporate tax rate on the level of corporate taxable income. An obvious difficulty with such an exercise is that the tax rate itself is determined by the level of taxable income. Thus, a regression of taxable income on tax rates will suffer from potential reverse causality.

We address this problem by following the approach applied by Gruber and Saez (2002) to the analysis of the impact of the tax rate on the individual income tax base. In particular, we model the effective tax rates faced by firms in one period and the effective tax rate that would be faced by firms *with that same income* in the next period. The difference between these two is exogenous to firm behavior. This forms a natural instrument for a regression of the change in taxable income as a function of the change in effective tax rates.

We carry out this exercise using data from Compustat. This provides longitudinal data on the universe of publicly traded firms in the United States, allowing us to model the change in taxable income as a function of the change in tax rates. These data have the weakness, however, of being accounting based rather than tax based. They also lack information on a host of tax credits used by corporations and consist only of publicly traded firms. In future work we, therefore, plan to extend this analysis to incorporate tax data from Internal Revenue Service (IRS) industry-level files.

We find strong evidence that the corporate tax base is elastic with respect to the marginal effective tax rate. Our central estimate is that the elasticity of the corporate tax base with respect to the rate is -0.2. This is a fairly small elasticity relative to those found for individual income taxation. Absent external effects, this suggests that the inefficiency of corporate taxation may be lower than that of individual income taxation.

Our chapter proceeds as follows. In Section 1, we review the relevant literature on corporate and individual income taxation. In Section 2, we describe our data and the construction of our key measures. Section 3 discusses our regression approach. Section 4 presents our results, and Section 5 concludes.

1. Literature Review

1.1. Corporate Taxation and Corporate Tax Revenues

As noted above, there is no work of which we are aware that directly assesses how changes in the effective corporate tax rate affect the size of the corporate tax base. There is, however, a huge body of work that speaks to aspects of this relationship. In this section, we provide a brief review of that literature.

A large number of studies assess the impact of corporate taxation and the user cost of capital on investment decisions. This literature is obviously relevant because if a higher tax rate leads to less investment, it may lead to lower corporate tax revenues in the long run. The conclusions of this literature are varied. Goolsbee (1998a) finds that most of the benefit of tax incentives goes to capital suppliers through higher prices, explaining traditionally small investment elasticities. Auerbach and Hassett (1992) estimate an elasticity of equipment investment with respect to the user cost of capital of approximately −0.25, whereas the results of Cummins, Hassett, and Hubbard (1994, 1996) and Caballero, Engel, and Haltiwanger (1995) imply elasticities of −0.5 to −1. Recent attention has also been paid to the bonus depreciation rules of 2002 and 2003, with the literature finding generally modest effects (see Goolsbee and Desai, 2004, and House and Shapiro, 2006).

There is also a large number of studies that assess the impact of corporate taxation on corporate financing decisions. Once again, this literature is relevant because if higher tax rates cause firms to shift to forms of financing that are tax favored, it will lower the firm's tax burden. In the equilibrium of Miller (1977), taxes are irrelevant to the form of finance for all but the marginal firm. Empirical studies have found mixed evidence of tax effects on financial policy. MacKie-Mason (1990) demonstrates an effect of tax loss carryforwards on the marginal financing decision, but Graham (2000) suggests that substantial tax benefits are left unused and that, from a tax perspective, debt policy is pervasively conservative.

A number of studies have also investigated the impact of corporate taxation on the incorporation choice and the choice of corporate form. Economic activity that is not incorporated is taxed at individual income tax rates. Incorporated firms may organize in a variety of forms, some of which (such as S corporations) avoid the corporate entity-level tax, whereas others (such as C corporations) must pay corporate tax on corporate earnings.

If incorporated entities cannot escape the corporate tax, then as the corporate tax rate rises relative to the individual tax rate, it may cause economic activity to be shifted from the corporate to the noncorporate sector. This organizational form response margin has been modeled by Gravelle and Kotlikoff (1989), who show that excess burdens can be quite large if less efficient noncorporate production is substituting for more efficient corporate production. Goolsbee (1998b) and Gordon and MacKie-Mason (1994, 1997) find relatively small elasticities of substitution between the corporate and noncorporate sector. Goolsbee (2004), however, finds much larger responses of organizational form to tax rates using cross-sectional data – an increase in the corporate tax rate by 10 percentage points reduces the corporate share of firms in a state by 0.25 percent, and his results suggest that organizational form is in fact a more important adjustment margin than the firm's operations.

Incorporated firms may respond to tax policy by electing to organize as S corporations rather than C corporations. Plesko (1994) found that firms were more likely to organize as S corporations after the Tax Reform Act of 1986 (TRA86), and Carroll and Joulfaian (1997) estimate a tax elasticity of

0.2 for the probability of a firm electing to be an S corporation. Firms that are publicly traded are required to have C corporation status, placing an effective limit on this response margin.

1.2. The Elasticity of Individual Taxable Income

In contrast to corporate income taxation, there is a burgeoning literature on the elasticity of the individual income tax base to individual income taxation; a very recent comprehensive review of this literature is provided by Giertz (2004). This literature grew out of early work by Lindsey (1987) and Feldstein (1995). The literature has evolved to deal with a number of difficult issues, such as the fact that changes in taxation by income group may be correlated with other underlying trends in taxable income that are unrelated to the tax system.

The broad consensus from this literature is that the elasticity of taxable income with respect to the tax rate is roughly 0.4. Moreover, the elasticity of actual income generation through labor supply or savings, as opposed to reported income, is much lower. And most of the response of taxable income to taxation appears to arise from higher income groups. An important recent contribution is Kopczuk (2005), who shows that the elasticity of taxable income to tax rates is a function of the elasticity of the tax base: When the tax base is less fungible, taxable income is less elastic.

1.3. Why Does This Parameter Matter?

Saez (2004) provides a useful framework for interpreting this literature. He highlights that, if there are no external effects of tax changes, the full welfare consequences of a tax change are summarized by the impact on the base of taxable income. For example, unless there is some additional social cost to individuals working less hard, the full welfare cost of higher labor taxes can be represented by the resulting decline in labor income.

In the context of both individual and corporate income taxation, a major source of such externalities can be spillovers to other tax systems. When the corporate income tax rate rises, then individuals might avoid incorporation and therefore report more income within the individual income tax system. In this way, the elasticity of the corporate tax base with respect to the corporate tax rate overstates the welfare costs of corporate taxation. A similar issue arises with individual income taxation. In absolute dollar terms, the externalities are symmetric under the two systems. However, as a percentage of the total base of revenues, this externality will be proportionally larger in the corporate tax system.

Other externalities are harder to quantify. If, for some reason beyond tax wedges, the social return to investment is above its private return, then corporate taxation could have large welfare costs even with a modest decline in corporate taxable income. There is a large debate on this point, but certainly no consensus for external returns to investment.

Thus, the elasticity of the corporate tax base with respect to the corporate tax rate seems a natural place to start for assessing the welfare consequences of corporate taxation. Additional work beyond this chapter will clearly be necessary to consider the external effects of corporate taxation and whether they, on the whole, change the conclusions of our analysis.

2. Methodology and Data

This section reviews and motivates the use of the marginal effective tax rate (ETR), discusses the data, and presents the construction of the ETR and the instruments. It also reviews the important corporate tax law changes that are the source of our variation in marginal tax incentives.

2.1. The Marginal Effective Tax Rate

The marginal effective tax rate is defined as the share of a firm's required return on capital that goes to the federal government rather than to investors (Fullerton, 1984). The marginal effective tax rate is to be distinguished from what in accounting literature is called the (average) effective tax rate, which is taxes paid divided by a measure of income. We refer to the marginal effective tax rate as simply the effective tax rate, or ETR. The ETR captures features of the tax code such as the present discounted value of depreciation allowances and investment tax credits, as well as the statutory marginal tax rate.

Our measure of the effective tax rate is closest in spirit to the King and Fullerton (1984) application of Hall and Jorgenson (1967): For each firm and its chosen capital structure, we estimate the ETR for each type of capital asset separately. One major difference is that we do not account for shareholder taxes. Our construction can also be compared to Gravelle (1994, 2001), who constructs marginal effective tax rates at the industry level, although our constructions also allow discount rates to reflect financing choices at the firm (and hence industry) level. Gravelle (2001) shows that these types of effective tax rates display substantial variation by industry over time. Auerbach (1983) illustrates that differential asset taxation results in a social cost of misallocated capital and that this cost has varied over time.

This is not, of course, the only possible way to measure the effective tax burden on firms. Gordon, Kalambokidis, and Slemrod (2003) review several possible ways of measuring the marginal effective tax rates and propose an alternative measure based on the difference between the tax collected under existing rules and hypothetical tax collected under the nondistortionary R-based tax (as in Gordon and Slemrod, 1988). This alternative measure may capture some complications omitted by the more traditional ETR, and future work on this topic could consider this alternative to the traditional ETR.

In its most basic form, the traditional ETR is written as

$$ETR_t = \frac{f'(k_t) - \delta - \rho_t}{f'(k_t) - \delta}, \tag{1}$$

where ρ is the required return on capital (or after-tax discount rate) that is ultimately demanded by investors, δ is economic depreciation, and $f'(k)$ is the marginal product of capital. In calculating the effective tax rate, it is usually assumed (as in Hall and Jorgensen, 1967) that firms set the marginal product of capital equal to the implicit rental value of capital services:

$$f'(k_t) = \frac{(\rho_t + \delta)(1 - ITC_t - \tau z_t)}{(1 - \tau_t)}. \tag{2}$$

Here, ρ and δ are as before, τ is the relevant statutory marginal tax rate, ITC_t is the investment tax credit per dollar as of time t, and z_t is the present discounted value of depreciation allowances as of time t. These derivations are reviewed in Gravelle (1982, 1983) and Fullerton (1987, 1999).

2.2. Data

The data for this exercise come from several sources. Financial data for 1960–2003 were extracted from the Compustat industrial, full-coverage, and research files. This is the broadest available source of annual data on publicly traded companies and is compiled by Standard & Poor's from corporate financial statements. Because the main variation in the tax code that we exploit takes place at the industry level, the tax and income variables constructed from the Compustat data are averaged or aggregated to the industry level for our regression analysis. This procedure also avoids the problem of the rather substantial number of firm-year observations for which taxable income is zero (approximately 10 percent of the sample overall and approximately 25 percent after TRA86).

The use of Compustat for these purposes presents two major challenges. First, the sample does not represent the entire corporate sector. It consists only of C corporations, and only those C corporations whose stock is publicly traded. Although the incidence of firms actually going private and exiting the Compustat database is not large, the estimates in this chapter must be taken as representing only the effects of the corporate tax code on the behavior of publicly traded C corporations.

The second challenge is the fact that Compustat only reports income as presented by the corporation in its financial statements. Taxable income and the gross income for the purposes of tax books are not reported. The problem of inferring taxable income from financial statements is discussed in Plesko (2003), Manzon and Plesko (2002), Mills and Plesko (2003), and Hanlon (2003). We follow Stickney and McGee (1982) and define taxable income as pretax book income (before interest) minus the deferred tax expense divided by the statutory marginal tax rate. We calculate taxes paid as the total tax expense minus the deferred tax expense.

In future work, we intend to use an industry-level panel of tax data from the IRS Statistics of Income Division to confirm and deepen the analysis undertaken in this chapter. This dataset, currently under construction, will allow us to include firms of all organizational forms and will contain industry-year level aggregates for taxable income as reported to the IRS.

Compustat does not contain sufficient information on the activities of each firm to derive an estimate of the present discounted value of the firm's depreciation allowances. We rely on benchmark input-output accounts from the Bureau of Economic Analysis (BEA) at the industry level to measure the extent to which a change in depreciation allowances affects a firm in a given industry. These matrices are published approximately every five years by the BEA and are obtainable at the level of the BEA's 2-digit industry classification for 1958, 1963, 1967, 1972, 1977, 1982, 1987, 1992, and 1997. Each firm in our analysis was assigned a BEA 2-digit output industry based on its 4-digit Compustat industry code, and the vector of capital inputs for that output industry in the last published year prior to the observation was assigned to the observation. In other words, for a given observation, we always use the lagged vector of capital shares used by firms in that industry. We renormalized the vector of inputs to reflect only capital inputs, not raw materials. (We explored alternative constructions using the BEA's capital flow tables, but these were not available as frequently as the input-output tables and their industry categories were less consistent.) Finally, each different type of capital input was matched to one of the standard 28 asset categories used by the BEA. These are the same 28 asset categories used in Hulten and

Wykoff (1981), Cummins, Hassett, and Hubbard (1994), and Gravelle (1994, 2001).

The combination of a firm's output industry, the vector of capital inputs used by that industry, and the asset category that each capital input belongs to creates a mapping between each firm and the share of its capital in each of the 28 different asset types. For each year, we also collected and coded annual corporation income tax brackets and rates from the U.S. Department of Treasury, Internal Revenue Service (2003), annual nominal corporate bond rates from the Federal Reserve, and annual inflation rates from the Bureau of Labor Statistics.

2.3. Constructing Effective Tax Rates

Our ultimate unit of analysis is the 2-digit Standard Industrial Classification (SIC) industry level. We analyze the data at this level because a key input into our effective tax rate, for computing the value of depreciation deductions, is the asset mix. While we know the capital structure (debt/equity ratio) of the firm and can approximate its taxable income, the only information about the asset mix is the imputation based on industry-level data as described above. Using this imputation, we create effective tax rates at the firm level and then aggregate back to the industry level for analysis. At the firm level, assuming a constant asset mix could result in biases due to measurement error.

We proceed as follows. Each of the 28 asset categories is matched to economic depreciation rates, taxable asset lives, depreciation rules, and investment tax credit (ITC) rules using the tables in Gravelle (1994). This gives us a vector of tax treatments by asset category. Effective tax rates are then calculated for each firm for each of the 28 BEA asset categories and weighted using the vector of capital usages for that firm's industry. Finally, these firm-level effective tax rates are averaged to the 2-digit SIC level for our regression analysis.

Combining Equations (1) and (2), the ETR for asset category j at firm i in year t is

$$ETR_{it}^{(j)} = \frac{[(\rho_{it} + \delta_j)(1 - ITC_{jt} - \tau_{it}z_{jt})/(1 - \tau_{jt})] - \delta_j - \rho_{it}}{[(\rho_{it} + \delta_j)(1 - ITC_{jt} - \tau_{it}z_{jt})/(1 - \tau_{jt})] - \delta_j}. \tag{3}$$

This calculation parallels that of Gravelle (1994, 2001). The discount rate ρ_{it} depends on the firm's capital structure. Letting α be the share financed from debt,

$$\rho_{it} = \alpha_{it}\left(r_t^D(1 - \tau_{it}) - \pi_t\right) + (1 - \alpha_{it})r_t^E, \tag{4}$$

where r^D is the highest quality corporate bond rate (AAA rating), r^E is calculated assuming a 4 percent equity premium, and p_t is the inflation rate in year t. Investment tax credits, statutory marginal tax rates, and economic depreciation rates are collected and applied as described above.

The calculation of the present discounted value of depreciation deductions z for asset category j in year t is a function of the asset recovery rules specified by the tax code in year t. These rules are tabulated for Gravelle (1994) for most years, though we also augment them with the bonus depreciation of 30 percent implemented for 2002 and 50 percent implemented for 2003. The possible asset recovery rules consist of straight line, sum of year digits, double declining balance, 150 percent double declining balance, 175 percent double declining balance, and variations on these that allow for the 30 percent or 50 percent bonus depreciation. The present value calculations are based on the formulas in Hall and Jorgensen (1967), extended to allow a flexible rate of declining balance and for the immediate expensing of a portion of the investment under the bonus depreciation. So for a given bonus depreciation α (e.g., 30 percent in 2002), a declining balance n (e.g., 2 for equipment in 1981), an asset life T, and a nominal interest rate ρ, the present discounted value of depreciation deductions for a given asset class and year is

$$z = \alpha \left(\frac{1}{1 + \rho} \right) + (1 - \alpha) \left\{ \frac{(n/T)}{\rho + (n/T)} \left[1 - e^{-(\rho + (n/T))T^*} \right] \right.$$
$$\left. + \frac{e^{-(n/T)T^*}}{\rho(T - T^*)} \left[e^{-\rho T^*} - e^{-\rho T} \right] \right\}, \tag{5}$$

where $T^* = T/n$.

In summary, the effective tax rate calculations for each asset category are essentially as in Gravelle (1994, 2001), but they also reflect variation in marginal tax rates resulting from differences in taxable income and capital structure shares at the firm level and incorporate some of the more recent tax changes. Note that in these constructions τ is the current statutory rate faced by the firm, which is zero if the firm has no taxable income or has a taxable loss. An alternative construction is to assume that the statutory rate returns to the top bracket level the following year. This changes effective tax rates for firms running operating losses but does not change the general distribution of the estimated effective tax rates. The appropriateness of the use of the current marginal tax rate in this calculation depends on the extent of mobility out of the state of tax exhaustion (see Auerbach, 1983, and Altshuler and Auerbach, 1990).

One notable complication is the corporate alternative minimum tax (AMT), which is not included in the classical definition of the effective tax rate (ETR). This is problematic, as the alternative minimum tax does alter the tax schedule for firms that take large amounts of deductions, and this was particularly the case during the period 1987–1997, after the implementation of the AMT but before the 1997 changes that brought AMT depreciation deductions more in line with those of the rest of the tax system. Marginal incentives to invest may be affected by the AMT in ways that are not captured by the ETR. On the other hand, to the extent that the AMT broadens the tax base by disallowing deductions, it should perhaps generate lower elasticities with respect to the corporate tax rate, if the arguments of Kopczuk (2005) carry over to a corporate setting.

This measure of the effective tax rate is "myopic" in the sense that we assume firms base expected future values of their marginal tax rates on their current values. A more sophisticated measure would account for the fact that firms expect changes to occur in the marginal tax rate, and in that case the present value of depreciation deductions would depend on the expected path of statutory tax rates rather than the current rate. Auerbach and Hines (1988) offer one way of accounting for expectations of changing tax policy by calculating moving averages of future realized costs of capital with weights declining as the time horizon gets longer. Furthermore, if there are large adjustment lags, lagged costs of capital are also useful in this context. Given the difficulties with measuring the expected future cost of capital, we focus in this chapter on the one-period myopic user cost of capital but caution that more sophisticated models should account for the fact that firms have expectations over future tax parameters.

Table 1 shows mean marginal effective tax rates by consolidated industry categories. The table illustrates that there is substantial variation in the effective tax rate both across industries and within industries over time. Consider the case of Chemical, Plastic, and Drug manufacturing. This industry had one of the highest effective tax rates in the 1960s and early 1970s, one of the lowest during the mid-1970s through the early 1980s, and then returned to an above-average tax rate by the late 1980s. Note that for illustrative purposes the industry categories in this table are more consolidated than those in our regressions where the standard 2-digit industry categories are employed.

In addition to considering the effects of marginal effective tax rates on taxable income, we also test for effects of the simple marginal tax rate on an extra dollar of currently earned income. This latter rate is simply the federal statutory rate if the firm has positive taxable income and zero if it has zero or negative taxable income. As with the ETR, we create this rate

Table 1. *Marginal Effective Tax Rates and Means (%) by Industry*

Consolidated Industry Categories	1964–1968	1969–1973	1974–1978	1979–1983	1984–1988	1989–1993	1994–1998	1999–2003
Mining and Extraction	29.4	38.7	16.5	-2.0	4.3	17.2	20.1	16.8
Food and Tobacco	21.7	47.0	6.7	1.6	13.0	26.3	23.3	18.3
Manufacturing; Paper Products	29.3	49.9	5.2	6.6	12.8	24.3	27.6	17.1
Manufacturing; Chemicals, Plastics, Drugs	30.4	49.7	2.5	-2.3	14.5	25.7	24.4	22.3
Manufacturing; Stone and Metal	31.5	50.3	14.5	10.1	16.6	26.2	24.7	19.7
Manufacturing; General Industrial	31.9	52.7	14.1	13.9	14.5	22.6	25.4	16.0
Computer, Office, and Household Appliances	32.6	46.0	16.8	-4.6	10.2	23.5	20.0	12.6
Audio, Video, Communications, Electronics	34.5	54.6	18.7	10.4	14.5	25.7	23.4	17.1
Motor Vehicles and Aircraft	29.7	56.1	21.2	8.4	13.6	24.6	25.5	20.6
Scientific Instruments and Defense	25.8	48.1	11.2	13.1	15.3	22.0	23.6	17.3
Transportation	23.9	42.2	-1.7	18.3	29.2	33.2	23.4	15.6
Utilities	19.7	42.4	1.8	0.0	20.4	22.9	23.6	19.9
Wholesale and Retail Trade	18.0	37.1	10.4	8.0	23.4	21.9	25.4	17.7
Finance and Real Estate	24.5	42.6	11.3	0.7	11.2	26.6	21.0	15.5
Professional Services	28.1	38.9	20.3	4.4	3.7	12.0	25.9	25.4
Health and Educational Services	-4.9	25.0	16.1	1.5	-3.3	17.6	15.6	7.2

These industries represent the authors' consolidations of the actual 2-digit industries used in the empirical analysis.

at the firm level and then aggregate back to the industry level for analysis. The simple marginal tax rate on an additional dollar of earned or reported income does not capture the effects of depreciation allowances or investment tax credits on the marginal tax burden. However, firms can change taxable income directly through means unrelated to investment – for example, by increasing leverage to make higher interest payments or by various methods of tax avoidance, such as moving income offshore. The marginal tax rate on an additional dollar of earned income defines the firm's incentives to engage in these activities.

3. Empirical Approach

3.1. Regression Framework

Gruber and Saez (2002) derive an equation for relating the change in marginal tax rates to the change in taxable income. Following their derivation, we estimate equations of the form:

$$\log \left(\frac{y_{h,t+1}}{y_{h,t}} \right) = \alpha_t + \beta \log \left(\frac{1 - ETR_{h,t+1}}{1 - ETR_{h,t}} \right) + \varepsilon_{h,t}, \qquad (6)$$

where y is taxable income, α_t is a year effect, ETR is the effective tax rate constructed as described in the previous section, and each h represents an industry.

In this equation, the coefficient β estimates the effect of a 1 percent change in the after-tax earnings on a dollar of investment in terms of percent changes in taxable income. A coefficient of zero indicates that taxable income does not respond to changes in tax rates; a coefficient of one indicates that for every percent increase in after-tax earnings, after-tax income rises by 1 percent. All estimates are weighted by industry-aggregate firm size (assets) so that the estimates more closely reflect the relative contribution to total revenues; the results are very similar if we instead weight by sales.

Of course, a problem with such a regression is that common factors determine both effective tax rates and taxable income, such as a firm's mix of productive assets or capital structure. Thus, an equation such as Equation (1) is not identified. We address this concern by following the instrumental-variables strategy of Gruber and Saez (2002). For each pair of years t and $t + 1$, we compute the ETR for both years using the same set of constant firm characteristics from year t, but allowing tax rules and macroeconomic factors to change. The difference between these sets of ETRs is correlated with the change in the actual ETR, but is uncorrelated with any changes in firm decisions.

As Gruber and Saez (2002) highlight, however, there remains an important identifying assumption with this approach: that lagged characteristics of the firm do not affect the change in taxable income. This was a particularly important concern in the context of studying the tax reforms of the 1980s at the individual level. These reforms reduced tax rates at the top of the income distribution in particular, so that the instrument in that context was showing a particular decline in tax rates for high-income taxpayers. But the income distribution was widening over this same interval, so that high-income taxpayers were seeing a rise in their taxable income independent of tax reform. As a result, the instrument was naturally correlated with the change in taxable incomes.

To address this concern, Gruber and Saez (2002) suggest including detailed controls for lagged taxable income. In this way, any underlying trends correlated with lagged characteristics will be captured. Thus, we include in our regression specification a 10-piece spline in lagged taxable income.

Given this instrumental-variables strategy and the included controls, the identification of the ETR effects in our empirical model comes from two sources: the differential effects of tax law changes and macroeconomic factors across firms. To be clear, because our models include year dummies, the overall effects of tax reform and macroeconomic changes are purged from the model, and identification only comes from differential impacts of these changes across firms.

The appendix table outlines the tax law changes that affect the ETR and that are incorporated into our model. The tax brackets changed numerous times over the years 1960 to 2003. These bracket changes apply to all firms, and there is relatively little graduation of the corporate income tax rate, especially relative to the personal schedules. However, firms often have zero taxable income, and so there is cross-sectional variation in the extent to which they are affected by rate changes. There have been numerous changes in depreciation rules, notably the liberalization of asset lives effective in 1971, the implantation of accelerated cost recovery system (ACRS) accounting in 1981, the modification of these by the 1982 tax act, the implementation of the modified accelerated cost recovery system (MACRS) accounting through TRA86, the changes in structure lives in the 1993 legislation, and the bonus depreciation in the 2002 and 2003 tax laws. There have also been many changes to the investment tax credit over time, beginning with the Kennedy-era laws and culminating with the repeal of the investment tax credit in the 1986 legislation.

Appendix Table. *Corporate Tax Law Changes in the Model (1960–2003)*

Year*	Brackets		Depreciation	Credits
1962				ITC introduced
1964	First $25,000	22.00%		ITC basis adjustment
	Over $25,000	50.00%		removed
1965	First $25,000	22.00%		
	Over $25,000	48.00%		
1968	First $25,000	24.20%		
	Over $25,000	52.80%		
1969			Change in structure lives	ITC eliminated
1970	First $25,000	22.55%		
	Over $25,000	42.90%		
1971	First $25,000	22.00%	Change in asset lives	ITC reinstated
	Over $25,000	48.00%		
1975	First $25,000	20.00%		ITC revised
	$25,000–$50,000	22.00%		
	Over $50,000	48.00%		
1979	First $25,000	17.00%		
	$25,000–$50,000	20.00%		
	$50,000–$75,000	30.00%		
	$75,000–$100,000	40.00%		
	Over $100,000	46.00%		
1981			ACRS	ITC revised
1982	First $25,000	16.00%		
	$25,000–$50,000	19.00%		
	$50,000–$75,000	30.00%		
	$75,000–$100,000	40.00%		
	Over $100,000	46.00%		
1983	First $25,000	15.00%	TEFRA	ITC basis adjustment
	$25,000–$50,000	18.00%	modifications	
	$50,000–$75,000	30.00%		
	$75,000–$100,000	40.00%		
	Over $100,000	46.00%		
1984	First $25,000	15.00%		
	$25,000–$50,000	18.00%		
	$50,000–$75,000	30.00%		
	$75,000–$100,000	40.00%		
	$100,000–$1,000,000	46.00%		
	$1,000,000–$1,405,000	51.00%		
	Over $1,405,000	46.00%		

(continued)

Appendix Table *(continued)*

Year*	Brackets		Depreciation	Credits
1987	First $25,000	15.00%	MACRS	ITC ended
	$25,000–$50,000	16.50%		
	$50,000–$75,000	27.50%		
	$75,000–$100,000	37.00%		
	$100,000–$335,000	42.50%		
	$335,000–$1,000,000	40.00%		
	$1,000,000–$1,405,000	42.50%		
	Over $1,405,000	40.00%		
1988	First $50,000	15.00%		
	$50,000–$75,000	25.00%		
	$75,000–$100,000	34.00%		
	$100,000–$335,000	39.00%		
	Over $335,000	34.00%		
1993	First $50,000	15.00%	Change in structure	
	$50,000–$75,000	25.00%	lives	
	$75,000–$100,000	34.00%		
	$100,000–$335,000	39.00%		
	$335,000–$10,000,000	34.00%		
	$10,000,000–$15,000,000	35.00%		
	$15,000,000–$18,333,333	38.00%		
	Over $18,333,333	35.00%		
2002			30% bonus	
2003			50% bonus	

* The year in this column is the year that the law or bracket went into effect.

Figure 1 illustrates the variation across firms in the effective tax rate over time. This figure shows the effective tax rate at the mean and at the 25th, 50th, and 75th percentiles of the effective tax rate distribution over time. There was very little effective tax rate variation across firms until the 1961 tax reforms, which opened up some variation across firms. This variation then narrowed again through the late 1960s and early 1970s, until the major liberalization of asset lives in 1972, which led to enormous increases in variation in effective tax rates across firms. This variation was then considerably narrowed by the Tax Reform Act of 1986, although the 25th percentile of firms still had an effective tax rate of zero, while the 75th percentile had an effective tax rate of the statutory 34 percent. Finally, recent tax reforms combined with depressed levels of corporate profits have substantially reduced effective tax rates to zero at the median. Figure 2 shows this distribution at the industry

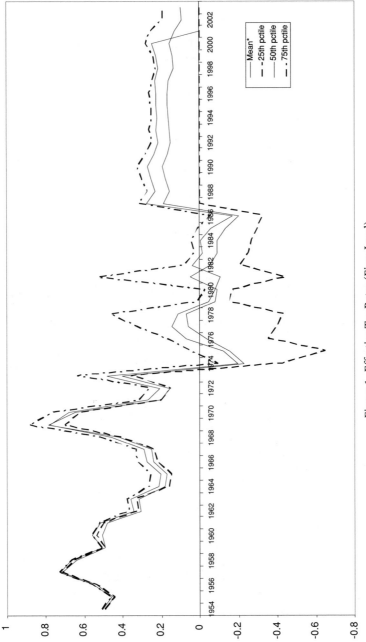

Figure 1. Effective Tax Rates (Firm Level)

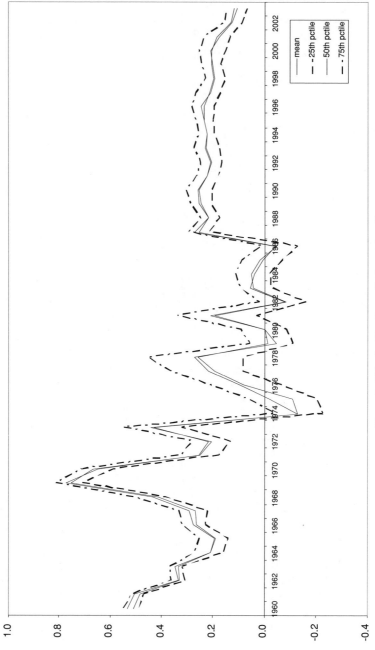

Figure 2. Effective Tax Rates (Industry Level)

Table 2. *Effects of the Effective Tax Rate (ETR) on Taxable Income*

Dependent Variable:	$\ln[(1 - ETR_{t+1})/$ $(1 - ETR_t)]$	$\ln[(Taxable\ Income_{t+1})/$ $(Taxable\ Income_t)]$	
$\ln[(1 - ETR_{t+1})/$ $(1 - ETR_t)]$	0.944*** (0.064)	0.174** (0.076)	0.197*** (0.075)
Spline control	None	None	Taxable income
Description	1st stage	IV	IV
Observations	2481	2481	2481
R-squared	0.81	0.17	0.19

The first column is an OLS regression, and the second two columns are IV regressions. Each statistic is from a separate industry-level regression. All regressions contain year fixed effects. Standard errors are clustered by industry.

*** significant at 1 percent, ** significant at 5 percent.

level where we conduct our analysis. The distribution is somewhat more compressed, but the patterns remain broadly similar as would be expected.

4. Results

Table 2 reports the basic results of our analysis. In all regressions, we cluster the standard errors at the industry level, following the strategy suggested by Bertrand et al. (2004). In the first column, we show the first-stage relationship between our instrument for the change in after-tax shares and the change in those shares. There is a very strong correlation between these measures. The coefficient is 0.944, and it is very highly significant with a *t* statistic of around 15.

The second column shows the instrumented regression for taxable income. We first show the results without a control for lagged taxable income. The coefficient of the change in after-tax share is 0.174, indicating that each 10 percent change in after-tax share leads to a rise in taxable income of 1.74 percent. While significant, this is a considerably smaller response than is found for individual taxable income responsiveness to tax changes. The next column includes the splines in lagged income. Controlling for these splines has a relatively small effect on the estimate, with the coefficient rising to 0.197.

In Table 3, we show the results of a similar specification but now with two explanatory tax variables: the log change in the ETR and the log change

Table 3. *Effects of the Effective Tax Rate (ETR) and Marginal Tax Rate (MTR) on Taxable Income*

Dependent Variable:	$\ln[(1 - ETR_{t+1})/(1 - ETR_t)]$	$\ln[(1 - MTR_{t+1})/(1 - ETR_t)]$	$\ln[(Taxable\ Income_{t+1})/(Taxable\ Income_t)]$	
$\ln[(1 - ETR_{t+1})/(1 - ETR_t)]$	0.944*** (0.064)		0.172 (0.105)	0.216** (0.104)
$\ln[(1 - MTR_{t+1})/(1 - MTR_t)]$		0.928*** (0.204)	−0.113 (2.836)	1.122 (2.625)
Spline control	None	None	None	Taxable income
Description	1st stage	1st stage	IV	IV
Observations	2481	2481	2481	2481
R-squared	0.81	0.38	0.17	0.15

All regressions are at the industry level and contain year fixed effects. Standard errors are clustered by industry.

*** significant at 1 percent, ** significant at 5 percent.

in the marginal tax rate on an additional dollar earned. This latter rate is simply the federal statutory rate if the firm has positive taxable income and 0 if it has zero or negative taxable income. The first two columns show the first-stage equations in which the log change in the tax rate measures are regressed on the log changes calculated based on time t characteristics and time $t + 1$ rules. The last two columns show the results of the IV estimation. Without controls for the spline in taxable income, the ETR coefficient is almost identical to its value in Table 2, although it is now less statistically significant (t statistic of 1.64). When the spline in taxable income is included as a control, the coefficient value and standard error are both slightly larger than in Table 2.

The statutory marginal tax rate appears with a large coefficient but an enormous standard error. In this context, the effective tax rate seems to have a greater effect on corporate taxable income than the statutory rate on an additional dollar of income earned, but given the potential issues with expected changes in the firm's tax status and tax law, this result is only suggestive.

Table 4 shows this same specification as Table 2, estimated on different outcome variables. It is natural to ask whether the effect we observe on taxable income is due to a reduction in actual output or simply an ability on the part of the firm to engage in tax avoidance or tax sheltering. One

Table 4. *The Effective Tax Rate (ETR), Production Inputs, and Corporate Profits*

Dependent Variable:	$\ln[(Labor\ Expense_{t+1})/(Labor\ Expense_t)]$	$\ln[(Investment_{t+1})/(Investment_t)]$	$\ln[(EBIT_{t+1})/(EBIT_t)]$
$\ln[(1-ETR_{t+1})/(1-ETR_t)]$	−0.015	0.101	0.213**
	(0.075)	(0.082)	(0.100)
Spline control	None	None	None
	IV	IV	IV
Observations	1999	2704	2614
R-squared	0.36	0.19	0.20
$\ln[(1-ETR_{t+1})/(1-ETR_t)]$	−0.009	0.115	0.219**
	(0.079)	(0.085)	(0.099)
Spline control	Labor expense	Investment	EBIT
	IV	IV	IV
Observations	1999	2704	2614
R-squared	0.40	0.20	0.21

All columns are IV regressions. Each statistic is from a separate industry-level regression. All regressions contain year fixed effects. Standard errors are clustered by industry.

*** significant at 1 percent, ** significant at 5 percent.

preliminary way we investigate this question is to examine labor expenses and corporate capital expenditures as dependent variables.

There are several issues with this approach. First, data on labor expenses are only available for a subset of Compustat firms and are computed on an accounting basis. Second, even if labor were measured precisely, the effective tax rate essentially measures the tax on output from an additional unit of capital, and higher tax rates could, in theory, induce substitution away from capital inputs and toward labor inputs. So even the theoretical direction of the coefficient on labor expense is ambiguous. Third, there are general equilibrium issues with interpreting these kinds of production input specifications. The classic treatment of Harberger (1962) shows that if a capital tax is increased for a less capital-intensive sector relative to a more capital-intensive sector, the aggregate quantity of capital demanded will actually increase.

The results on production inputs in Table 4 are generally inconclusive. The main coefficient in the labor expense equation is essentially zero. In the investment equation, the coefficient has the right sign but is statistically not significant. Taking a magnitude of 0.1 literally in the investment equation would imply an investment elasticity of 0.1 with respect to the effective tax rate, but the estimation is not precise enough to draw such a conclusion.

Table 4 also shows the results of examining a traditional definition of corporate profit, earnings before interest and tax (EBIT). Similar to Table 2, this measure displays an elasticity of around 0.2 with respect to the effective tax rate. This specification shows that the main taxable income elasticity we measure is not an artifact of our procedure for deriving estimates of taxable income from corporate accounting data. Confirmation of the result from IRS industry-level administrative data, however, is an important step for future research.

5. Conclusions

Despite the growing literature on the elasticity of household taxable income with respect to parameters of the federal tax code, there have not been similar attempts to measure the elasticity of corporate taxable income. This is partly due to the fact that the corporate setting is more complex. Corporations face taxation at both the corporate and the personal level. They may be more rational or forward-looking about future changes in the tax code than individuals. Furthermore, different marginal tax rates may be more relevant in defining the different margins of corporate behavior that affect corporate taxable income. Effective tax rates have been shown to matter for capital investment, whereas the marginal tax rate on an additional dollar of income impact the corporate financing decision that affects taxable income through interest deductions.

This chapter considers a simplified version of the corporate tax setting and leaves a number of these complications for later work. At the industry level, we find a moderate elasticity of the corporate tax base with respect to current effective tax rates, on the order of -0.2. Our preliminary evidence suggests that corporate taxable income may be more responsive to effective marginal tax rates than to the marginal tax rate on an additional dollar earned. An important area for future research is to examine the robustness of these results to different assumptions about the importance of lagged and future expected tax policy and to examine the elasticity of corporate taxable income to tax parameters over longer time horizons.

References

Altshuler, Rosanne, and Alan J. Auerbach. 1990. "The Significance of Tax Law Asymmetries: An Empirical Investigation." *Quarterly Journal of Economics* 105(1): 61–86.

Auerbach, Alan J. 1983. "Corporate Taxation in the United States." *Brookings Papers on Economic Activity* (2): 451–513.

Auerbach, Alan J., and Kevin A. Hassett. 1992. "Tax Policy and Business Fixed Investment in the United States." *Journal of Public Economics* 47(2): 141–170.

Auerbach, Alan J., and James R. Hines Jr. 1988. "Investment Tax Incentives and Frequent Tax Reforms." *American Economic Review Papers and Proceedings* 78(2): 211–216.

Bertrand, Marianne, Esther Duflo, and Sendhil Mullainathan. 2004. "How Much Should We Trust Differences-in-Differences Estimates?" *Quarterly Journal of Economics* 119(1): 249–275.

Caballero, Richard J., Eduardo M. R. A. Engel, and John C. Haltiwanger. 1995. "Plant-Level Adjustment and Aggregate Investment Dynamics." *Brookings Papers on Economic Activity* (2): 1–54.

Carroll, Robert, and David Joulfaian. 1997. "Taxes and Corporate Choice of Organizational Form." Working Paper 73. (Washington, DC: U.S. Department of the Treasury, Office of Tax Analysis).

Cummins, Jason G., Kevin A. Hassett, and R. Glenn Hubbard. 1994. "A Reconsideration of Investment Behavior Using Tax Reforms as Natural Experiments." *Brookings Papers on Economic Activity* (2): 1–74.

Cummins, Jason G., Kevin A. Hassett, and R. Glenn Hubbard. 1996. "Tax Reforms and Investment: A Cross-Country Comparison." *Journal of Public Economics* 62(1–2): 237–273.

Feldstein, Martin. 1995. "The Effect of Marginal Tax Rates on Taxable Income: A Panel Study of the 1986 Tax Reform Act." *Journal of Political Economy* 103(3): 551–572.

Fullerton, Don. 1984. "Which Effective Tax Rate?" *National Tax Journal* 37(1): 23–41.

Fullerton, Don. 1987. "The Indexation of Interest, Depreciation, and Capital Gains and Tax Reform in the United States." *Journal of Public Economics* 32(1): 25–51.

Fullerton, Don. 1999. "Marginal Effective Tax Rate." In Joseph J. Cordes, Robert D. Ebel, and Jane G. Gravelle, eds., *The Encyclopedia of Taxation and Tax Policy*. (Washington, DC: Urban Institute Press), pp. 270–272.

Giertz, Seth. 2004. "Recent Literature on Taxable-Income Elasticities." Technical Paper 2004–16. (Washington, DC: Congressional Budget Office).

Goolsbee, Austan. 1998a. "Investment Tax Incentives, Prices, and the Supply of Capital Goods." *Quarterly Journal of Economics* 113(1): 121–148.

Goolsbee, Austan. 1998b. "Taxes, Organizational Form, and the Deadweight Loss of the Corporate Income Tax." *Journal of Public Economics* 69 (1): 143–152.

Goolsbee, Austan. 2004. "The Impact and Inefficiency of the Corporate Income Tax: Evidence from State Organizational Form Data." *Journal of Public Economics* 88(11): 2283–2299.

Goolsbee, Austan, and Mihir A. Desai. 2004. "Investment, Overhang, and Tax Policy." *Brookings Papers on Economic Activity* (2): 285–355.

Gordon, Roger H., and Jeffrey K. MacKie-Mason. 1994. "Tax Distortions to the Choice of Organizational Form." *Journal of Public Economics* 55(2): 279–306.

Gordon, Roger H., and Jeffrey K. MacKie-Mason. 1997. "How Much Do Taxes Discourage Incorporation?" *Journal of Finance* 52(2): 477–505.

Gordon, Roger H., and Joel Slemrod. 1988. "Do We Collect Any Revenue from Taxing Capital Income?" In Lawrence Summers, ed., *Tax Policy and the Economy*, vol. 2 (Cambridge, MA: MIT Press), pp. 89–103.

Gordon, Roger H., Laura Kalambokidis, and Joel Slemrod. 2003. "A New Summary Measure of the Effective Tax Rate on Investment." NBER Working Paper 9535 (Cambridge, MA: National Bureau of Economic Research).

Graham, John. 2000. "How Big Are the Tax Benefits of Debt?" *Journal of Finance* 55(5): 1901–1941.

Gravelle, Jane G. 1982. "Effects of the 1981 Depreciation Revisions on the Taxation of Income from Business Capital." *National Tax Journal* 35(1): 1–20.

Gravelle, Jane G. 1983. "Capital Income Taxation and Efficiency in the Allocation of Investment." *National Tax Journal* 36(3): 297–306.

Gravelle, Jane G. 1994. *The Economic Effects of Taxing Capital Income*. (Cambridge, MA: MIT Press).

Gravelle, Jane G. 2001. "Whither Depreciation?" *National Tax Journal* 54(3): 513–526.

Gravelle, Jane G., and Laurence J. Kotlikoff. 1989. "The Incidence and Efficiency Costs of Corporate Taxation When Corporate and Noncorporate Firms Produce the Same Good." *Journal of Political Economy* 97(4): 749–780.

Gruber, Jonathan, and Emmanuel Saez. 2002. "The Elasticity of Capital Income: Evidence and Implications." *Journal of Public Economics* 84(1): 1–32.

Hall, Robert E., and Dale W. Jorgensen. 1967. "Tax Policy and Investment Behavior." *American Economic Review* 57(3): 391–414.

Hanlon, Michelle. 2003. "What Can We Infer About a Firm's Taxable Income from Its Financial Statements?" *National Tax Journal* 56(4): 831–863.

Harberger, Arnold C. 1962. "The Incidence of the Corporation Income Tax." *Journal of Political Economy* 70(3): 215–240.

House, Christopher, and Matthew D. Shapiro. 2006. "Temporary Investment Tax Incentives: Theory with Evidence from Bonus Depreciation," NBER Working Paper W12514. (Cambridge, MA: National Bureau of Economic Research).

Hulten, Charles, and Frank Wyckoff. 1981. "The Measurement of Economic Depreciation." In Charles Hulten, ed., *Depreciation, Inflation, and the Taxation of Income from Capital*. (Washington, DC: Urban Institute Press), pp. 45–60.

King, Mervyn A., and Don Fullerton. 1984. *The Taxation of Income from Capital: A Comparative Study of the United States, the United Kingdom, Sweden, and West Germany*. (Chicago: University of Chicago Press).

Kopczuk, Wojciech. 2005. "Tax Bases, Tax Rates and the Elasticity of Reported Income." *Journal of Public Economics* 89(11–12): 2093–2119.

Lindsey, Lawrence. 1987. "Capital Gains: Rates, Realizations, and Revenues." In Martin Feldstein, ed., *The Effects of Taxation on Capital Formation*. (Chicago: University of Chicago Press), pp. 69–97.

MacKie-Mason, Jeffrey. 1990. "Do Taxes Affect Corporate Financing Decisions? *Journal of Finance* 45(5): 1471–1493.

Manzon, Gil B., Jr., and George A. Plesko. 2002. "The Relation Between Financial and Tax Reporting Measures of Income." *Tax Law Review* 55(2): 175–214.

Miller, Merton. 1977. "Debt and Taxes." *Journal of Finance* 32(2): 261–275.

Mills, Lillian, and George A. Plesko. 2003. "Bridging the Reporting Gap: A Proposal for More Informative Reconciling of Book and Tax Income." *National Tax Journal* 56(4): 865–893.

Plesko, George A. 1994. "Corporate Taxation and the Financial Characteristics of Firms." *Public Finance Quarterly* 22(3): 311–334.

Plesko, George A. 2003. "An Evaluation of Alternative Measures of Corporate Tax Rates." *Journal of Accounting and Economics* 35(2): 201–226.

Saez, Emmanuel. 2004. "Reported Incomes and Marginal Tax Rates, 1960–2000: Evidence and Policy Implications." In James Poterba, ed., *Tax Policy and the Economy*, vol. 18. (Cambridge, MA: MIT Press): pp. 117–174.

Stickney, C. P., and V. E. McGee. 1982. "Effective Corporate Tax Rates: The Effect of Size, Capital Intensity, Leverage, and Other Factors." *Journal of Accounting and Public Policy* 1(2): 125–152.

U.S. Department of the Treasury. Internal Revenue Service. 2003. "Corporation Income Tax Brackets and Rates: 1909–2002." (Washington, DC: Internal Revenue Service Data Release).

Comments

Jane Gravelle

Congressional Research Service

The authors of this chapter have put together an impressive data set on effective tax rates. However, I do not believe they can use this methodology to estimate the efficiency effects of the corporate income tax.

Their approach is inspired by the body of work estimating the response of the individual income tax base to changes in tax rates. In my view, these taxable elasticity estimates for individual taxpayers are not very useful because tax changes are heterogeneous and it is difficult to control for the changes (for example, in a complex piece of legislation, such as the Tax Reform Act of 1986).

The analysis of corporate taxable income is somewhat better in this regard, because the user cost can capture the important changes that do not arise from rates. But the taxable income elasticity approach does not transfer to the corporate income tax because the pre-tax corporate return is not common to all firms; rather, it is a function of the capital stock and other production and output variables.

Consider the normal focus of corporate tax inefficiency, as embodied in its simplest form in the two-sector Harberger model, with a tax on capital income in one sector and no depreciation. The tax is recycled either through a lump sum payment to individuals or it goes to the government, which spends it in the same fashion as consumers. The efficiency cost arises from the shift of capital from the corporate to the noncorporate sector with the imposition of the corporate profits tax. Assume that both the utility function and production functions are Cobb-Douglas functions. In this case, the pre-tax capital income of the corporation is a fixed share of national output.

The views in these comments do not reflect those of the Congressional Research Service.

Imposing a capital income tax does not alter pre-tax earnings in the new equilibrium: the capital stock falls, but the pre-tax return rises just enough to offset it.

And when taxable earnings do rise or fall, they reflect a relatively complicated mix of factor substitution elasticities, product substitution elasticities, capital intensities, and the role of depreciation. Without knowing those relationships, one cannot determine the relationship between the change in income and the change in the capital stock, which governs the efficiency effect.

These complications are the reason that it is difficult to estimate the corporate/noncorporate distortions directly. Rather, they are estimated on the basis of estimates of factor and product substitution elasticities and some underlying model structure.

These complications do not arise in the case of most individual taxable income. If labor income falls, it falls either because labor is reduced or compensation is shifted to non-taxable forms of compensation, but not because the wage rate has also changed.

Even if there were a direct method of estimating these effects, there is an additional issue of lags. No one would expect that these adjustments take place immediately or even very quickly. If the existing capital stock cannot be moved to other productive uses, a decline in the capital stock must occur through changes in investment – and even investment may be delayed through planning lags or the need to change the technology of production.

Finally – in some cases, but not others – unincorporated businesses are getting benefits. They benefit from investment credits and accelerated depreciation but not from corporate rate cuts. Unless the differential between the corporate and noncorporate sectors is modeled, the relative tax rates are not correctly specified.

Thus, this approach cannot address the usual central focus of corporate tax efficiency – the misallocation of capital between the corporate and noncorporate sectors.

There are other potential behavioral reactions – reactions that might occur more quickly and clearly. One is a change in the debt share, which, at least in theory, could happen quickly. The other is a change in tax avoidance or evasion. But both of these are likely to be driven not by the effective tax rates derived from user cost but by the statutory tax rate. But profitable firms all face the same tax rate, so this technique cannot be used for that purpose unless one can focus on profitable versus loss firms. Moreover, even in this case, loss firms may have non-tax reasons for changing their debt-to-equity ratio.

Finally, a firm can, while leaving its entire capital stock intact, shift orga-nizational form to a S corporation or partnership. In this case, one would need to have a full data set that can identify these shifting firms and also identify the changes in tax rates facing both types of firms. In practice, this option is probably not available for large publicly traded firms, and my own feeling is that it is not really an important margin for change for the vast majority of corporate production that exists.

A final possibility is a change in the total capital stock from a change in savings, but this effect will happen over a long time horizon as well. Its direction is uncertain because it depends on what type of model is used, how the revenue changes were offset, and even the particular type of change. Moreover, not only can savings rise or fall, as an empirical matter, the effect of a shift in capital on the pre-tax return, while constrained by the change in output, is still affected by the other elasticities.

The authors do find a statistically significant result indicating that taxable income falls in response to marginal tax rates. The effect is small, but it is not clear what meaning to assign to it in any case. In addition, there is at least some possibility that causality is reversed: When manufacturing firms, for example, are having troubled times, Congress may enact a provision (such as investment credit) especially beneficial to them.

I do have some suggestions for the authors about a different use of their data, which is to focus on investment and to consider investment with the tax rate change lagged. Certainly, a contemporaneous change of any magnitude would be unlikely if there is a planning period involved. This approach would also present an opportunity to examine shifts in the com-position of investment as different types of capital were treated differently via investment credits, if there are data that differentiate equipment from structures.

In such an analysis, it would also be important to differentiate results across broad industry sectors, such as all manufacturing retail and whole-sale trade and services. The shift between capital is greatest in those indus-tries where there is a substantial pre-existing noncorporate sector, and thus it is feasible to shift into a noncorporate form. That argument would be particularly true in the model developed by Gravelle and Kotlikoff (1989), where output price effects are governed by the corporate tax variables. The price effects depend on capital intensity, and there is a more powerful shift in industries. An industry that is largely corporate and not especially capi-tal intensive as compared to the economy at large (such as manufacturing) might experience very little, if any shift, while an industry that is largely non-corporate and capital intensive, such as rental housing, would experience a larger shift. Thus, it is important to include largely noncorporate industries in the database.

Reference

Gravelle, Jane G., and Laurence J. Kotlikoff. 1989. "The Incidence and Efficiency Costs of Corporate Taxation When Corporate and Noncorporate Firms Produce the Same Goods." *Journal of Political Economy* 97(4): 749–780.

Comments

Casey B. Mulligan
University of Chicago

Gruber and Rauh raise an interesting question and offer an empirical answer. Before interpreting their estimates, it helps to think about what economic theory predicts for this elasticity and what structural economic hypotheses are at stake in an empirical exercise like this. Perhaps a good start assumes that the corporate income tax base is proportional to national capital income, so the question becomes "How elastic is capital income to capital income taxation?" Furthermore, let us assume, as in the closed-economy neoclassical growth model, that the amount of capital supplied is the primary determinant of capital income:

$$B = kf'(k),$$

where f' denotes the marginal product of capital k and B is the corporate income tax base. The elasticity of the base can be related to the elasticity of capital supply:

$$d \ln B = \left[1 - \frac{-f''}{f'} k \right] d \ln k.$$

Hence, as long as the marginal product of capital diminishes, the tax base elasticity is less than the elasticity of capital supply. Intuitively, as the corporate tax discourages capital accumulation, it has an offsetting effect on the corporate income tax base because the marginal product of capital rises. The tax base elasticity is probably a lot less than the capital supply elasticity, because in the Cobb-Douglas case the term in square brackets is equal to the capital's share of national income, or about 0.3. Hence, it would be surprising to see the corporate income tax base to be very elastic, unless we thought shifts between corporate and noncorporate forms of capital income (neglected above) were particularly important.

The elasticity of interest to Gruber and Rauh is with respect to the after-corporate-tax share, which I denote q. Capital theory more often refers to

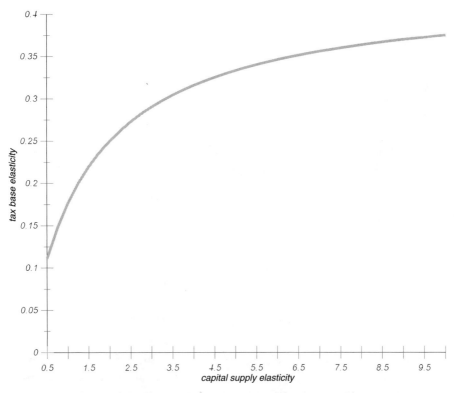

Figure 1. Tax Base Elasticity as a Function of Capital Supply Elasticity (Marginal Product Elasticity assumed to be −0.7)

the elasticity ε of capital supply with the after-tax return, which I denote r, but the two elasticities are readily related if we ignore the distinction between corporate income and capital income because $r = qf'(k)$:[1]

$$\frac{d\ln k}{d\ln q} = \left[\frac{1}{\varepsilon} + \frac{-f''}{f'}k\right]^{-1} \Rightarrow \frac{d\ln B}{d\ln q} = \frac{1 - \frac{-f''}{f'}k}{\frac{1}{\varepsilon} + \frac{-f''}{f'}k}.$$

Figure 1 graphs the Gruber-Rauh elasticity as a function of the elasticity ϵ of capital supply with respect to the after-tax return, assuming that the elasticity of the marginal product with respect to capital is −0.7, as it would be with a constant capital share of 0.3.

Figure 2 shows how the tax base is inelastic with respect to q regardless of how elastically capital is supplied. This tells us something about practical

---

[1] The left equation is calculated by differentiating the definition $r = qf'(k)$ and then substituting using the definition $\varepsilon = (d\ln k)/(d\ln r)$.

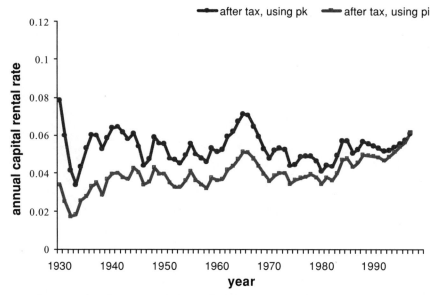

Figure 2. The After-Tax Capital Rental Rate, 1930–1997 (*Source:* Mulligan, 2002)

public finance matters, such as the short-run forecasting of corporate income tax revenues. However, estimates like Gruber and Rauh's leave us in the dark about the capital supply elasticity, and therefore any structural economic questions that depend on it, because a wide range of capital supply elasticities is consistent with essentially the same tax base elasticity.

Another empirical calculation reported by Mulligan (2002) suggests that capital is in fact elastically supplied, so that capital income taxes are significantly distortionary even if the corporate income tax base is inelastic with respect to the after-corporate-tax share. Namely, as heavy capital income tax rates emerged since the 1940s, there has been little if any depression of the after-tax capital rental rate. Figure 1 displays two of Mulligan's measures of the after-tax capital rental rate for the years 1930–97.

Reference

Mulligan, Casey B. 2002. "Capital, Interest, and Aggregate Intertemporal Substitution." NBER Working Paper 9373. (Cambridge, MA: National Bureau of Economic Research).

FIVE

An Empirical Examination of Corporate Tax Noncompliance

Michelle Hanlon

University of Michigan

Lillian Mills

University of Texas

Joel Slemrod

University of Michigan

We appreciate guidance on data questions from Richard Denesha, Donald Lee, John Miller, and Dick Teed. We are grateful for comments on a presentation of preliminary results received from Charles Brown, James Hines, and other members of the University of Michigan public finance workshop and for comments received at the conference from discussants Joe Bankman and Brian Erard, and several other participants.

The Internal Revenue Service (IRS) provided confidential tax information to one of the authors pursuant to provisions of the Internal Revenue Code that allow disclosure of information to a contractor to the extent necessary to perform a research contract for the IRS. None of the confidential tax information received from the IRS is disclosed in this chapter. Statistical aggregates were used so that a specific taxpayer cannot be identified from information supplied by the IRS. Information in this chapter that identifies specific companies was not provided by the IRS and came from public sources, such as reports to shareholders.

1. Introduction and Motivation

This chapter examines the extent and nature of corporate tax noncompliance using previously undisclosed Internal Revenue Service (IRS) operational audits and appeals data merged with confidential tax return data. The extent of tax noncompliance is primarily measured as the level of proposed tax deficiencies under IRS audit, although we also investigate the amount of the proposed deficiencies that are upheld after taxpayer appeals. We examine the relation between corporate noncompliance and various corporate characteristics, such as firm size, industry, multinationality, being publicly traded, the form of executive compensation arrangements, and governance characteristics. In addition, we examine the relationship between corporate tax noncompliance and average or effective tax rates (ETRs) calculated on the basis of publicly available data.

Our results are consistent with larger firms, firms in the large-case audit program, and privately held firms having larger proposed audit deficiencies relative to the "true" tax liability. In general, we find that firms that are foreign-controlled have a smaller deficiency than their purely domestic counterparts and that multinational firms have a greater deficiency relative to nonmultinational firms. We find that both the percentage of annual compensation that is bonus and the level of equity incentives from exercisable stock options are positively related to the proposed deficiency, indicating that executive compensation may be associated with tax aggressiveness. Finally, we find no relation between a measure of governance quality and the proposed deficiency. We find little evidence that lower ETRs are related to deficiencies.

Understanding the extent and nature of tax noncompliance is important because it has potentially serious implications for both the equity and efficiency of the tax system. Tax noncompliance can change the distribution of the tax burden from what was intended or from what a reading of the tax law might suggest. In the case of individual taxation, the distributional pattern of personal income tax noncompliance could, on average, be offset by Congress adopting an appropriate level of the nominal progressivity of the personal tax rate schedule that delivers the desired after-noncompliance degree of progressivity.

The equity implications of corporate tax noncompliance are not as straightforward.[1] According to the economic theory of taxation, the incidence of corporation taxes must be traced back to which *people* ultimately bear the burden of taxation – be they the company's shareholders, managers, workers, or customers From this perspective, it is not interesting or even meaningful to say *corporations* are worse off, or better off, as a result of a particular tax change. How the burden of the corporation income tax is distributed among these groups of individual people remains highly controversial. Note, though, that the theory of corporation income tax incidence

---

[1] These issues are discussed in greater detail in Slemrod (2004).

addresses a tax policy that applies generally to all corporations. A particular act of noncompliance does not, by definition, apply to all corporations. Although a tax policy that facilitates noncompliance for *all* corporations might attract entry and thereby be shifted, for example, to customers through lower output prices, a successful act of noncompliance by one corporation will not be met by increased pressure from competitors. Thus, the windfall gains to those companies that successfully play the tax lottery by acting aggressively probably accrue to the shareholders in their role as residual claimants, shared to some extent with the corporate executives through incentivized compensation contracts.

If there are particular characteristics of corporations in certain sectors that facilitate noncompliance or abusive avoidance, such as the presence of corporate intangibles, the apparent gains that accrue to shareholders of firms in these sectors via a lower effective tax rate will be partially eroded to the extent that competitors have similar characteristics that facilitate noncompliance; in this case, the noncompliance-facilitating characteristic will benefit some other constituency, notably this sector's customers. The same argument applies to the incidence of altering policy instruments related to deterrence, such as the penalties for detected noncompliance. The industrial organization of the tax shelter promoter business may also be a factor in determining how the tax savings are shared among taxpayers and tax shelter promoters. For example, if the promoter business is perfectly competitive with free entry, in the long run most of the gains from tax shelter "innovation" will accrue to the taxpayers; if not, some of the gain will accrue to the promoters via high fees.[2]

Tax noncompliance has efficiency as well as equity implications, because opportunities for tax noncompliance can distort resource allocation in a variety of ways. It can cause intersectoral distortions because, for example, companies that otherwise would not find it attractive might have a financial subsidiary, or set up operations in a tax haven, to facilitate or camouflage abusive avoidance or noncompliance. In general, resources flow more than otherwise to activities that facilitate tax noncompliance.

An important and fascinating question concerns the relationship between noncompliance and real corporate activity. Could cracking down on this behavior decrease corporate investment, because it eliminates what was essentially a do-it-yourself tax cut? The answer depends on the relationship between the marginal cost (if there were *no* cost, no tax would be paid) to the taxpayer of avoiding tax and the volume of investment it

---

[2] See Gergen (2002) and Hines (2004) for related discussions.

undertakes.[3] If there is no relationship, then cracking down on noncompliance and thereby increasing its cost will not decrease investment. More likely, the private cost of a given (absolute, not relative) level of avoidance is lower when the scale of real operations is higher, so that there is an implicit subsidy to investment. For example, if the IRS effectively overlooks noncompliance that constitutes a constant fraction of true income, then this is equivalent to a reduction in the effective marginal tax rate on income-earning investment.[4]

This discussion of the policy relevance of corporate tax noncompliance raises a number of research issues:

- The relationship of noncompliance to size, because this sheds light on whether it is inframarginal or an implicit subsidy to investment.
- The relationship of noncompliance to sector, because this sheds light on to what extent the benefit is bid away via competition.
- The relationship of noncompliance to particular characteristics of companies, such as the presence of intangibles or multinationality, because this sheds light on whether the possibility of noncompliance affects the full cost of acquiring these characteristics.

2. Previous Literature

Most existing analysis of tax noncompliance in the United States is based on the IRS Tax Compliance Measurement Program, or TCMP, which featured intensive examinations of random samples of tax returns. Although developed primarily to improve case-selection techniques, the data has been central to attempts to estimate an economy-wide measure of a corporate "tax gap" – the difference between taxes owed and taxes actually paid. The TCMP featured intensive examinations of a random sample of tax returns filed for tax years from the early 1960s until 1988, and the current corporate tax gap measures are primarily based on simple extrapolations from TCMP studies done in 1977, 1980, and 1983 and on routine operational audits from the mid-1980s.[5] The estimates for the corporation income tax gap came from three sources. For small corporations, the IRS used TCMP data adjusted for

---

[3] This reasoning is developed in Slemrod (2001).

[4] The empirical relationship between corporate tax avoidance and the effectiveness of tax incentives to invest is examined in Slemrod, Dauchy, and Martinez (2005).

[5] The IRS has recently issued updated estimates of components of the tax gap on the basis of the TCMP successor project known as the National Research Program (NRP). However, the new estimates cover individual income tax and employment tax, not the corporation income tax.

underreporting unlikely to be detected by the TCMP. For medium-sized corporations, the gap was calculated by estimating, on the basis of operational audits, how much tax revenue would have been generated if the IRS examined all these corporations' tax returns. Finally, for large corporations, because the IRS routinely examines a high percentage of these companies, examination results of the type analyzed in this chapter were used as the basis of estimates of the tax gap.[6]

The IRS has made corporate tax gap estimates for tax year 2001, but not later, on the basis of a rough projection from the 15- to 20-year-old TCMP and other data, assuming that the compliance rates for each major component have not changed.[7] Corporate underreporting in 2001 is estimated at $29.9 billion, of which corporations with over $10.0 million in assets make up $25.0 billion.[8] As a benchmark for comparison, estimated individual underreporting in 2001 is $148.8 billion. Compared to estimated 2001 tax year receipts paid voluntarily and in a timely fashion of $142.4 billion and $930.1 billion for corporate and individual income tax collections, respectively, the estimated underreporting rate in 2001 (calculated as underreported tax divided by receipts plus underreported tax) was 17.4 percent and 13.8 percent for corporations and individuals, respectively.

The Bureau of Economic Analysis (BEA) also calculates an annual measure of corporate "misreporting," in order to adjust the National Income and Product Accounts (NIPA) measure of corporate profits, which is based on data from corporate tax returns as filed.[9] The BEA estimate for corporations reporting a profit is based on actual tax settlements – the change in income recommended by the IRS examination team reduced by the overall ratio of actual settlements to recommendations.[10] For loss companies, the

---

[6] This description is based on U.S. General Accounting Office (1988).

[7] The tax gap numbers are drawn from Internal Revenue Service (2004). A data-gathering effort known as the National Research Program has collected similar data for tax year 2001 that have been used to produce updated but preliminary estimates of the tax gap; this project has not yet, however, updated the corporate tax gap estimates.

[8] Underreporting is only one of the three components of the total tax gap, which is estimated to be $282.5 billion. The other two components are nonfiling and underpayment. There is no estimate for corporate nonfiling, and underpayment is a quite different issue.

[9] The BEA methodology is discussed in Petrick (2002, p. 7). The official BEA term is "misreporting," although the BEA description of its methodology uses the terms "misreport" and "evade" interchangeably.

[10] In contrast, the IRS tax gap measures are based on the recommendations of the return audit, unadjusted for how much tax was ultimately assessed after any appeals process. This is defended in part as an approximate adjustment for the fact that IRS examiners do not detect all underreporting. Another methodological difference is that the BEA projects the average amount of recommended adjustment per return to all returns by multiplying this

adjustment is calculated by multiplying total losses by an estimate of the percentage by which losses are reduced during audit. The BEA procedure calculates that in 2000 corporate tax misreporting as a percentage of misreporting plus total receipts less deductions (the tax-return-based measure that the BEA procedures begin from)[11] was 13.8 percent, compared to the 17.4 percent figure on the basis of the IRS methodology that extrapolates from two-decades-old data assuming no change in compliance rates. The BEA series shows an increase in the misreporting rate since the mid-1990s, but puts the 2000 misreporting rate below the rates of the 1989-through-1992 period.

There has been very little analysis of the micro data underlying the TCMP-based corporate tax gap studies. One exception is Rice (1992), who studied the 1980 TCMP data of small (with assets between $1 and $10 million) corporations. This analysis found that compliance is positively related to being publicly traded and in a highly regulated industry, so that characteristics that assure public disclosure of information also tend to encourage better tax compliance.[12] Second, more profitable corporations are relatively less compliant. Finally, Rice finds that firm size and tax compliance are not positively related but instead that the reporting gap grows with the amount of a firm's value added (total revenue).

In a study of large-case audit firms (the Coordinated Industry Cases (CIC), formerly the Coordinated Examination Program) in the manufacturing industry from 1982 to 1992, Mills (1998) studies the relation between tax deficiencies and book-tax differences. Using corporate tax return Schedule M-1 data, she finds that the excess of book income over taxable income is positively related to proposed audit adjustments. Cloyd (1995) finds

---

figure by the total number of returns, thus implicitly assuming that the examined returns are representative of all corporate returns. In contrast, the IRS tax gap methodology for midsized corporations (with assets between $10 million and $100 million) projects the results of audited returns to the whole population, with some acknowledgment that returns audited are not representative of the entire population and indeed have higher unreported income than unexamined returns. The first methodological difference would make the BEA estimates of underreporting lower than the IRS tax gap measure, while the second methodological difference would make it higher. We are grateful to Alan Plumley and Eric Toder of the IRS for insights about these issues.

[11] Note that the NIPA table refers to misreported *income*, not understated *tax liability*, as in the IRS corporate tax gap studies.

[12] Tannenwald et al. (1993) argued that Rice's finding that publicly traded companies have higher compliance may have nothing to do with public disclosure and instead might reflect the fact that publicly traded companies are more likely to have managers who are independent of its owners and therefore are less fearful of commingling the owners' personal affairs with those of the corporation.

that tax preparers believe that when book-tax differences are greater, audit probabilities increase and the probability of a successful defense against the IRS decreases.

A related literature investigates the level, variation, and determinants of effective tax rates (ETRs). To the extent that low ETRs, defined as total (or current) income tax expense divided by pre-tax earnings (from public financial statements), are a proxy for tax noncompliance or aggressive tax positions, variables that explain differences in ETRs may help explain tax deficiencies. The organization Citizens for Tax Justice (CTJ) has published several studies using ETRs to classify firms as tax aggressive. Their initial study was one of the factors causing additional inquiry into firms' tax practices that eventually led to the Tax Reform Act of 1986 (TRA86).[13] In addition, in a study of the benefits of investments in tax planning, Mills, Erickson, and Maydew (1998) find, using data from Slemrod and Blumenthal (1996), that corporate expenditures on tax planning are negatively associated with the worldwide current effective tax rate. They also find that corporate ETRs are decreasing in size and leverage (because their ETR denominator is pre-tax income before interest expense), but higher for firms with foreign assets.

3. Data

3.1. Details

This paper is the first to use operational data from the Voluntary Compliance Baseline Measurement (VCBLM) program compiled by the Large and Mid-Size Business (LMSB) Research Division of the IRS to systematically examine the magnitude and nature of corporate tax noncompliance.[14] The LMSB Division contains Coordinated Industry Case (CIC) and Industry Case (IC) returns. Although LMSB handles all returns for taxpayers with assets exceeding $10 million, about 1,200 taxpayers per year (in the 1990s) are placed in the CIC group due to their large size and complexity. The CIC is often referred to as the "large-case audit program," and nearly all of these cases are audited. The IC returns are audited with less regularity, especially as the size of the firm decreases, although IC returns are audited

---

[13] We note, however, that the CTJ makes several adjustments to the firms' reported ETRs, and its calculations are not undisputed by the firms on which it reports.

[14] Mills (1998) and Mills and Sansing (2000) use these data to investigate the relation between book-tax differences and audit adjustments. Mills and Newberry (2001) explain the determinants of book-tax differences. Gleason and Mills (2002) use proposed deficiencies to evaluate financial statement disclosures of contingent tax liabilities.

more frequently than small businesses (less than $10 million of assets) and Schedule C businesses.

The VCBLM audit data include Audit Information Management System (AIMS) closed examinations from 1990 through 2003.[15] These data include extensive information about the audit and any subsequent appeal, including the tax deficiency (if any) proposed by the examination team, the amount the taxpayer agrees to at examination, and the results of the appeals or in the IRS counsel process (court decisions or out-of-court settlements). Henceforth, we refer to the entire appeals and counsel process as simply "appeals." The dataset records tax paid on the return as originally filed, ignoring amended returns and carryback claims.[16]

The initial dataset includes 114,257 firm-year observations, consisting of 37,995 unique employer identification numbers (EINs).[17] It covers tax return periods from 1960 to 2002 (although most return years are between 1986 and 1999) for examinations closed between 1990 and 2003 (although most closures occurred between 1993 and 2001). Both public and private companies are covered.

We merge the VCBLM data with two separate sources of data. First, we match the VCBLM data with corporate tax return data extracted by the LMSB Research Division at the IRS. Merging the VCBLM audit data (114,257) with the tax return data (545,021) by tax return period and EIN yields 45,121 merged observations. Because the tax return data for non-CIC firms are not available to us until 1994, we are unable to make full use of approximately 60,000 observations for VCBLM data for tax return years before 1994. Because the data are scarce in early years and include only relatively less complicated returns in the later years (an issue we discuss further below), we consider only the data for tax years from 1983 through 1998. Additional data requirements detailed in Appendix A reduce the sample to 29,141, which is the basis of our primary regressions.

---

[15] Readers of this and other studies must remain alert to the use of the word "closed." The AIMS data (which are also used in GAO, 1995, p. 19 are organized by year in which *examinations* are closed. Audit data do not enter the system until the examination team has released the return with the deficiency agreed in full, unagreed (in full or part), or released with other information (such as a change that does not generate a deficiency), or a no change audit. In the VCBLM data, however, the return is assigned a status of closed only if it has been settled through appeals, counsel, and all claims that relate to the return year. We refer to this as a closed "case."

[16] The VCBLM data do not contain information concerning the types of issues identified during the audit, although the IRS is developing an Issue Based Management Information System (IBMIS) that will track issue types for all exams.

[17] Note that taxpayers can change EIN over the sample period, so we cannot say that there are only 37,995 companies.

Appendix A. *Sample Selection Details*

		Observations
VCBLM Audit Data	114,257	
Tax Return Data		
LMSB 1994–2002	526,610	
CIC 1981–1993	18,411	
Merge VCBLM, Tax Return Data		45,121
Drop Observations Where:	Drop	Subtotal
Year < 1983, > 1998	6,207	38,914
Financial Services Industry	8,720	30,194
Status Code < 80 (Exam Not Finished)	215	29,979
Industry Code Missing	4	29,975
Tax Deficiency < 0	312	29,663
Total Ending Assets = 0	248	29,415
Total Sales = 0	274	29,141
Final Sample		29,141

We also merge this combined data with Standard and Poor's (S&P) Compustat financial statement data, using the employer identification number recorded in Compustat as of the 2003 tape year. We are likely unable to match some observations because EINs can change over time due to mergers and acquisitions, and thus a public company in the VCBLM data may not match into Compustat because the Compustat data will have the new EIN of the merged company. Thus, some of the observations designated as private could actually be public, especially in the earlier return years. Of the 29,141 observations in the sample, 12,100 (42 percent) of the return years are designated as public.

3.2. Discussion

We will argue below that these operational data shed light on corporate tax noncompliance. This claim must be accompanied by several caveats. First, the deficiencies proposed by the examination team are not a perfect measure of actual noncompliance. Due to the many complexities of the tax law, exactly what is actual tax liability – and therefore what is actual tax noncompliance – is often not clear. Second, any given examination is not perfect. Some noncompliance may be missed, and there will also be mistakes in characterizing as noncompliance what is legitimate tax planning. For this reason, the data reflect not only the reporting behavior of the companies but also the enforcement behavior of the tax authority. Knowing that the resolution of the ultimate tax liability is often a long process of negotiation that may or may not involve the judicial system, the tax liability per the originally filed return, as well as the initial deficiency assessed by the examination team, may be partly a tactical "opening bid" that is neither party's best estimate of the "true" tax liability. Partly in response to this issue, we also examine the amount of proposed adjustments that are sustained after the taxpayer exhausts any appeals. Whether the final settlement is a more accurate measure of noncompliance is an open question.

Another issue is that the proposed deficiency as reported in the VCBLM data does not necessarily capture the long-term effect of tax noncompliance on revenues collected. There are two situations that have opposite effects with respect to timing. First, some of the proposed tax deficiency may involve temporary adjustments. As an example, consider a corporation that expensed an item, but the examination team decided that this item should have been amortized instead. The tax effect of a difference between the expense and the first-year allowable amortization would be recorded in the VCBLM as a deficiency; however, the repercussion in future years – that taxable income would be lower than otherwise – is not accounted for anywhere. The result is that the present value of the tax effects of this adjustment is likely to be substantially less than the first-year adjustment recorded in the VCBLM data. Unfortunately, we cannot tell what fraction of adjustments relates to temporary differences.

A related issue applies to adjustments made to the taxable income of corporations whose taxable income in the examination year is negative and that could not carry back these losses against earlier years' positive taxable income. In this case, an upward adjustment of taxable income (from a negative number to a smaller – in absolute value – number) would not increase that year's tax liability. The adjustment would, though, in general increase the present value of tax liability to the extent that it reduces the expected amount of further carryforward of losses. The VCBLM data record an estimate of the tax effect of adjustments as "revenue protection" with no discounting, but only for companies in the CIC program. Valuing the revenue protection amounts the same as other adjustments presumes that the expected present value of a dollar of reduced carryforward is exactly a dollar. In fact, that fraction will vary depending on the expected pattern of future taxable income amounts. Compared to the treatment of temporary adjustments, treating revenue protection amounts as worth a full dollar in present value terms represents the opposite extreme of methodologies. Largely because of the limited data availability, in what follows we have not included revenue protection amounts in our calculations of proposed deficiency.

There is one other important qualification to keep in mind in interpreting the results we present below. We examine the outcomes of tax filings for tax years between 1983 and 1998 that were included in an IRS extract of audit data for AIMS closed cases from 1990 to 2003. Over this time period, the coverage of the data changes, most notably but not only because we only have tax return data that include non-CIC companies beginning in return year 1994. Because it can be several years before the audit and especially the appeals process are completed, for some of the tax returns the appeals process has not been completed: The "case" has not been closed. For these returns, we can measure the deficiency as per the audit but not how much of the disputed tax liability was upheld by the appeals process. The later the tax return year, the higher the likelihood that a tax return case is still "open" and, holding the tax return year constant, the more substantive and complex are the tax issues that are disputed for the open cases. For this reason, presenting a time series of our noncompliance measures would probably not reveal anything about true trends in corporate reporting behavior (or tax enforcement vigilance), and we have refrained from reporting such a time series. We do, though, include a year dummy in the regression analysis to control for possible time trends, either real or due to sample selection. This caveat also applies to the time-aggregated figures that we do report. The returns that are closed are by no means a random sample of all returns – they are more likely to pertain to earlier tax years and to less complicated and less disputed tax returns. When this issue is especially pertinent below, we note its implications for how to interpret the results.

We make two adjustments to the data as compiled by the IRS in constructing the VCBLM data. First, the dataset records $1 in the deficiency field to represent the presence of a change (such as shrinking a tax loss) that did not actually increase tax due. We re-code the deficiency to zero, removing this tag. Second, where taxpayer-agreed amounts (in exam, appeals, or counsel) exceeded the deficiency, we constrain the settlement to the deficiency, essentially capping the settlement percentage on a firm-year basis at 100 percent.

4. Patterns of Proposed Deficiency, Agreements, and Appeal Results

4.1. Aggregate

Table 1 presents some summary statistics based on the VCBLM data. We present statistics for the full sample (29,141 observations) and for a subsample of observations for which the tax after proposed deficiency (i.e., reported

Table 1. *Sample Statistics*

	All Returns	Closed Returns	Open Returns
Total Observations	29,141		
Percentage with Deficiency > 0	55%		
Deficiency / Assets	0.0017		
Deficiency / Sales	0.0022		
Observations with Proposed Tax > 0	25,266	22,552	2,714
Percentage with Deficiency > 0	63%		
Deficiency / Proposed Tax	0.136	0.094	0.207
Agreed to at Exam / Deficiency	0.320	0.487	0.193
Agreed to at Appeals / Deficiency		0.113	NA
Agreed / Final Tax		0.059	NA

Notes: The data come from the VCBLM for return-years between 1983 and 1998 as shown in Appendix A, on the basis of an IRS (LMSB) extract in 2004 of AIMS closed-case data from 1990–2003. *Deficiency* is the proposed tax deficiency. *Proposed Tax* (*Prop. Tax*) is the sum of *Tax on Return* plus *Deficiency*. *Tax on Return* is the total tax after credits from the U.S. Corporation Form 1120. *Agreed to at Exam* is the payments posted to the taxpayer's account, field X300R, during the examination process with respect to that return year's examination. *Agreed to at Appeals* is the sum of payments posted to the taxpayer's account during the appeal (A300R) or counsel (C300R) processes with respect to that return year's examination. *Final Tax* equals *Tax on Return* plus *Agreed to at Exam* plus *Agreed to at Appeals*. *Agreed* is the total amount of *Deficiency* agreed to by the taxpayer when the case is closed through appeals and counsel. We limit the amounts *Agreed* to the *Deficiency*. In the VCBLM dataset, deficiencies are coded at $1 if there is a change that did not increase tax. We restore these observations to zero deficiency. *Assets* is the total year end assets from Form 1120, Schedule L. *Sales* is the gross receipts from Form 1120, page 1, line 1.

tax plus the proposed deficiency, or proposed tax) is positive (25,266 observations). In the full sample, 55 percent of the observations have a proposed deficiency, and in aggregate the deficiency is 0.17 percent of aggregate assets and 0.22 percent of total sales.[18] For the subsample of observations for which the tax after proposed deficiency is positive, the aggregate proposed deficiency is 13.6 percent of the tax reported plus deficiency (henceforth, the "proposed deficiency rate"). Thus, the aggregate deficiency rate we measure is similar, but slightly below the lower of the 13.8 and 17.4 percent figures discussed earlier that have been calculated by the BEA and IRS, respectively. Of the total proposed deficiency, just under one-third, or 32.0 percent, was agreed to by the taxpayer at the examination.

[18] In calculating this and all subsequent aggregate ratios, we report the ratio of the sum of the numerators to the sum of the denominators, and not the mean of the ratios. The deficiency-to-assets ratio is higher than found by Mills (1998) or Mills and Sansing (2000). When we constrain our sample to approximate the same years and other data constraints (e.g., manufacturing, book-tax differences), we obtain qualitatively similar results.

We separately analyze the 22,552 firm-years for which the return year has closed in our data, meaning that all appeals and court disputes are settled, and the 2,714 firm years for which the return was still open. We find that the amount of the proposed deficiency agreed to by the taxpayer at the time of the exam varies sharply between open and closed cases – 48.7 percent for the closed cases, but only 19.3 percent for the open cases. This difference is not surprising, and reflects the fact that it is precisely when the discrepancy between the proposed deficiency and the tax liability agreed to by the taxpayer is large that the case is likely to be subject to a protracted appeals process. For the closed cases only, we can measure the ultimate resolution of the unagreed deficiencies. The data indicate that another 11.3 percent of the proposed deficiency, or 22.0 percent of the unagreed amount $(.113/(1 - .487))$, was sustained. All in all, 60.0 percent of the proposed deficiency was either agreed to by the taxpayer or upheld at a later stage. This 60 percent sustention rate is almost certainly an upper-bound estimate of the rate for all companies, because it excludes the tax return years that had not been closed when the dataset was compiled. Because taxpayers are more likely to agree to smaller and less controversial proposed deficiencies and will fight longer and harder against larger and more controversial proposed deficiencies, the overall average including the still-open returns will likely be lower than 60 percent.

Consistent with taxpayers fighting larger deficiencies more, Table 1 shows that on average the open returns in our sample have a proposed deficiency/proposed tax of 20.7 percent compared to the closed returns, which have an analogous rate of only 9.4 percent. In untabulated computations of the aggregate proposed deficiency for our sample firms, a disproportionate amount of the deficiency is related to open returns. Although the open returns represent only 10.7 percent of the number of return years in the sample, 57 percent of the proposed deficiency is related to the open returns.

4.2. Firm Size

Table 2 presents the audit data by size of the firm. We divide the sample into seven groups by the amount of year-end assets reported on the tax return. The largest companies (those with assets greater than $5 billion) have the greatest percentage of firms with a deficiency (74 percent) and, for those with a positive proposed tax (reported tax plus deficiency), the highest proposed deficiency rate (14.6 percent, versus a range of 9.9 percent to 13.4 percent for the other six groups). The same pattern appears when the proposed deficiency is scaled by sales. (Although the reverse pattern appears when the

Table 2. *Audit Results by Asset Class*

Panel A: Full Sample, All Returns

Asset Class	Obs.	% with Deficiency > 0	Deficiency / Assets	Deficiency / Sales	Obs.w/Prop. Tax > 0	% with Deficiency > 0	Deficiency / Prop. Tax	Agreed to at Exam / Deficiency
A(assets) < $100M	11,196	49	0.0027	0.0015	9,280	59	0.099	0.457
$100M ≤ A < $250M	4,198	48	0.0028	0.0019	3,530	57	0.117	0.293
$250M ≤ A < $500M	3,032	53	0.0025	0.0017	2,629	61	0.115	0.329
$500M ≤ A < $1B	3,067	56	0.0023	0.0018	2,737	63	0.109	0.345
$1B ≤ A < $2B	2,746	62	0.0023	0.0020	2,479	69	0.121	0.281
$2B ≤ A < $5B	2,519	66	0.0021	0.0021	2,345	71	0.134	0.314
A > $5B	2,383	74	0.0014	0.0024	2,266	78	0.146	0.323
TOTALS	29,141	55	0.0017	0.0022	25,266	63	0.136	0.320

Panel B: Full Sample, Closed versus Open Returns

| | Closed Returns | | | | | Open Returns | | |
Asset Class	Obs.	Deficiency / Prop. Tax	Agreed to at Exam / Deficiency	Agreed to at Appeals / Deficiency	Agreed / Final Tax	Obs.	Deficiency / Prop. Tax	Agreed to at Exam / Deficiency
A(assets) < $100M	8,898	0.073	0.611	0.059	0.050	382	0.465	0.104
$100M ≤ A < $250M	3,336	0.086	0.403	0.076	0.043	194	0.443	0.067
$250M ≤ A < $500M	2,423	0.086	0.435	0.082	0.046	206	0.336	0.124
$500M ≤ A < $1B	2,476	0.083	0.479	0.096	0.050	261	0.272	0.084
$1B ≤ A < $2B	2,134	0.080	0.441	0.106	0.046	345	0.290	0.097
$2B ≤ A < $5B	1,839	0.091	0.471	0.134	0.057	506	0.251	0.159
A > $5B	1,446	0.104	0.510	0.115	0.068	820	0.188	0.221
TOTALS	22,552	0.094	0.487	0.113	0.059	2,714	0.207	0.193

Panel C: Coordinated Industry Cases (CIC) Only, All Returns

Asset Class	Obs.	% with Deficiency > 0	Deficiency / Assets	Deficiency / Sales	Obs. w/Prop. Tax > 0	% with Deficiency > 0	Deficiency / Prop. Tax	Agreed to at Exam / Deficiency
A(assets) < $100M	85	51	0.0054	0.0026	74	58	0.147	0.227
$100M ≤ A < $250M	476	58	0.0105	0.0057	415	66	0.340	0.135
$250M ≤ A < $500M	1,123	63	0.0044	0.0029	1,020	70	0.192	0.246
$500M ≤ A < $1B	1,648	63	0.0029	0.0023	1,524	68	0.134	0.318
$1B ≤ A < $2B	1,861	67	0.0028	0.0023	1,728	72	0.137	0.258
$2B ≤ A < $5B	2,084	68	0.0023	0.0023	1,965	73	0.140	0.316
A > $5B	2,230	75	0.0015	0.0024	2,136	78	0.148	0.314
TOTALS	9,507	67	0.0017	0.0024	8,862	72	0.147	0.306

Panel D: Coordinated Industry Cases (CIC) Only, Closed versus Open Returns

	Closed Returns					Open Returns		
Asset Class	Obs.	Deficiency / Prop. Tax	Agreed to at Exam / Deficiency	Agreed to at Appeals / Deficiency	Agreed / Final Tax	Obs.	Deficiency / Prop. Tax	Agreed to at Exam / Deficiency
A(assets) < $100M	70	0.084	0.433	0.142	0.050	4	0.770	0.003
$100M ≤ A < $250M	388	0.266	0.170	0.118	0.095	27	0.669	0.074
$250M ≤ A < $500M	950	0.149	0.327	0.098	0.069	70	0.443	0.086
$500M ≤ A < $1B	1,390	0.107	0.425	0.110	0.060	134	0.334	0.075
$1B ≤ A < $2B	1,500	0.095	0.387	0.117	0.050	228	0.303	0.102
$2B ≤ A < $5B	1,549	0.098	0.469	0.130	0.061	416	0.256	0.156
A > $5B	1,359	0.105	0.491	0.119	0.067	777	0.189	0.221
TOTALS	7,206	0.104	0.459	0.120	0.063	1,656	0.207	0.198

(continued)

185

Table 2 (continued)

Panel E: Non-Coordinated Industry Cases (Non-CIC) Only, All Returns

Asset Class	Total Obs.	% with Deficiency > 0	Deficiency / Assets	Deficiency / Sales	Obs. w/Prop. Tax > 0	% with Deficiency > 0	Deficiency / Prop. Tax	Agreed to at Exam / Deficiency
A(assets) < $100M	11,111	49	0.0026	0.0015	9,206	59	0.098	0.464
$100M ≤ A < $250M	3,722	47	0.0016	0.0011	3,115	56	0.071	0.447
$250M ≤ A < $500M	1,909	46	0.0013	0.0009	1,609	55	0.062	0.510
$500M ≤ A < $1B	1,419	49	0.0015	0.0013	1,213	57	0.074	0.410
$1B ≤ A < $2B	885	52	0.0011	0.0012	751	61	0.073	0.404
$2B ≤ A < $5B	435	56	0.0012	0.0013	380	64	0.092	0.297
A > $5B	153	61	0.0009	0.0017	130	72	0.100	0.645
TOTALS	19,634	49	0.0013	0.0013	16,404	58	0.081	0.453

Panel F: Non-Coordinated Industry Cases (Non-CIC) Only, Closed versus Open Returns

Asset Class	Closed Returns					Open Returns		
	Obs	Deficiency / Prop. Tax	Agreed to at Exam / Deficiency	Agreed to at Appeals / Deficiency	Agreed / Final Tax	Obs.	Deficiency / Prop. Tax	Agreed to at Exam / Deficiency
A(assets) < $100M	8,828	0.073	0.614	0.057	0.050	378	0.457	0.108
$100M ≤ A < $250M	2,948	0.054	0.606	0.040	0.036	167	0.314	0.058
$250M ≤ A < $500M	1,473	0.044	0.678	0.045	0.032	136	0.224	0.204
$500M ≤ A < $1B	1,086	0.051	0.634	0.056	0.036	127	0.205	0.099
$1B ≤ A < $2B	634	0.040	0.789	0.039	0.034	117	0.241	0.072
$2B ≤ A < $5B	290	0.046	0.496	0.185	0.032	90	0.220	0.181
A > $5B	87	0.089	0.891	0.041	0.083	43	0.130	0.217
TOTALS	15,346	0.055	0.688	0.062	0.042	1,058	0.213	0.138

Notes: Asset classes are based on total ending assets from the Form 1120, Schedule L. All variables are as defined in Table 1.

scaling factor is assets, this pattern is probably spurious and caused by the fact that the returns in this table are categorized by the denominator of the deficiency rate (i.e., assets). To the extent that asset size mismeasures the ideal scaling factor, this will induce a negative association between assets and the deficiency/assets ratio.)

Panel B shows that the largest firms were also much less likely to have had their returns closed over our observation period: 36.2 percent (820/2,266) were open, compared to only 8.2 percent (1,894/23,000) for all other companies. As already noted, because a return is not closed until it is through both audit and appeals, it is not surprising that the returns of large and complex taxpayers remain open longer.

Although the largest companies were much more likely to have open returns, the proposed deficiency *rate* in those open cases was much less than for smaller companies, just 18.8 percent compared to rates ranging from 25.1 percent to 46.5 percent for the other asset-size classes. This pattern is consistent with the existence of a fixed cost of fighting a proposed deficiency, so that small firms will contest only proposed deficiencies that are relatively large compared to the size of their operations. Among closed returns, the proposed deficiency rate was slightly higher than average for the largest companies, and the fraction of these proposed deficiencies agreed to at exam shows no linear size-related pattern.

In interpreting these data, one must keep in mind two potentially confounding factors – the probability of audit and the intensity of audit, conditional on audit, may be related to the size of the company. This issue applies more generally to any characteristic that is correlated with the probability or conditional intensity of an audit. If the IRS is good at choosing for audit those companies with a higher probability of being noncompliant, then our data on audited firms will overstate the noncompliance rate among all firms, audited or not. This issue does not, however, apply to the approximately 1,200 companies in the CIC program, which are mostly audited at some level of intensity every year. For this group, the sample averages are much closer to the population characteristics.

For the (generally smaller) non-CIC companies, to the extent that the audit selection rules are effective at identifying those companies with higher tax deficiencies, the sample population of audited companies should have a higher proposed deficiency rate than a random sample of companies would have had, if subject to audit. Thus, we might draw an incorrect inference as to the relationship between size and noncompliance.

To investigate this issue further, in Panels C and D of Table 2 we repeat the cross-tabs for only the CIC companies. The data reveal that, similar to

Table 3. *Audit Results for Full Sample by Firm Characteristic*

Panel A: All Returns

	Total Obs.	% with Deficiency > 0	Deficiency / Assets	Deficiency / Sales	Obs. w/Prop. Tax > 0	% with Deficiency > 0	Deficiency / Prop. Tax	Agreed to at Exam / Deficiency
Private	17,041	52	0.0020	0.0025	14,410	62	0.171	0.265
Public	12,100	58	0.0015	0.0021	10,856	65	0.125	0.345
Domestic	23,892	56	0.0016	0.0021	21,054	64	0.125	0.343
Foreign-Controlled	5,249	47	0.0023	0.0027	4,212	59	0.254	0.202
Domestic	16,676	52	0.0013	0.0018	13,919	62	0.135	0.286
Multinational	12,465	58	0.0018	0.0025	11,347	64	0.137	0.333
Non-CIC	19,634	49	0.0013	0.0013	16,404	58	0.081	0.453
CIC	9,507	67	0.0017	0.0024	8,862	72	0.147	0.306
Agriculture	229	45	0.0010	0.0013	172	59	0.096	0.413
Mining & Utilities	2,975	59	0.0010	0.0023	2,694	65	0.090	0.285
Manufacturing	12,765	56	0.0020	0.0026	11,289	63	0.162	0.308
Trade & Transport.	7,192	55	0.0016	0.0014	6,182	64	0.133	0.319
Insurance & Other	4,250	50	0.0012	0.0024	3,530	60	0.087	0.421
Education & Health	676	45	0.0031	0.0048	527	58	0.221	0.275
Arts & Food Services	837	52	0.0016	0.0020	700	62	0.114	0.446
Other Services	217	43	0.0012	0.0015	172	54	0.068	0.442
TOTALS	29,141	55	0.0017	0.0022	25,266	63	0.136	0.320

Panel B: Closed versus Open Returns

	Closed Returns					Open Returns		
	Obs.	Deficiency / Prop. Tax	Agreed to at Exam / Deficiency	Agreed to at Appeals / Deficiency	Agreed / Final Tax	Obs.	Deficiency / Prop. Tax	Agreed to at Exam / Deficiency
Private	13,332	0.100	0.470	0.098	0.060	1,078	0.335	0.122
Public	9,220	0.092	0.495	0.119	0.058	1,636	0.175	0.228
Domestic	18,739	0.091	0.487	0.115	0.057	2,315	0.183	0.222
Foreign-Controlled	3,813	0.129	0.493	0.095	0.080	399	0.438	0.077
Domestic	12,798	0.104	0.394	0.106	0.055	1,121	0.202	0.168
Multinational	9,754	0.089	0.535	0.116	0.060	1,593	0.208	0.201
Non-CIC	15,346	0.055	0.688	0.062	0.042	1,058	0.213	0.138
CIC	7,206	0.104	0.459	0.120	0.063	1,656	0.207	0.198
Agriculture	155	0.066	0.499	0.156	0.044	17	0.413	0.267
Mining & Utilities	2,340	0.082	0.349	0.111	0.039	354	0.107	0.188
Manufacturing	10,028	0.104	0.520	0.123	0.069	1,261	0.257	0.171
Trade & Transport	5,698	0.091	0.414	0.095	0.048	484	0.234	0.231
Insurance & Other	3,092	0.074	0.592	0.086	0.051	438	0.101	0.284
Education & Health	465	0.105	0.528	0.049	0.063	62	0.331	0.199
Arts & Food Services	622	0.092	0.529	0.169	0.066	78	0.223	0.281
Other Services	152	0.047	0.595	0.085	0.032	20	0.224	0.201
TOTALS	22,552	0.094	0.487	0.113	0.059	2,714	0.207	0.193

Notes: *Public* includes those taxpayers whose Employer Identification Number (EIN) on Form 1120 matches the firm-year EIN on S&P Compustat and for which total financial statement assets (Data item 6) is nonmissing. If no EIN match is found for the firm on Compustat, the firm is classified as *Private*. Firms are classified as a Foreign-Controlled Corporation (FCC) if the answer to Question 7 on Form 1120 Schedule K is yes (the question asks whether during any time of the year one foreign person owned at least 25 percent of the stock of the company). If the answer to Question 7 is no, the firm is classified as *Domestic*. Firms are classified as being *Multinational* if they claim a foreign tax credit on Form 1120 or file Form 5471, indicating they owned a foreign subsidiary. If the firm does not claim an FTC or file a Form 5471, the firm is classified as *Domestic*. The CIC grouping of firms includes those firms that are part of the IRS's CICs (large-case audits). All other firms are labeled non-CIC firms. Industry classifications are taken from the North American Industrial Classification System (*NAICS*) codes, which are recorded in the IRS data for each return year.

189

the full sample, the largest companies have the greatest percentage of firms with a deficiency (75 percent versus a range of 51 percent to 68 percent for smaller-size groupings) and are much more likely to have had their returns remain open over our sample period (36.4 percent (777/2,136)) as compared to 13.1 percent (879/6,726) for all other companies. As before, the largest CIC taxpayers have a lower deficiency rate in the open years than the smaller companies (18.9 percent versus a range of 25.6 to 77.0 percent). However, in contrast to the full sample results described above, the largest firms within the CIC group do not have the highest deficiency rate for all returns (closed and open). For firms with a positive proposed tax, the largest firms' deficiency rate is 14.8 percent, while the smaller firms' rate ranges from 13.4 to (a notable outlier value of) 34.0 percent. Thus, the result that the largest firms in the full sample have the highest deficiency rate is apparently largely driven by the difference in the proposed deficiency rate between (large) CIC firms and (generally smaller) non-CIC firms.

The second confounding factor is the possibility that the intensity of an examination – and therefore the likelihood of uncovering a deficiency – depends on the reported tax situation of the company. It is not clear how, if at all, this biases the interpretation of the size-deficiency relationship. If there are economies of scale in examining big companies, then audit intensity of an audit might be larger for larger companies. On the other hand, like the independent auditors who certify financial statements, the Internal Revenue Service can only sample the transactions of a complex multinational taxpayer, so that the possibility of undetected noncompliance may increase.

Panels E and F complete the picture by detailing results for non-CIC firms. Again, the largest asset grouping has the highest percentage of firms with positive deficiency, the highest deficiency rate relative to other asset classes (10 percent versus a range of 6.2 percent to 9.8 percent), a much higher proportion of open returns (33 percent versus 6 percent for all other asset groups), and the lowest deficiency rate when considering only open returns (13 percent versus a range of 20.5 percent to 45.7 percent for the other groups).

4.3. Other Firm Characteristics

Table 3 presents audit data across partitions of firm characteristics other than size. The first comparison is private versus public companies. Considering only firms with a positive proposed tax (reported tax plus proposed deficiency), the data reveal that private companies have higher proposed deficiency rates than public companies (17.1 percent versus 12.5 percent), even though private companies have a lower proportion of firms with tax deficiencies (62 percent versus 65 percent).[19] The first result is consistent with Cloyd (1995) and Cloyd, Pratt, and Stock's (1996) survey results that privately held firms are more tax aggressive because they are less constrained by financial reporting incentives (i.e., they have fewer capital market pressures and thus can sacrifice reporting high financial accounting earnings and take more aggressive tax positions).

Panel B shows that public companies are much more likely to have their returns still open, with the percentage of open returns in our sample being 15.1 (1,636/10,856) percent versus 7.5 percent (1,078/14,410) for private companies. This is probably because public companies are generally larger and have a greater ability to contest the IRS proposals.

The next partition of Table 3 compares foreign-controlled companies (FCCs) and domestic companies. We classify a firm as foreign-controlled if the firm declares that its ownership is 25 percent or more foreign.[20] The data reveal that FCCs have a much greater aggregate deficiency ratio than domestic companies, even though a lower fraction of FCCs have a deficiency. For the subsample of observations that includes only firms with a positive proposed tax (the 25,266 observations), the FCCs have more than double the proposed deficiency rate as domestic companies, 25.4 percent versus 12.5 percent.[21] These results are consistent with Grubert, Goodspeed, and Swenson (1993) and Grubert (1999), who find that FCCs on average have lower rates of return (and thus lower tax liabilities) than U.S.-owned corporations. Although much of the lower relative rate of return can be explained by cross-sectional variables such as age, investment income, reliance on outside suppliers, dividends, and depreciation and interest expense differentials, Grubert (1999) suggests that between a quarter and a half of the difference cannot be explained by economic factors and may be due to more aggressive tax reporting (e.g., transfer pricing and income shifting). Mills and Newberry (2004) find that taxable income reported by FCCs is related to the incentives to shift in or out of the United States in response to the difference between the United States and the worldwide effective tax rate, consistent with FCCs responding to income-shifting opportunities.

---

[19] The private firms also have a larger aggregate deficiency over assets measure (0.19 percent versus 0.15 percent for public firms) and a slightly larger aggregate deficiency over sales measure (0.22 percent versus 0.21 percent).

[20] This comes from the answer to question 7 on Schedule K of Form 1120.

[21] The FCCs also have higher proposed deficiencies than domestic companies as a fraction of either sales or assets.

The separate analysis of open and closed returns in Panel B reveals that much of the difference between the FCCs and domestic firms can be attributed to the large difference in the proposed deficiency rate for the returns that are still open. Among this group of companies, the proposed deficiency rate is 43.8 percent for FCCs compared to the deficiency rate for open domestic firms of 18.3 percent.

The next partition of data compares multinational firms to domestic firms. We classify a company as multinational if it claimed a foreign tax credit or filed Form 5471 (indicating that it has a foreign subsidiary). Panel A of Table 3 reveals that for the subsample of firms with a positive proposed tax, a slightly higher percentage of multinational firms have a deficiency (64 percent) compared to domestic firms (62 percent). For this same sample, the aggregate proposed deficiency rate is only slightly higher for multinational firms (13.7 percent) versus domestic firms (13.5 percent), and multinational firms appear to settle at higher agreement percentages (33.3 percent) than domestic firms (28.6 percent).

We next partition the data between CIC firms and non-CIC firms. Consistent with the discussion above, the data reveal that for the subsample of firms with a positive tax, CIC firms have a higher proportion of firms with a deficiency (72 percent) relative to the non-CIC firms (58 percent), have a higher deficiency rate (14.7 percent versus 8.1 percent), and are less likely to agree to the deficiency upon exam (CIC firms agree on average with 30.6 percent of proposed deficiency, whereas non-CIC firms agree to 45.3 percent). Finally, a much higher percentage of CIC returns are still open during our sample period (18.7 percent (1,656/8,862)) compared to the non-CIC firms (6.5 percent (1,058/16,404)).[22]

---

[22] Our finding that for non-CIC companies 45.3 percent of the proposed deficiency is agreed to by the taxpayer at the exam stands in apparent contrast to the findings of GAO (1995) that estimates in Table II.9 that for non-CIC companies whose returns were examined between 1988 and 1994, 25 percent of the proposed deficiency is agreed to at exam. (The GAO report also includes an estimated "assessment rate," which apparently tracks the resolution of the appeals of unagreed amounts; however, because it does so only until 1994, it excludes many unresolved cases and thus suffers from a potentially severe sample selection bias, as we understand the compilation of the AIMS case data.) One reason why our estimates differ from those of the GAO is that the GAO study uses data on returns for which the audits (not the cases) were completed between 1988 and 1994, while we examine data for non-CIC firms that begin with the 1994 tax year; because the two samples do not overlap, our estimates will differ from GAO's to the extent that IRS or taxpayer behavior changed over this period. Indeed, the same GAO report indicates that the fraction of returns for which the taxpayer agreed to the proposed deficiency increased continually from 39 percent in 1988 to 51 percent in 1994. The percentage of the dollar amount agreed to by the taxpayer upon exam changed discontinuously over the period but was highest in 1994, when it reached 34 percent compared to the period average of 25 percent.

Table 3 also shows how the aggregate results differ by industry sector for eight single-digit North American Industry Classification System (NAICS) codes. While strong patterns do not emerge from this analysis, it appears that in aggregate, firms in the manufacturing industry; the trade, transportation, and warehousing industry; and the education, healthcare, and social assistance industry have a higher proposed deficiency rate and a lower proportion of deficiency agreed to upon exam relative to the other groups. As a result, we include industry effects in the regression analysis below.

5. The Determinants of Corporate Tax Noncompliance: Regression Analyses

5.1. Baseline Model and Variable Definitions

The cross-tabs presented in Tables 2 and 3, while suggestive, cannot provide a sense of the relationship between the proposed deficiency measures and any given company characteristic, holding other characteristics constant. For example, public companies, on average, are bigger than private companies, so the public-private and size breakdowns may reveal a mixture of the association with size and being public. To sort out the partial relationships, we turn to a multivariate regression analysis.

In so doing, we must address the potential problem that nonrandom sample selection may bias the regression results. One approach to this problem is to first estimate the probability that a given company will be audited and then, from the probit equation, construct an inverse Mill's ratio that is added to the equation that estimates noncompliance conditional on being audited. However, this method is unlikely to be convincing because it is difficult to identify independent variables that affect the probability of audit but do not affect the amount of noncompliance.

Rather than pursue this approach, we instead perform all the regression analyses both on the whole sample and then separately only on the CIC sample. For reasons already discussed, a large percentage of the CIC companies are audited every year, so the sample selection issue is not likely to be quantitatively important for the CIC subsample.[23] We estimate Tobit specifications, beginning with the same set of explanatory variables discussed in the previous section and some other variables that are discussed below.

---

[23] Although, note that Mills (1998) uses a Heckman two-stage test to control for sample selection bias even within the Coordinated Industry Cases, finding that size and profitability are the best predictors of full audits (versus surveyed returns). That is, tax returns with losses and smaller taxpayers are less frequently audited, even within the "large-case" audit population.

Our dependent variable is the proposed deficiency upon IRS audit scaled by one of two alternative measures of the size of the corporation: assets and sales.[24] We estimate the following model:

$$Deficiency/Scale = \alpha_0 + \alpha_1 LogAssets \ (or \ LogSales) + \alpha_2 CIC + \alpha_3 Public$$
$$+ \alpha_4 FCC + \alpha_5 Multinational + \alpha_6 - \alpha_{12} Sector + \varepsilon,$$

where

Deficiency	= the proposed tax deficiency, as recorded in the VCBLM database of the Internal Revenue Service,
Scale	= total year-end assets or sales per the tax returns
LogAssets (or *LogSales*)	= the natural logarithm of millions of dollars of total year-end assets or sales per the tax returns
CIC	= 1 if the taxpayer is a member of the Coordinated Industry Cases or its predecessor, the Coordinated Examination Program; 0 otherwise,
Public	= 1 if the taxpayer's EIN matches to a company in the Compustat database for whom total assets is present; 0 otherwise,
FCC	= 1 if the IRS designates the company as a U.S. foreign-controlled corporation on the basis of answering yes to question 7 in Schedule K of Form 1120, indicating that 25 percent or more of ownership is by a foreign person; 0 otherwise,
Multinational	= 1 if the taxpayer claims a foreign tax credit or files Form 5471, which must be filed by U.S. individuals, partnerships, corporations, and trusts with 5 percent or more stock ownership in a foreign corporation; 0 otherwise,
Sector	= 1 if the company is the relevant 1-digit North American Industry Classification System (NAICS) code from two through eight, omitting zero and nine; 0 otherwise.
Year	= 1 if the return is in a particular return year; 0 otherwise.

[24] We do not use the proposed deficiency rate (proposed deficiency/(tax reported + proposed deficiency)) as the dependent variable for two reasons. First, this ratio can be undefined when the reported tax and proposed deficiency are both zero, and it is not clear that we want to exclude these firms (i.e., we may overstate the rate of noncompliance if we leave them out of the analysis). Second, when the reported tax is zero but there is a proposed deficiency of any magnitude, the proposed deficiency rate becomes 100 percent, not distinguishing between firms that underreport $10 of tax and those that underreport $1 million of tax.

Prior to estimating the regression model above, we winsorize the continuous variables at the 1 percent and 99 percent values of their distributions by setting values outside those ranges to the values at those percentiles. Table 4 provides summary statistics for the winsorized regression variables and other variables of interest.

In order to minimize the spurious negative bias to the estimated effect of scale that results from errors in measuring the true scale variable, we use sales as the size measure when the dependent variable is scaled by assets and assets as the size measure when the dependent variable is scaled by sales.

5.2. Baseline Regression Results

Table 5 presents results for the baseline Tobit regressions, with and without the indicator variable for membership in the CIC, and for the CIC subsample only. The effect of size on the level of deficiency is positive and significant in the specifications that do not include the CIC variable separately, consistent with the CIC also proxying for size. Thus, on average, larger firms are more noncompliant than smaller firms, consistent with the reasonable explanation that larger, more complex firms have more opportunities for tax noncompliance (that is detected by the IRS) and consistent with the tendency noted in Table 2. In addition, we note that size remains positive and significant (at least at $p = 0.10$ for a two-tailed test) even when the model is estimated over only CIC firms, which suggests that size is more likely a determinant of noncompliance rather than just a determinant of being audited. The variable indicating that the firm is part of the CIC program is positive and significant after controlling for size. Thus, firms in the CIC have a greater deficiency on average than firms of the same size not in the CIC. This may be due to greater noncompliance or a higher intensity of audit for these firms.

As in the cross-tabulations of Table 3, public firms have smaller-scaled deficiencies in the full sample. This result is consistent with Cloyd (1995), Cloyd, Pratt, and Stock (1996), and Mills and Newberry's (2001) findings that private firms are less constrained by financial reporting incentives in their choices to be tax-aggressive. However, within the CIC subsample, controlling for other factors, public ownership does not explain deficiency when the deficiency/sales ratio is the dependent variable.

Within the full sample, after controlling for other factors, being a foreign-controlled corporation is negatively related to the tax deficiency. Note that this is the opposite of the finding reported in Table 3, where it appears that in aggregate the FCCs have a greater deficiency rate (in terms of assets,

Table 4. *Descriptive Statistics*

Variable	Obs.	Mean	Std. Deviation	Lower Quartile	Median	Upper Quartile
Deficiency / Assets	29,141	0.0020	0.0055	0.0000	0.0001	0.0013
Deficiency / Sales	29,141	0.0022	0.0068	0.0000	0.0001	0.0012
Log(Assets)	29,141	5.499	1.996	3.894	5.328	6.995
Log(Sales)	29,141	5.529	1.946	4.104	5.480	6.943
Assets ($ Millions)	29,141	1,623.500	4,244.680	49.116	206.001	1,091.340
Sales ($ Millions)	29,141	1,305.120	2,989.250	60.561	239.888	1,035.440
Coordinated Industry Cases	29,141	0.326	0.469	0	0	1
Public	29,141	0.415	0.493	0	0	1
FCC	29,141	0.180	0.384	0	0	0
Multinational	29,141	0.428	0.495	0	0	1
U.S. Current ETR	11,207	0.289	0.206	0.152	0.287	0.369
Advertising / Assets	11,515	0.013	0.033	0	0	0.006
R&D Expense / Assets	11,515	0.025	0.047	0	0	0.028
Market-to-Book Ratio	11,515	2.508	2.272	1.292	1.918	3.017
Bonus Percentage	3,875	0.228	0.151	0.112	0.226	0.328
Exercisable Option Sensitivity	3,842	0.110	0.182	0.011	0.044	0.125
Vested Holdings Sensitivity	3,869	0.648	1.388	0.076	0.204	0.547
Total Equity Sensitivity	3,875	0.768	1.466	0.116	0.291	0.728
Governance Index	3,875	7.283	4.685	4	8	11

Notes: All variables are winsorized at 1 percent and 99 percent, and ETRs are limited to be between 0 percent and 75 percent. *Coordinated Industry Cases, Public, FCC,* and *Multinational* are indicator variables set equal to 1 if the firm is identified as part of these groups (defined in Table 3), and set equal to 0 otherwise. *U.S. Current ETR* is the firm's effective tax rate calculated as the U.S. portion of current tax expense divided by U.S. pre-tax book income (Compustat data item 63 / data item 272). *Advertising* is the firm's advertising expense from their financial statements (Compustat data item 45). *R&D Expense* is the firm's research and development expense from their financial statements (Compustat data item 46). *Market-to-Book Ratio* is the firm's market value of equity divided by the book value of equity ((data item 99 × data item 25) / data item 60). *Bonus Percentage* is the proportion of compensation that is bonus. It is calculated as the sum over the five most highly paid executives of the annual bonus in the year prior to the year for which the tax deficiency is assessed, scaled by the sum of the bonus, salary, and the Black-Scholes value of the stock option grants for the five most highly paid executives in the year prior to the year for which the tax deficiency is assessed. *Exercisable Option Sensitivity* is the sensitivity of the holdings of exercisable (vested) executive stock options to a 1 percent change in stock price. This is the sum for the five most highly paid executives of the firm, and holdings are measured in the year prior to the year for which the deficiency is assessed. *Vested Holdings Sensitivity* is the sensitivity of the holdings of exercisable executive stock options and unrestricted stock to a 1 percent change in stock price. This is the sum for the five most highly paid executives of the firm, and holdings are measured in the year prior to the year for which the deficiency is assessed. *Total Equity Sensitivity* is the sensitivity of the holdings of all stock options, all unrestricted stock, and all restricted stock to a 1 percent change in stock price. This is the sum over the five most highly paid executives of the firm, and holdings are measured in the year prior to the year for which the deficiency is assessed. *Governance Index* is a measure of governance developed by Gompers, Ishii, and Metrick (2003). It is an index of shareholder rights that ranges from 0 to 24, a low value indicates high-quality governance. The index is set to 0 in regression when missing. *Governance Index Missing* is an indicator set equal to 1 if Governance Index is missing and 0 otherwise. All other variables are as defined in Tables 2 and 3.

Table 5. *Baseline Tobit Regressions (t-statistics in italics)*

Dependent Variable	Deficiency / Sales			Deficiency / Assets		
	Full Sample		CIC Only	Full Sample		CIC Only
Intercept	−0.0053	−0.0041	−0.0078	−0.0041	−0.0032	−0.0048
	−4.74	*−3.66*	*−3.52*	*−4.46*	*−3.49*	*−2.82*
Log (Size)	−0.0000	0.0002	0.0002	0.00004	0.00019	0.0001
	−0.67	*5.05*	*2.52*	*0.99*	*5.08*	*1.70*
CIC	0.0032	*dropped*	NA	0.0020	dropped	NA
	11.24			*8.78*		
Public	−0.0011	−0.0011	−0.0002	−0.0013	−0.0013	−0.0004
	−6.98	*−6.57*	*−0.87*	*−10.39*	*−9.72*	*−2.17*
FCC	−0.0009	−0.00095	−0.0002	−0.0013	−0.0013	−0.0005
	−4.89	*−5.12*	*−0.65*	*−8.49*	*−8.36*	*−1.76*
Multinational	0.0004	0.0005	0.0016	0.0002	0.0003	0.0013
	2.75	*3.08*	*6.81*	*1.97*	*2.43*	*7.25*
Return Year Dummies			Untabulated			
1-digit NAICS Codes			Untabulated			
Observations	29,141	29,141	9,507	29,141	29,141	9,507
L. R. Chi-squared	810.56	684.63	163.12	660.47	583.67	170.45

Note: Variables are as defined in Tables 2–4.

sales, and proposed deficiency rate) than domestic firms. This suggests that the FCCs are notably different from domestic companies with respect to other characteristics that are associated with our measure of noncompliance. Indeed, in untabulated results we find that FCCs are on average smaller, have a greater percentage of zero deficiencies, and have a greater percentage of zero tax paid on the return. Again, within the CIC subsample, controlling for other factors, FCC does not explain deficiency when the deficiency/sales ratio is the dependent variable.

The results for the multinationality variable are generally consistent with multinational firms having greater deficiencies. In the full sample, being a multinational firm is significantly positively associated with the level of deficiency. In the CIC-only subsample, the estimated coefficient on multinationality is also positive and significant, indicating that within the firms of the CIC program the multinational firms have a greater deficiency rate.

Although not presented in the interest of brevity, we note that in some specifications (specifically when the deficiency/assets ratio is the dependent variable), the industry effects are significant and that the year-effect coefficients are generally significant as well. In all cases, the model chi-squared statistic is higher if the industry and year effects are included.[25]

5.3. Additional Variable Definitions: Intangibles, Executive Compensation, and Governance

In this section, we add measures of intangible intensity, executive compensation and equity incentives, and governance quality as explanatory variables into the regression specification above to expand our understanding of the determinants of tax noncompliance as measured by proposed deficiency rates. These variables are only available for publicly traded firms with data available on Compustat or Execucomp. Those variables are defined as follows:

Advertising/Scale = advertising expense (Compustat data item 45) / assets (data item 6) or sales (data item 12).

R&D Expense/Scale = research and development (R&D) expense (Compustat data item 46) scaled by assets (data item 6) or sales (data item 12). If R&D expense is missing, we reset the value to 0.

Market-to-Book = market value of the firm at the end of the year (price per share, Compustat data item 199 × common shares outstanding, data item 25), divided by book value of equity (data item 60).

Bonus Percentage = proportion compensation that is bonus. Calculated as the sum over the five most highly paid executives of the annual bonus in the year prior to the year for which the tax deficiency is assessed scaled by the sum of the bonus, salary, and the Black-Scholes value of the stock option grants for the five executives in the year prior to the year for which the tax deficiency is assessed.

Exercisable Option Sensitivity = the sensitivity of the holdings of exercisable (vested) executive stock options to a 1 percent change in stock

---

[25] Because Mills (1998) finds that loss firms are audited less frequently than firms with positive taxable income, we also estimate a model that includes the variable reported tax/scale to control for the revenue potential of the firm. We expect that the IRS is more likely to audit high-tax firms more than low-tax firms. In untabulated results we find that, consistent with our conjecture, this variable is highly positively significant in all specifications. The other estimated coefficients are not greatly affected, although size becomes more significantly positive and multinationality becomes significantly negative in the model that does not include a CIC dummy variable.

price. This is the sum for the five most highly paid executives of the firm, and holdings are measured in the year prior to the year for which the deficiency is assessed. (The computation of sensitivity is explained in more detail below.)

Vested Holdings Sensitivity = the sensitivity of the holdings of exercisable executive stock options and unrestricted stock to a 1 percent change in stock price. This is the sum for the five most highly paid executives of the firm, and holdings are measured in the year prior to the year for which the deficiency is assessed. (The computation of sensitivity is explained in more detail below.)

Total Equity Sensitivity = the sensitivity of the holdings of all stock options, all unrestricted stock, and all restricted stock to a 1 percent change in stock price. This is the sum over the five most highly paid executives of the firm, and holdings are measured in the year prior to the year for which the deficiency is assessed. (The computation of sensitivity is explained in more detail below.)

Governance Index = measure of governance developed by Gompers, Ishii, and Metrick (2003). It is an index of shareholder rights that ranges from 1 to 24, a low value indicates high-quality governance – set to 0 in regression when missing.

Governance Index Missing = indicator set equal to 1 if Governance Index is missing, and 0 otherwise.

The calculation of the sensitivity of executive equity holdings to a change in stock price warrants further explanation. The expected wealth change from stock is estimated by multiplying the market value of the stock holdings at year-end (the year prior to the alleged accounting fraud for the alleged fraud firms) by 1 percent. For stock options, we use the method of calculating their sensitivity to stock price as described by Core and Guay (2002). Although details such as the number of options, exercise price, and time to maturity are available from Execucomp or the current-year proxy statement for current-year grants, much of these data are unavailable in the current-year proxy statement for prior grants. The 1-year approximation method described in Core and Guay (1999, 2002) requires information only from the most recent proxy statement to estimate the sensitivity of the option portfolio to a change in stock price. The sensitivity to stock price for each option held is estimated as

$$[\partial(optionvalue)/\partial(price)] \times [price \times 0.01] = e^{-dT}N(Z) \times [price \times 0.01]$$

where d is the natural logarithm of expected dividend yield over the life of the option, T is the time to maturity of the option in years, N is the cumulative normal probability function and Z is $[\ln(S/X) + T(r - d + \sigma^2/2)]/\sigma T^{1/2}]$, where S is the price of the underlying stock, X is the exercise price of the option, r is the natural logarithm of the risk-free interest rate, and σ is the expected stock-return volatility over the life of the option.

5.4. Results for Additional Variables

In Table 6, we introduce proxies for the tax planning opportunities afforded by firms that develop intangible assets, proxies for executive compensation contracts and equity holding incentives, and proxies for the governance quality at the firm. We present results only for the specifications in which the deficiency/sales ratio is the dependent variable. (In untabulated regressions using the deficiency/assets ratio as the dependent variable, the results are qualitatively similar, except where noted.) We first re-estimate the baseline regression over only those observations having the additional variables to confirm that the results from Table 5 hold for this subsample. This analysis is presented in the first column of Table 6. The results are qualitatively similar to Table 5. We also find that the results for our baseline variables are consistent with those reported in Table 5 when the new variables are included, indicating that they are not omitted correlated variables for our main variables of interest.

Intangible Assets
For intangible asset proxies, we use three variables: (1) the ratio of research and development expense (R&D expense) to the scale measure (assets or sales); (2) the ratio of advertising expense to the scale measure; and (3) the market-to-book ratio. We predict that firms with more intangible assets will have greater opportunities for tax planning, consistent with Grubert and Slemrod's (1998) finding in the context of Puerto Rico subsidiaries of U.S. parents that the presence of intangible assets facilitates transfer pricing.

The coefficients on R&D expense and the market-to-book ratio are significantly positive, indicating that the greater the intangible assets of the firm, the greater the tax deficiency, consistent with these firms having greater tax planning opportunities. However, the results for advertising expense are

Table 6. *Tobit Regression with Additional Variables. Dependent Variable: Deficiency / Sales (t-statistics in italics)*

Compensation Variable	Baseline Regression	Bonus Percentage	Exercisable Option Sensitivity	Vested Holdings Sensitivity	Total Equity Sensitivity
Intercept	−0.0073	−0.0102	−0.0080	−0.0095	−0.0095
	−3.22	−4.35	−3.44	−4.10	−4.08
Log (Assets)	0.0002	0.0003	0.0002	0.0003	0.0003
	1.35	2.29	1.61	2.23	2.06
CIC	0.0026	0.0021	0.0022	0.0021	0.0021
	7.45	6.07	6.31	6.19	6.08
FCC	−0.0031	−0.0035	−0.0034	−0.0035	−0.0034
	−2.78	−3.12	−3.03	−3.12	−3.11
Multinational	0.0010	0.0005	0.0006	0.0006	0.0006
	2.94	1.53	1.70	1.77	1.71
R&D Expense /		0.0173	0.0150	0.0164	0.0161
Assets		5.63	4.88	5.39	5.29
Advertising / Assets		−0.0073	−0.0078	−0.0077	−0.0080
		−1.89	−2.05	−2.03	−2.09
Market-to-Book		0.0004	0.0004	0.0004	0.0004
		6.81	6.14	6.39	6.19
Compensation		0.0024	0.0018	0.0002	0.0002
Variable		2.82	2.33	1.64	2.60
Governance Index		−0.0012	−0.0012	−0.0011	−0.0010
Missing		−2.02	−2.05	−1.78	−1.67
Governance Index		−0.0001	−0.0001	−0.0001	−0.0000
(0 if Missing)		−1.37	−1.28	−1.09	−0.95
Return Year Dummies			Untabulated		
1-digit NAICS Codes			Untabulated		
Observations	3,875	3,860	3,830	3,857	3,860
L. R. Chi-squared	187.85	293.78	292.19	288.14	292.56

Note: Variables are as defined in Tables 2–4.

marginally negatively significant, which is inconsistent with this explanation. One explanation is that firms with more advertising expense are more likely to be consumer products firms. As a result, these firms may be more compliant in efforts to avoid negative publicity from being a "bad" corporate citizen.

Executive Compensation
Executive compensation contracts may be set to induce or prevent tax avoidance activities on the part of firm management. In discussing the incentives that affected Enron, the Joint Committee on Taxation noted that Enron's

tax department was viewed as a profit center by the firm. This observation is consistent with increasing pressure of firms to report a relatively low effective tax rate during the 1990s.[26] Phillips (2003) provides evidence consistent with firms whose managers' bonus payments are based on after-tax income reporting lower effective tax rates. In other work, Desai and Dharmapala (2006) investigate the relationship between incentive compensation and proxies for tax sheltering. To examine the association between the form of executive compensation and tax noncompliance, we include measures of executive compensation in our regressions.

For compensation, we include four different proxies each in a separate regression: (1) bonus percentage; (2) exercisable option sensitivity; (3) vested holding sensitivity; and (4) total equity sensitivity, all defined above.[27] Table 6 shows that only total vested holding sensitivity is insignificant ($p = 0.101$), with the other three variables being positively related to the amount of tax deficiency, providing preliminary evidence that executive compensation is positively related to tax noncompliance.[28]

Governance Quality

Finally, we investigate whether the governance characteristics of the firm affect the level of noncompliance. To do so, we include the governance index compiled by Gompers, Ishii, and Metrick (2003). This index is a score ranging from 1 to 24 that combines data from the Investor Responsibility Research Center (IRRC) on firms' takeover defenses with information on antitakeover provisions in state statutes to calculate an index that reflects the extent to which the firm is protected from hostile takeovers. A lower value of the index indicates a higher quality governance (see Gompers, Ishii, and Metrick, 2003, for more details). If better-governed firms take fewer aggressive positions, we expect that better-governed firms will have lower tax deficiencies.

---

[26] For example, the Council for International Tax Education, Inc. previously publicized seminars designed to help corporations plan for lowering effective tax rates. However, as of 2005, the programs on their Web site (http://www.citeusa.org/programs/index.html) are more concerned with tax, financial reporting, and Sarbanes-Oxley compliance. Their SFAS109 course still includes a bullet "Using Export Sales to Reduce the Effective Tax Rate."

[27] See Erickson, Hanlon, and Maydew (2006) for a full discussion of how these variables relate to management incentives and may affect accounting aggressiveness.

[28] We recognize that the choice of compensation contract is endogenous in this regression. We include some likely controls for the type of compensation, such as book-to-market and research and development, which proxy for investment opportunity set. We leave a more detailed analysis of compensation more formally dealing with the endogeneity issue for future research.

Table 6 shows that governance is not associated with the tax deficiency, indicating that governance quality of the firm does not alter the level of tax aggressiveness. However, because our sample period is prior to the passage of the Sarbanes-Oxley Act, we cannot test whether this relation became more important after its passage.[29]

6. Correlations among Measures of Tax Aggressiveness

The data examined in this chapter are one indicator of a company's tax aggressiveness. This indicator has the advantage of being based on extensive audits of a company's tax filings (and any subsequent appeals of the examination results), but for reasons we have already discussed, it is not perfect. Because these data are confidential, past researchers have for the most part relied on other indicators of tax aggressiveness that can be constructed from publicly available data. The most common of such indicators include the firm's effective tax rate, measured in a variety of ways, and the firm's book-tax differences, perhaps adjusted for known differences in these concepts that are not indicative of tax aggressiveness (see Plesko, 2003 and Desai and Dharmapala, 2006, for examples). In this section, we examine whether effective tax rates are associated with the audit-based measure studied in this chapter. In other words, does the tax aggressiveness that results in high audit deficiencies result in a low effective tax rate for the firm?

Effective tax rate measures based on financial statement information may not provide a good proxy for tax noncompliance. Depending on how it is defined, the numerator, total taxes, may reveal little about actual tax liability because it includes the effect of deferred taxes (i.e., future deductible and future taxable amounts). Moreover, even if one defines the numerator to

---

[29] Desai and Dharmapala (2006) (known as DD) develop a model and provide supporting empirical evidence based on book-tax differences from financial statements as a measure of tax aggressiveness, in which increasing the extent of incentive compensation can decrease the level of tax sheltering for firms with relatively poor governance. To investigate the interaction between governance and incentive compensation, we estimate a model including an indicator variable for well-governed firms (those with a governance score of 7 or below, consistent with DD), by itself and interacted with the compensation variables in Table 6. We find some evidence consistent with their premise in that well-governed firms have a more positive association between vested option sensitivity and our measure of deficiency, meaning well-governed firms engage in more avoidance when their compensation incentives are high relative to poorly governed firms. However, overall the results are mixed because in the other two equity incentive specifications the interaction term is insignificant and, in the bonus regression (not tested by DD), the interaction term is negative, meaning managers in well-governed firms avoid fewer taxes when the bonus is higher.

include only current taxes payable, in many cases this will not approximate the actual tax liability of the firm.[30] One important reason for this difference for our purposes is that when firms take an aggressive tax reporting position that they expect is probable of being denied, they are required for financial accounting purposes to accrue the estimated loss in the current period even though the tax is not being paid currently.[31] Thus, the aggressive position would not be fully reflected as a decrease in the firm's effective tax rate. As a result, it is an empirical question as to the association of tax deficiency and ETR.

Further, one must be cautious about how to interpret any observed correlation between ETR and proposed deficiency. For example, it is possible that the level of reported ETR affects the intensity of the audit examination and therefore the amount of deficiency uncovered, because a low ETR may be a signal to the IRS that the company has taken aggressive positions (even though the company is aware that a low ETR provides this signal, and the IRS is aware that the company is aware, etc.).[32] Conversely, as discussed above, it may be that the IRS is more likely to intensively examine companies that already have a substantial positive tax liability. In the extreme, uncovering an income understatement by a company making losses and that has exhausted its loss carryback capacity is unlikely to generate much revenue in a present-value sense. More generally, the more profitable a firm, the more likely is it true that uncovering a taxable income understatement will lead to a recovery of unpaid taxes.

We calculate a firm's effective tax rate using U.S. current tax expense divided by the firm's U.S. pre-tax income (U.S. current ETR). Because the audit data is U.S. only, we use the U.S.-based measure rather than the worldwide measure.[33] We delete observations for which the denominator of the ETR measure is negative, because the ratio becomes uninterpretable. In

---

[30] See Hanlon (2003) for a detailed explanation of why a firm's financial statements cannot be used to infer tax liabilities or taxable income in many cases. One material example is the effect of stock options.

[31] See Financial Accounting Standard Boards (1975): *Accounting for Contingencies.* In addition, see the Financial Accounting Standards Board's (2006) Financial Interpretation No. 48: *Accounting for Uncertainty in Income Taxes* which takes effect in 2007 and requires firms to disclose reserves for uncertain tax benefits. Gleason and Mills (2002) discuss how little the taxpayers disclose to shareholders about large tax deficiencies, even when they appear to be material.

[32] Mills and Sansing (2000) adopt such a game-theoretic approach to analyzing the effect of book-tax differences on audit outcomes.

[33] Although using a worldwide measure (untabulated), we find similar relationships between deficiency and the worldwide ETR as described above for the U.S. current ETR.

Table 7. *Correlation Matrix of Deficiency-Based Measures and ETRs*
(t-statistics in italics)

	Deficiency / Prop. Tax	Deficiency / Assets	Deficiency / Sales
Panel A: All Observations			
U.S. Current ETR	−0.095	0.027	0.055
P-Value	*0.0000*	*0.0034*	*0.0000*
Observations	10,545	11,778	11,778
Panel B: Observations with Positive Taxable Income (L.28)			
U.S. Current ETR	−0.055	−0.005	0.022
P-Value	*0.00*	*0.6412*	*0.0268*
Observations	9,737	9,776	9,776

Note: Variables are defined as in Tables 3 and 4.

addition, to ensure that our results are not unduly influenced by outliers, we reset any values greater than 75 percent to 75 percent and any values less than zero 0 to 0.

We first present in Table 7 simple correlations between the deficiency/proposed tax, deficiency/assets, or deficiency/sales ratios and the ETR measure. The correlation between the ETR and deficiency/proposed tax ratio is negative, consistent with lower ETRs representing more tax aggressive behavior, although this correlation could be caused by a small-denominator problem. If a zero-ETR corporation pays no tax on the return as originally filed, but has $1 (or any amount) of tax deficiency, the ratio of deficiency/proposed tax is its maximum value of 100 percent. In contrast, we find that the correlations between the ETR measure and our tax deficiency/assets and tax deficiency/sales measures are positive. This is not consistent with the tax aggressiveness reflected in the deficiency measure causing the firm to have a low effective tax rate.

To examine whether there is a relation between a firm's ETR and its proposed deficiency rate, holding other influencing factors constant, we next estimate a regression of each ETR measure on the tax deficiency measure and other controls. We first estimate the regression over all firms, and then we delete observations with negative or zero taxable income (Form 1120, Line 28) in order to eliminate the effect of loss firms.

The regression results, presented in Table 8, Column 1, reveal that the tax deficiency/sales variable is significantly positively related to the ETR measure when all return-years are included. Thus, consistent with the univariate

Table 8. *ETR Regressions (t-statistics in italics)*

	Tobit over All Available Observations (1)	Tobit over Positive Taxable Income Observations (L.28) (2)
Dependent variable (ETR) defined as	USCurETR	USCurETR
Intercept	0.0205	0.0431
	0.47	*1.10*
Deficiency / Sales	0.8502	−0.4339
	2.27	*−1.39*
Log (Assets)	0.0032	−0.0007
	1.86	*−0.45*
CIC	0.0022	−0.0037
	0.27	*−0.54*
FCC	−0.0390	−0.0110
	−2.94	*−0.92*
Multinational	0.0638	0.0261
	12.6	*5.84*
R&D Expense / Assets	0.0748	0.3823
	1.43	*8.04*
Advertising / Assets	0.0382	0.1589
	0.56	*2.74*
Market-to-Book	0.0059	−0.0020
	5.68	*−2.11*
Return Year Dummies	Untabulated	Untabulated
1-Digit NAICS Codes	Untabulated	Untabulated
Observations	11,208	9,346
L. R. Chi-squared	461.01	408.29

Note: Variables are defined as in Tables 3 and 4.

correlations, we find that the greater the tax deficiency (the more tax aggressive the firm) the higher the ETR, inconsistent with the ETR being an indicator of tax aggressiveness as measured by the proposed tax deficiency. This result could occur if a high ETR attracts a more intense audit because the IRS believes the revenue gains are greatest for these firms. Another explanation is that tax aggressive firms will record a tax cushion in order to provide an accounting reserve for its tax aggressive position. While this would not explain the positive relation, it does explain why a negative relation is not observed.

In Table 8, Column 2, where the loss firms are eliminated, the relation of the deficiency rate to the U.S. current ETR is insignificant, again providing no evidence consistent with financial statement ETRs reflecting the same noncompliance as shown in the deficiency rates from our data.

7. Conclusions

This chapter offers some exploratory analysis of an extraordinarily rich dataset of audit and appeals records, matched with tax returns and financial statements, of several thousand corporations. As with any exploratory analysis, it has raised at least as many questions as it has provided definitive answers. But it has provided preliminary answers to several important questions.

First, it has confirmed that corporate tax noncompliance, at least as measured by deficiencies proposed upon examination, amounts to approximately 13 percent of "true" tax liability. That estimate is in line with official IRS tax gap measures, which in one way is not surprising because the tax gap measures were largely based on audit data, but provides new information because the official IRS measures are in part based on nearly two-decade-old data.

Second, noncompliance is generally a progressive phenomenon, meaning that noncompliance as a fraction of a scale measure increases with the size of the company. Combined with other information that the noncompliance rate among very small businesses is significantly higher than 13 percent suggests that business tax noncompliance relative to scale is U-shaped, with medium-sized businesses having the lowest rate of noncompliance. This pattern is not consistent with noncompliance being an inframarginal benefit to doing business and implies that the opportunity for noncompliance provides some implicit subsidy to achieving greater scale through investment.

Third, noncompliance is related to some observable characteristics of companies, including sector and two measures of the presence of intangible assets. This suggests that the private benefits of successful tax noncompliance by any given firm are to some extent competed away because similar firms find tax noncompliance to be similarly available. Being a private company is also associated with higher noncompliance, corroborating the common suspicion that private companies are less affected by the financial reporting incentives to publicly report high earnings, which in turn constrains the ability to report low earnings to the IRS.

Fourth, we find some evidence that incentivized executive compensation schemes are associated with more tax noncompliance. We find no relation between a commonly studied measure of the quality of corporate governance and the extent of proposed (scaled) tax deficiency.

Finally, we find that there is no consistent simple or partial negative association between our measure of tax noncompliance and measures of the effective tax rate calculated from financial statements. This might mean that the financial statements are uninformative about tax aggressiveness, in part because of the tax cushion for future adverse judgments that is included in the tax expense amount on the financial statements. In addition, it may be that publicly available ETR measures affect the aggressiveness with which the IRS pursues tax noncompliance.

There are many reasons why we offer these conclusions with such tentativeness; we close by mentioning two. One is that our central measure of tax noncompliance is in fact the result of an imperfect and perhaps systematically intense audit of a tax return declaration that may itself be the opening bid in what is expected, often correctly, to be an intense negotiation and formal appeals process. Second, the causal links among tax aggressiveness, executive compensation, and corporate governance are potentially complex, and the analysis presented here at best establishes statistical associations, but certainly does not establish causal relations. Answering these, and other, questions in future research should help to clarify the magnitude and nature of corporate tax noncompliance as well as its economic and policy implications.

References

Cloyd, C. Bryan. 1995. "The Effects of Financial Accounting Conformity on Recommendations of Tax Preparers." *Journal of the American Taxation Association* 17(2): 50–70.

Cloyd, C. Bryan, Jamie Pratt, and Toby Stock. 1996. "The Use of Financial Accounting Choice to Support Aggressive Tax Positions: Public and Private Firms." *Journal of Accounting Research* 34(1): 23–43.

Core, John, and Wayne Guay. 1999. "The Use of Equity Grants to Manage Optimal Equity Incentive Levels." *Journal of Accounting and Economics* 28(2): 151–184.

Core, John, and Wayne Guay. 2002. "Estimating the Value of Employee Stock Option Portfolios and Their Sensitivities to Price and Volatility." *Journal of Accounting Research* 40(3): 613–630.

Desai, Mihir A., and Dhammika Dharmapala. 2006. "Corporate Tax Avoidance and High Powered Incentives." *Journal of Financial Economics* 79(1): 145–179.

Erickson, Merle, Michelle Hanlon, and Edward Maydew. 2006. "Is There a Link Between Executive Compensation and Accounting Fraud?" *Journal of Accounting Research* 44(1): 113–143.

Financial Accounting Standards Board. 1975. Statement of Financial Accounting Standards No. 5: "Accounting for Contingencies." (Norwalk, CT: FASB).

Financial Accounting Standards Board. 2006. Financial Interpretation No. 48: "Accounting for Uncertainty in Income Taxes." (Norwalk, CT: FASB).

Gergen, Mark P. 2002. "The Logic of Deterrence: Corporate Tax Shelters." *Tax Law Review* 55(2): 255–288.

Gleason, Cristi, and Lillian Mills. 2002. "Materiality and Contingent Tax Liability Reporting." *Accounting Review* 77(2): 317–342.

Gompers, Paul, Joy Ishii, and Andrew Metrick. 2003. "Corporate Governance and Equity Prices." *Quarterly Journal of Economics* 118(1): 107–155.

Grubert, Harry. 1999. "Another Look at the Low Taxable Income of Foreign-Controlled Companies in the United States." In *Proceedings of the Ninety-First Annual Confrence on Taxation 1998.* (Washington, DC: National Tax Association – Tax Institute of America), pp. 157–175.

Grubert, Harry, and Joel Slemrod. 1998. "The Effect of Taxes on Investment and Income Shifting to Puerto Rico." *Review of Economics and Statistics* 80(3): 365–373.

Grubert, Harry, Timothy Goodspeed, and Deborah Swenson. 1993. "Explaining the Low Taxable Income of Foreign-Controlled Companies in the United States." In Alberto Giovannini, R. Glenn Hubbard, and Joel Slemrod, eds., *Studies in International Taxation.* (Chicago: University of Chicago Press), pp. 237–275.

Hanlon, Michelle. 2003. "What Can We Infer about a Firm's Taxable Income from Its Financial Statements?" *National Tax Journal* 54(4): 831–864.

Hines, James R., Jr. 2004. "On the Timeliness of Tax Reform." *Journal of Public Economics* 88(5): 1043–1059.

Mills, Lillian. 1998. "Book-Tax Differences and Internal Revenue Service Adjustments." *Journal of Accounting Research* 36(2): 343–356.

Mills, Lillian, and Kaye Newberry. 2001. "The Influence of Tax and Nontax Costs on Book-Tax Reporting Differences: Public and Private Firms." *Journal of the American Taxation Association* 23(1): 1–19.

Mills, Lillian, and Kaye Newberry. 2004. "Do Foreign Multinationals' Tax Incentives Influence Their U.S. Income Reporting and Debt Policy?" *National Tax Journal* 57(1): 89–107.

Mills, Lillian, and Richard Sansing. 2000. "Strategic Tax and Financial Reporting Decisions: Theory and Evidence." *Contemporary Accounting Research* 17(1): 85–106.

Mills, Lillian, Merle Erickson, and Edward Maydew. 1998. "Investments in Tax Planning." *Journal of the American Taxation Association* 20(1): 1–20.

Petrick, Kenneth. A. 2002. "Corporate Profits: Profits Before Tax, Profits Tax Liability, and Dividends." Methodology Paper. (Washington, DC: U.S. Department of Commerce, Economics and Statistics Administration, Bureau of Economic Analysis).

Phillips, John. 2003. "Corporate Tax Planning Effectiveness: The Role of Compensation-Based Incentives." *Accounting Review* 78(July): 847–874.

Plesko, George. 2003. "Estimates of the Magnitude of Financial and Tax Reporting Conflicts." Working paper. (Cambridge, MA: Massachusetts Institute of Technology).

Rice, Eric. 1992. "The Corporate Tax Gap: Evidence on Tax Compliance by Small Corporations." In Joel Slemrod, ed., *Why People Pay Taxes.* (Ann Arbor: University of Michigan Press), pp. 125–161.

Slemrod, Joel. 2001. "A General Model of the Behavioral Response to Taxation." *International Tax and Public Finance* 8(2): 119–128.

Slemrod, Joel. 2004. "The Economics of Corporate Tax Selfishness." *National Tax Journal* 57(4): 877–899.

Slemrod, Joel, and Marsha Blumenthal. 1996. "The Income Tax Compliance Cost of Big Business." *Public Finance Quarterly* 24(4): 411–438.

Slemrod, Joel, Estelle Dauchy, and Claudia Martinez. 2005. "Corporate Tax Avoidance and the Effectiveness of Tax Incentives for Investment." Mimeo. (Ann Arbor: University of Michigan).

Tannenwald, Robert, with Jeannette Hargroves, Rachel Cononi, Pamela Larson, and Michele Mongiello. 1993. "Corporate Tax Disclosure: Good or Bad for the Commonwealth?" Paper prepared for the Massachusetts Special Commission on Business Tax Policy, May 28, Boston.

U.S. Department of the Treasury, Internal Revenue Service. 2004. "Interactive Tax Gap Map." (Washington, DC: U.S. DOT, National Headquarters, Office of Research).

U.S. General Accounting Office. 1988. "IRS' Tax Gap Studies." GAO/GGD-88-66BR. (Washington, DC: U.S. GAO).

U.S. General Accounting Office. 1995. "Audit Trends and Taxes Assessed on Large Corporations." GAO/GGD-96-6. (Washington, DC: U.S. GAO).

Comments

Joseph Bankman[1]
Stanford University

The authors here have provided a treasure trove of information with which to analyze important topics, ranging from how we collect taxes from corporations to the determinants of corporate tax aggressiveness. Their chapter does a terrific "first run" at the topic. It clearly frames issues, provides the information most of us would be most interested in, tests leading hypotheses, and so on. Future papers by the same authors will no doubt provide additional data and follow up on some of the questions raised by this chapter. With this (justified) high praise as an anchor for this commentary, I'd like to briefly discuss some inherent limitations of the data or analysis and then comment on some of the most significant findings.

1. Limitations of Data or Analysis

The authors do not provide time-series data, and as a result we do not get an idea of how, if at all, corporate tax aggressiveness and government enforcement behavior might have changed during the 15 years of their study. This is a potentially significant issue because there is some anecdotal and some hard evidence that the behavior of both sets of actors changed a great deal during this period. For example, beginning in 1992, the midpoint in their dataset, the government is widely thought to have aggressively pursued capitalization issues in the wake of an important Supreme Court decision: *INDOPCO v. Commissioner*.[2] Bankman (2003). In the middle and late years of that same decade, corporations are thought to have heavily invested in tax shelters, with the government responding to that behavior in the late years of that decade (Bankman, 2004). The authors correctly note the many

---

[1] Ralph M. Parsons Professor of Law and Business, Stanford Law School.
[2] *INDOPCO v. Commissioner*, 503 U.S. 79 (1992).

problems of attributing deficiencies to a single year, and they control for the year in their regressions. But I believe that a nuanced view of the issue requires time-series data. I do not believe the imperfections in that approach are so great as to outweigh its usefulness.

A more important limitation, which the authors note, is that the data tells us only the deficiencies found by the IRS on audit and the collections on those deficiencies. The data do not tell us the extent of actual corporate non-compliance. The authors sensibly compare their findings with estimates of noncompliance (which are also audit-based) from the Bureau of Economic Analysis and IRS estimates on the basis of the old Taxpayer Compliance Management Program data and other sources.

Manzon and Plesko (2002) have attempted to get a grip on tax shelters and other forms of noncompliance by looking at the gap between so-called "book" income (e.g., income reported under financial accounting standards) and taxable income (as inferred from other financial accounting data). The difference between these measures, after adjusting for depreciation, stock options, and other clearly permissible tax-planning techniques, and a host of other more specialized adjustments, is taken as a measure of evasion or at least aggressiveness. Other researchers, including Desai (2003) and Desai and Dharmapala (2006), have also used financial reporting data to estimate noncompliance. The great advantage of this technique is that, in theory, it can capture noncompliance that is undetected on audit. The great disadvantage is that there is no way of knowing whether it captures any noncompliance. One of the most interesting findings in this chapter is the suggestion that the financial reporting measures relied upon in these studies may not be correlated to noncompliance in the manner hypothesized by the authors of those studies.

Graham and Tucker (2006) avoid this latter problem, the danger of wrongfully inferring noncompliance from financial data, by looking only at publicly available information, chiefly from judicial records, that shows that a corporation has engaged in a shelter and gotten caught. Their approach yields a great deal of qualitative information that is missing from the authors' dataset. For example, their data can show not only that Y corporation had a $33 million deficiency, but that the deficiency was comprised of a tax shelter purchased from Investment Bank Z and used to offset gain on the sale of a subsidiary, that the shelter took advantage of a misreading of a certain regulation, and so on. The obvious disadvantage to their approach is that it covers only the tiny subset of deficiencies that are litigated or for some other reason publicly disclosed.

The IRS data the authors have are clearly the single best indicator of tax noncompliance. But the data are far from perfect. Ideally, this chapter would be paired with a careful examination and analysis of IRS enforcement strategies. To take but one issue, we know that IRS enforcement resources are redeployed from time to time – witness, for example, the recently constructed Office of Tax Shelter Analysis. It would be useful to know the determinants of this shift. Presumably, the shift is designed to maximize revenue, but how much revenue is lost by this kind of redeployment? More generally, how much does adherence to a cost–benefit rule of thumb (such as pegging enforcement so that, at the margin, $1 of enforcement yields $5 of revenue) cost in foregone revenue? Are there known concentrated pockets of noncompliance in the corporate sector that are left undisturbed under such a formula?

For obvious reasons, the IRS is loathe to provide a roadmap of its enforcement strategy, but without some idea of that strategy it is difficult to evaluate the fruits of enforcement efforts. Unfortunately, to my knowledge, very little has been written on this subject.

2. Major Findings

As noted earlier, the authors generally provide the results those of us in tax policy would most want to know – at least in what I take to be the first in a number of papers. Some of these results, of course, are consistent with prior expectations, and to that extent less interesting. For example, the authors test the correlation between multinational operations and tax deficiency and (as one would predict) find that it is positive. What follows is a brief discussion of some of the more surprising results.

2.1. The (Relatively) Low Deficiency Rate

The authors find a deficiency rate of 13.6 percent, substantially below IRS estimates and about at the level predicted by the Bureau of Economic Analysis. At first glance, at least, this seems inconsistent with the reports of shelter use and increasingly aggressive corporate tax management. I think most of the explanation lies in the fact that the authors' study began in 1983 and ended in 1998. The tax shelter boom is generally thought to have begun in the early or mid-1990s, with its peak years during 1999–2001. IRS enforcement efforts necessarily lag actual use (Bankman, 2004). As a result, not only were shelters relatively rare in all but the last few years of this study, the likelihood that the IRS would detect what shelters there were was low as well.[3] It would be interesting to test this hypothesis by comparing the

---

[3] An additional factor is that, in the late years of the boom, corporations comprised less of a percentage of the shelter market than is generally imagined. Under the California amnesty

deficiency rate for 1988 with 1998 – the latter being a year in which shelter use was high and with respect to which, by the time of audit, the IRS had developed effective detection techniques.

2.2. Effective Tax Rates and Noncompliance

As noted above, a number of scholars have adopted what might be referred to as a "reporting data" methodology to ferret out noncompliance: They have looked at the gap between income and taxes paid, as measured by financial reporting standards, adjusted that gap to account for some forms of expected and accepted tax planning, and viewed the remainder as indirect evidence of noncompliance or aggressive tax planning.

This study finds no correlation between low effective tax rates, as measured by financial accounting purposes, and deficiencies. This result does not directly contradict any of the results reached by those who have based their estimates on financial data. None of the other studies use as simple a measure as effective tax rate as the indicator of noncompliance. More generally, because the purpose of relying on financial data is to pick up noncompliance that the government misses on audit, the fact that we don't see evidence of this hypothesized noncompliance in the audit results does not deal anything close to a fatal blow to this methodology.

However, if aggressive tax planning accounts for some of the difference between income and taxes paid, as measured by financial reporting standards, one would expect that as that gap grows, deficiencies assessed by the IRS would increase. One would also expect that this result would show up even in the rough measure of effective tax rates used by the authors to test this theory. It will be interesting to see how those who derive estimates of noncompliance from reported data respond to the authors' results here.

2.3. Determinants of Corporate Tax Aggressiveness

Stock Options and Bonuses

Any study of corporate tax behavior is complicated by the presence of agency-principal conflicts between owners and management. What presumably motivates corporate actors to take aggressive tax positions is not the reward

---

provision, for example, taxpayers "gave up" approximately $15 billion of shelter-related losses. A majority of those losses had been taken by individual, rather than corporate, taxpayers. (Bankman and Simmons, 2003).

to the corporation's owners (which may be hard to determine in any case) but the reward to the corporate actor. Following up on the work of Slemrod (2004), Desai and Dharmapala (2006), and others, the authors test to see if the stock options or bonuses are positively correlated with noncompliance. The hypotheses are that managers will work harder if their interests are better aligned with shareholders; that stock options and bonuses will better align interests; and that in the tax context, harder work will lead to more aggressive tax positions and higher deficiencies.

While there is some intuitive appeal to these linked hypotheses, it may be worthwhile to note that there are hypotheses that might push in the opposite direction or other factors that might obscure the hypothesized relationships even if they in fact exist. One can imagine, for example, that bonus plans for top executives would focus on measures such as sales, before-tax profit, or market share that are easier to evaluate than taxes paid or after-tax earnings. If this is true, one might expect the presence of plans would lead managers to shift resources toward these bonus-related measures and away from tax planning. The use of stock options as a motivation tool to any but top officers has long been suspect, because the relationship between effort and reward is so attenuated (Oyer and Schaefer, 2005). Moreover, the relationship between option use and aggressive tax planning might be confounded by an industry effect. Options use is very high in the technology sector, and, in the past at least, that sector has had the reputation among tax lawyers and others as putting relatively less emphasis upon tax management techniques, including, most notably, tax shelters (Bankman, 1994). The authors include a control variable for research and development, but this is only imperfectly correlated with the technology sector. Finally, the authors' dataset only provides information on options and bonuses given to the five most highly paid executives. The executive most relevant to tax management decisions is the tax director, who will not be in that top-paid group. The presence of incentive compensation for the top executives is relevant only to the extent that it is correlated with incentive compensation to the tax director or to the extent such compensation aligns the incentives of the top executives, who either make tax management decisions or closely monitor the actions of the tax director.

The fact that, notwithstanding these confounding factors, the authors find a positive correlation between incentive compensation and tax deficiencies is somewhat surprising. It would be interesting to survey tax directors to see if this result comports with their beliefs about incentive compensation and even more interesting to see some examples of the compensation agreements, particularly those that cover tax directors.

Corporate Governance

The authors test the relationship between corporate governance and deficiencies. The underlying hypothesis appears to be that poor corporate governance is positively correlated with noncompliance: Let the management run the show, and they will cheat on taxes. This hypothesis is in apparent conflict with the hypothesis underlying the test for incentive compensation, described immediately above. Incentive compensation is all about reducing the agent-principal problem: There the hypothesis was that stock options or bonuses align management with shareholders, lead management to work harder and more aggressively manage taxes, and lead to more noncompliance. Noncompliance is therefore associated with aligned incentives. Good corporate governance is also all about reducing the agent-principal problem. The standard indicator of good (or bad) corporate governance measures whether management controls the board or has insulated itself from direct democracy in the form of shareholder votes on takeovers or other proxy issues. Here, the hypothesis is that it is when management is in control, and incentives are *mis*aligned, that corporations manage taxes more aggressively and deficiencies rise.

One can perhaps reconcile these hypotheses by assuming that the misalignment of incentives due to poor corporate governance can lead to the kind of fraud seen in Enron. Management will put out false financial data to boost stock price (and hopefully sell out before the deception is uncovered); and management will aggressively manage taxes to increase reported earnings and boost stock price even further, with the thought that it will also be years before an audit reverses the tax savings. Companies with good corporate governance but that lack incentive compensation suffer from a different form of misaligned incentives. Here, management gets lazy and, on the tax front, resigns itself to paying an average amount of tax. This reconciliation is not altogether satisfying, though. Why wouldn't entrenched management in companies with poor corporate governance sometimes reap their rewards by working less, acting like the lazy tax director described immediately above?

In any event, the authors find that there is no relationship (positive or negative) between noncompliance and good corporate governance. The authors measure good corporate governance under a definition proposed by Gompers, Ishii, and Metrick (2003), who found certain criteria of governance to be positively correlated with stock return. Unfortunately, this definition looks at factors (such as the presence of poison pills or independent directors) that many corporate scholars believe are irrelevant.[4] The index also classifies as "anti-shareholder" several provisions that are apt to be "pro-shareholder." For instance, the Gompers index considers it bad governance when a firm is able to reimburse its directors for expenses incurred in shareholder litigation. But given shareholders' need to attract and retain directors, it is certainly in shareholders' interest to shield directors from many (if not all) cases involving a director's duty of care.[5] Moreover, other scholars find no relationship between the Gompers index and shareholder returns in later years or find that the size of any effect depends on entirely different factors (such as the existence of monitoring shareholders).[6] The fundamental problem is that we do not have a good metric with which to measure corporate governance. This can be seen by the fact that some of the most spectacular frauds were committed by management in companies that appeared to have good corporate governance. Enron, for example, is sometimes used to illustrated the hypothesis that managers who can get away with cheating shareholders will also cheat the government. But Enron fares pretty well on most conventional measures of corporate governance. It had a board that was dominated (numerically) by outside directors and met frequently.

References

Bankman, Joseph. 1994. "The Structure of Silicon Valley Start-Ups." *UCLA Law Review* 41(7): 1737–1768.

Bankman, Joseph. 2003. "The Story of INDOPCO: What Went Wrong in the Capitalization v. Deduction Debate?" In Paul Caron, ed., *Tax Stories.* (New York: Foundation Press), pp. 183–206.

Bankman, Joseph. 2004. "The Tax Shelter Problem." *National Tax Journal* 57(4): 925–936.

Bankman, Joseph, and Daniel Simmons. 2003. "Has California Broken the Tax Shelter Logjam?" *Tax Notes* 101(9): 1111–1115.

Bhagat, Sanjai, and Bernard Black. 2002. "The Noncorrelation Between Board Independence and Long-Term Firm Performance." *Journal of Corporation Law* 27(2): 231–273.

Cremers, K. J. Martijn, and Vinay B. Nair. 2005. "Governance Mechanisms and Equity Prices." *Journal of Finance* 60(6): 2859–2894.

---

[4] Whether a corporation has a "poison pill" already in place is generally thought irrelevant because a company can generally get a pill in place at short notice. The lack of relationship between board independence and performance is discussed in Bhagat and Black (2002).

[5] I am indebted to Rob Daines for this point.

[6] See Cremers and Nair (2005).

Desai, Mihir A. 2003. "The Divergence Between Book Income and Tax Income." In James M. Poterba, ed., *Tax Policy and the Economy*, vol. 17. (Cambridge, MA: NBER and MIT Press), pp. 169–206.

Desai, Mihir A., and Dhammika Dharmapala. 2006. "Corporate Tax Avoidance and High-Powered Incentives." *Journal of Financial Economics* 79(1): 145–179.

Gompers, Paul, Joy Ishii, and Andrew Metrick. 2003. "Corporate Governance and Equity Prices." *Quarterly Journal of Economics* 118(1): 107–155.

Graham, John R., and Alan L. Tucker. 2006. "Tax Shelters and Corporate Debt Policy." *Journal of Financial Economics* 81(3): 563–594.

Manzon, Gil, Jr., and George Plesko. 2002. "The Relation Between Financial and Tax Reporting Measures of Income." *Tax Law Review* 55(2): 175–214.

Oyer, Paul, and Scott Schaefer. 2005. "Why Do Firms Give Stock Options to All Employees?: An Empirical Examination of Alternative Theories." *Journal of Financial Economics* 76(1): 99–132.

Slemrod, Joel. 2004. "The Economics of Corporate Tax Selfishness." *National Tax Journal* 57(4): 877–899.

Comments

Brian Erard

B. Erard and Associates

1. Introduction

Data on tax noncompliance are hard to come by, and the results presented in this study provide a rare glimpse into the compliance behavior of large corporations. Beyond presenting a broad set of summary statistics, Hanlon, Mills, and Slemrod (henceforth referred to as HMS) provide some intriguing results on the relationship between a measure of identified corporate tax deficiencies and various firm characteristics, including size, public ownership, multinational activity, and governance structure. I will begin by commenting on certain key data issues surrounding this study, including accuracy, representativeness, and interpretation. I will then propose some extensions to the econometric design used by HMS to account for the time-series nature of the data, allow for tax overstatements and undetected noncompliance, and address sample selection.

2. Data Issues

The data in this study include details from operational audits of the U.S. federal income tax returns of large corporations and subsequent appeals. This information has been matched against computer files containing line item details from the corporations' tax returns.

2.1. Accuracy

In my experience working with similar administrative datasets, I have found that there are often various data anomalies that can impact accuracy and interpretation, including miscoded results, inconsistencies between variables, missing returns or audit results, and duplicate sets of results from the same examination. In this regard, it would be useful if HMS could provide more details on what efforts have been undertaken to identify errors and "cleanse" the data.

It is also important to recognize that audit statistics for large corporations can be quite sensitive to differences in data definitions, such as cutoff dates for assigning case dispositions, the choice between audit and tax years, the time period of analysis, and the meaning of a "closed" case. As HMS note, for instance, past studies by the Government Accountability Office (formerly known as the General Accounting Office) that were based on somewhat different data sources and definitions have produced markedly different estimates than the current study for such population characteristics as the share of proposed deficiencies agreed to at the time of the exam and the share that is ultimately assessed. My sense is that the statistics from the current study are probably superior. However, even these results (which are arguably based on the best available direct evidence on corporate compliance) probably should be viewed as only rough estimates. There is simply a limit to how much accuracy one can reasonably expect from administrative data collected during a complex examination and appeals process that typically plays out over a period of many years.

2.2. Representativeness

An important question in this study is how representative the results are of large corporations. In this regard, it is useful to consider separately two different subsamples of the data. The first subsample contains results for corporations in the Coordinated Examination Program (CEP).[1] Based on publicly available Internal Revenue Service tabulations, it appears that audit coverage within the CEP population was rather high, ranging from about 66% percent to 77 percent over the sample period covered in this study (tax years 1983 through 1993).

The second subsample contains results for large corporations (with more than $10 million in assets) that were not part of the CEP. Audit coverage for large corporations not in the CEP appears to have been much lower than for CEP corporations, declining from roughly 22 percent in the first year in the sample period (tax year 1994) to approximately 16 percent in the final year of the period (tax year 1998).

Corporate returns were not randomly selected for either of the above subsamples. Rather, the IRS typically chose returns for operational audits on

---

[1] As noted by HMS, this program has evolved into what is now known as the Coordinated Industry Case (CIC) program.

the basis of judgments about their potential audit yield, taking into account the availability of examination resources and other factors. As well, HMS excluded from both of their subsamples cases involving financial service corporations.

Given the fairly high audit coverage of the CEP population, the results for the CEP subsample may be at least somewhat representative of the results that would have been achieved if all nonfinancial service corporations in the CEP had been subjected to comparable operational audits for the sampled tax years.[2] Conceptually, however, it is somewhat difficult to interpret the nature of the CEP population. To be sure, the CEP included many of the very largest corporations that filed U.S. federal income tax returns during the sample period. However, the CEP also included a significant number of corporations that were smaller than many of the corporations that were not in the CEP population. Presumably, these smaller corporations were selected for inclusion in the CEP, because they were deemed by the IRS to have complex or unique tax issues that made it preferable to subject them to the special team audit approach employed in the CEP program. So while the CEP is surely an interesting population, it is somewhat of a hodgepodge of different types of corporations that were chosen on the basis of operational considerations rather than any specific research criteria.

Given relatively low audit coverage rates and nonrandom selection into the non-CEP subsample, it would be dangerous to generalize from the results for this subsample to the overall non-CEP population. In particular, it seems likely that the sample results would, on average, overstate the proposed and final audit assessments that would have been applied to the unaudited large corporations in the non-CEP population had they been subjected to comparable audits. Nonetheless, the results for the non-CEP subsample are still of interest for understanding the nature of compliance and enforcement. More specifically, the results give us an indication of the sorts of corporations that were being audited, the results of those audits, and the amounts of additional tax that were ultimately assessed.

2.3. Interpretation

I have suggested that the results for the CEP subsample may be at least somewhat representative of the results that would have been achieved if all nonfinancial service corporations in the CEP had been subjected to comparable

[2] To the extent that IRS judgments regarding potential audit yield were accurate, assessments for unselected CEP corporations may have been somewhat lower had they been subjected to comparable operational audits to selected CEP corporations.

operational audits. On the other hand, I have argued that it would not be appropriate to generalize from the results for the non-CEP subsample. However, even if the combined CEP and non-CEP subsamples were perfectly representative of the results one would obtain if all large corporations were subjected to operational audits, these results still would not serve as a plausible measure of the "tax gap" – the difference between the amount of taxes large corporations truly owed and the amount that they reported. There are several reasons for this conclusion. First, operational audits tend to be selective examinations of specific issues on a tax return, not an exhaustive examination of all issues. For instance, my understanding is that audits of large corporations during much of the 1980s had a heavy emphasis on tax shelter issues, the emphasis shifted to other specific issues during the 1990s, and tax shelter issues are again receiving substantial attention in recent years.

Second, even when a specific tax issue is examined, it is not always possible for the IRS examiners to detect all tax violations relating to that issue. Over the period covered by this study, the IRS averaged only about one full-time-equivalent auditor per large corporation return examination. With limited time, resources, and available information about the corporation under examination, it seems highly unlikely that all instances of noncompliance could have been uncovered relating to what, in many cases, would have been some extremely complex tax issues.

Third, in many instances, the proper legal treatment of a tax issue is ambiguous and subject to differing legal opinions. In such cases, there may not be an objective definition of "true tax liability" against which reported tax liability can be compared.

As HMS have suggested, examinations and appeals of corporations are perhaps best thought of as elements of a negotiation process. In this light, one might interpret the proposed deficiency as a measure of the overall aggressiveness of the taxpayer and the IRS in the negotiation process. In cases where both parties take an aggressive stance toward negotiation, one would expect the proposed deficiency to be relatively large. Since the mid-1990s, it seems plausible that large corporations have become more aggressive, given the reported expansion in tax shelter activities and the recent wave of corporate accounting scandals. On the other hand, one wonders whether the IRS has become less aggressive as a result of the resource and administrative constraints it has faced. Consequently, it is unclear whether one would expect average proposed deficiencies to have increased or declined over this period. Therefore, changes in proposed deficiency amounts may not provide an accurate indication of the overall magnitude or even direction of trends in corporate tax noncompliance.

3. Econometric Issues

HMS have employed an econometric approach to examine the relationship between proposed tax deficiencies and various corporation characteristics. In this section I offer several suggestions for expanding and improving upon this analysis.

3.1. Time-Series Issues

In their econometric analysis, HMS do not account for the time-series nature of their data. Over the period being studied, there were significant variations in audit coverage, scope, and perhaps intensity. As well, there were important legislative and administrative changes. For instance, the CEP subsample spans the period before and after the Tax Reform Act of 1986 (TRA86). Presumably, the reduction in tax rates and elimination of many deductions under TRA86 would have important implications for proposed tax deficiencies. On the administrative side, various changes were instituted in an effort to improve examination performance and better coordinate the examination and appeals functions. To the extent possible, it would be helpful if HMS could expand their specification to account for the impact of such changes on proposed tax deficiencies.

An important consideration when accounting for the time-series nature of the data will be what time unit to employ. The most natural choice would seem to be the tax year. Unfortunately, though, it takes many years before all audits of corporate returns from a given tax year have been closed, particularly in the case of large corporations. Because the data sample used by HMS contains information only for closed audits, this means that they will have a reasonably complete set of audit cases only for the earlier tax years in their data sample. An alternative approach would be to use the year the audit was closed as the time unit for the analysis. This would complicate interpretations, but it has the advantage of having more years of complete information.

For most of the corporations in the CEP subsample, my understanding is that HMS have information on multiple audits from different tax years. For this subsample, it therefore would make sense to employ panel data techniques to account for unobserved heterogeneity among the sampled corporations. As well, HMS have noted that audits for one tax year can have implications for amounts assessed in other tax years, as a result of various timing issues (e.g., carrybacks and carryforwards). It may be possible to control for these timing issues in the CEP subsample, for instance by averaging proposed deficiencies across tax years.

3.2. Tobit Specification Issues

HMS employ a Tobit framework rather than an ordinary multiple regression specification in an effort to account for the mass of returns in their data sample that have a 0 proposed tax deficiency. Such a specification would seem appropriate if the zeros in the sample represented instances of perfect compliance. In many cases, however, it seems plausible that the zeros actually represent instances where noncompliance was present but went undetected. As discussed earlier, operational audits are neither comprehensive enough nor intensive enough to ensure that all noncompliance on a return will be detected. If the zeros are indeed part of a more general problem of undetected noncompliance, it would be desirable to employ a more comprehensive econometric specification of the data generation process that accounted both for the propensity to commit noncompliance and for the extent to which noncompliance is detected during an examination.[3]

A second issue relating to the Tobit specification is the handling of cases with negative proposed deficiencies (i.e., cases of apparent tax overstatement). In the Tobit framework employed by HMS, I assume that such cases are treated the same as the zeros. However, in some instances, overstatements of taxes may in fact represent a deliberate choice distinct from an attempt to correctly report tax liability. For example, my understanding is that a number of the corporations that were found in recent years to have improperly inflated their earnings to their shareholders either have filed or are considering filing for a refund of any taxes that were paid on their fictitious reported earnings. Depending on how many cases of negative proposed deficiencies there are in the data sample, it therefore may be desirable to employ a more general econometric specification that allows for positive, negative, and zero values for the proposed deficiency.

3.3. Sample Selection

Given the differences in audit coverage, audit methods, and sampled time periods for the CEP and non-CEP populations, I believe that HMS should perform a separate econometric analysis of their non-CEP subsample. Moreover, particularly for that subsample, their analysis should take into account, to the extent possible, the nonrandom selection of returns. While I understand that it may be difficult to find appropriate instruments to control for unobserved differences between returns that were and were not selected

---

[3] See Feinstein (1991) or Erard (1997) for examples of such an econometric framework.

for audit, HMS might at least attempt to control for observable differences between these two groups of returns. To do this effectively, however, they would need to obtain information from a sample of tax returns from the same time period that were not subjected to audit.

4. Conclusion

HMS have begun to tap a rich and valuable data source for learning about corporate income tax compliance and enforcement, thereby providing us with a window into a notoriously elusive, but important, research issue. As the earlier discussion indicates, the analysis of operational audit results poses some significant challenges. At the same time, such results arguably provide the best available direct evidence on the compliance behavior of large corporations. The preliminary results of this study are intriguing, and I look forward to learning about future findings as the authors refine and expand their analysis in the years to come.

References

Erard, Brian. 1997. "Self-Selection with Measurement Errors: A Microeconometric Analysis of the Decision to Seek Tax Assistance and Its Implication for Tax Compliance." *Journal of Econometrics* 81(2): 319–356.

Feinstein, Jonathan S. 1991. "An Econometric Analysis of Income Tax Evasion and Its Detection." *Rand Journal of Economics* 22(1): 14–35.

SIX

On the Extent, Growth, and Efficiency Consequences of State Business Tax Planning

Donald Bruce

University of Tennessee

John Deskins

Creighton University

William F. Fox*

University of Tennessee

1. Introduction

Traditionally, much of the literature on state corporate taxation has focused on how taxes affect the location of economic activity (see Wasylenko, 1997). A perpetual concern among policymakers is that higher tax rates or broader tax bases will retard regional economic development. In contrast, some recent research has begun to focus more on tax planning, or how firms expand after-tax profits by adjusting to tax policy through financial arrangements within related firms. Interest in tax planning among businesses is evidenced by the fact that each of the Big Four accounting firms and many banks maintain specific groups to deal exclusively with aiding firms in making arrangements to reduce their tax liability.

Tax planning is defined here as a broad set of tax avoidance and evasion schemes that affect only financial arrangements of firms. Tax planning is contrasted with strategies in which firms move physical operations to avoid higher taxes – herein termed locational distortions of tax

* The authors thank Dhammika Dharmapala, Brian Hill, LeAnn Luna, Matthew Murray, Michael McKee, Kenneth Anderson, and participants in the University of Tennessee Department of Economics Seminar Series and the 2004 National Tax Association Annual Conference for insightful comments on an earlier draft. The authors also thank Bill Gentry, Charles McLure, Joel Slemrod and participants in the OTPR corporate tax conference for many helpful comments and suggestions.

policy.[1] Firms may also respond to corporate taxation by altering the input mix or production technology, though no attempt is made here to measure the implications of this third effect. Tax planning exploits differences in state tax policies and often involves sophisticated arrangements wherein firms create one or more subsidiaries for the purpose of shifting income from high- to lower-tax jurisdictions. Tax planning strategies are often legal, but some may fall into a legally gray area or even be blatantly illegal methods of tax evasion, such as underreporting taxable income or overstating tax deductions.[2]

Policymakers' uneasiness surrounding increases in the use of tax planning techniques is grounded in these techniques' potential contribution to the decline of state corporate income tax bases. State corporate income tax revenues as a share of corporate profits fell by about one-third from 1989 to 2002 (controlling for rate changes), and some have asserted that tax planning is a significant contributor to this decline (Fox and Luna, 2002).[3] Policymakers' concerns are evidenced by the fact that, since 2002, as many as 18 states have considered adding or modifying a combined-reporting requirement with the intention of retarding tax planning activities (Houghton, Hogroian, and Weinreb, 2004). Other potential problems include lost neutrality when only a subset of firms is able to use tax planning to minimize taxes and increases in compliance and administrative costs associated with implementing tax planning practices.

If one is only concerned with the revenue consequences of tax planning, then the growing literature on the elasticity of taxable income is perhaps most relevant.[4] Specifically, locational distortions, tax planning, and other responses potentially change a state's corporate income tax base, so an analysis of the overall elasticity of reported taxable corporate income would give policymakers a good picture of the combined problem from a revenue

---

[1] Note that location distortions need not be restricted to the movement of an entire firm. Many location distortions may involve marginal changes in economic activity, such as when a firm makes decisions to expand output by employing excess capacity at facilities located in low-tax rather than high-tax areas.

[2] An aggregation of tax avoidance, tax evasion, and ambiguous practices differs from traditional analysis but is consistent with recent research. See Slemrod (2004) who refers to these actions as "tax selfishness." One advantage of this aggregation is the ability to avoid categorizing legally ambiguous practices along the gray area between evasion and avoidance.

[3] Other likely determinants of the tax base erosion are reductions in the federal corporate income tax base (to which essentially every state CIT base is coupled) and state policy decisions such as concessions for economic development purposes.

[4] See Slemrod (1998) and Slemrod (2001) for a general discussion.

perspective. However, the purpose of this chapter is to isolate tax planning effects from locational distortions in a broader consideration of economic efficiency. The extent to which tax planning might be substituting for locational effects is important, even though the combined revenue effects might be slight.

Unfortunately, the efficiency consequences of tax planning alone cannot be determined a priori. For example, prior to the adoption of tax planning strategies, firms might have moved real activity in response to tax policy, creating an inefficient allocation of resources. Tax planning strategies might allow firms to respond to tax policy through structural changes within the firm, removing the inefficiency from repositioning operations. Even if tax planning and locational distortions have identical effects on reported taxable income (and revenues), greater tax planning and correspondingly less locational distortions might have a net positive effect on overall economic efficiency.

Some would also assert that tax planning could be efficiency-enhancing when viewed within a Leviathan framework (i.e., it helps to constrain a government that is too large). On the other hand, tax planning may retard efficiency if it ignites a "race to the bottom" that yields tax rates on mobile capital below an efficient level, resulting in an economy that is too capital intensive (Inman and Rubinfeld, 1996). Further, overall efficiency changes depend on other factors, such as administrative and compliance costs (which could potentially be very large) and, in a revenue neutral framework, on the alternative revenue sources used to replace declining corporate tax revenues.

The degree to which tax planning has eroded state tax bases is yet to be empirically tested with a significant degree of rigor. It remains to be seen whether accounts of tax planning are anecdotal and isolated or whether tax planning has significantly reduced tax revenues. Indeed, as evidenced by the Associated Industries of Massachusetts (2004), a consensus regarding the extent of tax planning is elusive. Fully informed tax policy decision making requires a greater understanding of the causes, effects, and extent of tax planning.

The purpose of this chapter is to determine the extent to which tax planning in response to tax policy differences across U.S. states has lowered state corporate income tax revenues. This effect cannot be measured directly but will be accomplished indirectly by examining relationships between several state tax policy parameters and state corporate income tax bases. More specifically, evidence of the impact of tax planning can be inferred from an econometric model that examines the effects of tax structure variables on the corporate income tax base while holding state economic activity constant. This study also assesses the degree to which the effect of such activities on corporate income tax bases has changed over time. Further, the analysis allows us to examine whether state efforts to restore corporate income tax bases (i.e., combined-reporting requirements and throwback rules) are effective.

This chapter proceeds as follows. Section 2 reviews the relevant literature. Section 3 presents a more in-depth discussion of several tax planning strategies. Section 4 details the empirical strategy and the data that are used. Section 5 presents a discussion of the results, and Section 6 offers a conclusion. Results indicate that tax planning in response to state tax policy differences significantly diminishes state corporate income tax bases in higher-tax states. In addition, the evidence suggests that combined-reporting requirements are frequently effective in partially restoring state corporate income tax bases while throwback rules are not. Results do not indicate that tax planning has diminished the locational distortions of tax policy between 1985 and 2001.

2. Existing Literature

No studies have been identified that specifically measure the extent to which tax planning has eroded state tax bases. Fox and Luna (2002) review state corporate income tax revenue trends and assert that tax planning is a contributor to the decline of state corporate bases. They also discuss some of the methods that are intended to restore corporate income tax base erosion due to tax planning (some of which are discussed below). However, they do not specifically measure the effect of tax planning on state tax bases.[5]

Mintz and Smart (2004) investigate the extent to which income shifting among affiliated companies (which constitutes one form of tax planning) affects provincial tax bases in Canada. They develop a theoretical model that finds that taxable income for multijurisdictional firms is more mobile for firms that are able to shift income between affiliated companies than for those that are not. Their model also predicts that the responsiveness of real investment to tax rate differentials is reduced by the possibility of income shifting. Then, using administrative tax records for businesses operating in Canadian provinces, they test their hypothesis by estimating and comparing taxable income elasticities between firms that are able to engage in income shifting to firms that are not, and they indeed find that the elasticity of taxable income is much higher for firms that are able to shift income.

Two other areas of literature are relevant here. The first is literature on the effects of tax policy on location, or how tax policy affects the location

---

[5] Also see Mazerov (2003) and Schiller (2002).

of the physical operations of firms. This extensive literature represents, in large part, the traditional treatment of the effects of tax policy on business. This literature is important to this study because, (1) as previously stated, it may be possible that tax planning has reduced locational distortions, and (2) the methods below provide further information on the effects of tax policy on the location of economic activity. The literature on federal tax planning, which has likely grown significantly over the past decade or so, is also relevant[6] because nearly every state begins its determination of profits with the federal definition. In addition, the degree to which firms pursue tax planning at the federal level may be a signal of the intensity of planning at the state level.

2.1. Location Effects of Tax Policy

The literature on the effects of tax policy on the location of economic activity is vast, in part due to the great emphasis policymakers place on structuring tax policy to be conducive to economic development. Fortunately, Wasylenko (1997) examined over 75 studies in a review of this literature.[7] What follows is a brief overview of his review. A portion of the methodology below aligns with the standards of this literature.

Wasylenko begins with a review of issues associated with the design and estimation of economic development as a function of tax policy. Most studies are based on a profit or cost function that determines the profitability of locating in a particular region. The most common measures used to capture economic activity are employment, income, investment, or business location. Explanatory variables usually include measures of input costs, such as wages and energy prices; proxies of market size, such as population, median income, or unionization; and various measures of tax policy. The most common tax policy measures are statutory tax rates and tax revenues relative to some measure of income or population. Most studies fail to incorporate more detailed elements of tax structures, such as incentives for economic development.

According to Wasylenko, the general conclusion of the literature on the interregional effects of tax policy is that tax policy is a statistically significant determinant of economic activity. However, the magnitudes (and even direction) of the effects of tax policy on economic development are scattered. Wasylenko reports a wide range of tax elasticities, from −1.54 to 0.54, that depend primarily on data used for the dependent variable (particularly

---

[6] See Bankman (1999) for example.
[7] See also Bartik (1991 and 1994).

micro- versus aggregate-level data), methodology, and time period of analysis. However, the median tax elasticity in each of the dependent variable categories is negative and generally small. For example, studies that specify gross state product as the dependent variable (most relevant to the current study as discussed below) report a median tax elasticity of −0.07. That is, given a 1 percent increase in some tax parameter, gross state product declines by only 0.07 percent.

2.2. Federal Tax Planning

Federal concern about tax planning is evidenced by the U.S. Department of the Treasury (1999), which expresses significant unease with the use of corporate tax sheltering (similar to the tax planning definition used here) and represents an attempt to design better strategies to combat such practices. The study cites several potential problems with tax sheltering, such as revenue losses, disrespect for the tax system, increased complexity, and the cost to firms of pursuing such activities. The Internal Revenue Service (U.S. General Accounting Office, 2003) estimated that losses from abusive tax shelters amounted to $14.5 billion to $18.4 billion in 1998. The loss from sheltering amounts to between 7 and 9 percent of the $204.2 billion in corporate tax revenues. Following Slemrod (2004), if the average of this span is added to a recent estimate of corporate tax evasion of $53.0 billion (U.S. General Accounting Office, 1998), abusive tax sheltering combined with evasion amounted to 26.1 percent of corporate tax receipts in 1998.[8]

A few studies have examined more closely the causes of corporate tax sheltering and the policies with which it is most closely associated. Desai (2002) studies federal tax sheltering by using simulations to examine the growing divergence between corporate book income and taxable income. He finds that over half of the difference between book and taxable income in 1998 is due to differences in the treatment of depreciation, the reporting of foreign source income, and the shift from salaries to stock options as forms of employee compensation. Desai also finds evidence that the relationship between book and tax income has become much less stable over the past few years, indicating increasing tax sheltering activity. Desai and Dharmapala (2004) develop and test a model that explains how incentive compensation for management relates to the degree to which firms pursue tax sheltering strategies. Although their theoretical model yields ambiguous results, their empirical findings indicate that increases in incentive compensation lead to

---

[8] See Mackie (2000) for a discussion of the problems of using average tax rates to examine the effects of tax sheltering.

less tax sheltering activity. Rego (2003) finds that economies of scale exist in tax planning – that is, larger and more profitable multinational firms are better able to reduce their income tax liability through tax planning.

A highly publicized form of tax planning at the federal level involves corporate inversions, or when a corporation with a foreign subsidiary (usually in a low- or no-tax country) inverts its structure such that the foreign subsidiary becomes the parent company and the U.S. firm becomes the subsidiary. This tactic generally allows the corporation to reduce its tax liability on its foreign income and also to hold pre-tax profits until earnings are repatriated to the United States. Desai and Hines (2002) analyze the determinants of inversions and find that firms are more likely to invert if they are larger and more heavily leveraged and if they have more overseas assets and operate in low-tax foreign countries.

Gentry and Hubbard (1998, p. 193) discuss three general forms of tax planning under the current federal corporate income tax: "discouraging incorporation, encouraging borrowing, and altering the timing of transactions." They analyze how fundamental tax reform in the form of either (1) integrating the personal and corporate systems or (2) moving from the current income tax to a pure consumption tax would alleviate these tax planning incentives. They conclude that both types of reforms can significantly reduce the incentives to adopt these forms of tax planning.[9]

3. How Does State Tax Planning Work?

Firms employ numerous tax planning strategies to reduce their tax burden. An exhaustive review is impossible because known strategies are numerous and many strategies are likely unknown to tax analysts. Some forms of tax planning include:[10]

(1) Reclassifying business income as nonbusiness income,
(2) Exploiting P.L. 86–272,
(3) Using transfer pricing to shift income from high-tax to low-tax jurisdictions,
(4) Employing passive investment companies, and
(5) Using single-member limited liability companies (LLCs) to shift income out of state.

---

[9] See Hines (2002) for a discussion of how governments respond to the adoption of tax avoidance strategies.

[10] See Luna (2004) for discussion of state corporate tax planning.

Many firms have altered the characterization of business and nonbusiness income to reduce tax liability. The distinction is important because only business income is apportionable while nonbusiness income is allocated to the state in which it was earned. Therefore, a firm can reduce its tax liability by classifying some income as nonbusiness income where possible and shifting it to a low- or no-tax state.

Congress passed P.L. 86–272 as a temporary measure to limit state efforts to tax multistate corporations while the best means of taxing the firms was being studied. The temporary legislation remains in place decades later. P.L. 86–272 precludes a state from levying tax on a firm whose only linkage with the state is the solicitation of sales of tangible personal property. Thus, companies can avoid tax through the creation of "nowhere income" when they sell into states where they have no presence other than solicitation, because the destination state cannot attribute the sales for corporate tax purposes and the origin state generally does not attribute the sales for corporate tax purposes.

Manipulating transfer prices is a common type of tax planning. For example, consider a firm that is headquartered in Delaware and has two wholly owned subsidiaries, a retailer in Montana and a wholesaler in Wyoming. An increase in the price that the Wyoming firm charges the Montana firm shifts profits from Montana to Wyoming. This transaction will lower overall tax liability as long as Wyoming's tax rate is lower than Montana's (Wyoming does not impose a corporate income tax) and Montana does not impose a combined-reporting requirement (see below).

The fourth group of tax planning practices involves the creation of a passive investment company (PIC). This strategy often exploits the tax structure of either Nevada, which does not tax corporations, or Delaware, which does not tax income from intangible assets, but it can be effective in other circumstances as well. Perhaps the most famous example is with Toys "Я" Us© and its subsidiary Geoffrey, Inc. Toys "Я" Us© created Geoffrey, Inc. in Delaware to house the Toys "Я" Us© trademark. Geoffrey, Inc. has physical presence only in Delaware. Toys "Я" Us© stores across the states pay royalties to Geoffrey, Inc. and transfer income to Delaware, effectively eliminating the income from state tax bases. Numerous corporations have duplicated this practice. South Carolina challenged the use of Geoffrey[11] and prevailed, but some states have lost similar cases and other states fail to pursue income shifted through PICs (at least in part because of the state's corporate tax

---

[11] *Geoffrey, Inc. v. South Carolina Tax Commission*, 114 S. Ct. 50 (1993).

legislation). Further, states have the often daunting task of identifying firms that are employing PIC strategies.

Lastly, single-member limited liability companies (LLCs) can allow firms to shift income to the state where the member is located (see Fox and Luna, 2005). At the end of the 1980s, only two states permitted the LLC structure, but by the end of 1997 all states had enacted LLC legislation and all but Massachusetts permit single-member LLCs. The simplest way for a corporation to use LLCs to avoid taxes is to create a single-member LLC to house its operating company for a particular state and to own this LLC with a Delaware corporation that does not otherwise have nexus in the state. Income earned in the LLC state flows through to the Delaware member without tax unless the corporate tax law is changed. Delaware does not tax a firm that only administers an intangible investment, and interest in an LLC is considered an intangible. This arrangement effectively removes all of the operating firm's profits from state taxation unless the state where the LLC is located imposes an entity-level tax on LLCs.

3.1. State Strategies to Offset Revenue Losses Arising from Tax Planning

States use a variety of strategies to lessen the effects of tax planning, several of which are reviewed here. Combined-reporting requirements can at least partially restore corporate income tax (CIT) bases by precluding some tax planning strategies based on transfer pricing, such as the use of PICs. Combined reporting requires firms that are part of a unitary group to file a single corporate income tax return and thereby eliminates many of the effects of intragroup transactions.[12] Combined reporting can only partially restore tax bases (see Fox and Luna, 2002, for a discussion).[13] For example, foreign corporations are seldom included in the combined report, meaning a foreign PIC can help shift income. Also, only the unitary group can be

---

[12] One firm in the unitary group is designated to file the return on behalf of all members of the group. Some states require all firms that are part of the unitary group to be combined and other states only require those firms that are part of the unitary group and that individually have nexus in the state to file as part of the combined group.

[13] Combined reporting does not always lessen the capacity for tax planning, as evidenced by the frequent use of California, a combined-reporting state, as situs for PICs. Firms that have a nexus in California and sell into separate reporting states are not disadvantaged by locating their PIC in California to shift income from the separate reporting states to the PIC in California. This practice does not alter the firm's California taxable income since this is determined by apportionment.

required to file a combined return.[14] Fourteen states imposed combined reporting in 2001 (5 of those 14 states added the requirement during the time frame of this analysis).[15]

States employ several other strategies in efforts to lessen the effects of PICs and transfer-pricing strategies, though these should generally be less effective than combined reporting. For example, a number of states disallow deductions for payments to PICs and require the in-state firm to add back the expenses. Other states have argued that certain PICs have no economic substance and that the payments should be disallowed. Still other states have argued that the out-of-state PIC has nexus by virtue of licensing intangible property to an in-state corporation.[16]

A number of states use throwback rules to eliminate the nowhere income that arises because of P.L. 86–272. Slightly over half of corporate income taxing states (24 out of 44) imposed throwback rules in 2001 (6 states either added or removed this rule during the time frame of this analysis). Throwback rules require corporations to include sales in the numerator of the origin state in cases where the sale is not or cannot be included in the numerator of the destination state. This can lessen the effectiveness of tax planning strategies that attempt to shift income to states where corporations do not have nexus, though firms may easily plan around the throwback rules by selling from nonthrowback-rule states (see Fox, Luna, and Murray, 2005). Indeed, throwback rules are a form of origin-based taxation and give firms an incentive to locate sales in states that do not impose such rules.

4. Empirical Design and Data

The primary hypothesis in this study is that cross-state differences in corporate tax policies have led to tax planning that has significantly lowered state corporate income tax bases. The effect of tax planning on tax bases cannot be measured directly but can be tested in the following way. A state's total CIT base is determined by three factors: (1) a set of state-determined institutional parameters that define taxable income, (2) the magnitude of economic activity in the state that is taxed under the CIT structure, and (3) the ability of firms to make financial or accounting adjustments to lower

---

[14] Also, combined reporting legislation in some states, such as the recently enacted legislation in Kentucky, only includes companies that individually have a nexus in the state in the combined group.

[15] See also McIntyre, Mines, and Pomp (2001).

[16] See Bureau of National Affairs (2004) for a discussion.

their tax liability. The third determinant of the CIT base is tax planning – the myriad ways in which firms adjust and restructure to lower tax liabilities. Tax planning to reduce taxable profits may be spurred by any tax policy change that raises the effective tax rate that firms face, by differences in tax structures between states, or by changes in state law that make planning easier.[17]

State tax policy can affect firm behavior along a number of different margins, some of which entail tax planning responses and others that change real behavior. We seek to separate these two types of responses by estimating the regression model that explains state CIT bases as a function of the set of government parameters that define the CIT base, Gross State Product (GSP), and variables that change the effective tax rate that firms face. GSP is included in the model to account for the effect that tax structures have on tax bases, through changes in the real behavior of firms, with the goal being to isolate the effects of tax planning by separating out real effects.

Firms can make two real economic responses to the higher relative price of capital caused by an increase in the effective corporate tax rate. They can relocate production to lower-cost-of-capital states, or they can change the capital/labor ratio (either within the existing technology or by using a new technology) used within the taxing state. Changes in the location of production are accounted for through GSP and are isolated from tax planning. Changes in the capital/labor ratio are accounted for through GSP to the extent that firms reduce output as they alter relative input use. That said, substitution of labor for capital will presumably also reduce firms' before-tax profits, and this will get reflected in a lower CIT base. The extent of tax planning is overstated in the empirical results to the extent that a lower tax base results from firms' changes in their input mix.[18]

A foremost econometric issue in this context is the potential endogeneity of GSP in explaining the CIT base because changes in the CIT base could also affect state economic activity. Therefore, we use both a standard model that does not control for endogeneity as well as a two-stage instrumental variables regression model that estimates GSP in the first stage and CIT base in the second. Of course, the two-stage model requires at least one instrumental

---

[17] Of course, other effects complicate this picture and render the relationship between higher-tax structures and tax planning theoretically ambiguous. See Crocker and Slemrod (2004) and Slemrod (2004) for recent models of corporate income tax evasion.

[18] The same can be said about other distortions, such as those regarding debt and equity policies, organizational form, and incorporation decisions. To the extent that distortions along these margins reduce the CIT base but are not accompanied by output changes, their influence will be part of our estimated tax planning effects.

variable in the GSP equation that does not have an independent effect on the CIT base. Technical details are discussed below.

A second hypothesis is that tax planning has begun to substitute for the location distortions of tax policy. More specifically, firms may be increasingly able to avoid higher taxes simply by engaging in tax planning strategies rather than actually moving physical operations to lower-tax jurisdictions. This hypothesis can be tested by examining how the effect of the CIT rate on its base (holding GSP constant) and on GSP differs over time. This approach is accomplished in the regression framework by including an interaction between the CIT rate and a time variable. If tax planning activity is rising and if tax planning and location responses are substitutes, the CIT rate (and other tax policy instruments) is of waning importance over time in determining state economic activity. The CIT rate would also have a growing effect on its base over time if tax planning were becoming more prevalent. Both of these hypotheses, that real investment would be *less* responsive and that taxable income would be *more* responsive to tax policy differentials, are consistent with the theoretical model of Mintz and Smart (2004).

4.1. Model Structure and Variable Description

We employ a panel of data from all 50 U.S. states for the years 1985 through 2001. The specific structure of the regression equations and the variables included in them are defined below.

Economic Activity and Corporate Income Tax Base Measures

Nongovernment gross state product (GSP) is used to measure economic activity. Government production is excluded because it is potentially not subject to corporate taxation.

The CIT base is approximated by dividing CIT collections by the highest marginal state CIT rate for those states with a corporate income tax.[19] This method suffers from measurement error given that a few states have progressive corporate income tax schedules. However, the consequences of this error are likely to be minor for two reasons. First, the majority of states (31 out of 44 that taxed corporate income in 2001) have a single rate. Second, in

---

[19] Nevada and Wyoming have no broad business tax. Michigan imposes a single business tax (sometimes described as a business activities tax or value added tax). Texas imposes a franchise tax on earned surplus. South Dakota imposes a corporate income tax on banks. Washington imposes a gross receipts tax termed the business and occupations tax (Federation of Tax Administrators, 2004). Michigan, Texas, South Dakota, and Washington are treated as if they have no CIT whatsoever.

the remaining 13 states that have progressive corporate income tax schedules, the threshold for the top bracket is relatively low, such that the majority
of income falls into the top bracket.[20]

The corporate income tax base is estimated for the six states without
a corporate income tax by regressing a measure of the federal corporate
income tax base by the state (U.S. Department of the Treasury, various
years) on state CIT bases using only data for states with a CIT. The parameter
estimates from this model are then applied to obtain predicted values for
CIT bases for states without CITs.[21] It is important to include these states
in the analysis to allow for the possibility that firms consider non-CIT states
in their tax planning decisions.

Tax Rates

The top marginal CIT rate is often the focal point of public attention surrounding business taxation because high rates could distort location distortions or justify the adoption of costlier and more effective tax planning
techniques. The omission of the CIT rates of lower brackets leads to specification error, but the error is relatively unimportant for the same reasons
offered above in the context of using the top marginal rate in calculating
corporate income tax bases.[22]

Tax planning or real economic effects could be encouraged by any parameter that affects the overall tax burden firms face, not just parameters directly
related to the corporate income tax. The state general sales tax rate is included
because it represents the largest component of the overall state tax liability
of many firms because it is imposed on the sales value of many business-
to-business transactions (Cline, Fox, Neubig, and Phillips, 2003a and 2003b;
Cline, Mikesell, Neubig, and Phillips, 2005). In a similar fashion, the top
marginal personal income tax (PIT) rate is included. Firms may be more
likely to reclassify themselves as corporations when faced with higher PIT

---

[20] Additionally, this overestimate of the CIT base is at least partially offset by an underestimate
due to our lack of consideration of CIT credits in the base calculation.

[21] This procedure uses a random-effects regression that results in an overall R-squared of
0.72. The federal corporate income tax base coefficient is statistically different from zero at
the 1 percent level. Results are omitted for brevity but are available upon request.

[22] Our use of the top statutory CIT rate might raise concerns about measurement error if
one truly believes that the firm's effective tax rate is a more appropriate measure. However,
our analysis of aggregate state data rather than individual firm data makes the use of
effective tax rates less compelling. Also, we view the statutory rate as an important policy
signal at the aggregate level and have thus elected to include it along with most other
factors in effective tax rate calculations (e.g., combined-reporting and throwback rules,
apportionment formula details, and other features of state CIT structures).

rates relative to CIT rates, or closely held corporations may choose to pay less in wages to owner or operators, meaning higher PIT rates could raise the CIT base.[23,24]

Corporate Tax Structure

Elements of the corporate tax structure could influence GSP and also have independent effects on CIT bases. The former is true because many of these parameters raise or lower effective corporate tax rates, which may create location distortions. The independent effects on CIT bases may occur because these variables help define the CIT base.

The first variable included in this group is the sales factor weight in the state corporate income tax apportionment formula. The apportionment formula uses a state's share of the corporation's national property, plant, and payroll to distribute the corporation's national profits to the state for tax purposes. These three factors are added together using weights that the states have been varying as economic development tools. Increasing the sales factor weight, which may entice firms (especially manufacturing firms) to expand production in a given state, has become a commonly used instrument for attracting production.

In general, for given tax rates, locating payroll and property in a state with a high sales factor weight while selling in many states will reduce tax liability compared with locating the payroll and property in a state with a low sales factor weight and higher weights on property and payroll factors (see Edmiston, 2002). States have aggressively increased the weight on the sales factor in the formula to lessen origin-based taxation and increase destination taxation. This also tends to lessen the corporate income tax on many multistate, and presumably more mobile, firms, without affecting the tax liability of domestic firms, which do not apportion income. For example, in 1990, 32 of the 44 income-taxing states applied equal weight to all three factors. By 2004, only 12 states applied equal weight to all factors, while

---

[23] There is a significant amount of variation in CIT, PIT, and sales tax rates, both between states and within states, during the time frame of this analysis. For each of these taxes, over half of states changed the rate at least one time from 1985 to 2001.

[24] A corporate franchise tax may also affect the CIT base. However, we chose not to include this variable because of the difficulty of capturing corporate franchise tax rates in a usable form. The use of a simple dummy variable for states that impose a corporate franchise tax was discarded because of the very small amount of variation in the states that impose such a tax. Omission of this variable does not bias the results because the state fixed-effects control for this tax and all other state-specific characteristics that are not included in the model.

23 states double-weighted the sales factor (a 50 percent weight), and the remainder applied more than 50 percent weight to sales.[25]

The apportionment formula for state corporate income taxes can be an important element in tax planning (as firms seek to exploit differences across states or across types of business structure) or location effects. For example, until Kentucky's 2005 corporate tax reform, LLCs' profits were apportioned using a single-factor sales formula, and other corporations were apportioned using double-weighted sales. Thus, the firm could lower its liability by producing inside Kentucky in its LLC and locating a sales office outside Kentucky inside a corporation to sell back into the state.

As previously stated, combined-reporting requirements can be an important element of state CIT structures and are thus included to help explain state CIT bases. Combined-reporting requirements could reduce economic activity in a state by driving away firms if such requirements effectively raise the CIT burden by disallowing some planning opportunities. Combined reporting is specified as a dummy variable to denote whether a state requires combined reporting. Other means of offsetting the use of PICs are not included because data are not available for a panel application. Whether a state has a throwback rule is included as a dummy variable. A throwback rule is intended to raise the CIT base as it narrows avoidance possibilities, but it could create location distortions because it raises the origin component of the CIT.[26]

State legislation permitting limited liability companies (LLCs) can create tax planning opportunities and may affect economic activity across states (see Fox and Luna, 2005). The option for LLC status could affect economic activity because firms may start in or relocate to states to exploit this organizational form. The LLC structure can be preferred over the C corporation structure because LLCs also offer limited liability, but in many cases they are treated as pass-through entities with the income taxed only under the PIT system.[27] Further, LLCs are often exempt from some other corporate taxes,

---

[25] A significant amount of this variation occurred during the time period of this analysis. Indeed, 24 states increased their sales factor weight at least once during this time period.

[26] It should be noted that we include two of the most common and most visible policies that have been used to offset the effects of tax planning but this does not represent a comprehensive set of such variables. States use several other policies, some of which were discussed in Section 3, to lessen avoidance opportunities. However, reliable data on these policies for all states and for the time period of this analysis are difficult to obtain. We leave this to future work.

[27] The LLC structure also offers some advantages over S corporations. For example, there is no limit on the number of members of an LLC whereas an S corporation is limited to 100 shareholders (75 before 2005).

such as the corporate license taxes in Louisiana. This arrangement allows these firms to avoid double taxation of the CIT and PIT systems, reducing CIT bases. In addition, single-member LLCs can erode CIT bases through the tax planning opportunities described above. This variable is specified as a dummy to denote whether states permit LLCs.

Allowing corporations to deduct their federal CIT liability will directly lower state CIT bases. We include a dummy variable to denote a federal CIT liability deduction from the state CIT. This variable essentially lowers the effective CIT rate that firms face in a state and, thus, may generate locational distortions. Economic development incentive programs are inherently difficult to capture in a simple metric because of the wide variation in incentive programs offered across states. They are incorporated in this analysis via a count of the number of incentive programs that states offer. The counts are divided into the number of tax-incentive programs and the number of non-tax-incentive programs. Both of these counts may increase economic activity by attracting firms to a state. Tax-incentive programs should lower the CIT base because states are providing tax breaks through these programs. Non-tax-incentive programs may increase real economic activity as they lower business costs, although no independent effect on the tax base is expected.[28]

The primary stage of the regression model is summarized below:

$$
\begin{aligned}
\text{CIT Base}_{i,t} \\
= \beta_0 + \beta_1 \text{ CIT Rate}_{i,t} + \beta_2 \text{ PIT Rate}_{i,t} + \beta_3 \text{ Sales Rate}_{i,t} \\
+ \beta_4 \text{ Sales Factor Apportionment}_{i,t} + \beta_5 \text{ Combined Reporting}_{i,t} \\
+ \beta_6 \text{ LLC}_{i,t}, + \beta_7 \text{ Throwback Rule}_{i,t} + \beta_8 \text{ Fed CIT Deductibility}_{i,t} \\
+ \beta_9 \text{ Tax Incentives}_{i,t} + \beta_{10} \text{ Non-Tax Incentives}_{i,t} + \beta_{11} \text{ GSP}_{i,t} + \varepsilon_{it},
\end{aligned}
$$

where i and t are state and year indices.

Instruments for GSP

As previously mentioned, GSP is likely to be endogenous with respect to the CIT base.[29] The first-stage GSP instrumenting equation includes all of the explanatory variables in the CIT base equation plus a set of socioeconomic

---

[28] See Zodrow (2003) for a discussion of tax incentives.
[29] To be precise, under perfect information the CIT base does not affect GSP directly, rather it is the parameters that define the base that affect GSP. However, given the complexity of CIT structures, firms may not separately consider every parameter that defines the CIT base and, under these circumstances, respond directly to the CIT base. A standard Hausman test revealed that GSP is endogenous in the CIT base equation (Hausman, 1978).

instrumental variables that explain GSP but do not have independent effects on CIT bases. This specification is consistent with the literature that explains the determinants of economic activity as discussed in the review of location effects of tax policy.[30] Most of this literature models locational decisions by constructing profit functions (or other related functions) to determine profitability and, correspondingly, the decision to locate into a region. The literature includes variables such as measures of regional market demand, costs of producing in a particular location, and, of course, taxes. The following summarizes this (first-stage) equation:

$$
\begin{aligned}
\text{GSP}_{i,t} = {} & \beta_0 + \beta_1 \text{ CIT Rate}_{i,t} + \beta_2 \text{ PIT Rate}_{i,t} + \beta_3 \text{ Sales Rate}_{i,t} \\
& + \beta_4 \text{ Sales Factor Apportionment}_{i,t} + \beta_5 \text{ Combined Reporting}_{i,t} \\
& + \beta_6 \text{LLC}_{i,t,} + \beta_7 \text{ Throwback Rule}_{i,t} + \beta_8 \text{ Fed CIT Deductibility} \\
& + \beta_9 \text{ Tax Incentives}_{i,t} + \beta_{10} \text{ Non-Tax Incentives}_{i,t} + \beta_{11} \text{ Population}_{i,t} \\
& + \beta_{12} \text{ Median Income}_{i,t} + \beta_{13} \text{ Population Density}_{i,t} \\
& + \beta_{14} \text{ Government Expenditures}_{i,t} + \beta_{15} \text{ Manufacturing Wage}_{i,t} \\
& + \beta_{16} \text{ Education}_{i,t} + \beta_{17} \text{ Energy Price}_{i,t} + \varepsilon_{it},
\end{aligned}
$$

where, as before, i and t are state and year indices.

Two measures of input costs are included. The first is the average hourly wage for manufacturing workers in a state. The second is a measure of overall energy prices in a state (including all forms of energy such as gas, electricity, etc.). State population and median income are included to control for state size and demand. Population density is included because a high population concentration may influence the ability of firms to achieve economies of operation. Total state government expenditures per capita control for government size. Government size has an ambiguous theoretical effect: Firms may be more likely to locate in a state with greater expenditures per capita, recognizing the associated benefits of more public services. Alternatively, they could focus on the higher taxes accompanying larger governments and choose to locate elsewhere to the extent that per capita taxes and expenditures are correlated. The percentage of a state's residents (over age 25) who hold a baccalaureate degree or higher would likely influence GSP because many firms require an educated workforce.[31]

---

[30] See, for example, Wasylenko and McGuire (1985).

[31] This education variable is not available for 1985–88, so values are imputed on the basis of the average rate of change in each state between 1980 and 1989.

All regressions include state- and year-specific fixed effects to control for state- and time-specific factors not included in the model.[32] CIT bases and GSP are entered as natural logs to control for the scaling effects from the wide variation in GSP and CIT bases between large and small states. The time period of analysis, 1985 through 2001, is advantageous in that it began just before the Tax Reform Act of 1986 (TRA86), which potentially affected tax planning by reducing marginal federal corporate income tax rates, thereby increasing the relative value of avoiding state business taxes from the perspective of firms. This time span also allows for broad changes across the business cycle. Appendix 1 presents summary statistics for all variables for the first and last years of the study, and Appendix 2 provides variable descriptions and source notes.

5. Results and Discussion

This section first discusses the results from the baseline model. It then turns to a modified baseline model that includes the CIT rate interacted with other CIT structural parameters to more precisely identify the effects of these parameters. The section closes with another modification of the baseline model that considers the possibility that tax planning has replaced the location distortions of tax policy over time.

5.1. Baseline Model

GSP Results

Table 1 presents results from the primary regression model. Estimates from the first-stage equation indicate that the top CIT rate does not have a statistically identifiable effect on private-sector economic activity. However, increases in top PIT rates and sales tax rates are associated with lower levels of output growth. One possible explanation is that the sales tax and PIT each account for about one-third of state tax revenues (and large shares of business costs), while the corporate income tax currently generates only about 6 percent of state tax revenue. The magnitude of the PIT rate effect is relatively small: a one-percentage-point increase in the top PIT rate decreases GSP by

---

[32] Note that this will influence our interpretation of the regression results, as statistical significance will be identified on the basis of changes in variables over time as well as cross-state differences. We also estimated the model using a random-effects specification, but a Hausman (1978) test revealed correlations between the explanatory variables and the random effects.

Appendix 1. *Summary Statistics*

	1985		2001	
	Mean	Std. Dev.	Mean	Std. Dev.
Nongovernment gross state product (millions)	72,000	87,300	178,000	217,000
Corporate income tax collections (thousands)	265,564	334,276	590,840	1,091,370
Top corporate income tax rate	6.5	3.2	6.6	2.9
Top personal income tax rate	6.9	4.9	5.6	3.2
Sales tax rate	4.1	1.7	4.6	1.8
Sales factor apportionment	32.6	16.1	42.2	22.6
Combined reporting	0.18	0.39	0.28	0.45
Throwback rule	0.49	0.50	0.46	0.50
LLC	0	0	1	0
Federal CIT deductibility	0.09	0.28	0.06	0.22
Tax incentives	10.2	1.9	8.6	6.1
Non-tax incentives	4.7	2.7	12.56	7.99
Population (thousands)	4,745	5,068	5,694	6,300
Median income (thousands)	32.0	4.0	62.0	9.0
Population density	160	228	184	253
State expenditures per capita (thousands)	1.8	1.1	4.3	1.2
Average wage	9.4	1.2	14.5	1.6
Education	18.5	3.6	25.4	4.3
Energy price	8.5	1.1	10.0	1.6

Notes: All percentages are on a 0–100 scale.

All dollar amounts are expressed as current-year dollars.

only 0.6 percent. In contrast, a one-percentage-point increase in the sales tax rate lowers GSP by 3.6 percent.[33]

The sales factor weight in the state CIT apportionment formula is also a statistically significant determinant of GSP. The model predicts that a sales factor weight increase from 33 percent to 50 percent would increase GSP by 1.7 percent. Deductibility of federal CIT liability from state CITs tends to reduce GSP growth, though the estimated effects are larger than seems reasonable. As variation in this factor is limited to a very small number of states, it may be picking up other influences common to those states. In addition,

---

[33] The sales tax effect translates into an elasticity of −0.2. That is, a 1 percent increase in the sales tax rate yields a −0.2-percent decrease in GSP (based on the average sales tax rate of 4.6 percent in 2001). This magnitude is within the range of tax elasticity estimates discussed in Wasylenko (1997).

Appendix 2. *Data Descriptions and Source Notes*

Variable	Definition
Nongovernment gross state product	Total gross state product less GSP from government sector (1)
Corporate income tax base	Corporate income tax (CIT) revenues divided by top marginal CIT rate (2)
Top corporate income tax rate	Highest marginal corporate income tax rate (3)
Top personal income tax rate	Highest marginal personal income tax rate (3)
Sales tax rate	General sales tax rate (3)
Sales factor apportionment	Weight given to sales factor in the apportionment formula (3)
Combined reporting	1 if a state has a combined reporting requirement, 0 otherwise (3)
Throwback rule	1 i if a state has a throwback rule, 0 otherwise (4)
LLC	1 if a state allows LLCs, 0 otherwise (5)
Federal CIT deductibility	1 if a state allows deduction of federal CIT liability from state CIT liability, 0 otherwise (12)
Tax incentives	Number of tax incentive programs a state offers (6)
Non-tax incentives	Number of non-tax-incentive programs a state offers (6)
Population (thousands)	State population (7)
Median income (thousands)	State median income (7)
Population density	Population/square miles in a state (8)
State expenditures per capita (thousands)	State government expenditures/population (9)
Average wage	Average hourly wage for manufacturing workers (10)
Education	Percent of population over age 25 that hold at least a bachelor's degree (7)
Energy price	Estimate of energy costs for all forms of energy, measured per million BTU (11)

Source Notes:
 (1) *Regional Economic Accounts*, Bureau of Economic Analysis, various years.
 (2) Author's calculations based on data from *State Government Finances*, U.S. Census Bureau, various years; and *State Tax Handbook*, Commerce Clearning House, various years.
 (3) *State Tax Handbook*, Commerce Clearing House, various years.
 (4) *State Tax Handbook*, Commerce Clearing House (various years;) and various state revenue departments.
 (5) http://www.llcweb.com.
 (6) National Association of State Development Agencies, various years.
 (7) *Statistical Abstract of the United States*, U.S. Census Bureau, various years.
 (8) Author's calculations based on data from *Statistical Abstract of the United States*, U.S. Census Bureau, various years.
 (9) Author's calculations based on data from *State Government Finances*, U.S. Census Bureau, various years.
 (10) Employment and Wages. U.S. Bureau of Labor Statistics, various years.
 (11) *Energy Price Estimates by Source*, U.S. Department of Energy, various years.
 (12) We thank Justin Garosi for assembling these data from primary sources.

Table 1. *Baseline Model*

| Variable | Instrumental Variables Model Result | | OLS Results |
	First Stage Ln Gross State Product	Second Stage Ln CIT Base	
Top corporate income tax rate	−0.003	−0.066***	−0.064***
	(0.004)	(0.013)	(0.013)
Top personal income tax rate	−0.006***	−0.015**	−0.014**
	(0.002)	(0.006)	(0.006)
Sales tax rate	−0.036***	0.020	0.028
	(0.008)	(0.024)	(0.023)
Sales factor apportionment	0.001*	0.003**	0.002**
	(0.0004)	(0.001)	(0.001)
Combined reporting	−0.012	0.067	0.078*
	(0.016)	(0.047)	(0.046)
LLC	0.005	−0.027	−0.026
	(0.012)	(0.035)	(0.035)
Throwback rule	0.038	−0.019	−0.041
	(0.021)	(0.063)	(0.061)
Federal CIT deducibility	−0.107***	−0.301***	−0.271***
	(0.033)	(0.100)	(0.097)
Tax incentives	−0.001	−0.009***	−0.008***
	(0.001)	(0.003)	(0.003)
Non-tax incentives	−0.005***	0.007**	0.009***
	(0.001)	(0.003)	(0.003)
Population	0.054***	–	–
	(0.007)	–	–
Median income	0.004***	–	–
	(0.001)	–	–
Population density	0.0001	–	–
	(0.0003)	–	–
State expenditures per capita	−0.029**	–	–
	(0.013)	–	–
Average manufacturing wage	0.037***	–	–
	(0.006)	–	–
Education	0.004*	–	–
	(0.002)	–	–
Energy price	−0.011*	–	–
	(0.006)	–	–
Ln GSP	–	0.604***	0.915***
	–	(0.243)	(0.098)
Constant	17.71***	−0.025	−5.82***
	(0.15)	(4.54)	(1.84)
Within R-squared	0.950	0.575	0.580

Notes: Entries are fixed-effects panel regression coefficients with standard errors in parentheses.
*, **, and *** denote statistical significance at the 10 percent, 5 percent, and 1 percent levels.
Regressions include state and year fixed effects.
All percentages are on a 0–100 scale.
Population is measured in thousands.
Median income, GSP, and state expenditures per capita are measured in thousands of current-year dollars.

the number of non-tax incentive programs has a statistically distinguishable, but unexpectedly negative, relationship with GSP. The programs may offer lower benefits than the tax costs, so the net effect is a reduction of economic activity. Alternatively, this variable could be endogenous with gross output if more non-tax-incentive programs are developed in low-output states.

Some of the other control variables in the first stage of the model also deserve attention. As would be expected, states with higher population or median income growth relative to the national average have higher relative GSP growth. Interestingly, increases in state government expenditures per capita tend to yield lower GSP growth. The overall relationship between government spending and total output is not captured because the GSP measure excludes government spending; this result could simply reflect the crowding out of private output. States with higher growth in average wages for manufacturing workers have higher rates of growth in economic output. This likely suggests that more skilled workers, as evidenced by greater salaries, result in greater output. In addition, increases in a state's highly educated population are associated with higher GSP growth.

Corporate Income Tax Base Results
Results from the second stage of the model indicate that GSP is highly significant in explaining the CIT base with an estimated elasticity of 0.60. The lack of statistical significance on the constant term in this equation, combined with the significance of GSP, indicate that the CIT base fundamentally follows from GSP, as would be expected.

A one-percentage-point increase in the top CIT rate is associated with a 6.6 percent decrease in the corporate income tax base, holding GSP and all else in the model constant.[34] The relationship between the CIT rate and base is mostly attributable to tax planning activities because holding GSP constant eliminates the effect of location distortions on the base. However, effects on profitability arising from changes in the relative use of inputs can also be included in this coefficient. Further, the CIT base declines by 1.5 percent following a one-percentage-point increase in the PIT rate, again attributable to tax planning. As previously stated, when faced with higher tax rates in the PIT system, owners may be cost-justified in seeking more tax planning opportunities.

Several other tax variables are statistically significant in explaining the CIT base. Higher sales factor weights relative to the national average are

---

[34] This translates into an elasticity of −0.44 (based on the average top CIT rate of 6.6 percent for 2001).

associated with higher relative CIT base growth. Changing the apportionment formula does not create any additional tax base across the 50 states, but differences in state apportionment formulas appear to allow those states with higher sales ratios to tax a greater share of the corporate tax base. The model provides no evidence that state efforts to limit tax planning are effective. The imposition of combined-reporting requirements or throwback rules has no effect on CIT bases in this context. These policies receive more attention in the next section.

The model also fails to find evidence that allowing LLCs erodes the CIT base. Fox and Luna (2005) use a different CIT base measure and find that the advent of LLCs lowered tax revenues, but only when the analysis is run without fixed effects for time. The result found here might also be due to a high degree of correlation between the LLC dummy and the year fixed effects. As expected, allowing the deduction of federal CIT liability reduces state CIT base growth. In addition, more tax-incentive programs reduce growth in the CIT base. More non-tax-incentive programs are associated with higher CIT base growth, holding GSP constant. Perhaps firms pursue tax planning strategies less aggressively when offered more non-tax-incentive programs, thereby increasing the tax base.

We also present a set of results from a standard fixed-effects model that does not control for the possible endogeneity bias. Here our tax policy results are largely similar to those in the instrumental variables specification, indicating that any endogeneity bias is small. Nonetheless, because a Hausman test revealed GSP endogeneity, we will continue to focus on the two-stage results.

Several pieces of policy-relevant information can be drawn from these results. Sales and personal income tax rates have statistically significant and negative effects on economic activity in states, although the effect of the personal income tax is small. On the other hand, the corporate income tax rate does not have a significant effect on economic activity. Higher corporate income tax rates do appear to encourage tax planning, so policymakers should be aware of the large tax-planning-related base erosion that would likely follow an increase in corporate income tax rates.

5.2. Baseline Model Modified to Include CIT Rate Interactions

Table 2 presents a set of results similar to those in Table 1, with the difference being the inclusion of (1) interactions of the top CIT rate with the sales factor weight in the CIT apportionment formula, combined-reporting requirements, throwback rules, and LLC allowances, and (2) the CIT

Table 2. *Results with CIT Rate Interactions*

Variable	First Stage Ln Gross State Product	Second Stage Ln CIT Base
Top corporate income tax rate	0.028**	−0.016
	(0.013)	(0.040)
Top personal income tax rate	−0.007***	−0.015**
	(0.002)	(0.007)
Sales tax rate	−0.045***	0.002
	(0.008)	(0.025)
Sales factor apportionment	0.002	−0.002
	(0.002)	(0.006)
CIT rate × Sales apportionment	−0.0003	−0.0002
	(0.0003)	(0.001)
Combined reporting	0.230**	0.670**
	(0.095)	(0.300)
CIT rate × Combined reporting	−0.0004	−0.030
	(0.007)	(0.020)
LLC	0.075***	−0.030
	(0.016)	(0.052)
CIT rate × LLC	−0.011***	0.002
	(0.002)	(0.006)
Throwback rule	0.135*	0.336
	(0.072)	(0.226)
CIT rate × Throwback rule	−0.020***	−0.071***
	(0.009)	(0.027)
Combined reporting × Sales appt	−0.001	−0.0004
	(0.001)	(0.003)
Throwback rule × Sales appt	0.002***	0.006*
	(0.001)	(0.003)
Combined reporting × Throwback rule	−0.190***	−0.376**
	(0.053)	(0.172)
Federal CIT deductibilty	−0.093***	−0.148
	(0.035)	(0.108)
Tax incentives	0.0001	−0.007**
	(0.001)	(0.003)
Non-tax incentives	−0.004***	0.007**
	(0.001)	(0.003)
Population	0.047***	–
	(0.006)	–
Median income	0.004***	–
	(0.001)	–
Population density	0.0010	–
	(0.0003)	–

(continued)

Table 2 *(continued)*

Variable	First Stage Ln Gross State Product	Second Stage Ln CIT Base
State expenditures per capita	−0.013	–
	(0.013)	–
Average wage	0.034***	–
	(0.006)	–
Education	0.004**	–
	(0.002)	–
Energy price	−0.011*	–
	(0.006)	–
Ln GSP	–	0.444*
	–	(0.252)
Constant	17.44***	2.75
	(0.16)	(4.68)
Within R-squared	0.954	0.580

Notes: Entries are fixed-effects panel regression coefficients with standard errors in parentheses.

*, **, and *** denote statistical significance at the 10 percent, 5 percent, and 1 percent levels.

Regressions include state and year fixed effects.

All percentages are on a 0–100 scale.

Population is measured in thousands.

Median income, GSP, and state expenditures per capita are measured in thousands of current-year dollars.

apportionment formula, combined reporting, and throwback rule variables interacted with each other in each possible two-way combination. This specification allows for a more in-depth examination of the effects of these variables because it more precisely identifies how the effect of each element of CIT structure differs across policy regimes defined by the other CIT factors. This framework is especially important given that it is likely that many firms consider state tax structures from a broad perspective (i.e., rates and other policies in conjunction) rather than from a narrower perspective that only considers each element of the tax structure in isolation. We focus our discussion of Table 2 on the CIT base results, leaving a more detailed analysis of the GSP results to the reader.

Our first result of note in Table 2 is that we find no separate effect of the CIT rate on tax planning. Instead, the CIT rate only reduces the base in states that impose a throwback rule. More specifically, the CIT base falls by 7.1 percent for every one-percentage-point increase in the top CIT rate. Combined-reporting requirements are effective in increasing CIT bases, but the effect depends on whether a throwback rule is also imposed. The CIT base increase from a combined-reporting requirement is large in states without a throwback rule but falls considerably in states with throwback rules. This suggests that the throwback rule may have reaped some of the gains that could be obtained with combined reporting. Increases in the sales factor weight only increase the CIT base in states that also impose a throwback rule. This is expected because the "throwing back" of sales into a state will have a greater impact in the formula when a greater weight is applied to sales. Results do not identify a significant relationship between LLC allowances and the CIT base.

One policy implication is that combined-reporting requirements aid in restoring corporate income tax bases in most cases without diminishing economic activity. Alternatively, results indicate that throwback rules often have the perverse effect of actually diminishing CIT bases.

5.3. Tax Planning Over Time

In the third and final component of our study, we examine whether tax planning has increased over time and whether tax planning has replaced locational distortions. We use two approaches to investigate this. First, we run the baseline model while fully interacting the top CIT rate with the year fixed effects. Second, we estimate a model in which the year fixed effects are replaced with a time trend in both level and interaction terms.[35] Results from the latter model are presented in Table 3, while similar yet more cumbersome results from the former model are omitted for brevity.[36]

The first goal is to understand how the effects of the tax rate on the tax base differ over time, holding GSP constant. The results from these models do not identify a significant difference in the effect of the CIT rate on the CIT base over time, providing evidence that tax planning was equally prevalent throughout the period of analysis.[37]

If tax planning and location responses to tax policy are substitutes, the effect of the CIT rate on GSP might decline over time if firms are beginning to use financial arrangements to avoid taxes, as opposed to location responses.

---

[35] The time trend takes on the values of 1 to 17 for the years 1985 through 2001, respectively.
[36] The only difference between the specification with year fixed effects and a year time trend is the effect of LLC allowances. In the latter model, the LLC allowance variable is positive and significant while it is not in the former. This variable is probably identifying a time effect in the time trend model given the pattern of LLC introductions.
[37] A third model is estimated that included a quadratic time trend and the corresponding CIT rate interaction. The coefficients on the quadratic terms are not statistically different from zero in this model, and other results are largely unchanged.

Table 3. *Results with CIT Rate Interacted with Time*

Variable	First Stage Ln Gross State Product	Second Stage Ln CIT Base
Top corporate income tax rate	0.005	−0.071***
	(0.005)	(0.014)
Top personal income tax rate	−0.008***	−0.016**
	(0.002)	(0.007)
Sales tax rate	−0.035***	0.028
	(0.008)	(0.025)
Sales factor apportionment	0.001**	0.002*
	(0.0004)	(0.001)
Combined reporting	0.010	0.089*
	(0.016)	(0.048)
LLC	0.021**	0.052*
	(0.010)	(0.031)
Throwback rule	0.034*	−0.032
	(0.020)	(0.065)
Federal CIT deductibility	−0.121***	−0.264**
	(0.033)	(0.104)
Tax incentives	0.0001	−0.011***
	(0.001)	(0.003)
Non-tax incentives	−0.005***	0.008***
	(0.001)	(0.003)
Population	0.043***	−
	(0.006)	−
Median income	0.003**	−
	(0.001)	−
Population density	0.001*	−
	(0.0003)	−
State expenditures per capita	−0.014	−
	(0.013)	−
Average wage	0.026***	−
	(0.006)	−
Education	0.004**	−
	(0.002)	−
Energy price	−0.009**	−
	(0.004)	−
Ln GSP	−	0.662**
	−	(0.284)
CIT rate × Time trend	−0.001***	0.0004
	(0.0002)	(0.001)

Variable	First Stage Ln Gross State Product	Second Stage Ln CIT Base
Time trend	0.049***	−0.015
	(0.003)	(0.020)
Constant	17.10***	−0.84
	(0.09)	(5.02)
Within R-squared	0.950	0.536

Notes: Entries are fixed-effects panel regression coefficients with standard errors in parentheses.

*, **, and *** denote statistical significance at the 10 percent, 5 percent, and 1 percent levels.

Regressions include state fixed effects.

All percentages are on a 0–100 scale.

Population is measured in thousands.

Median income, GSP, and state expenditures per capita are measured in thousands of current-year dollars.

This question is examined in the first stage of the model. However, results from this model indicate that the corporate income tax rate actually has a larger negative effect on GSP over time. A possible explanation for this puzzling result is that new technologies may enhance firms' abilities to produce remotely, by increasing firm mobility. Perhaps this effect dominates any tax planning effect. In other words, firms may have a growing ability to produce in one state and sell nationwide, given the increased use of online shopping and better information technologies. Therefore, firms can respond more strongly to taxes because they need not be in a particular location to serve their customers. Further research is required to verify this hypothesis. All other findings of this model are similar to the baseline model, with the exception of the combined-reporting variable (and LLC allowances, as noted). Here a combined-reporting requirement has a positive and statistically significant effect on the CIT base.

6. Conclusions

In this chapter, an econometric model is developed to test the extent to which tax planning activities in response to differences in state business tax policies have affected state corporate income tax bases. Results strongly suggest that tax planning activity significantly diminishes taxable corporate profits in high-tax states. In particular, state corporate income tax bases decline by nearly 7 percent following a one-percentage-point increase in the top corporate income tax rate, holding Gross State Product and other state policy parameters constant. More in-depth analysis provides evidence that throwback rules are not effective in restoring state corporate income tax bases in most states. This result can be interpreted as evidence that firms seek out more planning opportunities when they are cost-justified by high corporate tax rates combined with a throwback rule. In contrast, combined-reporting requirements are found to be somewhat effective in restoring corporate tax bases in most cases, but their effect is lessened in states with throwback rules.

No evidence is found that the effects of tax planning on state corporate income tax bases have grown over time. In addition, findings do not indicate that tax planning activity has replaced locational responses to tax policy over the past decade and a half.

These findings are very important for policymakers to consider in designing better corporate income tax systems. First, policymakers should consider significant tax-planning-related base erosion that would likely follow an increase in the corporate income tax rate. Second, if policymakers decide that restoring, or at least maintaining, the corporate income tax base is desirable, evidence suggests that combined-reporting requirements are often effective in partially achieving this goal. At the same time, there is no evidence that these requirements diminish economic activity in states. Next, results provide no evidence that increased tax planning activity is a contributor to the recent corporate income tax base erosion. Further research is needed to better understand the causes of this trend. Last, results indicate that the sales tax rate significantly diminishes economic activity in states while corporate income and personal income tax rates have either statistically insignificant or very small effects.

References

Associated Industries of Massachusetts. 2004. "A Response to Proponents of Combined Reporting: Combined Reporting Is Bad for Massachusetts." *State Tax Notes* 32(2): 135–136.

Bankman, Joseph. 1999. "The New Market in Corporate Tax Shelters." *Tax Notes* 83(12): 1775–1795.

Bartik, Timothy J. 1991. "Who Benefits from State and Local Economic Development Policies?" (Kalamazoo, MI: Upjohn Institute).

Bartik, Timothy J. 1994. "Jobs, Productivity, and Local Economic Development: What Implications Does Economic Research Have for the Role of Government?" *National Tax Journal* 47(4): 847–861.

Bureau of National Affairs (BNA). 2004. "Holding Companies." *BNA Tax Management Multistate Tax Report*. Vol. 11(4): S 65–S68.

Cline, Robert, John L. Mikesell, Thomas S. Neubig, and Andrew Phillips. 2005. "Sales Taxation of Business Inputs: Existing Tax Distortions and the Consequences of Extending the Sales Tax to Business Services." *State Tax Notes* 35(7): 457–470.

Cline, Robert, William Fox, Thomas S. Neubig, and Andrew Phillips. 2003a. "A Closer Examination of the Total State and Local Business Tax Burden." *State Tax Notes* 27(4): 295–303.

Cline, Robert, William Fox, Thomas S. Neubig, and Andrew Phillips. 2003b. "Total State and Local Business Taxes: Fiscal Year 2003 Update." *State Tax Notes* 30(3): 205–210.

Crocker, Keith J., and Joel Slemrod. 2004. "Corporate Tax Evasion with Agency Costs." NBER Working Paper 10690. (Cambridge, MA: National Bureau of Economic Research).

Desai, Mihir A. 2002. "The Corporate Profit Base, Tax Sheltering Activity, and the Changing Nature of Employee Compensation." NBER Working Paper 8866. (Cambridge, MA: National Bureau of Economic Research).

Desai, Mihir A., and Dhammika Dharmapala. 2004. "Earnings Management and Corporate Tax Shelters." NBER Working Paper 11241. (Cambridge, MA: National Bureau of Economic Research).

Desai, Mihir A., and James R. Hines Jr. 2002a. "Expectations and Expatriations: Tracing the Causes and Consequences of Corporate Inversions." *National Tax Journal* 60(3): 409–456.

Edmiston, Kelly. 2002. "Strategic Apportionment of the State Corporate Income Tax: An Applied General Equilibrium Analysis." *National Tax Journal* 55(2): 239–262.

Federation of Tax Administrators. 2004. "Range of State Corporate Income Tax Rates." Washington, DC.

Fox, William F., and LeAnn Luna. 2002. "State Corporate Tax Revenue Trends: Causes and Possible Solutions." *National Tax Journal* 55(3): 491–508.

Fox, William F., and LeAnn Luna. 2005. "Do Limited Liability Companies Explain Declining State Corporate Tax Revenues?" *Public Finance Review* 33(6): 690–720.

Fox, William F., LeAnn Luna, and Matthew Murray. 2005. "How Should a Subnational Corporate Income Tax on Multistate Businesses Be Structured?" *National Tax Journal* 58(1): 139–159.

Gentry, William M., and R. Glenn Hubbard. 1998. "Fundamental Tax Reform and Corporate Financial Policy." In James M. Poterba, ed., *Tax Policy and the Economy*, vol. 12. (Cambridge, MA: MIT Press), pp. 191–227.

Hausman, Jerry A. 1978. "Specification Tests in Econometrics." *Econometrica* 46(6): 1251–1271.

Hines, James R., Jr. 2002. "On the Timeliness of Tax Reform." NBER Working Paper 8909. (Cambridge, MA: National Bureau of Economic Research).

Houghton, Kendall L., Ferdinand Hogroian, and Adam Weinreb. 2004. "Unitary/Combined Filings: Old Concept, New Focus." *State Tax Notes* 33(6): 457–471.

Inman, Robert P., and Daniel L. Rubinfeld. 1996. "Designing Tax Policy in Federalist Economies: An Overview." *Journal of Public Economics* 60(3): 307–334.

Luna, LeAnn. 2004. "Corporate Tax Avoidance Strategies and Solutions." *Journal of Multistate Taxation and Incentives* 14(2): 6–17, 46–48.

Mackie, James B., III. 2000. "The Puzzling Comeback of the Corporate Income Tax." *Proceedings of the Ninety-Second Annual Conference on Taxation.* (Washington, DC: National Tax Association), pp. 93–102.

Mazerov, Michael. 2003. "Closing Three Common Corporate Income Tax Loopholes Could Raise Additional Revenue for Many States." (Washington, DC: Center for Budget and Policy Priorities).

McIntyre, Michael J., Paul Mines, and Richard D. Pomp. 2001. "Designing a Combined Reporting Regime for a State Corporate Income Tax: A Case Study of Louisiana." *Louisiana Law Review* 61(4): 699–761.

Mintz, Jack, and Michael Smart. 2004. "Income Shifting, Investment, and Tax Competition: Theory and Evidence from Provincial Taxation in Canada." *Journal of Public Economics* 88(6): 1149–1168.

National Association of State Development Agencies. Various years. "Directory of Incentives for Business Investment and Development in the United States: A State-by-State Guide." (Washington, DC: Urban Institute).

Rego, Sonja Olhoft. 2003. "Tax-Avoidance Activities of U.S. Multinational Corporations." *Contemporary Accounting Research* (20)4: 805–833.

Schiller, Zach. 2002. "Ohio's Vanishing Corporate Franchise Tax." *State Tax Notes* 26: 537–550.

Slemrod, Joel. 1998. "Methodological Issues in Measuring and Interpreting Taxable Income Elasticities." *National Tax Journal* 51(4): 773–788.

Slemrod, Joel. 2001. "A General Model of the Behavioral Response to Taxation." *International Tax and Public Finance* 8(2): 119–128.

Slemrod, Joel. 2004. "The Economics of Corporate Tax Selfishness." *National Tax Journal* 57(4): 877–899.

U.S. Department of the Treasury. 1999. "The Problem of Corporate Tax Shelters: Discussion, Analysis and Legislative Proposals." (Washington, DC: U.S. DOT).

U.S. Department of the Treasury. Internal Revenue Service. Various years. "Annual Report: Commissioner of the Internal Revenue Service and the Chief Counsel for the Internal Revenue Service." (Washington, DC).

U.S. General Accounting Office. 1998. "IRS' Tax Gap Studies." GAP/GGD-88–66BR. (Washington, DC: U.S. GAO).

U.S. General Accounting Office. 2003. "Challenges Remain in Combating Abusive Tax Shelters." Testimony before the Senate Finance Committee on Finance. (Washington, DC: U.S. GAO).

Wasylenko, Michael. 1997. "Taxation and Economic Development: The State of the Economic Literature." *New England Economic Review* (March/April): 37–52.

Wasylenko, Michael, and Therese McGuire. 1985. "Jobs and Taxes: The Effect of Taxes on States' Employment Growth Rates." *National Tax Journal* 38(4): 497–514.

Zodrow, George R. 2003. "Reflections on the Economic Theory of Local Tax Incentives." *State Tax Notes* 28(10): 891–900.

Comments

William M. Gentry
Williams College

Bruce, Deskins, and Fox (hereafter, BDF) have written an ambitious chapter on an important but relatively understudied topic: firms' tax planning response to state tax policy. As defined by BDF, tax planning refers to a "broad set of tax avoidance and evasion schemes that affect only financial arrangements of firms." The current concern over the possible explosion in corporate tax shelter activity for federal income tax purposes suggests that tax planning has grown rapidly in recent years. Variation in state tax policy offers a window of opportunity to study how firms respond to differences in tax policy while many other business factors are similar across states. The challenge for research in this area, however, is that tax planning activity is not well defined and, by its nature, is difficult to measure. Neither tax nor financial accounting requires firms to identify such activity on their accounting statements.

While tax planning is difficult to define, there is a common notion that, like pornography, we know it when we see it.[1] The slippery slope of defining tax planning plagues research in this area. BDF provide a list of the sorts of schemes that they have in mind when they refer to tax planning: reclassifying business income as nonbusiness income; creating "nowhere income"; using transfer pricing; and shifting income across states by choice of organizational form. As I will discuss more fully later, this list begs the question of where to draw the line as to what is included in tax planning. For example, if a firm

---

[1] The analogy to pornography refers to Justice Potter Stewart's U.S. Supreme Court opinion in which he struggled to define pornography but came to a plainspoken conclusion: "I have reached the conclusion, . . . , that under the First and Fourteenth Amendments criminal laws in this area are constitutionally limited to hard-core pornography. I shall not today attempt further to define the kinds of material I understand to be embraced within that shorthand description; and perhaps I could never succeed in intelligibly doing so. But I know it when I see it." See *Jacobellis v. Ohio*, 378 U.S. 184, 197 (1964).

borrows more in response to higher corporate tax rates, has it engaged in tax planning or is this debt something less sinister than what people have in mind by the term "tax planning"?

Before providing my specific comments, I have one general comment on tax planning, which is a helpful organizing principle in the framework of the multistate problem. With multiple jurisdictions, one can think of tax planning taking one of two general forms. First, some tax planning methods reduce overall corporate taxable income; for example, when a firm borrows with deductible interest, the size of the corporate income tax base falls (holding the level of investment constant). This form of tax planning should respond to the overall level of taxation across jurisdictions. Second, some tax planning methods shift income across jurisdictions; for example, firms can use transfer pricing to shift income from high-tax jurisdictions to low-tax jurisdictions. This form of tax planning depends on tax rate (or tax rule) differences across jurisdictions. If jurisdictions harmonized their tax rates and rules, the advantages of such schemes would disappear.

I have three goals in my comments. First, I want to overview and interpret the BDF methodology. Second, because the empirical methodology focuses on labeling a residual effect as the effect of tax planning, I want to ask whether this residual effect accurately reflects tax planning as the authors construe the term. Third, I have a methodological point about the use of instrumental variables in the empirical work.

1. Overview and Interpretation of the BDF Methodology

Given the difficulty of measuring tax planning, BDF resort to a clever empirical strategy of measuring tax planning as the residual effect of state tax policy on the size of the corporate tax base after controlling for the non-tax determinants of corporate income in each state during a year and the locational effects of the state tax policy. The empirical model is quite parsimonious. To capture non-tax determinants of the size of the state corporate income tax base, the model includes state and year fixed effects. The state fixed effects capture differences in endowments that might influence the amount of or profitability of corporate activity across states. The year fixed effects capture any national trends – either due to macroeconomics or changes in tax planning for federal taxes – that might affect the size of state-level corporate tax base.

One important direct effect of state corporate tax policy is that it may affect the location decisions of firms. Firms may prefer to locate in low-tax states instead of high-tax states. Such location decisions, presumably, would affect both the amount of capital and labor employed in the state.

To capture these location decisions, BDF include gross state product (GSP), which measures overall value added within a state. As they discuss, GSP and the corporate tax base are endogenously determined. For example, if a state became more attractive to corporations for non-tax reasons, then one would expect that GSP would increase. Thus, the error term in an ordinary least squares regression would be correlated with one of the regressors (GSP), which can bias coefficient estimates.

Because the empirical model includes state fixed effects, the estimated coefficients on the tax policy parameters are econometrically identified on the basis of changes in policy over time. The effects of differences in average state policy over time are captured in the state fixed effects. The effects of common trends in state policy over time are captured by the year fixed effects. Fortunately, the time period includes a fair amount of activity in changes in state tax policy. Given the crucial importance of changes in state tax policy, the results would be more convincing if the paper spent more effort documenting the magnitude of the shifts in tax policy.

2. Does the Residual Effect of Tax Policy Reflect "Tax Planning"?

To the extent that tax policy parameters affect the size of the corporate tax base, after including these controls, BDF attribute the effects to tax planning. The problem with this residual approach is that it sweeps any tax effects that are not captured by differences in GSP into the estimated parameters on the tax variables. The authors' definition of tax planning seems to be the sorts of tax effects that fly under the radar screen of many traditional analyses of corporate taxation. However, I am afraid that many of the more traditional effects of tax policy confound the interpretation of the results.

A partial list of the concerns of traditional tax policy, in terms of the responses to a higher corporate tax rate, includes: (1) the substitution of labor for capital by corporations; (2) the substitution across lightly taxed forms of capital for heavily taxed forms of capital (e.g., assets with different depreciation schedules) by corporations; (3) substitution of noncorporate for corporate output by consumers, in response to higher relative prices of corporate output (i.e., the output effect of the classic Harberger model); (4) the substitution of debt finance for equity finance by corporations; (5) the choice of noncorporate forms of organization, such as the S corporation form, by firms; and (6) the substitution of wages for the owners rather than dividends by employee-owned firms. None of these responses is included in the BDF list of tax planning schemes. Whether one wants to include such responses depends on one's definition of "tax planning." These judgments fall into the category of "we know it when we see it," but it turns out that not everyone agrees on the definition of tax planning. Few people would consider the first three items listed above as tax planning devices, while there is probably little consensus on whether the latter three items qualify as tax planning. BDF seem to categorize movements across states as the only "real" effects of tax policy. However, I would certainly categorize the first three items in the above list as "real" effects of tax policy.

Controlling for GSP does not purge the estimated parameters of the effects of any of these responses. The chapter claims that GSP accounts for changes in the capital-labor ratio to the extent that the substitution causes a reduction in output. Another way of putting this claim is that controlling for GSP accounts for the deadweight loss from substitution across inputs but does not account for the shift in factor income between factors. Because economists usually think in terms of the deadweight loss being measured as a triangle but factor incomes as being measured as rectangles, I would conclude that GSP does a poor job of controlling for these real effects.

The final conclusion of the chapter is that "tax planning activity significantly diminishes taxable corporate profits in high-tax states. In particular, state corporate income tax bases decline by nearly 7 percent following a one-percentage-point increase in the top corporate income tax rate, holding Gross State Product and other state policy parameters constant" (from the chapter's conclusion). The authors would suggest that the sorts of tax planning devices that they list are the main culprits for this response. I am not convinced that the narrow concept of tax planning drives the results. I am left wondering how to separate the "dog" from the "tail" in understanding the results. If the traditional effects of tax policy are large, then the tax planning aspects may just be a modest part of the story. One piece of evidence that suggests that some of the more traditional effects are substantial comes from Goolsbee (2004); he finds that corporate taxes play an important role in the organizational form decisions in the retail trade sector.

The conclusion that I draw from this chapter is that the size of the corporate tax base at the state level is quite sensitive to the state corporate income tax rate and other tax parameters. However, the source of the sensitivity is unclear. Nevertheless, state policymakers should be aware of the sensitivity, regardless of the source, because the revenue effects are invariant to the source of the sensitivity.

3. The Use of Instrumental Variables Techniques

As recognized in this chapter and mentioned above, GSP and the corporate tax base are endogenously determined, which can lead to biased coefficient estimates with an ordinary least squares regression of the corporate tax base on GSP. The common solution to this endogeneity problem is to use instrumental variables techniques. These techniques require that the model includes at least one variable that has a direct effect on GSP (i.e., the endogenous regressor) that does not have a direct effect on the corporate tax base (i.e., the left-hand-side variable). The authors recognize this important point by stating: "Of course, the two-stage model requires at least one instrumental variable in the GSP equation that does not have an independent effect on the CIT base." Unfortunately, the authors never make a case that any of the chosen instrumental variables meet this requirement. The instruments include variables that measure the size of the state, input quality, or input prices. I expect that all of these variables have a direct effect on either the amount of corporate activity in a state or the profitability of corporate activity in the state.

In the end, the authors report results from both ordinary least squares and instrumental variable models. They conclude that the results are similar under the two approaches. This similarity could result for one of two reasons. First, the endogeneity may not create much bias in the estimated coefficients (i.e., the instrumental variables are valid instruments, but the endogeneity problem is small). Second, the instrumental variables do not meet the necessary requirements (i.e., the endogeneity creates substantial bias in the estimated coefficients, but the chosen instruments are invalid so the technique has not eliminated the endogeneity bias). I am unsure as to how large the biases may be in the ordinary least squares estimates; but without a good story for why the instruments are valid, my guess is that the second reason underlies the similarity in the results from the ordinary least squares and two-stage models.

Reference

Goolsbee, Austan. 2004. "The Impact of the Corporate Income Tax: Evidence from State Organizational Form Data." *Journal of Public Economics* 88(11): 2283–2299.

Comments

Charles E. McLure, Jr.
Hoover Institution, Stanford University

Bruce, Deskins, and Fox have undertaken an important but difficult task: determining the extent of tax planning employed to avoid state corporate income taxes and the efficacy of state efforts to prevent it. The first problem is that the extent of tax planning cannot be observed; it can only be inferred. The authors infer that tax planning occurs when, all else equal, increasing the corporate tax rate causes a state's corporate tax base to fall. Because the tax base also cannot be observed, the authors deduce it by dividing corporate tax collections by the top corporate tax rate.

An increase in tax rates – or changes in other features of the tax system – could, of course, affect the tax base negatively by inducing a reduction in real economic activity, as well as by inducing tax planning. Thus, the authors distinguish between tax-induced changes in real economic activity undertaken in response to increased taxes and tax planning, which results in reductions in a state's tax base without any changes in real economic activity. The authors seek to account for the former effect – to hold state economic activity constant – by including gross state product (GSP) in the equation explaining the tax base. But, because gross state product is endogenous, in their primary model they employ a second equation to explain GSP; it also includes various features of the tax system. This is a further source of difficulty; many have bent their swords attempting to tease out the effects of taxation on economic activity.[1]

---

[1] The authors report, "According to Wasylenko, the general conclusion of the literature on the interregional effects of tax policy is that tax policy is a statistically significant determinant of economic activity. However, the magnitudes (and even direction) of the effects of tax policy on economic development are scattered." It seems to me that, when estimated effects are statistically significant, but differ in sign, something is wrong. Indeed, Wasylenko (1997, p. 38) notes, "In effect, the results are not very reliable and change depending on which variables are included in the estimation equation or which time period is analyzed."

Among the explanatory variables the authors include in the tax base and GSP equations of their baseline model are various features of the corporate income tax system that might arguably facilitate or prevent tax planning: the weight on the sales factor in the apportionment formula, whether the state employs combined reporting, the existence of legislation enabling businesses to be organized as limited liability partnerships, and throwback rules. The authors interpret the regression coefficients on these variables in the tax base equation as indicating whether the feature either facilitates tax planning or prevents it. A key finding is that combined reporting does not reduce tax planning, except in combination with other antiplanning features.

In part because the description of how tax planning works is not adequate,[2] there is a disconnect between that description and the empirical attempt to measure tax planning. According to the authors, "Some forms of tax planning include: reclassifying business income as nonbusiness income, exploiting P.L. 86–272, using transfer pricing to shift income from high-tax to low-tax jurisdictions, employing passive investment companies, and using single-member limited liability companies (LLCs) to shift income out of state." It would have been useful if the authors had described the building blocks of tax shelters more fully and explained in greater detail how they can be employed to reduce taxes, with no change in real economic activity.

The list of tax planning techniques does not include the use of separate reporting to isolate income for tax purposes in legally separate entities, although the introduction does say that subsidiaries may be created for tax planning purposes, and PICs (passive investment companies), LLCs, and subsidiaries are types of legally separate entities. It is only when the authors discuss the empirical results for combined reporting that they hint that separate reporting may be a source of tax planning. Explaining how tax planning works without mentioning separate reporting is a bit like producing *Hamlet* without the prince. Several of the techniques of tax planning that the authors describe would not work – or would not be as effective – if a state required combined reports for legally separate entities engaged in unitary activities (including those conducted through a PIC or an LLP).[3] For example, the Geoffrey–Toys "Я" Us© case would never have arisen if South Carolina had

---

[2] The authors repeatedly imply that *differences* in state tax policies are what make tax planning possible. But tax planning could occur even if all states had identical tax policies, for example, separate accounting and sales-only apportionment in a world constrained by P.L. 86–272.

[3] Thus in discussing their transfer-pricing example, the authors note that Montana, the state from which income is assumed to be shifted, does not require combined reporting. The option to report on a combined basis in some states may also be used for tax planning under some circumstances.

simply employed unitary combination. Thus, conducting business through separate legal entities should be listed as a separate category of tax planning. Indeed, because it is the sine qua non of some forms of tax planning, perhaps it should constitute a sort of "uber category."

The description of how tax planning works might give the impression that the various categories of tax planning do not interact. In fact, that is far from true. The ability to manipulate transfer prices allows the use of PICs to be a far more effective tool of tax planning than if all transactions occurred at arms-length prices. Because of the interaction of P.L. 86–272 and sales-only apportionment, a single firm could have little or no tax liability in a state if it had either (1) substantial sales in the state but no physical presence (that is, no nexus), or (2) a substantial physical and economic presence in a state, as indicated by payroll and property (and thus nexus) but minimal sales. With separate reporting by each legally separate entity, a corporate group could avoid paying taxes under this regime by lodging sales in affiliates that lack nexus in a state, even if other affiliates have nexus in the state.[4] The inclusion of interaction terms in the regression equations is presumably intended to take account of these interactions, but the description of how tax planning works provides no theoretical underpinnings for it.

Another disconnect between the description of how tax planning works and the empirical attempt to measure tax planning involves the weight a state places on the sales factor in its apportionment formula., which figures prominently in the report of empirical results, but is not mentioned in the discussion of how tax planning works. While this weight is not a "technique" of tax planning, it is an important building block of tax planning, as the previous paragraph shows. Also, it is commonly assumed that increasing the weight on the sales factor will attract productive activities and may create incentives for tax planning. But what is true of sales of tangible property need not be true for sales of services and intangible property, which many states effectively attribute to the state of origin of the intangibles. The regression coefficient on sales is likely to reflect the net effect of these two offsetting tendencies.

It does not make much sense for a state to impose throwback, if it is going to place a high weight on sales in its apportionment formula for economic development reasons. It would be taking away through throwback the economic development incentive it granted via the high weight on sales. One would thus expect to find absence of throwback in states that place

---

[4] The last example is taken from McLure (2002).

a high weight on the sales factor, and I think that that is what one does find. If I am right, the coefficient on the sales factor may be picking up the effect of throwback, and neither the coefficient on the sales weight nor that on throwback is meaningful. If, however, a state does employ throwback, its effect should be greater, the greater the weight that state puts on sales. So again, there is interaction between independent variables that is not explained.

As with planning techniques, there are interactions between antiplanning techniques. In particular, the power of throwback in preventing tax planning would inherently be much less if a state employed combined reporting than if it did not, because sales to affiliates would only be thrown back if they were not eliminated in preparing a combined report. Again, the tax base equation includes interaction between combination and throwback, with no theoretical foundation for doing so.

As the authors note, South Carolina and several other states have successfully asserted "Geoffrey nexus" (nexus based on the in-state presence of intangible assets) in an effort to combat the use of PICs for tax planning. It would seem only natural for the authors to include successful assertion of Geoffrey nexus as an explanatory variable in the equation for the tax base in future work.

A related comment involves the tax treatment of LLCs. If activities of LLCs engaged in unitary business with their owners were included in a combined report, the use of this device for tax planning would be significantly reduced. It seems the authors should examine the possibility of including some sort of explanatory variable that would take into account this feature of state laws and perhaps others that would limit the use of LLCs for tax planning.

In thinking about how corporations act to reduce taxes, it is useful to think of two prototypical types of corporation: one that produces in a state, but sells most of its output elsewhere, and one that makes sales in a state, but has little or no production there (and in the extreme case lacks nexus, due to P.L. 86–272). The effects on real economic activity and the tax planning opportunities open to the two types of corporations, depending on the tax structure of a given state, are likely to be quite different, as are the effects changes in the tax structure have on economic activity and tax liabilities, including the impact of antiplanning measures. Of course, many corporations, especially the large ones that dominate the U.S. economy, both produce and sell in many states (but they may use separate entities to do it). Moreover, a given state has corporations that produce there, out-of-state corporations that sell into it, and corporations that do both. Thus, the effects on state tax revenues, and thus the tax base, as estimated by the authors, will reflect the balance of positive and negative impacts on corporations of various kinds. It would have been enlightening for the authors to spin this story out and tell us its implications for their analysis. (For example, a throwback rule will have no effect on a corporation that only sells in a state.)

I am troubled by the specification of the equations. Consider first, the tax base equation. Essentially, the authors are regressing the tax base, as estimated, on GSP and a handful of tax variables (plus non-tax incentives for economic development). I should have thought it appropriate to include some measures of "corporateness," such as the fraction of GSP in such typically corporate sectors as manufacturing, mining, utilities, etc.

I am also troubled for several other reasons by the specification of the GSP equation. First, it would seem better to try to explain GSP per capita (and tax base per capita), rather than including population in an equation that explains aggregate GSP. (This would also take care of scale effects, without the need to use logs of GSP and the tax base, unless the analysis suggested it.) As it is, it seems that including population and median income as explanatory variables comes fairly close to estimating deviations from an identity (GSP = population times GSP per capita) – that is, deviations of median income from GSP per capita. Also, it seems strange to include government spending per capita in an equation explaining aggregate GSP, rather than GSP per capita.

This specification would highlight the fact that it is far from clear which way causality runs between GSP and many of the "independent" variables used to explain it. That is, high GSP per capita can be expected to yield high median income, high manufacturing wages, and high government spending per capita. See Wasylenko (1997, p. 43) on simultaneous equation bias.

The authors note that there has been considerable concern that resort to tax shelters has reduced the base of the federal corporate income tax, to which the state tax bases are related, but make no further mention of this issue. I wonder whether it might make sense to use the ratio of the federal tax base to GDP as an explanatory variable in the tax base equations (rewritten as suggested above).

The elasticity of the corporate tax base with respect to GSP, estimated to be only 0.60, seems extraordinarily low. The conventional wisdom is that the tax base is highly elastic cyclically, and perhaps secularly. I would have liked to have an explanation for this low elasticity.

Some of the tax base results have a "black box" feel to them. Thus, the authors say, "The relationship between the CIT rate and base is mostly attributable to tax planning activities because holding GSP constant eliminates the effect of location distortions on the base." But which techniques of tax planning?

In short, the authors have posed an important question, but I am not satisfied by either their explanation of how tax planning works, which is needed to understand how best to specify the regression equation and understand the empirical results, or by the specification of the regression equations. Beyond that, I am not sure I believe the empirical results.

References

McLure, Charles E., Jr. 2002. "The Nuttiness of State and Local Taxes – and the Nuttiness of Responses Thereto." *State Tax Notes* 25(12): 841–856.
Wasylenko, Michael. 1997. "Taxation and Economic Development: The State of the Economic Literature." *New England Economic Review* (March/April): 37–52.

SEVEN

Corporate Taxation and International Competition

James R. Hines Jr.
University of Michigan and NBER

1. Introduction

Many countries tax corporate income heavily despite the incentives that they face to reduce tax rates in order to attract greater investment, particularly investment from foreign sources. The volume of world foreign direct investment (FDI) has grown enormously since 1980, thereby increasing a country's ability to attract significant levels of new investment by reducing corporate taxation. The evidence indicates, however, that corporate tax collections are remarkably persistent relative to gross domestic product (GDP), government revenues, or other indicators of underlying economic activity or government need. If this were not true – if corporate income taxation were rapidly disappearing around the world – then such a development might be easily explained by pointing to competitive pressures to attract foreign investment and retain domestic investment. Hence, the question remains why growing international capital mobility has not significantly reduced reliance on corporate income taxation.

There are at least three possible resolutions of this puzzle, of which the simplest is that the continued taxation of corporate income at high rates reflects the politics of tax policy formation. Corporate taxation may be popular because its incidence is so uncertain, leading large numbers of voters and various interest groups to conclude that others, and not they, bear the burden of this tax. If this political phenomenon is important, then it would explain why greater international capital mobility might not be accompanied by sharp tax reductions around the world. Even when governments do not

I thank Justin Garosi and Claudia Martínez for excellent research assistance, and Jack Mintz, Jay Wilson, other conference participants, and an anonymous referee for very helpful comments and suggestions.

explicitly incorporate capital mobility in their deliberations over capital tax policies, capital mobility influences tax collections, tax revenue projections, and the observable experience of other countries. Hence there is ample scope for indirect effects of capital mobility on national tax policies, even in an environment that is largely dominated by distributional politics.

The second possible explanation for continued high rates of corporate taxation in an era of significant international capital mobility is that governments do not have incentives to reduce their taxation of mobile capital. This might be the case if, for example, the volume, location, and performance of FDI were insensitive to taxation. A large body of evidence suggests, however, that exactly the opposite is the case – international investment and international tax avoidance are strongly influenced by tax policies. Hence, there is every reason to expect countries to benefit from tax reductions as capital becomes more internationally mobile.

The third possible explanation is that countries subtly distinguish between more mobile and less mobile capital, subjecting the former to lower rates of taxation than the latter. Such a strategy permits tax systems to collect significant revenue from less mobile investments while affording highly mobile investments the benefits of reduced rates. This differentiation of tax burdens can be accomplished in any of several ways, of which the most obvious is negotiated tax reductions for certain investors. Other methods of favoring mobile investments include generous tax treatment of certain industries and rules that permit multinational firms to avoid taxes by using carefully constructed transactions with affiliates in tax haven countries.[1] While it might or might not be in a country's interest to continue taxing income earned by less mobile investments, whose volume and performance are undoubtedly influenced by taxation, it is clear that, for any given average level of corporate taxation, reducing the relative burden on more mobile capital improves efficiency.

The evidence suggests that countries have responded to greater international capital mobility by reducing the relative (and absolute) taxation of international investors while continuing to tax domestic investments at high rates. Statutory corporate tax rates fell noticeably since the early 1980s, but were accompanied by tax base broadening that maintained or even slightly

---

[1] The tax deductibility of interest expenses implies that there is no corporate tax burden on marginal debt-financed investments. Hence, to the extent that international debt investments are more mobile than international equity investments, the imposition of a high statutory corporate tax rate itself may impose a greater burden on less mobile equity investments than it does on more mobile debt investments.

increased overall average corporate tax burdens. Foreign investors, however, were increasingly relieved of corporate tax burdens, as evidenced by
the foreign affiliates of U.S. firms, which faced average foreign tax rates
of 43 percent in 1982 but only 26 percent by 1999. In drawing attention
to the divergent paths of corporate tax revenues and the income tax burdens of foreign subsidiaries of U.S. multinational firms, Desai (1999) suggests that foreign tax practices are designed to distinguish between mobile
and less mobile capital, offering increasingly attractive terms to mobile
capital.

The cross-sectional pattern of corporate income taxation likewise displays
aspects of increasing competition for mobile economic resources. Small
countries generally face more elastic supplies of world capital than do large
countries, because small countries are more likely to be price takers in world
markets. As a result, the efficient source-based tax on mobile capital is lower
for smaller countries, and indeed, the efficient capital income tax rate is zero
for a very small country facing an infinitely elastic supply of world capital.
The data reveal a change over time in the extent to which country size is
correlated with tax rates. In 1982, there was a strong positive correlation
between tax rates and country size, but by 1999 this correlation had largely
disappeared. Progressive elimination of the effects of country sizes on corporate tax rates is one of the implications of intensified international tax
competition, since it is the ability to exploit market power that permits large
countries to benefit from higher tax rates. Consequently, the evolution of
corporate taxation in the period of globalization is properly understood as
reflecting increased competition for mobile resources.

Section 2 of this chapter reviews evidence of rising international capital
mobility and the sensitivity of corporate activity to tax policies. Section 3
considers the implications of tax competition for international tax rate setting and cross-country evidence of the evolution of corporate taxation.
Section 4 analyzes the determinants of statutory and effective corporate tax
rates in 1982 and 1999. Section 5 is the conclusion.

2. Taxation and International Capital Mobility

The potential economic impact of international tax differences increased
significantly in the modern era due to the marked growth of FDI. Figure 1
plots annual ratios of total world outbound FDI to total world income, as
reported by the World Bank's *World Development Indicators*. As the figure
indicates, FDI increased rapidly in the 1980s and 1990s. While the evidence
of growing FDI does not by itself demonstrate that tax policies influence

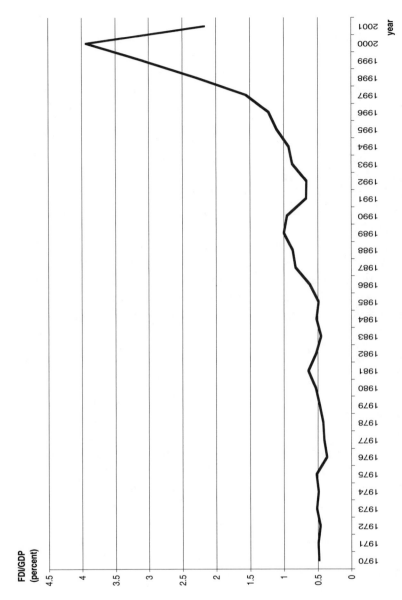

Figure 1. World Foreign Direct Investment as a Percent of World Product, 1970–2001
Note: The figure depicts annual ratios (measured in percent) of total world foreign direct investment to the sum of GDP for all countries.
Source: World Bank, *World Development Indicators.*

271

the magnitude and performance of international investment, there is ample separate evidence that they do.[2]

The available evidence of the effect of taxation on FDI comes in two forms. The first is time-series estimation of the responsiveness of FDI to annual variation in after-tax rates of return. Implicit in this estimation is a q-style investment model in which contemporaneous average after-tax rates of return serve as proxies for returns to marginal FDI. Studies of this type consistently report a positive correlation between levels of FDI and after-tax rates of return at industry and country levels.[3] The implied elasticity of FDI with respect to after-tax returns is generally close to unity, which translates into a tax elasticity of investment of roughly −0.6. The estimated elasticity is similar whether the investment in question is U.S. direct investment abroad or FDI by foreigners in the United States.

The primary limitation of aggregate time-series studies is that they are largely identified by yearly variation in taxes or profitability that may be correlated with important omitted variables. As a result, it becomes very difficult to identify the effects of taxation separately from the effects of other variables that are correlated with tax rates. Exceptions include Slemrod (1990), who distinguishes FDI in the United States by the tax regime in the country of origin, and Swenson (1994), who distinguishes investment by industry.

Other studies of investment location are exclusively cross-sectional in nature, exploiting the very large differences in corporate tax rates around the world to identify the effects of taxes on FDI. Grubert and Mutti (1991) and Hines and Rice (1994) estimate the effect of national tax rates on the cross-sectional distribution of aggregate U.S.-owned property, plant, and equipment (PPE) in 1982. Grubert and Mutti analyze the distribution of PPE in manufacturing affiliates in 33 countries, reporting a −0.1 elasticity with respect to local tax rates. Hines and Rice consider the distribution of PPE in all affiliates in 73 countries, reporting a much larger, −1, elasticity of PPE ownership with respect to tax rates. Desai, Foley, and Hines (2004a) report that high rates of indirect taxation have effects that are similar in sign and magnitude to high rates of corporate income taxation in depressing FDI by U.S. firms in data for 1982, 1989, and 1994. Altshuler, Grubert, and Newlon (2001) compare the tax sensitivity of aggregate PPE ownership in 58 countries in 1984 to that in 1992, reporting estimated tax elasticities

---

[2] See Hines (1997, 1999) for further elaboration and critical analysis of many of the studies surveyed in this section. This section draws on material from Hines (2005).

[3] See, for example, Hartman (1984), Boskin and Gale (1987), and Young (1988).

that rise (in absolute value) from −1.5 in 1984 to −2.8 in 1992. Altshuler and Grubert (2004) offer evidence of a −3.5 tax elasticity of investment in a sample of 58 countries in 2000, suggesting a continued, and possibly increasing, responsiveness to foreign tax differences.[4]

One of the important issues in considering the impact of taxation on international investment patterns is the ability of multinational firms to adjust the location of their taxable profits. It is often attractive to use debt to finance foreign affiliates in high-tax countries and to use equity to finance affiliates in low-tax countries, thereby accumulating income where tax rates are low and deductions where tax rates are high.[5] The evidence is broadly consistent with these incentives. Hines and Hubbard (1990) find that the average foreign tax rate paid by subsidiaries remitting nonzero interest to their U.S. parent firms in 1984 exceeds the average foreign tax rate paid by subsidiaries with no interest payments, while the reverse pattern holds for dividend payments. Grubert (1998) estimates separate equations for dividend, interest, and royalty payments by 3,467 foreign subsidiaries to their parent U.S. companies (and other members of controlled groups) in 1990, finding that high corporate tax rates in countries in which U.S. subsidiaries are located are correlated with higher interest payments and lower dividend payout rates. Desai, Foley, and Hines (2004b) report that, within groups of affiliates controlled by the same U.S. parents, debt levels are significantly higher among affiliates located in countries with higher tax rates.

Contractual arrangements between related parties located in countries with different tax rates offer numerous possibilities for sophisticated tax avoidance. Evidence of tax-motivated income reallocation comes in several forms. Grubert and Mutti (1991) and Hines and Rice (1994) analyze the

---

[4] Other cross-sectional evidence is consistent with these findings. Hines (2001) compares the distribution of Japanese and U.S. FDI around the world, finding Japanese investment to be concentrated in countries with which Japan has "tax sparing" agreements that reduce home-country taxation of foreign income; the estimated FDI impact of "tax sparing" is consistent with estimated large tax elasticities of foreign investment. Within the United States, Hines (1996) compares the distributions of FDI of investors whose home governments grant foreign tax credits for federal and state income taxes with those whose home governments do not tax income earned in the United States. One percent state tax rate differences in 1987 are associated with 10 percent differences in amounts of manufacturing PPE owned by investors from countries with differing home-country taxation of foreign-source income, and 3 percent differences in numbers of affiliates owned, implying a tax elasticity of investment equal to −0.6.

[5] Hines (1994) identifies exceptions to this rule that stem from the benefits of limiting equity finance in affiliates located in countries with very low tax rates in anticipation of reinvesting all of their after-tax profits over long periods.

aggregate reported profitabilities of U.S affiliates in different foreign locations in 1982. Grubert and Mutti examine profit/equity and profit/sales ratios of U.S.-owned manufacturing affiliates in 29 countries, while Hines and Rice regress the profitability of all U.S.-owned affiliates in 59 countries against capital and labor inputs and local productivities. Grubert and Mutti report that high taxes reduce the reported after-tax profitability of local operations; Hines and Rice come to a similar conclusion, their data indicating that 1 percent tax rate differences are associated with 2.3 percent differences in pre-tax profitability. Desai, Foley, and Hines (2006) find that foreign affiliates whose parent companies have nearby tax haven operations pay lower taxes as a fraction of sales than do other affiliates. While it is possible that high tax rates are correlated with other locational and firm-specific attributes that depress the profitability of foreign investment, competitive conditions typically imply that after-tax rates of return should be equal in the absence of tax-motivated income reallocation. The negative correlation of pre-tax profitability and local tax rates, together with the negative correlation of tax payments and ownership of foreign tax haven affiliates, is suggestive of active tax avoidance.

Harris et al. (1993) report that the U.S. tax liabilities of U.S. firms with tax haven affiliates are significantly lower than those of otherwise similar U.S. firms over the 1984–1988 period, which may be indirect evidence of aggressive income reallocation by firms with tax haven affiliates. Collins, Kemsley, and Lang (1998) analyze a pooled sample of U.S. multinationals over 1984–1992, finding a similar pattern of greater reported foreign profitability (normalized by foreign sales) among firms facing foreign tax rates below the U.S. rate. And Klassen, Lang, and Wolfson (1993) find that American multinationals report returns on equity in the United States that rose by 10 percent relative to reported equity returns in their foreign operations following the U.S. tax rate reduction in 1986.

Patterns of reported profitability are consistent with other indicators of aggressive tax-avoidance behavior, such as the use of royalties to remit profits from abroad and to generate tax deductions in host countries. Hines (1995) finds that royalty payments from foreign affiliates of U.S. companies in 1989 exhibit a –0.4 elasticity with respect to the tax cost of paying royalties, and Grubert (1998) likewise reports significant effects of tax rates on royalty payments by U.S. affiliates in 1990. Clausing (2001) finds that reported trade patterns between U.S. parent companies and their foreign affiliates, and those between foreign affiliates located in different countries, are consistent with incentives to reallocate taxable income. Controlling for various affiliate characteristics, including their trade balances with unaffiliated foreigners,

Clausing finds that 10 percent higher local tax rates are associated with 4.4 percent higher parent company trade surpluses with their local affiliates, which is suggestive of pricing practices that move taxable profits out of high-tax jurisdictions. Swenson (2001) finds a similar pattern in the reported prices of goods imported into the United States, in which high unit tariff rates appear to be associated with unusually low prices.

Taken together, this evidence implies that the volume of FDI, and accompanying economic activity and corporate tax bases, is highly responsive to local tax policies. It follows that countries contemplating lowering their corporate income tax rates can reasonably expect to receive greater foreign investment as a consequence. The incentive to reduce corporate tax rates in order to attract FDI has increased since the early 1980s, as levels of world FDI rose sharply during that time. The next section considers some of the implications of these developments for tax rate setting around the world.

3. International Tax Competition

Greater mobility of corporate economic activity produces incentives to reduce tax rates, particularly in small countries that face the most elastic supplies of foreign capital. This section considers the implications of simple models of tax rate setting in open economies and the available evidence of country reactions to these incentives.

3.1. Implications of Capital Mobility

Modern analysis of the corporate tax rate implications of international capital mobility dates to Diamond and Mirrlees (1971), who demonstrate that efficient taxation in a small, open economy entails zero taxation of income earned by foreign investors. The explanation for their result is that any positive taxation distorts the economy more than would other tax alternatives, without shifting any of the tax burden to foreign investors.[6] If international capital flows are increasingly sensitive to tax rate differences, then incentives to reduce tax rates are presumably rising as well. The analysis also implies that countries that nevertheless persist in taxing income earned by foreign investors will have lower incomes than those that do not.

The Diamond and Mirrlees result is commonly thought to imply that small countries have the least to gain from attempting to impose taxes on

[6] See Gordon (1986) for an elaboration of this argument, and Gordon and Hines (2002) for a further exposition.

foreign investment. Larger countries are able to extract some rents from foreign investors because prices in their economies need not respond to tax policies in a way that maintains unchanged the investors' after-tax profit margins. Possibly weighing against this is strategic competition among large countries, whose tax policies may be designed in a way that reflects their likely effects on the policies of other countries. Another consideration is that the inability to tailor tax and other policies perfectly might change efficient levels of corporate taxation from what they would be in the absence of other distortions. For example, trade barriers may distort local prices and thereby influence the efficient taxation of foreign direct investment. If countries are unable to impose corrective taxes or subsidies on externality-producing activities of corporations, then modifications to corporate income tax rates might serve as indirect remedies. Similarly, if personal income taxation cannot be tailored to achieve efficient redistribution, then there may be circumstances in which efficient third-best tax policies might include distortionary corporate taxes. Finally, large countries might have personal income tax rates that differ from those in small countries. Efforts to align top personal and corporate tax rates in order to prevent tax arbitrage would then produce correlations between corporate tax rates and country sizes that stem from the determinants of personal income tax rates rather than efficient taxation of inbound foreign investment.

Small countries are generally thought to face the most elastic corporate tax bases and therefore to have the strongest incentives to offer low corporate tax rates, despite possible mitigating factors such as strategic behavior and distortions induced by other policies. While there are few tests of the proposition that the supply of capital to small countries is more elastic than the supply of capital to large countries, this is more than a matter of faith, because, in most models, it follows as an implication of their relatively small domestic corporate tax bases. Whether countries actually design their policies based on these assumed elasticities is another matter.

3.2. Evidence of Country Reactions

Numerous studies have called attention to the significance of falling rates of corporate taxation around the world. Griffith and Klemm (2004) offer a recent survey of this literature, along with their own calculations showing that, while statutory corporate tax rates have declined, effective corporate tax burdens in Organisation for Economic Co-operation and Development (OECD) countries have remained roughly unchanged since the early 1980s. Thus, corporate tax revenues have remained constant, or even slightly risen, as a fraction of GDP in OECD countries. Corporate tax revenues as a fraction of total government tax revenues likewise remained roughly constant among OECD countries between 1980 and 2000. Keen and Simone (2004) note that the resiliency of corporate tax collections among OECD countries is not mirrored in the experience of developing countries, whose effective taxation of corporate income appears to have fallen between 1990 and 2001, due in part to the proliferation of tax holidays and other incentives directed at foreign investors.

The experience of U.S. multinational firms, whose foreign investments and foreign profitability are highly concentrated in OECD countries, is very different than that suggested by the aggregate OECD data. Desai (1999) notes that foreign taxes paid by U.S. firms began falling (as a fraction of income) in the mid-1980s, roughly coincident with passage of the U.S. Tax Reform Act of 1986. Altshuler and Grubert (2004) document a continued decline in average foreign tax rates faced by large controlled foreign corporations, a subset of the foreign affiliates of U.S. firms. Because average effective foreign tax rates may reflect endogenous taxpayer behavior as well as official action by foreign governments, it is not always easy to identify the source of tax reductions. One of the benefits of U.S. data, however, is that they are collected on a consistent basis over time, using unchanging tax base definitions, so falling effective tax rates are likely to correspond to reductions in actual tax burdens. Desai (1999) draws the very plausible conclusion from these patterns that foreign governments responded to increasing capital mobility and the implications of U.S. tax rate reductions by lowering their effective taxation of U.S. investors.

A number of studies probe the recent international experience for indications of the course of tax competition. Chennells and Griffith (1997) analyze tax rate setting among 10 OECD countries, reporting no evidence that smaller, more open countries tax capital at lower rates than do larger countries. Devereux, Lockwood, and Redoano (2002) report indications of tax policy interdependence among these 10 countries, in that they tend to mimic each other's statutory tax rate changes, which might represent a form of tax competition, though it could alternatively reflect policy coordination. Devereux, Griffith, and Klemm (2002) interpret the recent decline in statutory corporate tax rates together with roughly stable corporate tax collections as efforts on the part of governments to attract productive investments, and reported (taxable) income, from highly profitable multinational firms. Bretschger and Hettich (2002) revisit the relationship between country size and corporate tax rates in a panel of 14 OECD countries between 1967 and 1996, reporting that smaller countries have lower effective corporate tax rates, controlling for other considerations. And Altshuler and Grubert (2004) analyze changes in effective tax rates for foreign subsidiaries of U.S. firms between 1992 and 2000, reporting that tax rates fell most sharply for subsidiaries located in small countries. Given the inclusion of other regressors, among them lagged tax rates, it is, however, difficult to interpret this finding in the context of theories of tax rate setting.

3.3. Data

Information on country tax policies and their determinants comes from several sources. Top national statutory corporate tax rates, reported by the World Tax Database maintained by the University of Michigan's Office of Tax Policy Research (http://www.otpr.org), include data for several decades and a large number of countries. Comprehensive information on the tax obligations of the foreign affiliates of U.S. multinational firms is included among the data collected by the U.S. Bureau of Economic Analysis (BEA) on the basis of comprehensive surveys of American multinational firms in 1982, 1989, 1994, and 1999. Companies owning foreign affiliates with significant sales, assets, or net income are required to provide extensive information concerning their operations, which is then aggregated by country and reported by the BEA. Information is unavailable for countries in which very few U.S. firms have foreign operations, because reporting would then threaten to undermine the confidentiality promised survey respondents. In spite of these minor omissions, the BEA data are unique in their coverage and accuracy and therefore form the basis of the current analysis and much of what is known anywhere about the operations of multinational firms. National economic information is provided by the Penn World Tables, which compile national income account data on an internationally comparable basis for a large number of countries.[7]

Statutory corporate tax rates reported by the World Tax Database display the significant secular decline noted by other researchers. Using a matched sample of 68 countries, and weighting observations by GDP, average statutory tax rates fell from 45.9 percent in 1982 to 32.9 percent in 1999. The decline in statutory tax rates was most pronounced in large countries, but even unweighted average tax rates in this sample of countries fell from 41.3 percent in 1982 to 32.0 percent in 1999.

---

[7] The BEA data are available at http://bea.gov; the Penn World Tables are available at http://pwt.econ.upenn.edu.

Table 1. *Statutory and Effective Corporate Tax Rates*

	1982	1999
Statutory Corporate Tax Rates (%)		
Average weighted by GDP	45.9	32.9
Unweighted world average	41.3	32.0
Effective Corporate Tax Rates on U.S. Multinationals (%)		
Average weighted by GDP	42.6	26.2
Unweighted world average	36.5	23.9

Note: The table presents information for matched samples of countries in 1982 and 1999, for 68 of which it is possible to calculate average statutory corporate tax rates and for 45 of which it is possible to calculate average effective corporate tax rates.

Effective taxes paid by U.S. multinational firms to foreign governments fell over this time period along with statutory tax rates. These tax rates are calculated using BEA data and are defined as the ratio of corporate income taxes paid by all affiliates in a country to total pre-tax net income. In principle, this has the advantage of reflecting taxes that affiliates actually pay and thereby capturing the impact of tax holidays, tax credits, and tax base adjustments such as those to depreciation rules and loss carryforwards and carrybacks. In practice, however, companies may have negative earnings, so this measure tends to overstate actual effective tax rates faced by profitable firms. Hence, the effective tax rate is defined (as in Hines and Rice, 1994) as the (nonnegative) lesser of the statutory tax rate and the ratio of taxes paid to pre-tax income.

Effective tax rates exhibit more rapid declines than statutory tax rates over this time period. In 1982, the average effective tax rate (weighted by GDP) faced by U.S. firms in 39 foreign countries was 42.6 percent, whereas the corresponding average rate in the same countries in 1999 was 26.2 percent.[8] Unweighted average effective tax rates likewise declined markedly, from 36.5 percent in 1982 to 23.9 percent in 1999. Table 1 summarizes the average changes in statutory and effective tax rates. From the information in the

---

[8] Data availability dictates the choice of 1999 and 1982 as the reference years for these tax rate calculations, but it is noteworthy that the world economy performed poorly in 1982, whereas many economies expanded rapidly in 1999. It is not clear what impact, if any, these business cycle conditions might have on measured effective tax rates facing U.S. firms, though it is reassuring that effective tax rates exhibit the same secular trend as do statutory tax rates.

table it appears that, far from seeing some of the benefits of statutory tax rate reductions lost to tax base expansions, the foreign affiliates of U.S. firms enjoyed even greater foreign tax reductions than they might have in the absence of other adjustments to their tax positions.

4. Determinants of Corporate Taxation

The ability to exploit market power affords countries opportunities to extract rents from foreign investors by imposing high rates of tax on corporate profits. The incentive to raise corporate tax rates is greater for large countries whose stock of corporate investment is less elastic with respect to taxation than is the case for small countries. The purpose of this section is to consider the extent to which tax policy experience corresponds to this prediction.

4.1. Statutory Tax Rates

The evidence indicates that statutory tax rates were strongly positively correlated with country sizes in 1982 but that this positive correlation had largely disappeared by 1999. Figure 2 depicts average statutory corporate tax rates for 68 countries for which it was possible to obtain corporate tax rate, population, and GDP information for 1982. The two left-most bars in the chart correspond to 1982, the first bar presenting average statutory corporate tax rates for countries with below-median populations and the second presenting average statutory corporate tax rates for countries with above-median populations. As the bars reveal, smaller countries taxed corporate income at lower rates in 1982 than did larger countries, which is consistent with theoretical predictions. By 1999, however, this pattern has largely disappeared. Statutory corporate tax rates are lower for both sets of countries in 1999 and, in addition, the difference between large and small countries greatly narrowed.[9]

The average tax rates presented in Figure 2 are not adjusted to take account of differences in country incomes, and the simple division of the world into small and large countries is a bit crude from the standpoint of identifying the impact of country size on tax rates. Table 2 presents estimated coefficients from regressions in which the dependent variable is the statutory tax rate, and

---

[9] Figure 2 presents average statutory tax rates weighted by GDPs. In 1982, small countries had an average tax rate of 38.9 percent, while the average for large countries was 43.7 percent. In 1999, the average small country tax rate was 31.1 percent, and the average large country tax rate was 33.8 percent.

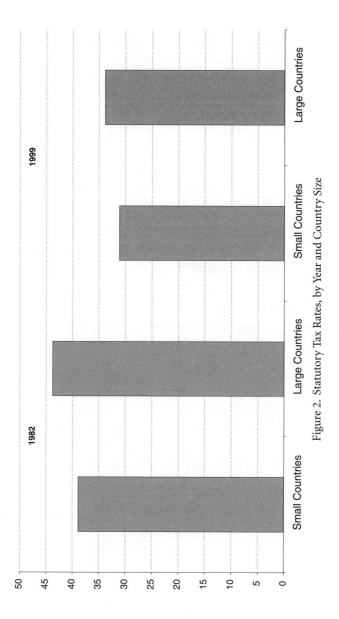

Figure 2. Statutory Tax Rates, by Year and Country Size

Table 2. *Determinants of Top Statutory Corporate Tax Rates (1982)*

	(1)	(2)	(3)	(4)	(5)
Constant	0.288	0.394	0.852	1.388	1.789
	(0.058)	(0.110)	(0.198)	(0.622)	(0.609)
Ln(Population 1982)	0.030	0.028	−0.193	0.027	−0.190
	(0.014)	(0.013)	(0.068)	(0.014)	(0.068)
Ln(Population 1982)^2			0.027		0.026
			(0.008)		(0.008)
Ln(Per capita GDP 1982)		−0.026	−0.028	−0.571	−0.548
		(0.026)	(0.026)	(0.351)	(0.350)
Ln(Per capita GDP 1982)^2				0.074	0.071
				(0.050)	(0.045)
Number of observations	69	69	69	69	69
R-squared	0.05	0.06	0.11	0.09	0.13

Note: Robust standard errors are in parentheses.

independent variables include powers of log population and log per capita GDP. The sample consists of 69 countries for which it is possible to obtain the necessary data. The estimated 0.030 coefficient on log population in the first column indicates that larger countries have higher statutory corporate tax rates; population doubling is associated with 3 percent higher rates in 1982. Adding the log of per capita GDP as an explanatory variable, as in the regression reported in column 2, reduces the estimated effect of population only slightly, to 0.028. The addition of a second power of log GDP has little effect on the population coefficient, as indicated by the regression reported in column 4. And the introduction of a second power of log population, as in the regressions reported in columns 3 and 5, reveals a nonlinear, indeed nonmonotone, effect of country size on corporate tax rates, the positive effect of country size on tax rates being strongest among the larger countries.[10]

The sizeable positive impact of national population on statutory corporate tax rates that is apparent in the 1982 data fails to materialize in 1999. Table 3 reports estimated coefficients from regressions in which the dependent variable is the 1999 statutory corporate tax rate, and independent variables

---

[10] Appendix Table 1 presents means and standard deviations of variables used in the regressions. The regressions presented in Table 2 are parsimonious, and resolutely so, despite the temptation to add other explanatory variables, including a standard measure of economic openness (the ratio of the sum of exports and imports to GDP). Explanatory variables are restricted to population and GDP in order to estimate the effect of largely exogenous determinants of tax policies and to focus on the impact of country size independent of other policy choices.

Table 3. *Determinants of Top Statutory Corporate Tax Rates (1999)*

	(1)	(2)	(3)	(4)	(5)
Constant	0.288	0.411	0.567	0.815	0.971
	(0.039)	(0.062)	(0.138)	(0.458)	(0.483)
Ln(Population 1999)	0.009	0.006	−0.071	0.005	−0.071
	(0.010)	(0.009)	(0.060)	(0.009)	(0.060)
Ln(Population 1999)^2			0.010		0.010
			(0.007)		(0.007)
Ln(Per capita GDP 1999)		−0.029	−0.031	−0.247	−0.249
		(0.013)	(0.013)	(0.242)	(0.243)
Ln(Per capita GDP 1999)^2				0.029	0.029
				(0.032)	(0.032)
Number of observations	111	111	111	111	111
R-squared	0.01	0.04	0.06	0.05	0.07

Note: Robust standard errors are in parentheses.

are the 1999 values of the same variables used in the regressions reported in Table 2. Thanks to greater data availability, the sample for the 1999 regression is considerably larger (111 countries) than that used to analyze the determinants of tax rates in 1982. The estimated coefficients reported in Table 3 have the same signs as their counterparts in Table 2, but are considerably smaller in magnitude and are statistically insignificant, save for the coefficients on log per capita GDP in the regressions reported in columns 2 and 3. In particular, the estimated 0.58 coefficient on log population reported in column 2 is less than one-fifth the size of the corresponding 1982 coefficient and is statistically indistinguishable from zero. To guard against the possibility that the 1999 results reflect mere differences in sample composition, the regressions were rerun using 1999 data for the 68 countries appearing in the 1982 sample;[11] the results, which are reported in Appendix Table 2, are very similar to those reported in Table 3.

4.2. Effective Tax Rates

Corporate tax obligations are the products not merely of statutory tax rates but also of specific rules by which tax bases are calculated. Figure 3 presents average effective foreign tax rates for U.S. firms in 1982 and 1999, distinguished by sizes of host countries. The height difference of the two left-most

---

[11] The 1999 data do not include information on Taiwan's GDP, so this observation is dropped from the regressions reported in Appendix Table 2.

Appendix Table 1. *Means and Standard Deviations of Regression Variables*

Variable	Mean	Standard Deviation
Statutory corporate tax rate, 1982	0.412	0.095
Statutory corporate tax rate, 1999	0.320	0.060
Ln(population), 1982	9.45	1.62
Ln(population), 1999	9.71	1.64
Ln(per capita GDP), 1982	8.70	0.94
Ln(per capita GDP), 1999	8.92	1.07
Effective corporate tax rate, 1982	0.341	0.224
Effective corporate tax rate, 1999	0.224	0.127
Effective corporate tax rate/Statutory corporate tax rate, 1982	0.897	0.249
Effective corporate tax rate/Statutory corporate tax rate, 1999	0.781	0.329
Indirect corporate tax revenue/Direct corporate tax revenue, 1982	3.75	3.90
Indirect corporate tax revenue/Direct corporate tax revenue, 1999	2.89	2.57

Appendix Table 2. *Determinants of Top Statutory Corporate Tax Rates (1999) (Sample Restricted to Countries in 1982 Sample)*

	(1)	(2)	(3)	(4)	(5)
Constant	0.292	0.326	0.452	0.508	0.663
	(0.042)	(0.061)	(0.172)	(0.439)	(0.486)
Ln(Population 1999)	0.007	0.006	−0.054	0.006	−0.057
	(0.010)	(0.010)	(0.075)	(0.010)	(0.076)
Ln(Population 1999)^2			0.007		0.007
			(0.009)		(0.009)
Ln(Per capita GDP 1999)		−0.008	−0.009	−0.106	−0.119
		(0.012)	(0.012)	(0.230)	(0.234)
Ln(Per capita GDP 1999)^2				0.013	0.015
				(0.031)	(0.031)
Number of observations	68	68	68	68	68
R-squared	0.01	0.01	0.02	0.01	0.02

Note: Robust standard errors are in parentheses.

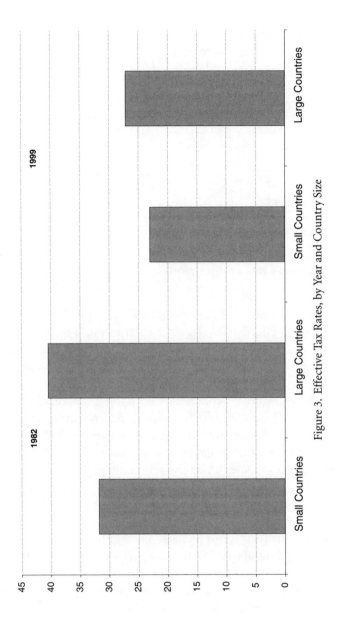

Figure 3. Effective Tax Rates, by Year and Country Size

285

Table 4. *Determinants of Effective Corporate Tax Rates (1982)*

	(1)	(2)	(3)	(4)	(5)
Constant	−0.236	−0.609	0.605	2.330	2.498
	(0.200)	(0.468)	(1.211)	(2.262)	(2.405)
Ln(Population 1982)	0.036	0.043	−0.112	0.039	−0.012
	(0.011)	(0.015)	(0.150)	(0.015)	(0.226)
Ln(Population 1982)^2			0.005		0.002
			(0.005)		(0.007)
Ln(Per capita GDP 1982)		0.029	0.034	−0.638	−0.582
		(0.028)	(0.029)	(0.505)	(0.566)
Ln(Per capita GDP 1982)^2				0.038	0.035
				(0.029)	(0.032)
Number of observations	45	45	45	45	45
R-squared	0.15	0.17	0.19	0.21	0.21

Note: Robust standard errors are in parentheses.

bars of Figure 3 indicates that U.S.-owned affiliates in small countries faced substantially lower effective tax rates in 1982 than did U.S.-owned affiliates in large countries. Effective tax rates were lower in 1999, as indicated by the two right-most bars of Figure 3, and the difference between average rates in small and large countries greatly attenuated.[12]

Table 4 presents estimated coefficients from regressions explaining effective tax rates in 1982 as functions of the same independent variables as those used in the regressions presented in Table 2. The estimated 0.036 coefficient in column 1 indicates that affiliates in larger countries paid greater taxes for a given level of income, a population doubling being associated with 3.6 percent higher effective tax rates. The estimated effect of country size increases somewhat with the addition of controls for per capita GDP in the regressions reported in columns 2 and 4, and does not exhibit important nonlinearities in the regressions reported in columns 3 and 5.

The positive and significant effect of country size on effective tax rates in 1982 is not repeated in data for 1999. Table 5 presents regressions estimating the determinants of effective tax rates in 1999. While the point estimates of the log population coefficients are positive in the regressions reported in columns 1, 2, and 4, they are considerably smaller in magnitude than the corresponding coefficients in Table 4 and are not statistically significant. The

---

[12] Figure 3 presents average effective tax rates weighted by GDPs. In 1982, U.S.-owned affiliates in small countries had average effective tax rates of 31.7 percent, while the average tax rate of affiliates in large countries was 40.5 percent. In 1999, the average small country effective tax rate was 23.0 percent, and the average large country tax rate was 27.1 percent.

Table 5. *Determinants of Effective Corporate Tax Rates (1999)*

	(1)	(2)	(3)	(4)	(5)
Constant	0.026	−0.317	−3.588	−1.023	−3.247
	(0.280)	(0.418)	(1.563)	(1.745)	(1.951)
Ln(Population 1999)	0.013	0.020	0.427	0.020	0.444
	(0.017)	(0.017)	(0.187)	(0.014)	(0.193)
Ln(Population 1999)^2			−0.012		−0.013
			(0.006)		(0.006)
Ln(Per capita GDP 1999)		0.025	0.015	0.185	−0.094
		(0.024)	(0.025)	(0.386)	(0.390)
Ln(Per capita GDP 1999)^2				−0.009	0.006
				(0.021)	(0.022)
Number of observations	45	45	45	45	45
R-squared	0.03	0.05	0.16	0.06	0.16

Note: Robust standard errors are in parentheses.

regressions reported in columns 3 and 5 of Table 5 suggest the possibility of a nonlinear effect of country size on effective tax rates, one in which the impact of greater population declines as populations grow, turning negative for larger countries. This nonlinear pattern differs from that evident in the regressions in which the statutory tax rate is the dependent variable. The pattern also differs from the implications of most models in which countries impose corporate taxes designed to extract rents from inelastic investors, because such models typically imply that the effects of given changes in country size on tax rates should increase in magnitude as countries grow larger and thereby affect world prices to greater degrees.

4.3. Corporate Tax Bases

One of the functions of the evidence presented in Tables 4 and 5 is to confirm that the disappearing effect of country size on statutory tax rates, implied by the regressions presented in Tables 2 and 3, is not merely an artifact of replacing narrow with broad tax bases, while reducing statutory tax rates, in larger countries. This leaves open the question of what happened to corporate tax bases in small and large countries in the period between 1982 and 1999. It is possible to examine this issue directly, and that is the purpose of the regressions presented in Tables 6 and 7.[13]

---

[13] It is worth noting that the chapter's calculations of effective corporate tax rates and corporate tax bases are based on data on U.S. multinational firms exclusively. Conceivably the experiences of investors from other countries might differ from those of U.S. investors, due

Table 6. *Determinants of Corporate Tax Bases (1982)*

	(1)	(2)	(3)	(4)	(5)
Constant	−0.167	−1.003	−2.606	2.977	1.570
	(0.405)	(0.870)	(2.024)	(4.074)	(4.271)
Ln(Population 1982)	0.064	0.080	0.284	0.075	0.505
	(0.023)	(0.030)	(0.257)	(0.026)	(0.401)
Ln(Population 1982)^2			−0.006		−0.013
			(0.008)		(0.012)
Ln(Per capita GDP 1982)		0.065	0.058	−0.838	−1.303
		(0.045)	(0.049)	(0.910)	(1.005)
Ln(Per capita GDP 1982)^2				0.052	0.078
				(0.052)	(0.057)
Number of observations	45	45	45	45	45
R-squared	0.15	0.19	0.19	0.20	0.23

Note: Robust standard errors are in parentheses.

Table 7. *Determinants of Corporate Tax Bases (1999)*

	(1)	(2)	(3)	(4)	(5)
Constant	0.047	−0.713	−10.792	−3.762	−10.433
	(0.849)	(1.217)	(4.847)	(4.928)	(5.464)
Ln(Population 1999)	0.045	0.059	1.313	0.058	1.331
	(0.051)	(0.051)	(0.591)	(0.039)	(0.541)
Ln(Population 1999)^2			−0.038		−0.038
			(0.018)		(0.016)
Ln(Per capita GDP 1999)		0.055	0.024	0.746	−0.090
		(0.070)	(0.072)	(1.090)	(1.093)
Ln(Per capita GDP 1999)^2				−0.038	0.006
				(0.061)	(0.061)
Number of observations	45	45	45	45	45
R-squared	0.04	0.05	0.18	0.06	0.18

Note: Robust standard errors are in parentheses.

The dependent variable in the regressions presented in Table 6 is the ratio of the effective corporate tax rate for U.S. firms to the statutory corporate rate. This is a measure of the corporate tax base, insofar as it applies to American firms, normalized by the U.S. accounting definition of

to national differences in the taxation of foreign income, industrial composition of foreign investment, and other factors. It is not clear whether any of these differences would affect measured correlations of tax rates and country sizes.

foreign income. As the estimated 0.064 coefficient in the regression reported in column 1 of Table 6 indicates, the corporate tax base was broader in large countries in 1982 than it was in small countries. The effect of country size persists, and indeed increases slightly in magnitude, as controls are added for per capita GDP in the regressions reported in columns 2 and 4. The 0.080 coefficient in column 2 implies that, controlling for per capita income, doubling the size of a country is associated with an 8 percent greater corporate tax base. Based on the regressions reported in columns 3 and 5, this effect of country size has little discernable nonlinearity. Total tax obligations are the product of tax rates and tax bases, and it appears that governments of large countries in 1982 used both higher tax rates and broader tax bases to tax corporations more heavily than did governments of small countries.

Table 7 reports the results of repeating these regressions using data for 1999. Point estimates of coefficients on log population in the regressions reported in columns 1, 2, and 4 are smaller, and associated standard errors larger, than in the 1982 regressions, making it impossible to reject the hypothesis that country size had no effect on corporate tax bases in 1999. The regressions reported in columns three and five suggest an anomalous nonlinear effect of population on corporate tax bases, in which the impact of greater country size diminishes and ultimately becomes negative as country populations grow. The pattern of corporate tax base regressions in 1982 and 1999 is similar to the pattern of effective corporate tax rate regressions for the same years, suggesting that whatever process was responsible for the correlation between country size and corporate tax provisions that imposed heavy burdens in 1982 had largely disappeared by 1999.

4.4. Indirect Taxes

Business activities generate government revenue from many taxes other than just corporate income taxes, including payroll and personal income taxes levied on employees, sales taxes, value added taxes, property taxes, excise taxes, and numerous others. Desai, Foley, and Hines (2004a) note that these indirect tax obligations generally exceed the corporate income tax obligations of foreign affiliates of U.S. multinational firms, and Christensen, Cline, and Neubig (2001) find the same to be true of firms in the United States. It is conceivable that, over the 1982–1999 period, larger countries simply replaced corporate income taxes with higher rates of indirect business taxes, thereby changing the tax mix without reducing effective rates of taxation of business activity. The data do not, however, support such an interpretation.

Appendix Table 3. *Determinants of Indirect/Direct Tax Revenue (1982)*

	(1)	(2)	(3)	(4)	(5)
Constant	7.307	−6.516	−38.145	−55.235	−63.744
	(7.405)	(13.255)	(29.352)	(72.798)	(77.951)
Ln(Population 1999)	−0.207	0.073	4.118	0.122	2.649
	(0.426)	(0.497)	(3.577)	(0.521)	(7.547)
Ln(Population 1999)^2			−0.123		−0.077
			(0.108)		(0.230)
Ln(Per capita GDP 1999)		1.005	0.847	12.141	9.451
		(0.683)	(0.727)	(16.301)	(18.349)
Ln(Per capita GDP 1999)^2				−0.641	−0.492
				(0.937)	(1.047)
Number of observations	40	40	40	40	40
R-squared	0.01	0.03	0.04	0.05	0.05

Note: Robust standard errors are in parentheses.

Appendix Table 4. *Determinants of Indirect/Direct Tax Revenue (1999)*

	(1)	(2)	(3)	(4)	(5)
Constant	2.408	2.026	−19.220	−74.154	−70.119
	(3.978)	(11.487)	(21.102)	(36.491)	(43.311)
Ln(Population 1999)	0.028	0.037	2.638	−0.068	−0.876
	(0.237)	(0.349)	(2.596)	(0.331)	(4.530)
Ln(Population 1999)^2			−0.077		0.024
			(0.079)		(0.134)
Ln(Per capita GDP 1999)		0.026	−0.020	17.670	18.272
		(0.663)	(0.695)	(8.174)	(8.940)
Ln(Per capita GDP 1999)^2				−0.987	−1.020
				(0.456)	(0.497)
Number of observations	41	41	41	41	41
R-squared	0.00	0.00	0.01	0.11	0.11

Note: Robust standard errors are in parentheses.

Appendix Tables 3 and 4 present regressions in which the dependent variable is the ratio of indirect tax payments by U.S. multinational firms to corporate income tax payments.[14] This ratio was not systematically related to country size in either the 1982 or the 1999 sample, suggesting that the determinants

---

[14] Indirect tax payments are defined in the BEA data to include any type of tax other than income and payroll taxes, as the BEA survey form asks for the sum of sales taxes, value added taxes, excise taxes; property taxes; and import and export duties. See Desai, Foley, and Hines (2004a) for further discussion of this variable.

Appendix Table 5. *Simple Effective Corporate Income Tax Rate (1982)*
(Revenue as a Fraction of GDP)

	(1)	(2)	(3)	(4)	(5)
Constant	5.19	9.18	15.66	−44.12	−42.46
	(3.62)	(4.70)	(13.53)	(24.60)	(27.82)
Ln(Population 1982)	−0.46	−0.53	−3.79	−0.47	−6.16
	(0.86)	(0.85)	(5.65)	(0.81)	(5.87)
Ln(Population 1982)^2			0.41		0.72
			(0.68)		(0.73)
Ln(Per capita GDP 1982)		−0.96	−1.01	28.34	33.57
		(0.87)	(0.93)	(14.14)	(17.25)
Ln(Per capita GDP 1982)^2				−3.98	−4.71
				(1.94)	(2.36)
Number of observations	50	50	50	50	50
R-squared	0.0088	0.0216	0.0296	0.0704	0.0933

Note: Robust standard errors are in parentheses.

of indirect tax rates are similar to the determinants of direct tax rates, a pattern that is consistent with the high correlation of the two taxes reported by Desai, Foley, and Hines (2004a).

4.5. Total Corporate Tax Collections

Total corporate income tax collections are the product of corporate investment, corporate profitability, the corporate tax base, and statutory corporate tax rates. Given the complexity of the factors involved, the endogeneity of tax policies to economic conditions, and the endogeneity of corporate investment to corporate income tax rates, it is perhaps naïve to expect total corporate income tax collections to be related in a systematic way to country size. Appendix Tables 5 and 6 nonetheless present regressions in which the dependent variable is the ratio of corporate income tax collections to GDP for countries for which it is possible to obtain the necessary data. The regressions reveal no discernable impact of country size on corporate tax collections in either 1982 or 1999, though, given the size of the associated standard errors, it is difficult to rule out many hypotheses on the basis of these results. Total corporate tax collections are the sum of revenues received from taxing inbound FDI and revenues from taxing income earned by domestic businesses. Hence, the absence of a country size effect on total corporate tax collections is consistent with the possibility of very different determinants of tax burdens facing foreign and domestic investors, particularly for 1982.

Appendix Table 6. *Simple Effective Corporate Income Tax Rate (1999)*
(Revenue as a Fraction of GDP)

	(1)	(2)	(3)	(4)	(5)
Constant	1.00	−3.57	−4.86	1.15	0.40
	(1.48)	(1.65)	(6.00)	(12.13)	(13.67)
Ln(Population 1999)	0.34	0.42	1.03	0.43	1.20
	(0.36)	(0.34)	(2.82)	(0.34)	(2.70)
Ln(Population 1999)^2			−0.07		−0.09
			(0.34)		(0.33)
Ln(Per capita GDP 1999)		1.08	1.09	−1.44	−1.89
		(0.40)	(0.40)	(6.46)	(6.12)
Ln(Per capita GDP 1999)^2				0.33	0.39
				(0.88)	(0.83)
Number of observations	63	63	63	63	63
R-squared	0.0264	0.1232	0.1244	0.1249	0.1268

Note: Robust standard errors are in parentheses.

5. Conclusion

The evidence points to a systematic change in the pattern of international tax rate setting during the period in which international capital mobility greatly increased. In 1982, large countries subjected corporate income to significantly higher rates of taxation than did small countries, but by 1999 these differences were no longer so apparent. Statutory corporate tax rates fell around the world over the same years, while corporate tax bases broadened to compensate for the revenue effects of tax rate reductions – except for foreign investors, whose average effective tax rates fell dramatically.

This pattern of international tax rate setting suggests that tax competition stiffened substantially since the early 1980s. Countries that previously exploited their positions as capital importers and as leaders in setting tax rates by imposing high corporate tax rates increasingly found themselves competing with other jurisdictions to attract mobile investment. As a result, tax rates on mobile investment fell, though countries maintained their (higher) rates of tax on less mobile domestic investment. This evolution of corporate tax policy is the logical outcome of greater competition between countries to attract investment, and, if anything, intensified corporate tax competition should be expected to lead to further pressures for corporate tax rate reductions. Whether this is a welcome or a regrettable development may turn on the form that these future tax changes take.

References

Altshuler, Rosanne, and Harry Grubert. 2004. "Taxpayer Responses to Competitive Tax Policies and Tax Policy Responses to Competitive Taxpayers: Recent Evidence." *Tax Notes International* 34(13): 1349–1362.

Altshuler, Rosanne, Harry Grubert, and T. Scott Newlon. 2001. "Has U.S. Investment Abroad Become More Sensitive to Tax Rates?" In James R. Hines Jr., ed., *International Taxation and Multinational Activity*. (Chicago: University of Chicago Press), pp. 9–32.

Boskin, Michael, and William G. Gale. 1987. "New Results on the Effects of Tax Policy on the International Location of Investment." In Martin Feldstein, ed., *The Effects of Taxation on Capital Accumulation*. (Chicago: University of Chicago Press), pp. 201–219.

Bretschger, Lucas, and Frank Hettich. 2002. "Globalisation, Capital Mobility and Tax Competition: Theory and Evidence for OECD Countries." *European Journal of Political Economy* 18(4): 695–716.

Chennells, Lucy, and Rachel Griffith. 1997. *Taxing Profits in a Changing World*. (London: Institute for Fiscal Studies).

Christensen, Kevin, Robert Cline, and Tom Neubig. 2001. "Total Corporate Taxation: 'Hidden,' Above-the-Line, Non-Income Taxes." *National Tax Journal* 54(3): 495–506.

Clausing, Kimberly A. 2001. "The Impact of Transfer Pricing on Intrafirm Trade." In James R. Hines Jr., ed., *International Taxation and Multinational Activity*. (Chicago: University of Chicago Press), pp. 173–194.

Collins, Julie H., Deen Kemsley, and Mark Lang. 1998. "Cross-Jurisdictional Income Shifting and Earnings Valuation." *Journal of Accounting Research* 36(2): 209–229.

Desai, Mihir A. 1999. "Are We Racing to the Bottom? Evidence on the Dynamics of International Tax Competition." In *Proceedings of the 91st Annual Conference on Taxation*. (Washington, DC: National Tax Association), pp. 176–187.

Desai, Mihir A., C. Fritz Foley, and James R. Hines Jr. 2004a. "Foreign Direct Investment in a World of Multiple Taxes." *Journal of Public Economics* 88(12): 2727–2744.

Desai, Mihir A., C. Fritz Foley, and James R. Hines Jr. 2004b. "A Multinational Perspective on Capital Structure Choice and Internal Capital Markets." *Journal of Finance* 59(6): 2451–2487.

Desai, Mihir A., C. Fritz Foley, and James R. Hines Jr. 2006. "The Demand for Tax Haven Operations." *Journal of Public Economics* 90(3): 513–531.

Devereux, Michael P., Ben Lockwood, and Michela Redoano. 2002. "Do Countries Compete over Corporate Tax Rates?" CSGR Working Paper 97/02. (Coventry, England: University of Warwick).

Devereux, Michael P., Rachel Griffith, and Alexander Klemm. 2002. "Corporate Income Tax Reforms and International Tax Competition." *Economic Policy* 17(35): 449–495.

Diamond, Peter A., and James Mirrlees. 1971. "Optimal Taxation and Public Production I: Production Efficiency; II: Tax Rules." *American Economic Review* 61(1, 2): 8–27, 261–278.

Gordon, Roger H. 1986. "Taxation of Investment and Savings in a World Economy." *American Economic Review* 76(5): 1086–1102.

Gordon, Roger H., and James R. Hines Jr. 2002. "International Taxation." In Alan J. Auerbach and Martin Feldstein, eds., *Handbook of Public Economics*, vol. 4. (Amsterdam: North-Holland), pp. 1935–1995.

Griffith, Rachel, and Alexander Klemm. 2004. "What Has Been the Tax Competition Experience of the Last 20 Years?" *Tax Notes International* 34(13): 1299–1315.

Grubert, Harry. 1998. "Taxes and the Division of Foreign Operating Income among Royalties, Interest, Dividends and Retained Earnings." *Journal of Public Economics* 68(2): 269–290.

Grubert, Harry, and John Mutti. 1991. "Taxes, Tariffs and Transfer Pricing in Multinational Corporate Decision Making." *Review of Economics and Statistics* 73(2): 285–293.

Harris, David, Randall Morck, Joel Slemrod, and Bernard Yeung. 1993. "Income Shifting in U.S. Multinational Corporations." In Alberto Giovannini, R. Glenn Hubbard, and Joel Slemrod, eds., *Studies in International Taxation.* (Chicago: University of Chicago Press), pp. 277–302.

Hartman, David G. 1984. "Tax Policy and Foreign Direct Investment in the United States." *National Tax Journal* 37(4): 475–487.

Hines, James R., Jr. 1994. "Credit and Deferral as International Investment Incentives." *Journal of Public Economics* 55(2): 323–347.

Hines, James R., Jr. 1995. "Taxes, Technology Transfer, and the R&D Activities of Multinational Firms." In Martin Feldstein, James R. Hines Jr., and R. Glenn Hubbard, eds., *The Effects of Taxation on Multinational Corporations.* (Chicago: University of Chicago Press), pp. 225–248.

Hines, James R., Jr. 1996. "Altered States: Taxes and the Location of Foreign Direct Investment in America." *American Economic Review* 86(5): 1076–1094.

Hines, James R., Jr. 1997. "Tax Policy and the Activities of Multinational Corporations." In Alan J. Auerbach, ed., *Fiscal Policy: Lessons from Economic Research.* (Cambridge, MA: MIT Press), pp. 401–445.

Hines, James R., Jr. 1999. "Lessons from Behavioral Responses to International Taxation." *National Tax Journal* 52(2): 305–322.

Hines, James R., Jr. 2001. "'Tax Sparing' and Direct Investment in Developing Countries." In James R. Hines Jr., ed., *International Taxation and Multinational Activity.* (Chicago: University of Chicago Press), pp. 39–66.

Hines, James R., Jr. 2005. "Do Tax Havens Flourish?" In James M. Poterba, ed., *Tax Policy and the Economy*, vol. 19. (Cambridge, MA: MIT Press), pp. 65–99.

Hines, James R., Jr., and Eric M. Rice. 1994. "Fiscal Paradise: Foreign Tax Havens and American Business." *Quarterly Journal of Economics* 109(1): 149–182.

Hines, James R., Jr., and R. Glenn Hubbard. 1990. "Coming Home to America: Dividend Repatriations by U.S. Multinationals." In Assaf Razin and Joel Slemrod, eds., *Taxation in the Global Economy.* (Chicago: University of Chicago Press), pp. 161–200.

Keen, Michael, and Alejandro Simone. 2004. "Is Tax Competition Harming Developing Countries More Than Developed?" *Tax Notes International* 34(13): 1317–1325.

Klassen, Kenneth, Mark Lang, and Mark Wolfson. 1993. "Geographic Income Shifting by Multinational Corporations in Response to Tax Rate Changes." *Journal of Accounting Research* 31(Supplement): 141–173.

Slemrod, Joel. 1990. "Tax Effects on Foreign Direct Investment in the United States: Evidence from a Cross-Country Comparison." In Assaf Razin and Joel Slemrod, eds., *Taxation in the Global Economy*. (Chicago: University of Chicago Press), pp. 79–117.

Swenson, Deborah L. 1994. "The Impact of U.S. Tax Reform on Foreign Direct Investment in the United States." *Journal of Public Economics* 54(2): 243–266.

Swenson, Deborah L. 2001. "Tax Reforms and Evidence of Transfer Pricing." *National Tax Journal* 54(1): 7–25.

Young, Kan H. 1988. "The Effects of Taxes and Rates of Return on Foreign Direct Investment in the United States." *National Tax Journal* 41(1): 109–121.

Comments

Jack M. Mintz[1]
University of Toronto

The most remarkable result in Jim Hines's paper is that the differences in corporate tax rates (whether statutory or average rates – taxes divided by profits) are no longer important across different-size countries by the year 2000, compared to 1980, when size did matter. This surprising result goes against anecdotal evidence. For example, the typical statutory corporate tax rate among developed and many developing countries is now 30 percent (KPMG, 2004); and for the G-7 countries, only the UK has a corporate income tax rate at 30 percent (all other G-7 countries have corporate income tax rates that are more than 30 percent, with Japan being the highest at more than 41 percent). It is not hard to find small countries with corporate income tax rates far less than 30 percent, including Hungary (18 percent), Ireland (12.5 percent), Sweden (28 percent), and Switzerland (22 percent), to name a few.

Later, I will discuss each of these points in tandem. However, first I wish to provide some background on corporate tax policies set internationally, to be followed by some comments that raise some doubts about the findings but nevertheless suggest that further research is needed to confirm the results.

1. Some Background

In his discussion of results, Jim Hines demonstrates three important points about the evolution of corporate tax policy in the last two decades. In fact, his empirical results stop in 1999, just prior to rapid reductions in corporate tax rates that have occurred in Europe, Asia, and the Americas since the year 2000. Nonetheless, I agree with these trends.

---

[1] Professor of Business Economics, J. L. Rotman School of Management, University of Toronto.

296

The first point is that corporate income tax has declined quite significantly in the past 20 years. In 1980, the average corporate tax rate was 48 percent, falling to 30 percent by 2004 (KPMG, 2004). This trend is continuing – for example, Finland, Germany, and the Netherlands have announced further rate reductions.

The second point is that corporate tax revenues as a portion of the GDP have not fallen in the past 15 years across OECD countries. In fact, there has been a slight increase in revenues for many countries. In part, this reflects tax policies that have led to the scaling back of targeted tax preferences, such as investment tax allowances, accelerated depreciation, and tax credits in many countries. It also reflects income being shifted from personal to corporate accounts, given that corporate rates are less than top personal rates in many countries.

The third important change has been a shift in profit-sensitive to profit-insensitive taxes levied on businesses (Canada, 1998). The decline in corporate income tax rates is largely a result of the relatively high elasticity of taxable corporate profits to the statutory tax rates (see, for example, Grubert and Slemrod, 1998 and Mintz and Smart, 2004). Businesses can easily shift profits from high- to low-tax rate jurisdictions through financial transactions and transfer pricing – no real inputs that are more costly to move need to be used to shift income. To recoup revenues, governments have increasingly relied on user fees or asset-based payroll and sales taxes applied to businesses. They have also broadened tax bases by reducing or eliminating accelerated depreciation, investment tax credits, and other generous write-offs. The reason for the asymmetric result is that reported profits move more easily than real capital, so that tax competition is resulting in a reduction of corporate income tax rates but not necessarily reductions in taxes on businesses.

One final point, not mentioned by Hines, has been the dramatic shift away from taxation of services in many countries. This has arisen from increased mobility of intangible income, finance, and business services that are now sensitive to differences in tax rates across countries. In fact, many countries have changed tax incentive regimes in recent years to levy very low corporate income tax rates and eliminate withholding taxes on dividends, interest, and royalties for headquarter or financial income (Belgium, Hungary, Ireland (until recently), Luxembourg, Malaysia, Netherlands, Singapore, and Switzerland). Special regimes are quite common now in many countries that successfully attract FDI.

These trends in corporate tax policy are well understood. However, until Jim's paper, most analysts would expect from theory (Kanbur and Keen,

1993) and observe by practice that large countries tend to have higher corporate income tax rates than small ones. This is a truly unique contribution of this chapter.

2. Empirical Robustness

Jim Hines examines the relationship of corporate income tax rates to the size of the economy (population and per capita incomes). In 1982, the statutory and effective corporate tax rates seemed to be positively correlated with population size and perhaps negatively correlated with per capita GDP. For 1999, population size no longer seems to be a determinant. Not much is said about the potential negative relationship between corporate income tax rates and per capita incomes, but I found that to be striking, suggesting that perhaps the small countries are rich and tend to set lower corporate tax rates. Perhaps, the tax rates are explaining wealth rather than the other way around.

Although the tests were of interest, several variables, it struck me, should have been included in the regression. One omitted variable is the importance of the resource industry in a country – it is well known that resource-intensive industries tend to set higher corporate tax rates to capture the rents earned by resource companies. Further, financial services also can affect the choice of corporate tax rates. Several countries, such as Hong Kong, Luxembourg, and the Netherlands, have low corporate tax rates (or special regimes) to capture financial service income. The general or headline corporate income tax rate becomes more questionable to use in the case of some of these countries with special regimes. Also, the openness of the market to trade and capital flows would presumably impact the corporate income tax rates being chosen – countries that are quite open in nature may indeed be more likely to choose lower corporate income taxes rates.

It was not entirely clear to me that corporate income tax rates included subnational tax rates, which are important in a wide variety of countries, including Canada, Germany, Japan, and the United States, among others. My understanding of the statutory tax rate data is that that they do not include subnational tax rates.

As another point, the measure of indirect taxes used in the chapter may be problematic. Value added tax (VAT) is included, which arguably would be shifted onto consumers. Perhaps, the data are related primarily to input taxes that are not refunded under the VAT, but I would not be surprised that countries with high taxes tend to have high VAT collections.

3. Conclusions

As mentioned, theory would suggest that large countries would likely choose higher corporate tax rates in a game with Nash or Stackelberg strategies. The results in the chapter suggesting that large and small countries choose similar tax rates require some theorists to go back to the drawing board on these issues. In some ways, I am not surprised. In my view, the role of income shifting, worldwide tax-efficient financing structures that lead to multiple deductions for the same expense (Mintz, 2004), and the growth of international competition for services and intangibles make it harder for governments to raise corporate income taxes. Countries are shifting increasingly to other methods of taxing businesses, such as relying on user fees, origin-based value added taxes, and payroll taxes to fund their activities. Profits are too easy to shift and businesses are able to create tax structures that are significantly minimizing their taxes on worldwide income. The result is the slow erosion of corporate income taxes as governments look for other methods to tax businesses.

References

Canada, Technical Committee on Business Taxation. 1998. *Report*. (Ottawa: Department of Finance).

Grubert, Harry, and Joel Slemrod. 1998. "The Effect of Taxes on Investment and Income Shifting to Puerto Rico." *Review of Economics and Statistics* 80(3): 365–373.

Kanbur, Ravi, and Michael Keen. 1993. "Jeux Sans Frontières: Tax Competition and Tax Coordination When Countries Differ in Size." *American Economic Review* 83(4): 877–892.

KPMG. 2004. *Corporate Tax Survey*. (Toronto: KPMG).

Mintz, Jack M. 2004. "Conduit Entities: Implications of Indirect Tax-Efficient Financing Structures for Real Investment." *International Tax and Public Finance* 11(4): 419–434.

Mintz, Jack M., and Michael A. Smart. 2004. "Income Shifting, Investment, and Tax Competition: Theory and Evidence from Provincial Taxation in Canada." *Journal of Public Economics* 88(6): 1149–1168.

Comments

John Douglas Wilson
Michigan State University

The results in this chapter present an intriguing puzzle. On the one hand, average statutory corporate tax rates fell between 1982 and 1999. On the other hand, tax bases broadened, causing corporate tax collections to rise. Moreover, this increase in collections has taken place in a period that is widely thought to have been characterized by increasing international capital mobility, which should be causing countries to reduce their taxation of capital. Hines's solution to the puzzle is to argue that countries are indeed attempting to tax mobile capital at lower effective rates, through reduced tax burdens on foreign investors, but they are continuing to tax domestic investments at high rates. In addition, he argues that the elimination of the positive relation between country size and corporate tax bases and rates can be explained by increasing competition for mobile resources.

To explain these results, Hines relies on the standard result from tax theory that a small open economy, facing an infinitely elastic supply of capital, should not impose a source-based tax on capital income. This result is an implication of the Diamond and Mirrlees (1971) production efficiency theorem, which has been applied directly to international taxation by Gordon (1986) and Bucovetsky and Wilson (1991). Despite this theorem, however, there are several reasons for why capital taxes can survive in a small open economy.

First, the zero-tax result for a small country assumes that a marginal investment there does not impose nonprivate costs on the country, such as the costs associated with providing public infrastructure, or various congestion or pollution externalities. The more general rule calls for a tax on capital equal to these marginal costs.

Second, the Diamond-Mirrlees theorem itself assumes that sufficient commodity taxes are available and that there are no untaxed profits.[1] In Bucovetsky and Wilson (1991), only a tax on wage income is needed to eliminate the taxation of capital at source, but the model assumes constant returns to scale and, therefore, no profits. If there do exist untaxed profits, then a capital tax may be desirable on efficiency grounds. By raising capital costs and thereby reducing these profits, this tax provides a means of indirectly taxing profits. As another example, consider the Mirrlees model of optimal income taxation, specialized by assuming that there are two types of labor, "skilled" and "unskilled." If these two types are imperfect substitutes, then a small open economy should tax or subsidize capital, depending on whether a fall or rise in the supply of capital reduces the difference between the skilled and unskilled wages (see Huber, 1999). The problem here is that both types of labor face the same income tax schedule. In other words, the absence of separate taxes on the incomes from the two labor types represents a violation of the Diamond-Mirrlees assumption of optimal commodity taxation. More generally, applying the Diamond-Mirrlees theorem to the issue of capital tax policy in an open economy requires strong assumptions about the availability of other tax instruments.

Third, the Diamond-Mirrlees analysis ignores the administrative issues involved in collecting taxes, such as the problems associated with tax evasion. If capital income is exempted from taxation, then taxpayers have an incentive to shift their form of compensation from wage income and toward capital income, creating the need for the government to engage in the costly monitoring activities needed to limit such income-shifting activities. Gordon and MacKie-Mason (1995) formally develop this argument.

Fourth, even if capital is perfectly mobile across countries, there may still exist countries with productivity advantages that create economic rents for the firms operating there. These rents can then be taxed without inducing firms to relocate. A potentially important source of such advantages is agglomeration economies, whereby firms locating in a particular region enjoy productivity advantages arising from the presence of other firms there. The literature on tax competition has begun to examine models with agglomeration economies. In particular, Ludema and Wooton (2000) present an argument for why lower mobility costs may *raise* equilibrium taxes on mobile factors, contrary to the results from standard tax competition models. Borrowing from the literature on economic geography, they develop

---

[1] The theorem has also been extended to the case where there are untaxed profits, but then profits must be optimally taxed, using firm-specific profits taxes. See Mirrlees (1972) and Sadka (1977).

a two-country model in which the forces of agglomeration cause manufacturing activities to locate in one country, leaving the other country with only a traditional constant-returns "agricultural sector." The concentration of manufacturing takes place through the movement of manufacturing workers from the "periphery" country to the "core" country, but the model could presumably be recast with mobile capital instead. The two countries play a Nash game in the tax rates collected from manufacturing workers by their country of residence, and the tax revenue is used to maximize the well-being of immobile agricultural workers. For our purposes, the most important result to come out of this model is that a decline in worker preferences for location per se (which are heterogeneous) decreases the amount by which the core has to reduce its tax rate to induce the marginal worker to reside there. The basic idea is that agglomeration forces raise the real wages of mobile workers above those wages available elsewhere, and low mobility costs increase the rents that the core is able to extract from these workers. See Baldwin and Krugman (2004) and Kind, Knarvik, and Schjelderup (2000) for similar models, but with different equilibrium concepts.

Fifth, a small capital-importing country has an incentive to tax mobile capital if the source country follows the common practice of providing credits for foreign tax payments. By raising its tax, the importing country increases the credit that investors receive from their home governments, thereby transferring income between government treasuries, with no effect on investment incentives. This argument holds whenever the host country taxes capital at a rate less than the source-country rate.

Sixth, whereas Hines convincingly argues that governments possess various methods for taxing more mobile and less mobile capital at different rates, there are undoubtedly limits to which such differentiation can be implemented in practice, in part because of the practical difficulties involved identifying the "mobility properties" of different types of investments. To the extent that mobile capital cannot be perfectly targeted for favorable tax treatment, taxes on this capital will not be driven to zero.

To summarize, the claim that efficient taxation for a small open economy entails zero taxation of internationally mobile capital rests on a series of assumptions that are likely to be violated in practice. The empirical importance of these violations deserves further study. While the assumptions about the availability of optimal commodity taxes are clearly violated in practice, for example, the importance of such violations for the taxation of mobile capital is not clear.

An issue related to the last (sixth) consideration is whether the countries that compete for capital would benefit from an explicit or implicit agreement not to give preferential tax treatment to more-mobile capital. The answer can go either way, depending on a host of factors, as described by Janeba and Smart (2003) and Wilson (2006). But there exist important cases where preferential treatment is not desirable (see, e.g., Janeba and Peters, 1999). While this possibility calls into question the desirability of the trend toward more unequal treatment suggested by Hines's empirical results, his finding that corporate tax collections have not significantly declined can be interpreted as strengthening the case for preferential regimes.

Perhaps the most interesting empirical finding is that the relation between country size and corporate tax policy appears to have disappeared in recent years. Hines attributes this finding to "intensified international tax competition, since it is the ability to exploit market power that permits large countries to benefit from higher tax rates." But the chapter does not fully explain why intensified international tax competition should take this form. In standard tax competition models, a large country chooses to tax mobile capital at a relatively high rate because the tax is partially borne by capital owners throughout the world economy in the form of a lower world return, thereby lessening the investment disincentives created by the tax (see Bucovetsky, 1991 and Wilson, 1991). But this market-power argument holds even if investors are able to costlessly move their capital between home and abroad.

One possibility is that "large countries" are becoming relatively less "large," due to an expansion in investment opportunities outside the set of the traditional host countries. Another possibility is that corporate tax bases have become more mobile in a manner that levels the playing field between small and large countries. Mintz and Smart (2004) emphasize the growing ability of firms to shift taxable income across country boundaries, independently of where physical investments are located, and Mintz builds on this research in his comment on the current chapter. Another consideration is how the dynamics of capital mobility interact with country size in tax competition games. Once a firm constructs a production facility abroad, relocating the facility to another country becomes costly. The host government then has an incentive to increase its taxes on the foreign firm. To limit such tax increases, the firm can attempt to reduce relocation costs, such as by purposely creating a state of excess capacity through the construction of plants in multiple countries. Janeba (2000) models this activity. If modern multinationals are able to reduce such relocation costs, independent of the size of their host countries, then perhaps large countries are losing their competitive advantage.

Though the chapter focuses on growing capital mobility, another important trend has been the reduction in barriers to trade in goods, through lower tariffs and transport costs. It is well known that large countries have an incentive to use tariffs to manipulate the terms of trade. In the presence of regional or multilateral trade agreements limiting the use of such tariffs, countries have an incentive to use other methods for achieving desirable changes in the terms of trade. Janeba and Wilson (2000) demonstrate that a capital-importing country may choose to subsidize capital if it cannot employ a tariff, though it would tax capital if the tariff could be optimally set.[2] Since such terms-of-trade arguments do not apply to small countries, this result explains how tariff reductions can lead to Hines's finding that corporate tax burdens have fallen in large countries relative to small countries.

The conclusion that large countries possess the incentive to tax mobile capital at relatively high rates is based on tax competition models with competitive market structures. Models with imperfect competition can lead to strikingly different results. For example, Haufler and Wooton (1999) consider a large and small country competing to attract a mobile monopolist. Each country is willing to subsidize the firm's profits earned within its borders, since the country's residents would otherwise incur the transport costs associated with importing the good. But the large country is willing to pay a higher subsidy, in part because there are more residents to share the burden of the subsidy. In equilibrium, the firm always locates in the large country, where it benefits from a larger home market, and this country may be able to tax the firm. It is difficult to compare the two countries' equilibrium tax or subsidy policies, since the small country never obtains access to the firm's profits. But the analysis does suggest a scale-economy argument that might apply to more general settings with multiple firms, whereby large countries choose low taxes or high subsidies because the lost revenue from doing so can be pooled over a larger group of residents. Such a possibility is consistent with Hines's finding that corporate tax burdens are no longer relatively high in large countries, though why a positive relation previously existed is then left unanswered. One other avenue of attack would be to examine the political economy of trade and tax policy, an approach that has increasingly occupied the attention of trade economists (see, e.g., Riezman and Wilson,

---

[2] Janeba and Wilson focus on the inefficiencies that result when capital taxes are chosen noncooperatively by regions within the country, rather than by the central government, but a similar relation between the tariff and capital tax holds in both cases.

1995), but it is unclear how such an approach would generate the changing relation between corporate tax policy and country size over the last few decades.

To conclude, this chapter has uncovered some fascinating trends in corporate tax policy, including the disappearing importance of country size. These trends raise some intriguing theoretical puzzles that deserve further study.

References

Baldwin, Richard E., and Paul Krugman. 2004. "Agglomeration, Integration and Tax Harmonization." *European Economic Review* 48(1): 1–23.

Bucovetsky, Sam. 1991. "Asymmetric Tax Competition." *Journal of Urban Economics* 30(2): 167–181.

Bucovetsky, Sam, and John D. Wilson. 1991. "Tax Competition with Two Tax Instruments." *Regional Science and Urban Economics* 21(3): 333–350.

Diamond, Peter A., and James Mirrlees. 1971. "Optimal Taxation and Public Production I: Production Efficiency; II: Tax Rules." *American Economic Review* 61(1, 2): 8–27, 261–278.

Gordon, Roger H. 1986. "Taxation of Investment and Savings in a World Economy." *American Economic Review* 76(5): 1086–1102.

Gordon, Roger H., and Jeffrey K. MacKie-Mason. 1995. "Why Is There Corporate Taxation in a Small Open Economy? The Role of Transfer Pricing and Income Shifting." In Martin Feldstein, James R. Hines Jr., and R. Glenn Hubbard, eds., *The Effects of Taxation on Multinational Corporations.* (Chicago: University of Chicago Press), pp. 67–91.

Haufler, Andreas, and Ian Wooton. 1999. "Country Size and Tax Competition for Foreign Direct Investment." *Journal of Public Economics* 71(1): 121–139.

Huber, Bernd. 1999. "Tax Competition and Tax Coordination in an Optimum Income Tax Model." *Journal of Public Economics* 71(3): 441–458.

Janeba, Eckhard. 2000. "Tax Competition When Governments Lack Commitment: Excess Capacity as a Countervailing Threat." *American Economic Review* 90(5): 1508–1519.

Janeba, Eckhard, and John D. Wilson. 2000. "Tax Competition and Trade Protection." *Finanzarchiv* 56(3/4): 459–480.

Janeba, Eckhard, and Michael Smart. 2003. "Is Targeted Tax Competition Less Harmful Than Its Remedies?" *International Tax and Public Finance* 10(3): 259–280.

Janeba, Eckhard, and Wolfgang Peters. 1999. "Tax Evasion, Tax Competition and the Gains from Nondiscrimination: The Case of Interest Taxation in Europe." *Economic Journal* 109(452): 93–101.

Kind, Hans Jarle, Karen Helene Midelfart Knarvik, and Guttorm Schjelderup. 2000. "Competing for Capital in a 'Lumpy' World." *Journal of Public Economics* 78(3): 253–274.

Ludema, Rodney D., and Ian Wooton. 2000. "Economic Geography and the Fiscal Effects of Regional Integration." *Journal of International Economics* 52(2): 331–357.

Mintz, Jack, and Michael Smart. 2004. "Income Shifting, Investment, and Tax Competition: Theory and Evidence from Provincial Taxation in Canada." *Journal of Public Economics* 88(6): 1149–1168.

Mirrlees, James. 1972. "On Producer Taxation." *Review of Economic Studies* 39(1): 105–111.

Riezman, Raymond, and John D. Wilson. 1995. "Politics and Trade Policy." In Jeffrey S. Banks and Eric A. Hanushek, eds., *Modern Political Economy*. (Cambridge: Cambridge University Press), pp. 145–170.

Sadka, Efraim. 1977. "A Note on Producer Taxation and Public Production." *Review of Economic Studies* 44(2): 385–387.

Wilson, John D. 1991. "Tax Competition with Interregional Differences in Factor Endowments." *Regional Science and Urban Economics* 21(3): 423–452.

Wilson, John D. 2006. "Tax Competition with and without Preferential Treatment of a Highly Mobile Tax Base." In James Alm, Jorge Martinez-Vazquez, and Mark Rider, eds. The Challenges of Tax Reform in a Global Economy. (New York: Springer), pp. 193–206.

EIGHT

The Changing Role of Auditors in Corporate Tax Planning

Edward L. Maydew

University of North Carolina

Douglas A. Shackelford

University of North Carolina and NBER

We acknowledge the thoughtful comments of conference participants, Robert Bushman, Courtney Edwards, Steve Kaplan, Lil Mills, Jana Raedy, Kevin Raedy, John Robinson, Richard Sansing, Joel Slemrod, and numerous practitioners at leading accounting firms and corporations. We appreciate the research assistance of Scott Dyreng, Allison Evans, and Vincent Thorn. A prior version of this chapter was titled "Corporate Tax Planning in a Sarbanes-Oxley World."

1. Introduction

This chapter examines the changing role that auditors play in corporate tax planning in the face of recent events, including the well-known accounting scandals, passage of the Sarbanes-Oxley Act, and regulatory actions by the Securities and Exchange Commission (SEC) and the Public Company Accounting Oversight Board (PCAOB). Although the events are recent, still being debated, and the data limited, one thing is clear in the preliminary data. The amount of tax services that audit firms provide to their audit clients has declined dramatically during the period 2001–2004. Furthermore, most of the tax work appears to have shifted among accounting firms because the amount of tax work that accounting firms perform for non-audit clients has increased sharply.

We find that in 2001, S&P 500 companies, on average, paid their auditors about the same fees for their audit work as they did for their tax work (i.e., the combination of tax compliance, tax advice, and tax consulting). Two years later, in 2003, the S&P 500 were paying twice as much for audit work as tax work. By 2004, we estimate that the average S&P 500 firm was paying its auditor four times more for audit work than tax work. This striking shift has occurred because audit clients are both paying more for audit work and spending less for tax services from their auditor. The total tax practice of the largest accounting firms (from both audit and non-audit clients) has held steady during this period, indicating that what we are observing is a shift in clients among the providers of tax services rather than a general decline in tax services.

Several related events likely contributed to the decline in auditor-related tax services and the increase in non-auditor-provided tax services. A rash of accounting scandals in 2001 and 2002 led to increased scrutiny of auditors and auditor independence. Congress responded by enacting SOX in the summer of 2002.[1] A primary purpose of SOX is to ensure (some would argue, restore) the independence of the auditor. To ensure that auditors are independent in fact and in appearance and therefore are not facing conflicting incentives when issuing an audit opinion, the sweeping legislation, among other things, restricts the tax services that accountants can provide to their audit clients.[2] Specifically, SOX requires that before an auditor is retained to perform tax services, the client must seek and obtain specific approval from the audit committee of the board of directors. No pre-approval is required when clients obtain tax services from a firm that is not their auditor. Follow-on regulations from the SEC place further restrictions on auditors by prohibiting them from providing certain types of tax planning services to their audit clients.[3] Because accounting firms historically provided their audit clients with substantial tax planning, these restrictions are altering the process by which corporations manage their tax liabilities.

Regulation, however, does not fully account for the decline in auditor-provided tax services. Some companies have gone beyond the SOX

---

[1] The nine months preceding the passage of Sarbanes-Oxley were marked with several major criminal investigations involving corporate managers. Among these were: Enron's earnings restatement on November 8, 2001; Adelphia's report of unbooked family loans on March 27, 2002; the tax evasion indictment of Tyco's CEO on June 4, 2002; the arrest of ImClone's CEO for insider trading on June 12, 2002; and WorldCom's admission of earnings overstatements on June 25, 2002.

[2] Note that the restrictions are placed on the accounting firm, not on an individual auditor. That is, tax consultants working at accounting firms are restricted in the services that they can provide audit clients, even if they had no role in the audit. Likewise, tax consulting opportunities are limited, even if no one associated with the audit played any role in the tax plan.

[3] SEC Release No. 33–8183, "Strengthening the Commission's Requirements Regarding Auditor Independence" (2003).

restrictions. They no longer accept any non-audit services from their audit firm, including tax work. One reason for these self-imposed restrictions is to signal a high-quality audit – that is, the auditors are not compromised by fees they receive from non-audit services. Companies completely dropping non-audit services are attempting to disassociate themselves from the negative publicity of accounting scandals involving perceived auditor compromise. One such case is Enron, where Arthur Andersen reportedly received over $52 million in 2000, mostly from non-audit services (McLean and Elkind, 2003, p. 145). Shareholder pressure also may be contributing to the decline in non-audit services. For example, the California Public Employees' Retirement System has a policy of opposing the election of audit committee members who approve non-audit services.[4] In addition, they generally vote against retaining auditors that provide non-audit services.[5] In sum, the combination of regulatory and self-imposed restrictions is decoupling the long-standing link between audit and tax services.

Why did firms obtain most of their tax services from their audit firm prior to the accounting scandals, the SOX Act, and regulatory changes by the SEC and PCAOB? The answer is that because all publicly traded firms are required to have an audit and all privately held businesses of any consequence acquire one, the firm conducting the audit historically enjoyed at least two significant advantages compared to other accounting firms. First, auditors learn a great deal about the client's business during the course of the audit and operate on the "inside," having access to the client's internal financial information. Consequently, the auditors are often able to identify consulting opportunities, including tax consulting, more readily than other service providers. Second, the auditors typically have a working relationship with both the tax director and the CFO, who historically were the key people involved in the selection of tax providers. Often the CFOs and tax directors began their careers with the accounting firm that does the audit. They therefore understand the firm's audit and tax approach and have long-standing, close relationships with the firm's personnel.

Compared to non-accounting providers of tax services, specifically law firms, accounting firms also enjoy some advantages. Because of long-standing financial accounting rules that are beyond the scope of this chapter, whole classes of tax strategies (in general, those that defer taxable income or accelerate tax deductions) do not actually reduce the tax expense that

---

[4] See http://www.calpers-governance.org/viewpoint/speeches/anson041403.asp.
[5] See http://www.boardmember.com/network/index.pl?section=1024&article_id=11985& show=article.

shows up in the firms' financial statements.[6] Paradoxically, this develop-ment means that only certain kinds of tax planning are actually useful at increasing the earnings that are reported to shareholders. With experts in both financial reporting and tax planning, accounting firms have a compet-itive advantage over law firms in designing corporate tax plans that reduce the actual taxes paid in a manner that also translates into reduced tax expense (and increased earnings) in the financial statements. Because earnings and earnings per share are viewed by CFOs as the most important determinants of share price (Graham, Harvey, and Rajgopal, 2005), the ability to reduce taxes for financial accounting purposes is often critical to selling tax planning ideas.

In addition, the financial reporting perspective of accountants has shaped corporate tax planning. Accountants were central in positioning tax depart-ments as corporate profit centers, where reducing effective tax rates was seen as a means of enhancing accounting earnings. This synergy meshes nicely with the managerial goal of enhancing shareholder value because earnings are a key component in valuation.

Accounting firms have also enjoyed advantages in providing tax services that require number crunching, something law firms typically do not do, and tax services that require coordination across offices in different coun-tries, as the largest accounting firms have global footprints that dwarf those of even the largest law firms. On the other hand, law firms have had an advantage in providing high-end legal analysis, such as writing opinion let-ters and, naturally, in tax litigation. Law firms also have the advantage of attorney-client privilege, although it has been curtailed to some extent in recent court cases involving tax shelters.

Over time, accounting firms became key providers of corporate tax exper-tise to their audit clients, and accountants became the leading designers of many corporate tax plans. One recent example is the role accountants played in the proliferation of corporate tax shelters around the turn of the millen-nium. Many of the alleged shelters were developed by the largest accounting firms (Bankman, 2004). It is not obvious how corporate tax planning would have evolved without the central role of accountants. Similarly, it is not apparent how it will evolve with the pressure to decouple audit and tax so profoundly altering the process and systems by which corporations approach

---

[6] For details, see Appendix 2.2 of Scholes et al. 2005. These rules are contained in Statement of Financial Accounting Standards (SFAS) 109, which was promulgated by the Financial Accounting Standards Board (FASB). The FASB is the private rule-making body primarily responsible for promulgating generally accepted accounting principles (GAAP).

taxes. While the future is hazy, we will nevertheless hazard three predictions, which should be testable with more research and more data.

First, there will be disruptions to the tax function that should, to some extent, increase the cost of tax planning and increase corporate taxes paid. The development and implementation of a tax plan for a large corporation is a complex undertaking. It requires extensive knowledge of the company, its history, and how the organization operates. It requires the coordination of parties with diverse interests and information, involving domestic and foreign operations across multiple segments of the business, including production, marketing, finance, financial reporting, management, human resources, and technology. Various professionals – accountants, attorneys, economists, bankers, insurers, and appraisers, both within and outside the company – provide the tax expertise. Any major disruption to the team of tax professionals, such as the loss of tax consultants within the auditing firm, should make it more costly for firms to reduce their tax liabilities.

To test this prediction, one would need data on taxes paid by corporations following the reduction in auditor-provided tax services. One would predict that taxes paid would increase the most in those firms that had the largest declines in auditor-provided tax services. There also could be a general time effect on tax collections to the extent that the tax industry is experiencing a period of conservatism following the accounting scandals, SOX, and the recent crackdown on corporate tax shelters by the Internal Revenue Service (IRS).

Two, we expect to see the tax provision (the tax expense reported in the financial statements) as an increased source of conflict between the auditor and the client. Because financial statement auditors today are less likely to be reviewing the tax strategy developed by a colleague down the hall, they are more likely to question the tax strategy. All else equal, we expect that auditors will require their clients to record more tax cushion (a financial accounting reserve for tax positions that may be disallowed by the IRS) for a given level of aggressive tax positions than they did in the past. We expect that auditors will also maintain increasingly detailed audit workpapers related to the tax provision and that these workpapers will serve as a road map for the IRS to the client's most sensitive tax positions.

Three, we predict significant long-run changes to the accounting industry. The synergies that have long kept audit and tax professionals together in the same firms are now eroded. Given the shift away from obtaining tax services from one's audit firm, it is possible that there is no net positive synergy to having large tax practices together with the audit firms. This is far from certain, but we predict that over time portions of the Big Four tax practices will be sold or spun off to entities that do not face the regulatory challenges the auditors face. In addition to stand-alone tax practices, potential buyers of parts of the Big Four tax practices include law firms, strategy consulting firms, human resource consulting firms, IT consulting firms, and even banks. Even without a sale or spin-off, portions of the Big Four tax practice may migrate to these same potential buyers as they enter the market or expand their existing tax services. Time will be necessary to test this prediction. We should note, however, that the short-run data do not support our long-run prediction. The total tax practices of the Big Four are currently expanding, not contracting, as they pick up business from each other's audit clients.

The remainder of the chapter develops as follows: The next section provides background on the related literature and on the legislative and regulatory changes affecting auditor-provided tax services. Section 3 provides some preliminary empirical evidence in terms of tax and audit fees. Section 4 speculates on the ultimate effects of the changes in tax service providers on the structure of the accounting industry. Section 5 discusses possible unintended consequences of SOX on aggregate corporate taxes. Concluding remarks follow.

2. Background

2.1. Related Literature

Prior research has tended to ignore the role of auditor-provided tax services. The closest stream of research among tax papers examines the interplay between tax planning and financial reporting (see review in Shackelford and Shevlin, 2001; examples in Scholes et al., 2005). That literature, however, tends to focus either on firm-level coordination between tax planning and financial reporting incentives (e.g., LIFO versus FIFO) or on capital market responses to earnings in the presence of book-tax differences (e.g., Hanlon, 2005). When auditors are mentioned in the tax literature, they almost always are employees of the IRS, rather than accounting firms. In short, tax papers tend to ignore the role of the financial statement auditor.

In the accounting literature, numerous papers study the market for auditors (e.g., Antle et al., 2002; Whisenant, Sankaraguruswamy, and Raghunandan 2003), auditing and the capital markets (e.g., Francis, Maydew, and Sparks, 1999; Francis and Ke, 2004), and auditor independence (e.g., Antle, 1984; Ashbaugh, Lafond, and Mayhew, 2003; DeFond, Raghunandan, and Subramanyam, 2002; Frankel, Johnson, and Nelson, 2002; Kinney, Palmrose, and Scholz, 2004; Reynolds, Deis, and Francis, 2004; Simunic,

1984). The independence literature is mixed on whether non-audit services compromise auditors. Using several tests for the presence of compromised auditors (e.g., the extent of earnings management), Frankel, Johnson, and Nelson (2002) conclude that having auditors provide non-audit services impairs auditor independence. Conversely, Ashbaugh, Lafond, and Mayhew (2003) find that the results in Frankel et al. are sensitive to research design choices. Similarly, Reynolds, Deis, and Francis (2004) find no relation between non-audit services and discretionary accruals after controlling for certain firm characteristics. In a sample of financially stressed manufacturing companies, Geiger and Rama (2003) find no association between non-audit fees and the likelihood of receiving a going-concern audit opinion (loosely speaking, a going-concern audit opinion indicates that the firm may face financial distress). On the whole, the evidence is inconclusive regarding whether non-audit services impair auditor independence.

Not surprisingly, researchers are beginning to analyze SOX from numerous angles (e.g., Asthana, Balsam, and Kim, 2004; Cohen, Day, and Lys, 2004; Griffin and Lont, 2005; Lai, 2003). However, we are aware of only one other study that examines the changing market for auditor-provided tax services, Omer, Bedard, and Falsetta (2006). Among other things, that study finds a decline in auditor-provided tax services in 2002, the last year of its sample.

2.2. Legislative and Regulatory Changes Affecting Auditor-Provided Tax Services

To understand the legislative and regulatory changes to what auditors can do, it is important to understand the two categories of tax services that accounting firms typically provide. The first category of tax services are those that are not essential to the completion of the audit, including tax compliance, tax advice, and tax consulting. Tax compliance involves filing tax returns and providing other information to the taxing authorities. Tax advice involves responding to inquiries about the specific treatment of transactions or other taxable endeavors. Tax consulting is the design and implementation of tax strategies designed to manage tax liabilities. Of the three, consulting is the highest-margin activity and includes profitable engagements such as restructuring organizations, shifting income across jurisdictions or time, or reclassifying the tax treatment of transactions. As detailed below, SOX discourages, and in some cases prohibits, accounting firms from providing these tax services to their audit clients.

The other services that tax professionals provide are those that are an essential part of the audit. Tax experts typically assist their audit brethren in the review of what is called the "tax provision," that is, the income tax expense in the corporation's financial statements. The tax provision is not the actual taxes paid during that year. Rather, it estimates the total taxes over the life of the firm related to the current year's activities.[7] Auditing the provision estimates requires extensive knowledge of both tax law and generally accepted accounting principles (GAAP). Because reviewing the provision is part of the audit, SOX does not prohibit auditors from provision work. However, as discussed below, SOX indirectly affects the nature of the provision work.

Sarbanes-Oxley builds on three principles of auditor independence: (1) the auditors cannot audit their own work; (2) the auditors cannot function as part of management; and (3) the auditors cannot serve in an advocacy role for the client.[8] In other words, SOX is designed to ensure that the auditors remain independent, that is, not conflicted in their audit of the financial reports. To that end, SOX specifically prohibits the firm that provides the audit from also providing: (1) bookkeeping or other services related to the accounting records or financial statements of the audit client; (2) financial information systems design and implementation; (3) appraisal or valuation services, fairness opinions, or contribution-in-kind reports; (4) actuarial services; (5) internal audit outsourcing services; (6) management functions or human resources; (7) broker or dealer, investment advisor, or investment banking services; (8) legal services and expert services unrelated to the audit; and (9) any other service deemed by regulators to be impermissible.

SOX does not prohibit auditors from providing tax services to their audit clients and, in fact, specifically identifies tax services as services that the auditor can perform so long as pre-approval is obtained from the clients' audit committees (Goodman, 2004).[9] Nonetheless, Congress has given both the SEC and the newly created PCAOB, discussed below, the authority to write

---

[7] There are some exceptions to this general rule. For example, the tax provision can be affected by revisions in deferred tax assets and liabilities due to changes in tax rates, changes in the APB 23 election for permanently reinvested foreign earnings, changes in the valuation allowance, changes in the tax cushion, and settlements with the IRS.

[8] The SEC based its November 2000 amendments to the auditor independence rules on these same principles. They also guide the PCAOB, which Sarbanes-Oxley created to further oversee auditor-provided tax services. In addition, a Treasury Regulation known as Circular 230 regulates some aspects of tax practice – for example, writing opinion letters.

[9] If Congress had been sufficiently concerned about tax impairing auditor independence, then it could have prohibited firms from offering both tax and audit services, much like the Glass-Steagall Act did for commercial and investment banking. See Kroszner, 1998; Kroszner and Rajan, 1994; and Kroszner and Rajan, 1997.

rules regulating auditor independence. In 2003, following passage of the Sarbanes-Oxley Act, the SEC revised its auditor independence regulations. The revisions continue the SEC's long-standing position that accountants can provide audit clients with certain tax services. The SEC considers tax services unique among non-audit services, noting that auditor-provided tax services predate the congressional passage of the securities laws in the 1930s. The SEC, however, has ruled that independence is impaired by representing an audit client before a tax court, district court, or federal court of claims.[10]

The PCAOB was established by SOX as a new regulator of auditors. The PCAOB has proposed regulations that, among other things, delineate between acceptable and unacceptable tax services.[11] It has ruled that auditor independence is compromised if the auditor participates in corporate tax planning under confidentiality or involving a "listed" transaction.[12] In addition, the PCAOB forbids the accounting firm from participating in "aggressive" tax planning with its audit clients. Aggressive tax planning is defined as any plan or opinion where (1) the auditor provides any service related to the plan or opinion; (2) the client did not initiate the idea; (3) a significant purpose of the idea was to avoid taxes; and (4) the plan has a less than a 50–50 chance of prevailing if challenged by the IRS. The PCAOB restrictions even extend to personal tax return preparation, barring the audit firm from preparing the personal tax returns for corporate officers with oversight authority over financial statements (Gary, 2004).

In addition to the SEC and PCAOB auditor regulations, SOX prohibits the audit firm from providing other tax services (e.g., ones that are not already prohibited) unless the audit committee approves the services in advance on a case-by-case basis. Audit committee approval can be a significant hurdle for at least four reasons. First, a primary responsibility of the audit committee is to ensure that the auditor's independence is not compromised (potentially resulting in a failed audit). Thus, audit committees are predisposed toward limiting non-audit utilization of the audit firm. Second, audit

---

[10] See Section B.11 of http://www.sec.gov/rules/final/33-8183.htm#footbody_103 for more details about the SEC's position on auditor-provided tax services.

[11] PCAOB *Interim Professional Auditing Standards*, issued April 18, 2003 and approved by the SEC on April 25, 2003.

[12] A "listed" transaction is one identified by the IRS as structured for the significant purpose of tax avoidance or evasion. Participants in listed transactions are required to disclose expected tax benefits and the identities and nature of involvement of all parties to the transaction. Among the 31 transactions currently listed are sale-in, lease-out transactions, intercompany financing through partnerships, offsetting foreign currency option contracts, abusive foreign tax credit transactions, and S corporation ESOP abuses.

committees historically have had little, if any, tax responsibility. It is unclear that corporate boards will add tax experts just to facilitate audit committee approval of auditor-provided tax services. Third, tax plans often demand rapid implementation for maximum effectiveness. To the extent audit committees cannot respond quickly, the audit firm may be precluded from some time-sensitive tax plans or dominated by non-auditor providers. Fourth, ignoring these tax approval responsibilities, SOX has already substantially increased the workloads of audit committees. Thus, it is unclear whether audit committees will place high priority on approving auditor-provided tax services. All in all, requiring audit committee pre-approval discourages firms from retaining their auditor to provide tax services.

2.3. The Tax Provision as a New Source of Conflict

Suppose a company adopts a tax plan designed to permanently reduce its taxes (as compared with intertemporal shifting). The tax savings from the plan will only boost book income if the tax provision is reduced. Recall that the tax provision refers to the tax expense reported in the financial statements. The tax provision is not the same as the actual taxes currently paid because the tax provision estimates the total taxes over the life of the firm related to the current year's financial reporting revenues and expenses. Thus, temporary differences between tax and financial accounting income, such as accelerated tax depreciation, have no effect on the amount of tax expense reported for financial reporting purposes.[13] If the only difference between tax and financial reporting income was due to accelerated depreciation for tax purposes, then financial reporting tax expense would exceed the actual tax liability in the early years of the asset's life. The pattern would reverse in the later years of the asset's life, and over the entire life of the asset the cumulative tax expense for tax and financial reporting would be equal. On the other hand, permanent differences between tax and financial reporting, such as tax-exempt interest or nondeductible fines and penalties, do affect financial reporting tax expense.

Even when a tax plan creates a permanent difference and would seemingly reduce financial reporting tax expense, if the auditor does not believe that the tax plan will prevail under the scrutiny of the taxing authorities, the auditor

---

[13] The composition of tax expense, however, will be affected. Tax expense for financial reporting is composed of current tax expense and deferred tax expense. Temporary differences between tax and financial reporting income give rise to deferred tax expense. See Scholes et al. (2005) for details.

may not allow the booking of the tax benefit in the financial statements. In other words, if the auditor believes that the taxes foregone in the current year will be paid in future years after an IRS audit, the auditor may require the client to record a tax cushion (a reserve) to keep the tax provision from being understated. Because financial reporting earnings are important to a company's valuation, if the auditor does not permit a reduction in the provision, then the tax plan is less valuable and may not be marketable at all.

Before the changes brought about by SOX and related events, purchasing tax services from one's auditor for the most part eliminated concerns that the auditor would oppose the firm's book treatment of the tax plan because the tax consultants would not promote a product that the auditors in their firm would not support. Because the same firm handled the tax and audit work, accounting firms were ideally positioned to sell corporate tax shelters. Auditors were not necessarily compromised under these arrangements, but the potential for conflicts of interest existed, and the perception of compromise was unavoidable.

The shift away from hiring one's audit firm for tax services has substantially reduced these arrangements. Consequently, auditors today are less likely to be faced with attesting to the propriety of aggressive tax plans originated by their own firms. Instead, with the audit-tax link broken, the auditor's interests are contrary to those of the tax service provider. Tax planners needs a favorable tax and financial reporting outcome to promote their tax idea. The auditor, however, will be concerned that the actual taxes over the life of the firm may exceed those reported in the financial statements. The auditor has no financial interest in the success of the tax plan. Because the company must have an audit and its auditor cannot be conflicted by the success of the tax plan, the auditor today wields unprecedented clout in determining the tax strategies that the firm undertakes and how it accounts for them.

Consequently, the auditor now impedes, rather than assists, corporate tax avoidance. In fact, Hardesty (2004) intimates that with tax shelters it is now easier to prevail in an IRS audit than to convince an auditor to accept favorable accounting. This outcome results from two influences: namely, information and time. The auditor is more likely to know about the tax position and can command more cooperation and disclosure than the IRS can. In addition, pressure from the auditor to have more documentation supporting the tax provision and the reserves, or "tax cushion," for future IRS audit adjustments is likely to increase the ease with which the IRS can find aggressive tax positions in those cases where it requests copies of the provision workpapers.[14] Furthermore, legal delays of years that increase the costs of IRS investigation are not possible with the auditor because the large SEC registrants are required to release their financial statements within 60 days of year-end.

In short, a (perhaps unintended) consequence of the pressure not to hire one's auditor for tax planning is that the auditor has switched from opposing to aiding the taxing authorities. The result of this role reversal should be increased taxes for financial reporting to the extent that auditors have become more conservative when reviewing the provisions of audit clients. In addition, the chilling effect on the ability to record the benefits of tax planning in the financial statements should reduce the amount and aggressiveness of tax planning and increase actual corporate tax payments.

3. Initial Evidence from Audit Fees

This section documents initial changes in auditor-provided tax services among the largest U.S. corporations. The operative word here is "initial." Because the accounting industry appears to be in transition from the effects of the accounting scandals, Sarbanes-Oxley, and related regulatory changes, it is too soon to know for sure how extensive the long-run effects will be. However, these preliminary findings provide some sense of the magnitude of change. The remainder of this section details the fees paid by the largest U.S. companies to their auditors from 2001 to 2003.

3.1. Audit and Tax Fee Data

The primary tests compare the fees that a company pays to its auditors for audit work with the fees that it pays them for tax work. We collect the fee information from disclosures in the company's proxy statements. In January 2003, the SEC required companies to disclose a finer breakdown of the fees paid to their auditors: audit fees, audit-related fees, tax fees, and all other fees. Before the rule change, tax fees were typically aggregated with other non-audit fees in the proxy statement disclosures. The finer partition disclosures were required for years ending after December 15, 2003, but corporations were required to report two years of information. Many companies chose

---

[14] The tax cushion is an increase in current tax expense beyond actual current tax payments to account for tax positions the firm has taken but believes it may lose upon IRS audit. In a related development, beyond the scope of this chapter, the Financial Accounting Standards Board (FASB) has recently proposed changes to the financial accounting treatment of "uncertain tax positions."

to adopt the disclosure early and included information for 2001 and 2002 in their 2002 proxy statements. These early adopters are the companies that we principally analyze in this study.

The SEC defines "audit fees" as the total fees for professional accounting services for the audit or other services related to statutory or regulatory filings. "Audit-related fees" are payment for ". . . assurance and related services by the principal accountant that are reasonably related to the performance of the audit." Throughout the study, we compare the tax fees both with the audit fees alone ("audit fees") and also with the audit fees combined with the audit-related fees ("expanded audit fees"). Inferences are similar for both measures.

"Tax fees" include fees for tax compliance, tax advice, and tax planning, which is this chapter's definition of tax services. The tax fees do not include review of the tax provision. Those fees are included in the audit fees. "All other fees" are for products and services provided by the auditor and not included in the other three categories. We largely ignore these fees in our analysis. See the Appendix for a reproduction of Allstate's auditor fee information in its 2002 financial statements.

Because the fee classifications are self-reported (as are all other financial statement data), the empirical analysis below assumes that corporations can segregate the fees they pay to their auditors into these different categories and furthermore that they do so. To the extent that the fee data are unreliable or manipulated in some manner to affect users of the financial statements, the results may be erroneous. We have no reason to think that the data are misleading, but the possibility exists. Furthermore, if the precision in the categorical classification has changed over the 2001–2003 period, this also could introduce error into the study.

3.2. Sample Selection

We draw our sample from the S&P 500 as of December 31, 2003. We exclude the 16 companies that do not detail their audit fees for 2001, 2002, and 2003 and the 235 companies that do not report the tax fees paid to their auditor for 2001, 2002, and 2003. One other company is dropped because data are missing from Compustat. Our sample consists of the remaining 248 companies that report both the audit and tax fees that they paid to their auditor in all three years. By definition, all of these firms adopted the SEC disclosures early.

If the companies that adopt early are systematically different from other firms, then our selection criteria may introduce bias. To assess how representative our sample is, we compare the 248 early adopters to the 247

S&P 500 firms that did not adopt early and for which we have complete data.

We find that the early adopters are larger. In 2003, on average, early adopters' assets were 159 percent greater; sales 164 percent higher; and market capitalization 174 percent larger than those of other S&P 500 firms. Sales and market capitalization are significantly different at conventional levels. Book-to-market ratios, however, are insignificantly different (42 percent for early adopters in 2003 versus 44 percent for other firms). Both early adopters and other firms are evenly distributed across sectors.

More importantly, we find no difference in the tax-to-audit ratios between early adopters and other firms for 2002 and 2003. By definition, the early adopters are the only firms that disclosed fee information for 2001. However, all firms had to disclose audit and tax fees for 2002 and 2003. When we compare the tax-to-audit ratios for 2002 and 2003, we find no significant difference. In 2002, the mean ratio for the early adopters is 0.71 versus 0.60 for the other firms. In 2003, the mean ratio for the early adopters is 0.48 versus 0.47 for the other firms. In summary, we find no evidence to suggest that the tax and audit fees of the early adopters are systematically different than those for other firms.

As expected, the Big Four accounting firms dominate the auditing market for the sample. For the three years combined in the study, both Ernst & Young and PricewaterhouseCoopers audited 32 percent of the firms. Deloitte & Touche audited 20 percent, and KPMG audited 11 percent. Arthur Andersen audited 10 percent of the sample in 2001. Arthur Andersen folded the following year, with all of their S&P 500 clients scattering among the remaining Big Four firms.

Eight companies changed auditors in 2001; 27 in 2002; and 4 in 2003. Twenty-five of the 2002 changes were Arthur Andersen clients who were forced to change after Arthur Andersen's demise. Thus, the sample only experienced 14 non-Andersen switches over the three years, or 0.6 percent annually. To ensure that fee changes are not simply caused by changes in the auditors or by the forced Arthur Andersen switches, we repeat our analysis excluding firms that experienced an auditor change. Inferences are unaltered.

3.3. Empirical Analysis

Table 1 presents descriptive statistics for the 248 S&P 500 companies for which we have data from 2001, 2002, and 2003. The mean (median) firm in 2003 had a market capitalization of $25 ($10) billion, assets of $48 ($15) billion, and sales of $16 ($8) billion. Both market value and sales show a dip in 2002, lingering effects of the 2001 recession.

Table 1. *Descriptive Statistics Sample Consists of S&P 500 Firms with Available Tax and Audit Fee Data for 2001 to 2003 (N = 248)*

Variable	Year	Mean	Std. Dev.	Median	75th Percentile	Mean of Yearly Differences	Median of Yearly Differences
Effective Tax Rate	2001	0.37	0.53	0.35	0.39		
	2002	0.27	0.44	0.32	0.37	−0.11**	−0.01***
	2003	0.43	1.82	0.33	0.37	0.16	0.00***
Return on Assets	2001	0.04	0.10	0.03	0.07		
	2002	0.02	0.12	0.03	0.07	−0.01**	0.00***
	2003	0.05	0.07	0.04	0.08	0.03***	0.01***
Market Value of Equity	2001	25,339.14	49,114.19	8,122.73	23,505.92		
	2002	20,302.69	36,099.98	7,259.04	17,602.39	−5,013.80***	−790.62***
	2003	25,043.94	44,319.41	9,729.73	23,824.91	4,741.25***	2,080.21***
Total Assets	2001	40,968.09	105,274.56	12,473.50	28,617.61		
	2002	43,086.41	112,548.50	13,833.50	29,577.50	2,322.99**	342.65***
	2003	47,615.94	128,285.59	14,565.25	30,375.77	3,899.24***	737.71***
Sales	2001	15,579.06	25,518.33	7,125.32	16,937.50		
	2002	14,785.10	24,783.36	6,964.18	15,756.00	−793.96**	−40.55***
	2003	16,125.55	26,957.91	7,771.50	17,235.25	1,340.45***	417.09***

*** indicates significance at the 1 percent level; ** at the 5 percent level; and * at the 10 percent level. Market Value of Equity is price multiplied by shares outstanding at the fiscal year end. Total Assets and Sales are Compustat items 6 and 12, respectively. Effective Tax Rate is income tax expense divided by pre-tax income. Return on Equity is Net Income divided by Shareholders Equity at the fiscal year end. Means and medians of yearly differences are means and medians of firm-specific differences. Means are tested using a *t* test; medians are tested using the sign-rank test.

Of more central interest to this study are the audit and tax fees paid to the auditing firm. Table 2 shows that from 2001 to 2003 the mean (median) audit fees grew by 43 (30) percent, from $4.0 ($2.3) million to $5.7 ($3.0) million. Mean (median) audit-related fees declined by 12 (17) percent, from $1.7 ($0.72) million to $1.5 ($0.60) million. One possible explanation for the decline in audit-related fees is that some firms are no longer purchasing their audit-related services from their auditor. Combining audit and audit-related fees to form expanded audit fees, we find mean (median) expanded audit fees rose by 26 (26) percent, from $5.7 ($3.1) million to $7.2 ($3.9) million. Meanwhile, from 2001 to 2003, mean (median) tax fees for auditor-provided tax services tumbled by 20 (27) percent, from $3.2 ($1.5) million to $2.5 ($1.1) million. These findings are consistent with companies voluntarily reducing their demand for auditor-provided tax services.[15]

The combination of increased audit fees and decreased tax fees halves the mean (median) ratio of tax-to-audit fees, from 96 (68) percent in 2001 to 48 (36) percent in 2003. Similarly, when we compute the ratio using expanded audit fees, the mean (median) ratio falls from 68 (49) percent to 39 (31) percent. Untabulated results show that the decrease in the ratio occurred for the firms that relied most heavily on their auditors for tax services. To demonstrate this difference, we split the sample on the median ratio in 2001, using audit fees in the denominator. The 124 firms above the median had an average ratio of 1.6. The 124 firms below the median had an average ratio of 0.3. Two years later, the ratio for the above-median group had slipped to 0.7. The below-median group was unchanged at 0.3. Although regression toward the mean may explain part of this decline, it appears unlikely to account for all of it, as there was no regression to the mean for the below-median firms.

The tax-to-audit ratios fell steadily from 2001 to 2003. Initial reports indicate that the decline continued in 2004. The *Public Accounting Report* (April 29, 2005) reported that the 430 Fortune 500 companies, for which data had been disclosed, paid 54 percent more for audit work in 2004 than they paid in 2003.[16] They added that the companies paid their auditors 11 percent less for tax work in 2004 than in 2003.[17]

---

[15] As an aside, All Other Fees fell precipitously with a mean (median) decline of 88 (95) percent, from $3.7 ($0.4) million to $0.5 ($0.0) million. This slump in All Other Fees is consistent with SOX restrictions on non-audit services; companies no longer looking to auditors for services, other than audit and tax work; and auditors divesting their consulting practices.

[16] Audit fees soared even higher for Fortune 501 to Fortune 1000 companies, with an average increase of 75 percent.

[17] The article specifically identified tax work for audit clients as one fee area "getting pinched for auditors."

Table 2. *Tax Fees and Audit Fees and Paid to Auditors Sample Consists of S&P 500 Firms with Available Tax and AuditFee Data, for 2001 to 2003 (N = 248)*

Variable	Year	Mean	Std. Dev.	25th Percentile	Median	75th Percentile	Mean of Yearly Differences	Median of Yearly Differences
Tax Fees	2001	3.16	4.47	0.55	1.50	3.48		
	2002	2.83	4.17	0.49	1.20	2.98	−0.33***	−0.07***
	2003	2.53	4.03	0.43	1.11	2.35	−0.30**	−0.10***
Audit Fees	2001	3.99	5.15	1.16	2.31	4.37		
	2002	5.05	6.23	1.31	2.70	5.72	1.06***	0.38***
	2003	5.70	7.31	1.59	3.01	6.12	0.65***	0.34***
Audit-Related Fees	2001	1.70	2.65	0.27	0.72	1.99		
	2002	1.44	2.71	0.21	0.50	1.53	−0.26**	−0.04***
	2003	1.50	2.81	0.27	0.60	1.35	0.06	0.01***
Expanded Audit Fees (Audit Fees + Audit-Related Fees)	2001	5.70	7.17	1.63	3.10	6.40		
	2002	6.49	8.33	1.77	3.42	7.46	0.80***	0.24***
	2003	7.20	9.54	1.92	3.92	8.50	0.70***	0.39***
All Other Fees Paid to Auditor	2001	3.72	9.01	0.04	0.43	2.50		
	2002	2.06	8.48	0.00	0.11	0.89	−1.66***	−0.10***
	2003	0.45	2.09	0.00	0.02	0.16	−1.61***	−0.03***
Total Fees Paid to Auditor	2001	12.57	17.28	3.05	6.21	14.15		
	2002	11.38	16.99	2.73	5.32	11.32	−1.19**	−0.10***
	2003	10.17	13.64	2.71	5.43	10.75	−1.20***	0.03***
Tax-Fee-to-Audit-Fee Ratio	2001	0.96	1.07	0.33	0.68	1.26		
	2002	0.71	1.15	0.23	0.48	0.85	−0.25***	−0.12***
	2003	0.48	0.47	0.16	0.36	0.62	−0.24***	−0.08***
Tax-Fee-to-Expanded-Audit-Fee Ratio	2001	0.68	0.76	0.24	0.49	0.86		
	2002	0.53	0.66	0.17	0.38	0.68	−0.15***	−0.06***
	2003	0.39	0.39	0.13	0.31	0.53	−0.14***	−0.05***

*** indicates significance at the 1 percent level; ** at the 5 percent level; and * at the 10 percent level. Audit Fees, Audit-Related Fees, Tax Fees, Other Fees, and Total Fees are as reported in the footnotes to the financial statements. The Tax-Fee-to-Audit-Fee Ratio is Tax Fees divided by Audit Fees. Means and medians of yearly differences are means and medians of firm-specific differences. Means are tested using a *t* test; medians are tested using the sign-rank test.

Assuming that these 430 Fortune 500 companies are comparable with the S&P 500 for which we have 2003 data, we estimate that the 2004 tax-to-audit ratio was 0.26, or almost half the ratio in 2003.[18] In other words, on average, the audit fees from audit clients were four times larger than the tax fees from them. In short, providing tax services to publicly traded audit clients is a significantly diminished revenue source for the major accounting firms.

Initial audits of internal control documentation, as required by section 404 of Sarbanes-Oxley, were responsible for much of the increase in 2004 audit fees. Because it was the first year of section 404 documentation, 2004 may have been an aberration. However, a November 2004 Corporate Executive Board survey reported that only 12 percent of corporations expected their SOX costs to abate in 2005.[19] So, it is not clear that the tax-to-audit ratio will rebound in the near future. For now, the audit so dominates all other sources of fees from audit clients that actual or perceived audit compromise seems highly unlikely.

3.4. Analysis of Big Four Audit and Tax Fees

Further examination of detailed information from the Big Four accounting firms confirms the diminished role for auditor-provided tax services. In private conversations with top management at one of the Big Four accounting firms, we were told that approximately three-quarters of their tax work was conducted for audit accounts for 2002. That figure declined 7 percent in 2003, another 7 percent in 2004, and will decline another 3 percent for 2005. Thus, they estimate that about 60 percent of their tax work is now with audit clients. They anticipate the continuing erosion of their audit-client tax work until the percentage levels around 50 percent or slightly less.

These managers also asserted regional and industry differences in the retention of auditors for tax work. Companies in the southwest and in the financial services industries are more likely to retain their auditors for tax services. They attribute the reticence of the financial service industry to the long-standing close relationship required between the auditors and the tax consultants in the regulated industries. In other words, they claim that the audit-tax coordination required for statutory filings in the

---

[18] Dropping Table 2's 2003 Tax Fees of $2.53 million by another 11 percent produces estimated 2004 Tax Fees of $2.25 million. Increasing Table 2's 2003 audit fees of $5.70 million by 54 percent yields estimated 2004 Audit Fees of $8.78 million. $2.25 divided by $8.78 is 0.26.

[19] The survey results can be found at http://www.cfo.executiveboard.com/Images/CTLR/PDF/Key%20Insights%20from%20MHF.pdf on the fifth page of a report titled, "SOX 404 Triggering Delayed Filings and CEO Turnover."

regulated industries increases the costs of decoupling the auditor and the tax professional.

This assertion is consistent with evidence at another Big Four firm, Ernst & Young. In its 2004 review, Ernst & Young reports that audit clients now account for 63 percent of its business, down from 80 percent in 2000. This decline is remarkable for at least two reasons. First, the shift toward non-audit clients is largely limited to publicly traded firms. Privately held businesses are mostly unaffected by SOX and usually have no need to signal uncompromised audits. Second, fees from audits have soared in recent years. Thus, for the percentage of business from audit accounts to have declined by 17 percentage points (from 80 percent to 63 percent), at least one of two changes must have happened: (1) work for non-audit clients has soared (i.e., doing non-audit work for other firms' audit clients) or (2) non-audit work for the firm's audit clients has plunged. More likely, both conditions have occurred. That is, Ernst & Young's non-audit professionals are winning work from other firms' audit clients, and Ernst and Young's audit clients are looking to other firms for their tax and consulting services.

To quantify these shifts, we reviewed Ernst & Young revenues by business lines. In 2000, we estimate that 60–87 percent of Ernst & Young's tax work was done for audit clients. By 2004, we estimate that no more than 21 percent of its tax work was for audit firms. In short, if our estimates are accurate, most of Ernst & Young's tax work now comes from non-audit clients. Even if our estimates somewhat overstate the shift, the data still suggest a radical decline in tax work for audit clients in recent years.[20]

---

[20] For the year ended June 2000, their Assurance business line (which should comprise audit and audit-related services) generated $5.2 billion, or 57 percent, of worldwide revenues. Assume that 90 percent of these audit services were provided to audit clients and recall that 80 percent of their 2000 work was conducted on audit clients. This fact pattern implies that another 29 (80 percent less [90 percent of 57 percent]) percentage points of audit revenues (or $2.6 billion) must have come from their other three business lines (Tax, Transaction Advisory, and Other).

Next, we attempt to estimate upper and lower bounds for auditor-provided tax work. Suppose no Transaction Advisory or Other services were provided to audit clients. Then, because Tax generated total fees of $3.0 billion, the maximum percentage of tax work on audit accounts in 2000 was 87 percent ($2.6÷$3.0). Conversely, suppose all Transaction Advisory services of $0.6 billion and Other services of $0.2 billion were conducted for audit clients, then the minimum percentage of tax work on audit accounts in 2000 was 60 percent ([$2.6–$0.6–$0.2]÷$3.0). In summary, the data are consistent with 60–87 percent of Ernst & Young's tax fees in 2000 coming from audit clients.

Let's compare those figures with 2004 data. For the year ended June 2004, the Assurance business line generated $9.0 billion (62 percent of worldwide revenues), up 72 percent from 2000. With 63 percent of Ernst & Young's 2004 work conducted on audit clients, if we continue to assume that 90 percent of the audit services were provided to audit clients,

3.5. Has the Overall Amount of Corporate Tax Work Declined?

An alternative explanation for the declining tax-to-audit ratios is that corporations are purchasing fewer tax services in total. In other words, perhaps auditor-provided tax work is not declining alone. Rather, accountants are providing fewer tax services to all clients, including their non-audit clients.

The Big Four data reject this proposition. In Ernst & Young's case, worldwide tax fees from both audit and non-audit clients rose 27 percent from 2000 to 2004. Although this increase pales in comparison to the 72 percent leap in worldwide audit fees, it is consistent with Ernst & Young continuing to generate large fees from tax work, albeit perhaps not for audit clients. Ernst & Young, however, reports worldwide fees. If tax work outside the United States soared, then these calculations may mask an underlying shrinkage in U.S. tax revenues. To test this possibility, we turn to financial information from another Big Four firm, Deloitte & Touche.

Deloitte & Touche reported U.S. tax fees of $1.2 billion for the year ended May 2002. Two years later, total U.S. tax fees were $1.8 billion, a 43 percent jump. During the same period, U.S. audit revenues rose 50 percent, from $1.8 billion to $2.8 billion. Thus, the Deloitte & Touche data suggest that its U.S. tax work is not receding at all. In fact, it appears to be growing at a rapid pace, although probably much stronger for non-audit clients than for audit accounts.

We also find evidence of a sharp increase in non-U.S. tax work. From 2002 to 2004, Deloitte & Touche's worldwide tax revenues leapt 58 percent (from $2.4 billion to $3.8 billion), while worldwide audit fees rose 51 percent (from $4.9 billion to $7.4 billion). This increase means that non-U.S. tax fees rose 74 percent in two years, from $1.2 billion to $2.0 billion. Meanwhile, non-U.S. audit revenues were up 52 percent, from $3.1 billion to $4.6 billion.

Other data, however, suggest that Deloitte & Touche's increase in tax fees may be exceptional. Data from the trade publication *Public Accounting Report* reveal that aggregate U.S. tax fees for the Big Four increased from approximately $5.5 billion in 2002 to approximately $6.0 billion in 2003, a one-year increase of approximately 9 percent. Excluding Deloitte & Touche,

then only 6 percentage points of audit revenues (or $0.9 billion) came from their other three business lines (Tax, Transaction Advisory, and Other). Again, suppose no Transaction Advisory or Other services were provided to audit clients. Then, because Tax generated total fees of $4.3 billion, (up 27 percent from 2000), the maximum percentage of tax work on audit accounts in 2000 was 21 percent ($0.9÷$4.3). Conversely, if all of Ernst & Young's non-audit, non-tax services (Transaction Advisory services of $1.1 billion and Other services of $0.2 billion) were for audit clients, then none of their tax work related to audit accounts.

however, aggregate U.S. tax fees increased by only 2.6 percent. Nevertheless, at least for 2002–2003, we detect no evidence of a drop in aggregate U.S. tax fees.

Finally, it appears that attorneys have increased market share as a result of restrictions on auditor-provided tax services. PricewaterhouseCoopers' vice-chairman John O'Connor reportedly estimates that his firm has lost about 3 percent of its tax practice to law firms.[21] Because law firms do not routinely disclose the percentage of their revenue from areas of legal practice (e.g., general corporate, litigation, tax), we are unable to further quantify the extent of this possible shift in market share to law firms.

4. Industry Restructuring

As would be expected, restrictions on auditor-provided tax services are affecting both auditors and tax professionals. In its review of 2004, Ernst & Young notes "The shifting market [for publicly traded audit clients] is having an unprecedented impact on our people, with our assurance and risk services resources strained to capacity, while activity has softened in other service areas, most notably tax planning" (*Global Review 2004*, p. 14).

As the tax work has moved among firms, some tax experts have switched accounting firms. Others have left accounting firms for other tax practices, such as law or consulting firms, that are unencumbered by these new restrictions. Also, new tax services providers are emerging in the wake of the SOX restrictions. For example, Alvarez and Marsal, a global professional service firm, expanded into tax consulting in 2004. In a January 2005 press release announcing the hiring of eight prominent tax professionals, Bob Lowe, head of their tax practice, said:

The need for management teams and boards of directors to maintain independence from their auditors has led to increased scrutiny of tax services provided by an audit firm. This need for independent tax advisors has begun to spur an exodus of senior tax professionals from Big Four accounting firms.... [W]e continue to attract the industry's leading tax professionals who are excited by the opportunity to work with a multidisciplinary firm that does not and will not perform audits. Since we will not offer audit services, our Managing Directors will not be faced with the types of independence conflicts that hinder a Big Four firm tax partner's ability to serve clients.

Alvarez and Marsal has met resistance in its attempt to build a major tax practice of former Big Four tax professionals. After Alvarez and Marsal hired

---

[21] http://www.cfoasia.com/archives/200402-05.htm.

13 tax consultants from Ernst & Young, the accounting firm sued them for raiding its personnel, interfering with its business, and misappropriating confidential information. In a *Wall Street Journal* article (March 18, 2005, C1), the tax consultants claimed that they were fleeing the constraints of SOX.

Leaving an accounting firm can be costly for partners. They can lose substantial capital and retirement benefits and face lengthy covenants-not-to-compete, which can thwart their ability to pursue clients of their former firm or recruit former colleagues. One tax partner privately told us that he switched Big Four firms so that he could continue to provide tax services to the clients that he had worked with for the last 20 years. However, his covenant-not-to-compete precludes his soliciting former clients or rebuilding his staff with former colleagues for two years. Nevertheless, he concluded that his skills were so client-specific that he would be better off to wait two years and pursue his former clients, rather than begin now to rebuild his tax practice with non-audit clients.

Moreover, firm-specific skills and relationships are costly to replicate. Entire careers are devoted to applying highly technical skills to a single firm. The tax director of one of the country's largest financial service firms privately told us that it would take years to develop the firm-specific tax and business expertise that currently resides among the tax consultants at the accounting firm that has conducted its audit for decades.

An alternative to employee reshuffling is that the Big Four accounting firms could spin off or sell their tax practices, thus eliminating the SOX constraints. Each firm acknowledges that it has considered dividing. However, to date, no firm has taken this final step. We understand that to facilitate division, one of the Big Four has moved its tax practice to a separate corporation, although retaining the same management.

In the past, significant opportunities existed to sell tax services more effectively and at lower cost to one's audit clients. This created an economic attraction that caused tax and audit specialists to operate synergistically in the large accounting firms. Today, it appears quite possible that the former attraction is now repulsion. As the data on the decline of tax fees coming from audit clients indicate, tax specialists in many cases appear effectively precluded from the very work that used to be nearly guaranteed. Based on the dramatic changes already evident in the data, we are skeptical that a net synergy remains to having tax and audit specialists in the same firm as their respective client bases diverge from one another. To be sure, auditing firms will always need some tax specialists to assist with the tax provision (e.g., auditing the tax numbers that appear in the financial statements).

But provision work would surely require only a small fraction of the tax specialists that currently work for the large accounting firms. In addition, the career path for a tax professional who only does provision work is likely less profitable than one involving tax consulting and planning.

Ironically, SOX is providing both the pressure to split audit and tax practices and the force to hold them together, at least for now. Tax partners, as discussed above, have an incentive to press for an organizational structure unencumbered by SOX restrictions.[22] However, Sarbanes-Oxley – particularly its section 404 internal control documentation – is currently generating unprecedented audit fees. Because audit and tax partners tend to share profits at least somewhat, Big Four audit partners today are said to be heavily subsidizing their tax colleagues. In other words, one explanation for the lack of audit-tax division within the Big Four is that the SOX boost to audit fees exceeds its disruption to tax practices. Thus, an audit-tax split may be inevitable, but it may be temporarily delayed until the audit profits from Sarbanes-Oxley dissipate. In the long run, however, large cross-partner subsidies could cause instability, as it reportedly did in the eventual breakup of Arthur Andersen and Andersen Consulting (now Accenture) in the 1990s.

Another factor that increases the incentive to sell or split off part of the Big Four tax practices is that the explicit and implicit restrictions on auditor-provided tax services substantially shrink the competition for both services. The restriction effect would be immaterial if the pool of prospective accounting firms were large. Instead, the Big Four accounting firms – Deloitte & Touche, Ernst & Young, KPMG, and PricewaterhouseCooopers – audit almost every large company in the country. Their audit market share exceeds 99 percent of the market capitalization of S&P 500, and they provide similar portions of the external tax accounting advice for these companies. Moreover, for most corporations, the pool of prospective auditors and tax accountants is even smaller than four firms because the firms specialize along industry lines. Consequently, once the auditor is removed as a tax service provider, many companies realistically have only one or two other accounting firms to access for tax expertise.

At first, it might seem natural that the large law firms acquire tax practices from the accounting firms or gradually acquire the underlying work and add personnel over time. Indeed, one could imagine a great deal of synergy in having tax accountants and tax lawyers working in the same firm. In fact, that is precisely the direction the Big Four were going in the 1990s as they hired

---

[22] The potentially catastrophic costs associated with failed audits (as seen in Arthur Andersen's collapse) is another reason for tax practitioners to separate from auditing firms.

a significant number of tax attorneys, sometimes at considerable premiums over what they were making in their former law firms.[23] Anecdotally, this migration is reversing, with tax attorneys returning to law firms.

Although synergies exist between the work that tax accountants and tax lawyers do, law firms are unlikely to acquire large portions of the Big Four tax practice for at least two reasons. The first reason is size. The law market is highly fragmented. Even the largest law firms are tiny compared with the Big Four accounting firms. Consequently, no law firm is large enough to acquire the entire tax practice of even the smallest Big Four firm. As of 2003, the largest law firm in the United States had revenues of approximately $1.3 billion, and only three other U.S. law firms had revenues in excess of $1 billion.[24] Moreover, the tax practice within the law firms would be only a fraction of the total revenues, the majority likely being general corporate work and litigation work. By comparison, the U.S. tax practice of the Big Four in 2003 ranged from nearly $1.2 billion for KPMG to almost $1.9 billion for Ernst & Young.[25] In short, the U.S. tax practices of the Big Four are indeed deserving of the "big" moniker, exceeding in size the entire tax and non-tax practices of all but the very largest U.S. law firms.

The second reason not to expect law firms to acquire major portions of the Big Four tax practice is regulatory – in this case, a restriction on law firms. We understand that, in most jurisdictions, law firms are not permitted to share profits with non-lawyers. In other words, law firms are regulated to be "pure" law firms, making it nearly impossible for law firms to expand into other lines of business. (These rules also effectively shield law firms from being taken over by anything other than another law firm.)

Furthermore, it is unlikely that large amounts of existing Big Four tax work could shift to law firms in the absence of their ability to hire tax accountants, because accounting tax and legal tax skills are not fully inter-changeable. A good deal of tax work, including most compliance work and some consulting work, is not well suited for lawyers because it is quantita-tive rather than verbal. As a gross simplification, tax lawyers tend to have a comparative advantage in verbal aspects of taxation (e.g., interpretation of the case law surrounding the assignment of income doctrine), while tax

---

[23] This practice led to several legal skirmishes about whether the tax attorneys working at the Big Four were improperly engaging in the practice of law and the limitations, if any, on them after they moved from a law firm to a Big Four accounting firm.

[24] These data come from the "Am Law 100" list compiled by *The American Lawyer* (July 2004). The four largest law firms per the Am Law 100 are Skadden Arps, Baker & McKenzie, Jones Day, and Latham & Watkins.

[25] These data are from the *Public Accounting Report* "Top 100 for 2004," September 14, 2004.

accountants tend to have a comparative advantage in quantitative aspects of taxation (e.g., analyzing the tax costs and benefits of various repatriation strategies).

However, other entities that do not face such constraints could have synergies with tax specialists. For example, strategic consulting firms, such as McKinsey, could have synergies with tax to the extent their existing work gives them enough knowledge of the client's business to facilitate cross-selling of tax services. Human resources consulting firms, such as Mercer, already employ some tax specialists and could see that work grows as they face less competition from their clients' audit firms. IT consulting firms, such as Accenture and IBM, could have synergies with process-oriented aspects of tax, such as compliance. Investment and commercial banks could conceivably find it worthwhile to offer a broad range of tax services, as the selling of tax services can sometimes lead to high-margin work implementing the transactions needed to carry out tax planning. In short, even with no wholesale split of the Big Four tax practices, portions of the tax work could move to non-audit professional firms over time, as those firms see an opportunity to enter the market or acquire pieces of the Big Four tax practices.

5. Unintended Consequences: More Corporate Tax Collections

We expect to see a chilling effect on tax avoidance activities. These strategies have been the subject of much research and speculation, and observers have pointed to the growing gap between book and tax income over the 1990s as evidence of increased corporate tax avoidance activities (see Hanlon and Shevlin, 2004; Mills, Newberry, and Trautman, 2002; and Plesko, 2004; among others). One unintended consequence of having a different provider of tax services than one's auditor could be to reduce the level of corporate tax aggressiveness and increase corporate tax collections.

We expect that auditors will be far less willing to accept tax planning strategies developed by a rival firm than by their tax colleagues down the hall. Anecdotal reports support the expectation that auditors are requiring much more detail in the workpapers supporting the "tax cushion." The tax cushion is the reserve that companies maintain to account for the positions they have taken on their tax returns that they may lose once audited by the IRS. Under certain conditions, IRS auditors can request or demand to see a company's tax accrual workpapers, including the tax cushion, which can serve as a road map to the parts of the tax return the company would rather the IRS not scrutinize. Now the road map, because of changes in the audit market, is increasingly detailed. It is possible that the financial statement auditor has become the single most effective deterrent against aggressive tax avoidance strategies. To test this prediction, one would need data on taxes paid, financial reporting tax expense, and the shift in obtaining tax services from one's auditor to other service providers.

Having said that, it is not obvious that collections will increase. Another possibility is that tax planners will become more aggressive now that they are no longer impeded by their audit partners. In the past, tax advisers from the audit firm suffered if the audit failed. No longer bearing the costs of an audit failure, tax advisers may press for increasingly aggressive positions. If so, the restrictions placed on auditor-provided tax services could actually serve to increase tax avoidance.

Another possible effect could come as auditors become privy to the latest tax technology at competitor firms and can share this information with the tax advisors in their firms. In equilibrium, this could cause tax consultants to reserve their best tax ideas – those that save taxes at low risk – for clients that continue to use them for both audit and tax.

It will take a good deal of research before we can conclusively resolve the revenue effects of decoupling audit and tax services. We expect that the net result of the restrictions on auditor-provided tax services will be an increase in tax collections. Auditors, as the final arbitrators of the financial statements, should prevail in most cases against highly aggressive tax advisers from other firms because auditors can demand complete disclosure in a timely manner from the tax adviser. Our expectation, however, relies critically on the assumption that auditors choose to maintain an aggressive posture toward manipulation of the financial statements and demand full disclosure of the firm's tax position. If auditors shrink from the heightened tension between them and tax advisers, then tax planning could indeed become more aggressive.

6. Conclusions

Following Sarbanes-Oxley, accountants have dramatically reduced the tax work that they conduct for audit clients, while increasing the amount of tax work that they do for non-audit clients. We estimate that from 2001 to 2004 the typical company went from paying its auditor the same for audit and tax services to paying the auditor only one-fourth as much for tax services as for audit services. This decline is reshaping the landscape for corporate tax consulting.

The future is still hazy, but a few predictions seem plausible. One, because auditors in the past had competitive advantages over other tax service providers, corporate taxes and the costs of tax avoidance will increase. Two, although SOX and related changes have reduced or eliminated the synergies that once existed between providing both audit and tax services to the same client, high audit fees are providing a short-term incentive for tax partners to stay in auditing firms. In the long run, if the trend away from auditor-provided tax services continues we anticipate instability and the possible sale or spin-off of significant portions of the Big Four tax practices. Even if no firm spins off or sells its tax line of business, some nontrivial amount of tax work will migrate to non-audit firms, including law firms, consulting firms, and investment and commercial banks. Three, a consequence of the decoupling of tax and audit services is that when auditors review the tax provision, they are no longer judging tax strategies developed by their own firm. Consequently, we predict that auditors will be more likely to require that their clients record a tax cushion for aggressive tax positions to protect against the financial reporting tax expense from being understated. Furthermore, the financial auditors are increasingly requiring detailed workpapers backing up the tax provision. This documentation will serve as a road map for the IRS in subsequent corporate tax return audits. These forecasts reflect the massive impact that the accounting scandals, Sarbanes-Oxley, and related regulatory changes have already had on the world of corporate tax planning – effects that will continue to reverberate for years to come.

APPENDIX

Allstate's Disclosure of the Fees Paid ($) to Deloitte & Touche in its 2002 Financial Statements

The following fees have been, or will be, billed by Deloitte & Touche LLP, the member firms of Deloitte Touche Tohmatsu, and their respective affiliates, for professional services rendered to Allstate for the fiscal years ending December 31, 2002 and December 31, 2001.

	2002 ($)	2001 ($)
Audit fees(1)	6,063,752	5,275,465
Audit-related fees(2)	963,328	213,365
Tax fees(3)	81,551	99,374
All other fees(4)	61,807	624,735
Total fees	7,170,338	6,212,939

(1) "Audit fees" include fees for audits of annual financial statements, reviews of quarterly financial statements, statutory audits, audit services, comfort letters, consents, and review of documents filed with the SEC.

(2) "Audit-related fees" relate to professional services, such as accounting consultations relating to new accounting standards, due diligence assistance, and audits of non-consolidated entities (i.e., employee benefit plans, various trusts, Allstate Foundation, etc.) and are set forth below. The fees associated with the 2001 audits of these entities (totaling $416,150) were not included in last year's proxy statement.

	2002	2001
Adoption of new accounting standards	16,610	169,612
Due diligence	479,861	23,903
Audits of non-consolidated entities	432,010	–
Other	34,747	19,850
Audit-related fees	963,228	213,365

(3) "Tax fees" include fees for tax compliance, consultation, and planning.

(4) "All other fees" primarily include professional fees for consulting services related to financial and nonfinancial information systems, as well as fees for other consulting services.

	2002	2001
Strategic planning	40,727	–
Nonfinancial information systems	–	445,353
Business consulting	–	67,580
Lease consulting	7,710	62,804
Financial information systems design and implementation	–	9,160
Other	13,370	39,838
All other fees	61,807	624,735

References

Antle, Rick 1984. "Auditor Independence." *Journal of Accounting Research* 22(1): 1–19.

Antle, Rick, Elizabeth Gordon, Ganapathi Narayanamoorthy, and Ling Zhou. 2002. "The Joint Determination of Audit Fees, Non-Audit Fees and Abnormal Accruals." Working paper. (New Haven, CT: Yale University).

Ashbaugh, Hollis, Ryan Lafond, and Brian Mayhew. 2003. "Do Nonaudit Services Compromise Auditor Independence? Further Evidence." *Accounting Review* 78(3): 611–639.

Asthana, Sharad, Steven Balsam, and Sungsoo Kim. 2004. "The Effect of Enron, Andersen, and Sarbanes-Oxley on the Market for Audit Services." Working paper. (Philadelphia: Temple University/New Brunswick, NJ: Rutgers University).

Bankman, Joseph. 2004. "The Tax Shelter Battle." In Henry J. Aaron and Joel Slemrod, eds., *The Crisis in Tax Administration.* (Washington, DC: Brookings Institution), pp. 9–37.

Cohen, Daniel, Aiyesha Day, and Thomas Lys. 2004. "The Effect of the Sarbanes-Oxley Act on Earnings Management: What Has Changed?" Working paper. (Evanston, IL: Northwestern University, Kellogg School of Management).

DeFond, Mark, Kannan Raghunandan, and K. R. Subramanyam. 2002. "Do Non-Audit Service Fees Impair Auditor Independence? Evidence from Going Concern Audit Opinions." *Journal of Accounting Research* 40(4): 1247–1274.

Deloitte & Touche. 2006. "Facts & Figures." Available online at http://www.deloitte.com.

Deloitte Touche Tohmatsu. 2004. *Worldwide Member Firms 2004 Review.* (New York: Deloitte Touche Tohmatsu).

Ernst & Young. 2004. *Global 2004 Review.* (London: Ernst & Young).

Francis, Jere, and Bin Ke. 2004. "Disclosure of Fees Paid to Auditors and the Market Valuation of Earnings Surprises." Working paper. (Columbia: University of Missouri/University Park: Pennsylvania State University).

Francis, Jere, Edward Maydew, and H. Charles Sparks. 1999. "The Role of Big 6 Auditors in the Credible Reporting of Accruals." *Auditing: A Journal of Practice and Theory* 18(2): 17–34.

Frankel, Richard M., Marilyn F. Johnson, and Karen K. Nelson. 2002. "The Relation Between Auditors' Fees for Non-Audit Services and Earnings Management." *Accounting Review* 77(Supplement): 71–105.

Gary, K. 2004. "PCAOB Approves Proposed Auditor Independence Rules." *Tax Notes* (December 20): 1603–1604.

Geiger, Marshall, and Dasaratha Rama. 2003. "Audit Fees, Nonaudit Fees, and Auditor Reporting on Stressed Companies." *Auditing: A Journal of Practice and Theory* 22(3): 53–69.

Goodman, George. 2004. "The Taxpayer's and Tax Adviser's Guide to Sarbanes-Oxley." *Tax Notes* (August 4): 691–712.

Graham, John R., Cam Harvey, and Shiva Rajgopal. 2005. "The Economic Implications of Corporate Financial Reporting." *Journal of Accounting and Economics* 40(1): 3–73.

Griffin, Paul, and David Lont. 2005. "The Effects of Auditor Dismissals and Resignations on Audit Fees: Evidence Based on SEC Disclosures under Sarbanes-Oxley." Working paper. (Davis: University of California).

Hanlon, Michelle. 2005. "The Persistence and Pricing of Earnings, Accruals, and Cash Flows When Firms Have Large Book-Tax Differences." *Accounting Review* 80(1): 137–166.

Hanlon, Michelle, and Terry J. Shevlin. 2005. "Book-Tax Conformity for Corporate Income: An Introduction to the Issues." In James M. Poterba, ed. *Tax Policy and the Economy*, vol. 19. (Cambridge, MA: MIT Press), pp. 101–134.

Hardesty, David. 2004. "Sarbanes-Oxley Compliance in the Corporate Tax Department." *State Tax Notes* (November 29): 589–596.

Kinney, William, Zoe-Vonna Palmrose, and Susan Scholz. 2004. "Auditor Independence, Non-Audit Services, and Restatements: Was the U.S. Government Right?" *Journal of Accounting Research* 42(3): 561–588.

KPMG. 2004. *International 2004 Annual Report*. (London: KPMG).

Kroszner, Randall. 1998. "Rethinking Bank Regulation: A Review of the Historical Evidence." *Journal of Applied Corporate Finance* 11(2): 48–58.

Kroszner, Randall, and Raghuram Rajan. 1994. "Is the Glass-Steagall Act Justified? A Study of the U.S. Experience with Universal Banking Before 1933." *American Economic Review* 84(4): 810–832.

Kroszner, Randall, and Raghuran Rajan. 1997. "Organization Structure and Credibility: Evidence from Commercial Bank Securities Activities Before the Glass-Steagall Act." *Journal of Monetary Economics* 39(3): 475–516.

Lai, Kam-Wah. 2003. "The Sarbanes-Oxley Act and Auditor Independence: Preliminary Evidence from Audit Opinion and Discretionary Accruals." Working paper. (Hong Kong: City University of Hong Kong).

McLean, Bethany, and Peter Elkind. 2003. *The Smartest Guys in the Room: The Amazing Rise and Scandalous Fall of Enron*. (New York: Penguin Group).

Mills, Lillian, Kaye Newberry, and William Trautman. 2002. "Trends in Book-Tax Income and Balance Sheet Differences." *Tax Notes* 96(8): 1109–1124.

Omer, Thomas C., Jean C. Bedard, and Diana Falsetta. 2006. "Auditor Provided Tax Services: The Effects of a Changing Regulatory Environment." *Accounting Review* (forthcoming).

Plesko, George. 2004. "Corporate Tax Avoidance and the Properties of Corporate Earnings." *National Tax Journal* 57(3): 729–737.

PricewaterhouseCoopers. 2004. *2004 Global Annual Review*. (London: PricewaterhouseCoopers).

Reynolds, J. Kenneth, Donald Deis, and Jere Francis. 2004. "Professional Service Fees and Auditor Objectivity." *Auditing: A Journal of Practice & Theory* 23(1): 29–52.

Sarbanes-Oxley Act of 2002. P. L. No. 207–204. (Washington, DC: Government Printing Office).

Scholes, Myron, Mark Wolfson, Merle Erickson, Edward Maydew, and Terry Shevlin. 2005. *Taxes and Business Strategy*, 3rd ed. (Upper Saddle River, NJ: Pearson/Prentice Hall).

Securities and Exchange Commission. 2000. *Final Rule: Revision of the Commission's Auditor Independence Requirements*. (Washington, DC: Government Printing Office).

Securities and Exchange Commission. 2003. *Final Rule: Strengthening the Commission's Requirements Regarding Auditor Independence*. (Washington, DC: Government Printing Office).

Shackelford, Douglas, and Terry Shevlin. 2001. "Empirical Tax Research in Accounting." *Journal of Accounting and Economics* 31(1–3): 321–387.

Simunic, Dan. 1984. "Auditing, Consulting, and Auditor Independence." *Journal of Accounting Research* 22(2): 679–702.

Whisenant, Scott, Srinivasan Sankaraguruswamy, and Kannan Raghunandan. 2003. "Evidence on the Joint Determination of Audit and Non-Audit Services." *Journal of Accounting Research* 41(4): 721–744.

Comments

Steven N. Kaplan*

Graduate School of Business University of Chicago

In this chapter, Maydew and Shackelford examine the effects of the Sarbanes-Oxley Act (SOX) on the market for tax planning and the role that auditors play in that planning. In so doing, they provide (1) a helpful discussion and summary of the new laws and regulations; (2) interesting preliminary information on spending for audit work and for tax work; and (3) thought-provoking predictions concerning the future impact of SOX. Overall, the chapter is informative and thought provoking. I learned a lot. I suspect that will be true for most readers, like me, who are not tax accountants. (I suspect that tax accountants will also enjoy the chapter.) At the same time that the chapter and, particularly, the future predictions are thought provoking, the thoughts they provoked in me were not always in agreement with the predictions. Below, I describe the authors' findings in more detail and provide my reactions to them.

As noted above, the chapter has three basic parts. First, the authors provide a helpful discussion of the SOX provisions as well as the subsequent SEC and PCAOB regulations or interpretations regarding what auditors can do. In short, the new rules push companies away from hiring their audit firms to do much of their tax work. The authors also provide a useful discussion arguing that separating the audit firm and the tax firm introduces a new set of conflicts regarding a company's tax plan. In short, the authors argue that the separation will increase the extent to which auditors question tax plans and generate information that will subsequently help the IRS. This is particularly true for tax plans that reduce book taxes (and increase book income).

Address correspondence to Steven Kaplan, University of Chicago Graduate School of Business, 5807 South Woodlawn Avenue, Chicago, IL 60637, or e-mail at skaplan@uhicago.edu.

Second, the authors study the fees paid by S&P 500 companies to auditors from 2001 to 2004. They find that mean fees paid to auditors for audit work increased while the mean fees paid to auditors for tax work declined. At the same time, "The total tax practice of the largest accounting firms (from both audit and non-audit clients) held steady during this period, indicating that what we are observing is a shift in clients among the providers of tax services rather than a general decline in tax services."

Third, the authors make two predictions concerning the medium- and long-term effects of the legal and regulatory changes. Their first prediction is that it is likely that tax work will shift away from the Big Four audit firms to other firms. The second, more interesting, prediction is that the separation of audit and tax firms will reduce the aggressiveness of tax planning, which will lead to an increase in actual corporate tax payments.

As I noted above, these predictions are not entirely convincing. First, consider the prediction that tax work will tend to move away from the Big Four firms. As the authors point out, the early evidence for this prediction is not at all supportive. Tax work done by the Big Four has actually increased by 27 percent from 2000 to 2004. The fact that this increase is less than the (72 percent) increase in audit fees is not surprising, given the substantial increase in audit fees effectively required by SOX and its section 404.

There is an argument to be made that this trend will continue rather than reverse (as the authors predict). A large S&P 500 company will prefer to choose a tax firm that can evaluate, coordinate, and optimize the company's global tax activities. The reason for this is that a company's tax payments are affected by the company's activities in all the countries in which it operates. This means, of course, that a company will prefer to choose a tax firm with operations around the world. This, in turn, creates a strong preference for choosing one of the Big Four firms, all of which have operations around the world. This also makes it increasingly difficult for new entrants. They have to operate around the world and understand tax issues around the world.

Now, let's look at the prediction that taxes will increase because companies will be less aggressive with regard to tax avoidance. The author's arguments are reasonable and identify forces that may indeed reduce tax avoidance and, therefore, increase taxes. At the same time, however, there are forces that may retard, if not cancel, the forces stressed by the authors. First, the authors effectively assume that companies and investors focus on short-term book net income. The conflict between audit work and tax work concerns getting book accounting treatment that reflects the increase in cash flows from tax reduction. It is conceivable that post-SOX and post-advances in behavioral finance, companies and investors care less about book accounting treatment and more about increased cash flow. If this is true, companies will have an incentive to focus more on legal tax avoidance or reduction while focusing less on the effects on book taxes and income.

Second, the authors argue that as audit and tax work is separated, auditors will have more of an incentive to be critical of tax avoidance behavior. While this is true, there is a question as to how big the effect will be. The reason for the question is that with only four large accounting firms, the same accounting firms will repeatedly come into contact with one another. It seems reasonable to assume that as the auditor of firm 1 is tough on the tax accountant at firm 2, the auditor at firm 2 for another client will be tough with the tax accountant at firm 1. In equilibrium, auditors will have incentives to be less tough on tax accountants at other firms than the authors suggest.

Despite the fact that I am not entirely convinced by the predictions in the chapter, I enjoyed the chapter a great deal. It provides a fair amount of useful information and puts forth predictions that are very much worth thinking about.

Comments

Richard Sansing

Tuck School of Business at Dartmouth and Tilburg University

Maydew and Shackelford (hereinafter, MS) examine the effects of the Sarbanes-Oxley Act (SOX) on corporate tax planning and corporate tax collections. The basic idea of the chapter is that corporations can choose a tax consultant from a variety of sources, such as public accounting firms or law firms. Prior to SOX, firms often chose a tax consultant from the public accounting firm that provided its audit services. If this choice minimized the sum of the corporation's tax payments and consulting costs, then the restrictions in SOX that make it more difficult to use a tax consultant from the firm that provides audit services will increase the cost of tax consulting services. This, in turn, will induce the corporation to purchase fewer tax consulting services, thus leading to an increase in corporate tax collections. The chapter provides empirical support for these predictions.

The first section of my discussion suggests three other possible effects of SOX on corporate tax planning decisions that could lead to decreases instead of increases in corporate tax collections. The second section examines the chapter's empirical results.

1. Alternative Effects of SOX on Corporate Tax Collections

1.1. Tax Minimization Versus Effective Tax Planning

Scholes et al. (2005) argue that the most effective tax plan will often not be the tax plan that minimizes the taxpayer's tax payments to the government. Taxes change the pre-tax rates of return on assets, so the optimal tax plan features a tradeoff between tax-induced differentials in pre-tax rates of return (implicit taxes) and taxes paid to the government (explicit taxes). If the corporation's choice of tax consultant induces a particular three-way tradeoff between implicit taxes, explicit taxes, and tax consulting fees, a SOX-induced change

341

in one's tax consultant could lead to a decrease in explicit taxes and an increase in implicit taxes.

The most effective tax plan is one that considers the explicit taxes paid by all the parties to a transaction. Many transactions to which a corporation is a party, such as deferred compensation arrangements and incentive stock options, feature outcomes that increase corporate taxes but decrease individual taxes. Again, if SOX induces a change in a corporation's tax consultant, this change could yield higher individual taxes and lower corporate taxes instead of the higher corporate taxes that MS hypothesize.

2. Financial Reporting Effects

There is ample evidence that firms consider the financial reporting consequences of tax planning, sometimes paying more in taxes for the sake of financial reporting considerations (Engel, Erickson, and Maydew, 1999; Matsunaga, Shevlin, and Shores, 1992; Maydew, Schipper, and Vincent, 1999). If SOX causes a corporation to change its tax consultant, the new consultant may be less sensitive to financial reporting consequences, in which case SOX could lead to lower corporate tax payments and lower book income being reported.

Tax planning ideas with identical effects on the present value of a firm's current and future tax payments could have very different effects on the tax expense that a firm reports on its income statement prepared in accordance with generally accepted accounting principles (GAAP). Converting a deduction into a credit reduces a corporation's tax expense shown on its GAAP income statement (the book tax expense); converting a depreciable capital expenditure into a current deduction does not, but instead transforms part of the corporation's current income tax expense into a deferred income tax expense. It may be that tax consultants working for accounting firms pay less attention to the latter because it does not lower a firm's accounting effective tax rate. Perhaps non-accounting tax consultants will be more interested in tax planning ideas that defer taxes. In addition, MS argue that SOX will induce more conservative tax planning because the auditor will be less willing to recognize the tax benefits associated with a risky tax planning idea by insisting that the corporation accrue a liability (the so-called "tax cushion") until the tax year has been audited. However, this argument does not hold for tax planning ideas that defer taxes because tax deferral does not reduce the corporation's book tax expense. Therefore, SOX may have the effect of inducing an increase in tax planning ideas that generate tax deferral, thereby decreasing the present value of corporate tax payments, although not changing the book income tax expense that corporations report on their income statement under GAAP.

2.1. Risk-Return Tradeoffs from Aggressive Tax Planning

The authors argue that using auditors and tax consultants from different firms will deter aggressive tax planning because the auditor has no financial stake in the success of the tax consultants' ideas. This will lead to less aggressive tax planning and higher corporate tax collections.

I believe that the authors' conjecture only captures half the story. When the tax consultant and auditor are from the same accounting firm, each has a stake in the success of the other. While separating the audit and tax work will make the auditor more conservative, it will likely make the tax consultant more aggressive for two reasons. First, when the audit and tax consulting work is done by the same firm, a failed tax plan would reflect badly on the accounting firm as a whole, which could lead to the loss of both tax and audit work. Thus, the costs of a failed tax plan are lower in a post-SOX world. Second, when different firms provide audit and tax work, there is more pressure on the tax consultant to come up with tax-saving ideas because the cost of switching to a different tax consultant is lower. So while SOX will induce the auditor to be more conservative, it will also induce the tax consultant to be more aggressive. It is not clear which effect will dominate, but it is certainly possible that SOX will lead to more aggressive tax planning and hence lower corporate tax collections.

3. Interpretation of the Data

3.1. Alternative Explanations

The authors find that tax consulting fees paid to the provider of audit services dropped after SOX was enacted, both in absolute terms and as a percentage of audit fees. It is important to draw a distinction between the effects of SOX and the effects of the economic climate in which SOX was enacted. In the aftermath of Enron's collapse, firms began pursuing more conservative financial policies in an effort to avoid being tainted by being involved in transactions that investors associated with Enron. For example, in February 2002, Krispy Kreme changed its plans to finance a new facility with a synthetic lease to avoid being associated with off-balance sheet financing vehicles (Weinberg, 2002). In addition, several firms began expensing stock options in an effort to create more transparent financial reporting (Jatras, 2002).

If firms also started adopting more conservative tax planning policies, the drop in tax planning fees documented in MS could be correlated with the enactment of SOX but not caused by it.

3.2. Economic Interpretations of Accounting Joint Costs

The empirical analysis in MS compares changes in audit fees and tax fees between 2001 and 2003. The authors interpret the decrease in ratio of tax fees to audit fees over time as evidence that firms providing audit services are providing fewer tax services over time. I would be cautious in drawing this inference because the data represent the division of an economic joint cost. The audit firm provides audit services (A) and tax services (T) in exchange for a fee, $f(A,T)$. The data reflect an allocation of this joint cost between the audit portion (α) and the tax portion ($1 - \alpha$). The authors make a strong case that the tax services are more efficiently provided by the firm that also provides the audit services, so cost function separability is absent. Interpreting a change in the ratio as a change in the value of tax services provided per dollar of audit services provided requires one to assign an economic interpretation to an allocation of accounting joint costs, an interpretation that is suspect in the absence of cost function separability (Demski, 1994).

References

Demski, Joel. 1994. *Managerial Uses of Accounting Information.* (Boston: Kluwer Academic Publishers).

Engel, Ellen, Merle Erickson, and Edward Maydew. 1999. "Debt-Equity Hybrid Securities." *Journal of Accounting Research* 37(2): 249–274.

Jatras, Todd. 2002. "Expensing Options." *Forbes* (July 24). Available online at http://www.forbes.com/2002/07/24/0724stockoptions.html.

Matsunaga, Steven, Terry Shevlin, and D. Shores. 1992. "Disqualifying Dispositions of Incentive Stock Options: Tax Benefits versus Financial Reporting Costs." *Journal of Accounting Research* 30(Supplement): 37–76.

Maydew, Edward, Katherine Schipper, and Linda Vincent. 1999. "The Effect of Taxes on Divestiture Method." *Journal of Accounting and Economics* 28(2): 117–150.

Scholes, Myron, Mark Wolfson, Merle Erickson, Edward Maydew, and Terry Shevlin. 2005. *Taxes and Business Strategy*, 3rd ed. (Upper Saddle River, NJ: Pearson/Prentice Hall).

Weinberg, Ari. 2002. "Krispy Kreme Changes Its Plant Financing." *Forbes* (February 12). Available online at http://www.forbes.com/2002/02/12/0212synthetic.html.

NINE

Taxation and the Evolution of Aggregate Corporate Ownership Concentration

Mihir A. Desai

Harvard University and NBER

Dhammika Dharmapala

University of Connecticut

Winnie Fung

Harvard University

We would like to thank Alan Auerbach, Steve Bank, Steve Bond, Bill Gale, Bill Gentry, Jim Hines, Emmanuel Saez, Richard Sansing, Gautam Tripathi, an anonymous referee, our discussants (Jeff Brown and Jeff Strnad) and participants at the Office of Tax Policy Research/Burch Center conference on "Taxing Corporate Income in the 21st Century" for valuable comments and suggestions on an earlier draft of this chapter. Mihir Desai acknowledges the financial support of the Division of Research of Harvard Business School.

1. Introduction

The extent to which corporate ownership is widely dispersed is an important dimension of an economy's corporate governance environment. The mechanisms by which diffuse owners police managers and the reasons why much of the world does not feature diffuse corporate ownership are major themes in the corporate governance literature. The comparative strand of this literature emphasizes legal origins as a critical determinant of the investor rights that facilitate ownership diffusion (e.g., La Porta et al., 1998). Subsequent efforts to trace the time-series patterns of governance and ownership concentration (e.g., Franks, Mayer, and Rossi, 2003; Rajan and Zingales, 2003) have questioned the singular role of legal investor protections, given the diffusion of ownership in the absence of legal protections at various times in the 20th century.[1] The dispersion of corporate ownership across households is also closely related to questions surrounding stock market participation that have attracted considerable interest in the recent literature (e.g., Griffin, Nardari, and Stulz, 2004; Vissing-Jorgensen, 2002). As a result, the question of what facilitates and propels ownership diffusion remains a central research question in corporate finance and asset pricing.

The role of taxes in retarding or promoting ownership diffusion has largely gone unexplored. This oversight is particularly surprising, as the seminal contribution that identified the issue of the separation of ownership and control (Berle and Means, 1932) was motivated by the observation that high tax rates during World War I marked a major turning point in this separation in the United States. Specifically, Warshow (1924) and Means (1930) analyze how these progressive taxes were associated with a sharp increase in the diffusion of ownership. This chapter extends that line of reasoning to analyze how personal taxes have shaped the level of ownership concentration over the rest of the 20th century.

The precise mechanism by which individual income taxation might facilitate ownership diffusion, as suggested originally in Means (1930), is illustrated with a simple extension to the Miller (1977) model of financial equilibrium. In Miller's model, firms endogenously issue both equity and bonds, with the corporate tax preference for debt financing being offset by a personal tax preference for equity among some investors. In equilibrium, each firm is indifferent about its debt-equity ratio, and investors sort into tax clienteles for stock and bonds. An extension of this model shows that an increase in the progressivity of the tax schedule leads to an increase in the fraction of investors holding equity and thus to a decrease in the concentration of stock ownership across investors. In essence, increased progressivity leads to a greater relative tax penalty on corporate bonds. Firms respond with increased equity issuance, and the identity of the marginal investor shifts to a lower income level, thereby generating a greater diffusion of equity ownership.

To analyze this hypothesis empirically, this chapter develops an index of corporate ownership concentration at the economy-wide level, following the methodology used to track income distribution pioneered by Kuznets (1953) and revived by Piketty and Saez (2003). Tax return data are used to

---

[1] Roe (2002) also notes that ownership is not diffuse in countries (such as Sweden and Finland) where corporate law and investor protections appear to be strong. He attributes this to the possibility that political forces would demand anti-shareholder actions in the absence of large blockholders.

construct a Herfindahl index that summarizes the degree of concentration of stock ownership across households over the 20th century. This index is characterized by significant time-series variation that undercuts the static view of the U.S. example as one where ownership has long been diffuse due to legal protections or political factors. It differs from measures used in existing studies of corporate governance (which typically track the ownership concentration of a sample of large public corporations across countries or through time) and is especially suited to time-series analysis within countries and for understanding the determinants of stock market participation across income groups. The advantages and disadvantages of such an economy-wide measure relative to the firm-specific approach typically employed are discussed in more detail below.

Time-series analysis of the determinants of this index reveals that increases in the progressivity of individual income tax rates are associated with statistically significant and economically meaningful increases in the diffusion of corporate ownership. Controlling for a variety of factors, a 1 standard deviation change in the top statutory rate is associated with close to a 1 standard deviation shift in the Herfindahl index. Analysis of the patterns of corporate equity ownership by each quintile of the income distribution confirms the impact of tax rates. This analysis can also be viewed as providing a new perspective on the determinants of equity market participation, suggesting that the progressivity of the tax code may be a contributing factor in stock market participation at lower income levels. This time-series analysis finds only weak evidence for the role of valuation levels on equity market participation.

The analysis finds support for the simple intuition that taxation can impact shareholding patterns and, consequently, levels of ownership concentration and stock market participation. Specifically, highly progressive rates shift the incentives for equity issuance and in response the distribution of ownership shifts across the income distribution. The empirical analysis is robust to controls for a variety of factors, including changes in economic conditions, income distribution, stock valuation, the fraction of households filing tax returns, and other tax rates. Analysis of various subperiods confirms that these findings do not reflect changing patterns in reporting or the increase in equity ownership through tax-advantaged accounts. While suggesting that taxes are an underappreciated determinant of the level of corporate ownership diffusion, the chapter does not claim that taxation alone can explain variations across time and countries in the level of ownership diffusion. The concluding section of the chapter locates these results within the broader literatures on the determinants of corporate governance and on the rationales for tax progressivity, and suggests possible avenues for further research.

The rest of the chapter proceeds as follows. Section 2 discusses the links to the relevant literatures. Section 3 develops a simple model of financial equilibrium and derives implications for the effects of taxation on ownership concentration. Section 4 develops the measures of ownership concentration and explains its relative merits and drawbacks. Section 5 presents the results, and Section 6 concludes with avenues for future research.

2. Related Literature

This chapter contributes to, and draws on, several distinct literatures. This section begins by reviewing historical and qualitative assessments of the interactions between the evolution of shareholding patterns and the income tax. Next, the more recent literature on the determinants of corporate governance is reviewed, with particular emphasis on political interpretations of corporate governance institutions. Finally, the emerging literatures on the links between taxation and governance and the reasons for limited equity market participation are also briefly reviewed.

2.1. The Evolution of the U.S. Income Tax and of Stock Ownership Diffusion

Historical, political, and early economic analyses of the evolution of the income taxation place much emphasis on the role of the income tax in determining corporate ownership patterns. Means (1930), building on the work of Warshow (1924), provides the classic statement of this argument. Without modern statistical techniques, Means argues that the dramatic rise in the diffusion of stock ownership from 1916 to 1921 was attributable to sharply progressive tax changes. Specifically, following Warshow, Means employs shareholder records for large, public firms and data compiled from tax records to show that stock ownership diffused sharply during this period, that other non-tax explanations for this diffusion are insufficient, and that wealthy individuals shifted toward tax-advantaged assets, including tax-exempt bonds, real estate, and life insurance. Means (1930, p. 589) argues that these tax changes made "the rich man not only a poor market for stocks but an actual seller of stock and the man of moderate income an excellent buyer."

Berle and Means (1932) go on to note that

the rise in popularity of [customer and employee ownership] was undoubtedly due in a considerable measure to the influence of Federal taxation. Both developed most vigorously during a period in which the weight of the Federal surtaxes was such as to make the individual with a large income an extremely poor market for corporate securities. The difficulty of obtaining new capital from the usual sources was thus increased and a new market for corporate securities was sought in the man of smaller income. . . ." (p. 59).

Such an analysis is an early statement of the tax clientele argument that is extended in this chapter. Means (1930, p. 592) concludes that the World War I taxes "accelerated that separation of ownership and control which has become a marked feature of our economy."

In addition to the portfolio effects emphasized by economists studying the separation of ownership and control, many early economic analyses of the income tax attributed the introduction and spread of income taxation in the United States and abroad in part to a desire to redistribute wealth and income.[2] Historical and political investigations of the evolution of the income tax mirror this emphasis on redistributional motives.[3] Taken together, these various qualitative assessments of the motivations and effects of income taxes indicate a plausible role for income taxation in shaping ownership patterns of corporate stock.

2.2. Determinants of Corporate Governance Arrangements

As discussed above, the arrangements that govern the relationship between shareholders and managers have drawn increased attention. Morck and Steier (2005) provide a useful overview of the factors that account for noted cross-country differences – ideology, legal rules, the role of trust in societies – as well as an overview of various country studies. While taxation is seldom discussed in these studies, a few exceptions stand out. Morck et al. (2004) study the evolution of ownership concentration in Canada and emphasize the role of estate taxes in determining when families choose to disgorge large shareholdings. Morck (2004) highlights the role of the double taxation of intercorporate dividends in the United States in discouraging the formation of business groups through pyramidal ownership structures.

Of course, tax policy reflects political impulses; Roe (1994) argues that the particularly diffuse nature of ownership in the United States was the result of political forces that prevented the persistence of large shareholders. Specifically, Roe emphasizes antitrust rules and financial regulation – particularly of banks and mutual funds – as being critical to

---

[2] See Seligman (1911), and Musgrave's (1992) critique of Schumpeter's views on the evolution of the income tax.

[3] Ratner (1942) and Brownlee (1996) provide detailed discussions of the political motivations for various changes in the tax code.

shaping the diffusion of ownership concentration. The potential role of taxes in shaping redistributions of corporate ownership is related to Roe's emphasis on politics in shaping corporate governance outcomes. It should be noted, however, that several dramatic tax changes in the United States – including the one emphasized by Berle and Means (1932) – were related to wartime efforts rather than conscious, politically motivated changes in the tax code.

2.3. Taxation and Corporate Governance

Studies of taxation and corporate governance have been converging in an emerging literature. Desai, Dyck, and Zingales (2004) note that the corporate tax makes the state the largest minority shareholder in most corporations. As a consequence, the workings of the corporate tax may well influence, and be influenced by, the relationship between managers and outside share-holders. Strong complementarities may exist between tax avoidance and managerial diversion because concealing income from the tax authorities through complex transactions reduces the ability of shareholders to monitor manager behavior, thereby making diversion less costly for managers. Such relationships appear to be operative based on evidence from Russia and cross-country differences in the way in which corporate tax revenues respond to corporate tax rate changes.

Desai and Dharmapala (2005, 2006) investigate the relevance of these ideas in the U.S. setting by developing a conceptual framework for understanding how changes in incentive compensation can change corporate tax avoidance activity and how such activity is valued by financial markets. Firm-level governance measures are found to be an important determinant of the role of high-powered incentives in changing sheltering decisions and of how markets value avoidance.

In addition to this work on the role of corporate taxation in influencing corporate governance outcomes, dividend taxation has also been shown to interact with governance arrangements. For example, Chetty and Saez (2005) and Brown, Liang, and Weisbenner (forthcoming) both note that managerial compensation patterns were an important determinant of firm responses to the 2003 dividend tax cut.[4] Similarly, Perez-Gonzalez

---

[4] Chetty and Saez (2004) show that increases in dividend payments in response to the tax cut were most pronounced among firms with high levels of managerial ownership, as well as those with high levels of institutional ownership. Managers with large stock option holding, however, were less likely to respond to the tax change (Brown, Liang, and Weisbenner (2004)).

(2003) finds that payout policy is significantly influenced by the presence of large individual shareholders. Each of these papers indicates that tax incentives interact with ownership and governance institutions in important ways.

2.4. Stock Market Participation and Portfolio Allocations

Heterogeneity in stock market participation rates across the income distribution has generated considerable interest among theorists and empirical researchers. For example, Haliassos and Bertaut (1995) and Vissing-Jorgensen (2002) argue that transaction costs, either in the form of explicit trading costs or informal psychic costs of information acquisition, can explain why many households do not participate in equity markets.[5] In one effort to explain these patterns, Poterba (2001) develops an after-tax capital asset pricing model and argues that tax rules are a potentially important determinant of household portfolio structure. Of particular note are the effects of tax incentives in influencing the location of assets across taxable and non-taxable accounts, as in Shoven and Sialm (2004) and Dammon, Spatt, and Zhang (2004). Their logic on the preferred habitat for assets is extended across the income distribution by the analysis in this chapter. In essence, the nature of tax progressivity, and changes to it, may constitute an underappreciated reason for heterogeneity in portfolio allocations across income classes and across time.

3. Hypothesis Development

The basic hypothesis developed in this section is that increases in the progressivity of the personal income tax system lead to a greater diffusion of stock ownership across the income distribution. This idea is illustrated using a simple extension to the model of financial equilibrium introduced in Miller (1977) (see also Auerbach, 2002, pp. 1271–1273). In Miller's model, firms endogenously issue both equity and bonds. The corporate tax system creates a preference for debt financing, as interest payments are tax deductible to the corporation while payouts to equityholders are not. Miller (1977) argues that this is offset, for some investors, by a personal tax preference for equity returns because of the lower personal tax rate on capital gains. This insight leads to the characterization of an equilibrium in which each firm is indifferent about its debt-equity ratio and in which investors sort into clienteles for stocks and bonds on the basis of their tax characteristics. In this section,

---

[5] Curcuru et al. (2005) review this and related literatures.

Miller's model is extended to consider the consequences of an increase in the progressivity of the tax schedule for shareholding patterns.

Assume that firms face an exogenously fixed corporate tax rate $\tau \in (0, 1)$ and can issue two kinds of assets: bonds and stock. Firms pay interest on the bonds they issue and pay out a fraction $d \in (0, 1)$ of the returns to equity holders as dividends (with the remaining fraction $(1 - d)$ being received by stockholders in the form of capital gains). The dividend yield d is assumed to be fixed and identical for all firms. There is no uncertainty about the returns from either bonds or equity. A continuum of investors exists, distinguished by income $y \in [0, y^{\max}] \subset \mathfrak{R}_+$. The distribution of investors over the interval $[0, y^{\max}]$ is represented by the pdf $f(y)$ and the corresponding cdf $F(y)$. The only restriction placed on this distribution is that the cdf $F(y)$ is strictly monotonically increasing (i.e., $f(y) > 0$) over $[0, y^{\max}]$. Investors are restricted to holding nonnegative amounts of the two kinds of assets – corporate bonds and equity – issued by firms.[6]

Investors are assumed to face a zero tax rate on capital gains; a positive tax rate on capital gains would reduce the extent of the personal tax preference for equity, but (as long as capital gains are tax favored relative to dividends and interest) would not affect the basic conclusions. An investor's tax liability on dividend and interest income is a function of her total pre-tax income y, and is determined by the tax schedule $t(y)$. This is assumed to be continuous and twice-differentiable over the interval $[0, y^{\max}]$ and to be strictly increasing and convex ($t'(y) > 0$ and $t''(y) > 0$) over $[0, y^{\max}]$, with $t(0) = t'(0) = 0$. As the marginal tax rate $t'(y)$ faced by an individual with income y is strictly increasing in income, $t(y)$ satisfies a stronger notion of progressivity (sometimes termed "marginal rate progressivity") than the standard definition (which requires only that the average tax rate increases with income). This appears appropriate in this context, as investors' portfolio decisions are based on their marginal tax rates. In addition,

---

[6] Tax-exempt assets (such as municipal bonds) could be introduced into the model without fundamentally affecting the results. The restriction on short sales is standard in the tax clientele literature, in order to rule out cases where investors can eliminate all taxes through arbitrage among assets with different tax characteristics. This also implicitly rules out the "tax irrelevance" view that taxpayers are able to use financial engineering to eliminate taxes on returns from equity. While doing so may be theoretically feasible, the empirical evidence suggests that taxes are important. Even in the context of capital gains taxation (where opportunities for avoidance are particularly abundant because of the realization doctrine), Auerbach, Burman and Siegel (2000) find that most realized capital gains are not sheltered by losses. Even in their sample of high-income taxpayers (some of whom are "sophisticated" in the sense that they trade in derivatives) "average effective tax rates on realized capital gains are very close to statutory rates" (p. 378).

further restrictions on $t(y)$ are imposed to ensure that the marginal tax rate is everywhere strictly less than 100 percent (i.e., $t'(y^{\max}) < 1$) and that it is sufficiently large to ensure the existence of an equilibrium in which investors hold both types of assets (i.e., $t'(y^{\max}) > \frac{\tau}{1-d(1-\tau)}$).

In Miller's (1977) equilibrium, the relative pre-tax returns on bonds and stock adjust so that the return to equity demanded by investors equals the after-tax interest rate (see also Auerbach, 2002, p. 1271). Given this, a dollar of interest income yields an after-tax amount of $\$(1 - t'(y))$ to an investor with income y (noting that the interest is deductible to the firm), while a dollar of equity returns leads to $\$d$ of dividends and so yields an after-tax amount of $\$(1-\tau)(1-dt'(y))$ (noting that the firm pays the corporate tax on the income paid out to the investor). Given the assumptions regarding $t(y)$ made above, an investor with income $y = 0$ strictly prefers interest income to equity returns (as $1 > 1 - \tau$), while an investor with income $y = y^{\max}$ strictly prefers equity to bonds (as $(1 - \tau)(1 - dt'(y^{\max})) > 1 - t'(y^{\max})$). By the continuity of $t'(y)$, there exists a marginal investor with income y^* who is indifferent between holding bonds and equity; y^* is defined by the expression:

$$1 - t'(y^*) = (1 - \tau)(1 - dt'(y^*)). \tag{1}$$

All other investors strictly prefer either bonds or stock. The degree of preference can be characterized by the ratio of the after-personal-tax value of \$1 of interest income to the after-personal-tax value of \$1 of equity income, denoted by $\theta(y)$:

$$\theta(y) \equiv \frac{1 - t'(y)}{1 - dt'(y)}. \tag{2}$$

As $d < 1$, $\theta(y) < 1$ for all $y > 0$. The smaller is the value of θ, the greater is the investor's tax preference for equity. It follows straightforwardly from Equation (2) that $\theta'(y) < 0$, so that the personal tax preference for equity increases with income.

The corporate tax preference can be analogously represented by $(1 - \tau)$; the higher the corporate tax rate, the greater the corporate tax preference for debt. The expressions $(1 - \tau)$ and $\theta(y)$ are depicted graphically in Figure 1. As shown in Figure 1, they characterize a financial equilibrium with the following features. All investors with incomes $y < y^*$ hold only debt, as the marginal personal tax rates they face are sufficiently low so that the personal tax preference for equity is outweighed by the corporate tax preference for debt. In contrast, all investors with incomes $y > y^*$ hold only equity because the marginal personal tax rates they face are sufficiently high so that

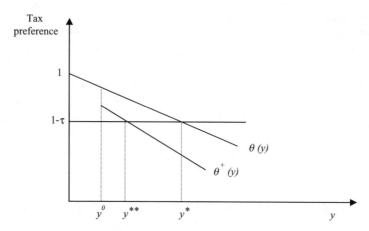

Figure 1. Changes in Tax Progressivity and Financial Market Equilibrium

the personal tax preference for equity outweighs the corporate tax preference for debt. Firms issue a sufficient quantity of bonds to satisfy the demand of investors with incomes $y < y^*$ and a sufficient amount of equity to satisfy the demand of investors with incomes $y > y^*$. The fraction of investors holding equity is $(1 - F(y^*))$. The aggregate debt-equity ratio for the corporate sector is determined by investors' demands for the two types of assets, but each firm is indifferent about its capital structure.

The primary question of interest here is how this equilibrium changes in response to an increase in the progressivity of the tax schedule $t(y)$. Suppose that the original tax schedule $t(y)$ is replaced by:[7]

$$t^+(y) = \begin{cases} t(y) & \text{if } y < y_0 < y^* \\ \alpha t(y) & \text{if } y \geq y_0 \end{cases}, \tag{3}$$

where y_0 is some arbitrary level of income chosen so that it is lower than the income of the marginal investor y^* and where $\alpha > 1$ (satisfying the constraint that the marginal tax rate is everywhere below 100 percent requires that α is also sufficiently close to 1: $\alpha < \frac{1}{t(y^{max})}$). The new tax schedule involves an increase in progressivity in a very general sense. The marginal tax rate faced by higher-income investors increases (as $\alpha t'(y) > t'(y)$), while the marginal rate for lower-income investors stays constant. There is also an increase in the convexity of the tax function for higher-income investors (as $\alpha t''(y) >$

---

[7] In the theoretical literature, the relative progressivity of different tax schedules is typically analyzed using the concept of Lorenz dominance (e.g., Kakwani, 1977); however, a simple example comparing two different tax schedules suffices to illustrate the basic point being made here.

$t''(y)$), so that (over the range $[y_0, y^{\max}]$) there is an increase in the rate at which the marginal tax rate increases with income.

Investors with incomes below y_0 are unaffected by the new tax schedule. The personal tax preference parameter (analogous to Equation (2)) over $[y_0, y^{\max}]$ is now:

$$\theta^+(y) \equiv \frac{1 - \alpha t'(y)}{1 - d\alpha t'(y)}. \tag{4}$$

For small changes in α, θ^+ is decreasing in α. Thus, it follows that $\theta^+(y_0)$ $< \theta(y_0)$ (as shown in Figure 1) and that the original marginal investor now strictly prefers equity (i.e., $\theta^+(y^*) < \theta(y^*) = 1 - \tau$). It can also be shown that $\frac{\partial^2 \theta^+(y)}{\partial y \partial \alpha} < 0$, so that over the range $[y_0, y^{\max}]$ and for α sufficiently close to 1, $\theta^{+\prime}(y) < \theta'(y)$. Thus, the new tax preference parameter in Equation (4) has a more negative slope (i.e., falls more rapidly with income) than does θ, as illustrated in Figure 1. In essence, all investors with incomes above y_0 now have a stronger personal tax preference for equity, and this preference now increases more rapidly with income. The increased progressivity of the tax schedule thus entails a greater relative personal tax disadvantage for bonds.

The corporate tax preference $(1 - \tau)$ and the new personal tax preference $\theta^+(y)$ characterize a new financial equilibrium. If $\theta^+(y_0) > 1 - \tau$, then (as shown in Figure 1) because $\theta^+(y^*) < (1 - \tau)$ and $\theta^+(y)$ is continuous over the interval $(y_0, y^*]$, there exists a new marginal investor with income $y^{**} \in (y_0, y^*)$, defined by the expression:

$$1 - t^{+\prime}(y^{**}) = (1 - \tau)(1 - dt^{+\prime}(y^{**})) \tag{5}$$

(i.e., $\theta^+(y^{**}) = 1 - \tau$, with $y^{**} < y^*$). In equilibrium, all investors with income $y > y^{**}$ hold equity, and all investors with income $y < y^{**}$ hold bonds.

Recalling that the distribution of investors $F(y)$ is strictly monotonically increasing, the fraction of investors holding equity rises from $(1 - F(y^*))$ (in the old equilibrium) to $(1 - F(y^{**}))$ (in the new equilibrium). Thus, the increased progressivity of the tax schedule leads to an increased diffusion of stock ownership, as some lower-income investors (those between y^{**} and y^*) switch from bonds to equity. The aggregate debt-equity ratio falls as firms issue more equity to satisfy the new demand from investors with incomes between y^{**} and y^* who enter the market for corporate stock.

If $\theta^+(y_0) \leq 1 - \tau$, the continuity argument above does not apply, but the basic conclusion is unchanged:[8] The fraction of investors holding equity

---

[8] Suppose that $\theta^+(y_0) = 1 - \tau$; then, the marginal investor has income y_0, so that $y^{**} = y_0 \leq y^*$. In equilibrium, all investors with income $y > y_0$ will hold equity, and all investors with

increases following an increase in the progressivity of the tax structure. Of course, this model is highly simplified. For example, it does not incorporate any uncertainty about asset returns (Auerbach and King, 1983), nor does it allow firms to respond to tax changes by adjusting their dividend yield. Nonetheless, it illustrates very simply a basic intuition regarding tax progressivity and financial equilibrium that is likely to be quite robust across a variety of settings in which investors form tax clienteles for different types of assets.[9]

4. The Index of Aggregate Ownership Concentration

4.1. Data Source

Individual income tax return data are compiled annually by the Statistics of Income Division (SOI) of the Internal Revenue Service (IRS). They are available in two forms: detailed statistical tables showing aggregated data by income brackets (for years 1916 to 2004)[10] and micro-files showing disaggregated data by individuals (for years 1960 to 1999).[11] The IRS processes more than 100 million tax returns each year, and the SOI uses about 200,000 returns to compute its statistics. The 1916–2004 statistical tables include information on the number of tax returns, the total amount of income reported, and the income composition for a large number of income

---

income $y < y_0$ will hold bonds, and the fraction of investors holding equity rises from $(1 - F(y^*))$ to $(1 - F(y_0))$. If $\theta^+(y_0) < 1 - \tau$ there is no investor who is indifferent between debt and equity (i.e., a marginal investor does not exist, as $t^+(y)$ has a discontinuity at $y = y_0$). However, all investors with income $y \geq y_0$ strictly prefer equity, and all investors with income $y < y_0$ strictly prefer bonds. As investors with income of precisely y^{**} constitute a set of measure zero, the equilibrium does not differ in any significant way from that when $\theta^+(y_0) = 1 - \tau$; the fraction of investors holding equity rises from $(1 - F(y^*))$ to $(1 - F(y_0))$.

[9] The previous version of this paper emphasized an alternative mechanism by which increased progressivity could lead to increased diffusion. Specifically, the supply of securities was held fixed, and increased progressivity led to wealth effects that generated similar results. In contrast, the model here emphasizes supply responses as the mechanism for the diffusion.

[10] In 1913, a constitutional amendment allowed the U.S. government to raise revenue by introducing an individual income tax. Later, the Revenue Act of 1916 mandated the annual publication of statistics related to internal revenue laws.

[11] These micro-files are made publicly available after identifiable taxpayer information has been deleted to ensure confidentiality. These 1960–1998 micro-files allow us to check that the method of interpolating data from the pre-1960 statistical tables produces accurate results. Note that there are three years during the 1960–1999 period (1961, 1963, and 1965) for which micro-files are not available, so aggregated data in the statistical tables are used instead.

brackets. More than 40 income brackets are used, with income defined as adjusted gross income (AGI) less deficit. For each income bracket, the different sources of income are broken down and reported separately. In particular, the amount of dividend income is reported for each income bracket.[12] Dividend income is used as a proxy for stock ownership, and the share of dividends accruing to each income group is used to measure the distribution of stock ownership.

Tax return data are in some respects more reliable and accurate than most other field survey data, because there are penalties for misreporting tax returns (although there are also incentives for underreporting, unlike in most field surveys). They also have the advantage of being available for many years, starting as early as 1916, enabling the analysis of the evolution of ownership concentration over the past 80 years or more. Although tax laws have changed over the years, it is quite feasible to track the changes and make necessary adjustments to preserve year-to-year consistency. Moreover, tax return data cover almost the entire population, and in particular, all middle- and high-income individuals. The data also oversample high-income individuals, thus enabling the breakdown of the top income group into finer fractiles, which is important because the top income group is very heterogeneous in terms of its income composition, with capital income being a major source of difference (Piketty and Saez, 2003).

4.2. Empirical Measures of Ownership Concentration Using Individual Tax Returns

The shares of total stocks owned by different income groups are first estimated and then used to construct a Herfindahl index of ownership concentration. As there is no data on the actual amount of stocks owned by individuals, dividend income reported in individual tax returns is used as a proxy for stock ownership. This is similar to the empirical strategy used by Means (1930) in his study of the diffusion of stock ownership in the 1920s.

The use of dividend shares as a proxy for stock ownership raises a number of issues. First, dividend income will be an exact proxy for stock ownership only if all stocks pay out dividends at the same rate. In practice, not all stocks pay out dividends, and not all stocks that pay out dividends pay at the same rate. However, this study is only concerned with *changes* in the

---

[12] Dividends are defined by the IRS as "distributions of money, stock, or other property received by taxpayers from domestic and foreign corporations, either directly or passed through estates, trusts, partnerships, or regulated investment companies."

proportions of total dividends received by different income groups. If one assumes that the propensity of different income groups to invest in stocks with different dividend policies remains relatively constant over time, then changes in dividend shares can be regarded as a reasonable proxy for changes in the distribution of stock ownership. It is possible that if firms lower their dividend payments in response to higher taxes, this methodology may misattribute the decline in dividend income to a fall in stock ownership. The empirical analysis described below controls for changes in the average dividend yield, and it is well known that firms are extremely reluctant to change their dividend policies (see Lintner, 1956 and Brav et al., 2005).

Second, recent studies documenting a decreasing propensity of firms to pay out dividends (Fama and French, 2001) may raise concerns about the use of dividends to measure corporate ownership concentration. However, total dividends, as reported on tax returns, increased by more than threefold, from $34 billion to $147 billion from 1916 to 2000 (in year 2000 dollars). Average dividend income (total dividends received divided by total number of tax units) lay mostly within the range of $600–$800 for the first half of the century and then increased to $800-$1,000 for the second half (in 2000 dollars), suggesting that dividends may provide a reasonable way as a proxy for corporate ownership over the century. An alternative series based on estate tax returns is also investigated to confirm the reliability of the dividend-based measure of ownership concentration.[13]

Finally, there are issues associated with the importance of trends in the direct ownership of corporate stock. For example, dividends received through pension plans and retirement saving accounts are not reported as dividends on individual income tax returns. The amount of total dividends reported on individual tax returns has always been less than the amount of dividends paid out by corporations, as reported in National Income and Product Accounts (NIPA), and the gap between the two has widened.[14] Part of the gap may be explained by dividends paid out to foreigners who are not required to file income tax returns, but the declining ratio in the 1980s and

---

[13] A related issue is that this measure relies on reported dividends received. As such, any observed changes in ownership shares may merely reflect changes in the reporting of income. A failure to report dividends will have no effect on this study if all income groups misreport by approximately the same proportion and this pattern is relatively steady through time. The relevance of underreporting is investigated below by controlling for the share of filers.

[14] The ratio of total dividends reported on tax returns to personal dividends paid out by corporations as reported in the NIPA has declined continuously over the period 1929 to 2000, starting from a level close to 90 percent in 1929, declining slowly to 60 percent in 1988, and dropping much more rapidly to less than 40 percent in 2000.

1990s is due mostly to the growth of funded pension plans and retirement saving accounts through which individuals receive dividends that are never reported on income tax returns. For rich investors, this additional source of dividends is likely to be very small relative to dividends directly reported on their tax returns (i.e., dividends from directly owned stocks or dividends received through mutual funds). If the dividends received through pension plans and retirement saving accounts are included in the estimates of dividend shares, then one should expect the middle-income group to experience a greater proportionate increase in dividend income and therefore a greater observed shift in stock ownership from the rich to the less-well-off. Investigation of subperiods where these effects are likely to be less relevant are employed below to determine whether the findings in this chapter are robust to the growth of these accounts. In particular, the analysis below undertakes a robustness check that restricts the sample to the 1929–1975 period and finds consistent results.

This subperiod analysis also illuminates whether the results reported are robust to concerns related to the rise of Subchapter S corporations and the rise of mutual funds. The growth of Subchapter S corporations may be problematic because – if this income is concentrated among those with higher incomes – the approach used here may lead to an underestimate of the degree of ownership concentration. The rise of mutual funds does not pose a fundamental problem, as dividend income received via mutual funds is reported on tax returns. However, interest income received via mutual funds may also be reported as dividends. If those with higher incomes tend to invest in funds with a relatively greater exposure to equity, then this may affect the concentration measure. These concerns about the growing importance of Subchapter S corporations and mutual funds can also be addressed by restricting the sample to the 1929–1975 period.[15]

---

[15] As noted by Luttrell (2005), the explosive growth of Subchapter S activity only began in 1986. On the rise of mutual funds, calculations based on the Federal Reserve Flow of Funds data are quite instructive. These data (specifically, table B100E) can be employed to compute the share of corporate equity held directly versus equity held through mutual funds, private retirement plans, public retirement plans and life insurance companies for the years 1952 to 2004. The direct share was close to unity in 1952, declined slowly to nearly 80 percent by 1975 and then dropped much more precipitously to 45 percent by 2004. From 1952 to 1975 the share of equity held through mutual funds stayed between 2 and 5 percent. Subsequent to 1975, the mutual fund share has exploded to nearly 20 percent. As such, restricting attention to the period prior to 1975 is instructive as it captures a period when direct ownership of equity was clearly dominant, when mutual funds were small and when Subchapter S activity was unimportant.

The total population is first divided into five income fractiles in such a manner that they can be consistently compared over time.[16] Following the notation used by Piketty and Saez (2003), the income fractiles are denoted by P0–P20 (the bottom 20 percent income group, i.e., the poorest 20 percent of the population), P20–P40 (the next 20 percent), P40–P60, P60–P80, and P80–P100 (the top 20 percent, i.e., the richest 20 percent of the population).[17] Top income fractiles are further divided into P90–P100 (the top 10 percent), P99–P100 (the top 1 percent), P99.9–P100 (the top 0.1 percent), and P99.99–P100 (the top 0.01 percent).[18] The share of dividend income is then calculated for the different income fractiles by dividing the amount of dividend income accruing to different income fractiles by the total amount of dividends reported. This is referred to as the "dividend share," and the time series as the "dividend series." Table 1 shows the dividend share for the different income fractiles from 1916 to 2000.

Next, the dividend shares of the five income fractiles are used to construct a Herfindahl index of concentration.[19] The concentration index for year t, denoted by C_t, is defined as:

$$C_t = \sum_{i=1}^{5} s_{it}^2, \tag{6}$$

where s_{it} is the dividend share of income quintile i in year t. The value of C_t lies between 0.2 and 1. A value of 0.2 indicates that stock ownership

---

[16] The term "income fractiles" is used in a sense distinct from the "income brackets" used by the IRS, which are problematic in two ways. First, the income bracket of, say, $3,000–$4,000 in 1916 is very different from the $3,000–$4,000 income bracket in 2000. Even if one adjusts for inflation, there is still a second problem: the income brackets do not contain the same proportion of total population. In that case, a change in dividend income reported by a particular income bracket may simply reflect a change in the number of individuals in that bracket and not a change in dividend share. A better way to define income groups is to divide the total population into groups with the same proportion of total population; these groups are referred to here as "income fractiles."

[17] Of course, the income thresholds for the different income fractiles vary over time. For example, in 2000, the bottom 20 percent income group earns less than $17,000 a year. The top 20 percent income group has an income of more than $70,000, while the top 10 percent has an income of more than $90,000.

[18] Since the top income group holds a majority of total stocks in the economy (the top 10 percent holds almost 70 percent of total stocks), considering only 0.01 percent of the total population still yields a significant share of stock ownership (for example, in 2000, the top 0.01 percent holds 9 percent of total stocks, which is greater than the share of stocks held by the bottom 40 percent income group).

[19] Using decile rather than quintile dividend shares (i.e., dividing the total population into ten income fractiles) leads to a concentration index that is highly consistent, with the same pattern of changes in ownership concentration.

Table 1. *Dividend Shares for Different Income Fractiles and the Herfindahl Index of Concentration of Stock Ownership, 1916–2000*

Year	P0–P20	P20–P40	P40–P60	P60–P80	P80–P100	Herfindahl index	Top 10% P90–P100	Top 1% P99–P100
	(1)	(2)	(3)	(4)	(5)	(6)	(7)	(8)
1916	1.15	0.95	2.82	8.70	86.38	0.7548	78.53	42.78
1917	1.12	1.53	2.74	5.85	88.77	0.7925	79.15	41.70
1918	1.13	1.43	2.18	4.44	89.47	0.8032	82.19	55.59
1919	0.98	1.24	2.32	4.41	91.04	0.8316	86.02	48.66
1920	1.08	1.23	2.02	3.73	91.95	0.8475	90.09	50.08
1921	7.82	1.46	2.23	3.58	83.52	0.7056	78.89	50.68
1922	4.73	1.23	2.27	3.98	87.78	0.7750	84.94	48.36
1923	2.19	1.88	2.93	5.64	86.22	0.7483	82.69	45.61
1924	2.00	1.74	3.08	5.77	87.41	0.7691	86.28	55.80
1925	1.24	1.90	3.22	5.75	87.90	0.7775	81.22	40.45
1926	1.28	1.57	3.32	5.98	87.86	0.7770	81.34	41.72
1927	2.98	2.98	2.98	3.57	87.48	0.7693	82.02	45.03
1928	2.09	2.09	2.09	3.31	90.43	0.8201	83.23	43.91
1929	3.02	3.02	3.02	4.21	86.72	0.7565	79.23	47.66
1930	2.98	2.98	2.98	3.66	87.40	0.7678	77.47	44.84
1931	4.17	4.17	4.17	4.17	81.98	0.6790	71.74	40.38
1932	4.82	4.82	4.82	4.82	80.72	0.6609	79.81	51.95
1933	5.06	5.06	5.06	5.06	79.77	0.6465	79.73	52.87
1934	4.32	4.32	4.32	4.32	81.74	0.6755	76.45	44.14
1935	4.23	4.23	4.23	4.23	83.10	0.6977	78.87	49.05
1936	4.25	4.25	4.25	4.25	82.27	0.6840	80.09	44.23
1937	3.00	2.31	4.11	5.86	84.23	0.7160	76.54	47.87
1938	6.38	2.86	6.19	6.92	77.62	0.6159	74.69	44.76
1939	5.71	3.01	4.88	6.44	79.96	0.6500	76.72	48.13
1940	6.08	4.56	4.13	5.04	80.07	0.6512	77.70	49.43
1941	7.12	4.53	4.33	5.64	78.38	0.6265	77.98	39.79
1942	6.68	4.59	4.26	6.39	78.08	0.6221	75.64	40.79
1943	6.16	4.25	4.52	4.75	80.32	0.6550	77.34	45.88
1944	3.77	5.47	5.75	7.14	77.86	0.6191	71.82	46.78
1945	2.32	4.88	5.29	6.93	80.59	0.6599	74.01	47.80
1946	1.74	3.23	3.41	5.08	86.54	0.7540	81.90	54.54
1947	2.16	3.52	3.60	4.58	86.13	0.7470	83.87	56.51
1948	2.06	3.01	2.99	4.24	87.70	0.7732	82.12	58.73
1949	2.12	3.68	3.98	5.67	84.55	0.7215	78.31	53.30
1950	2.49	2.07	3.10	2.38	88.21	0.7807	85.13	62.56
1951	1.73	3.29	3.69	6.48	84.81	0.7262	80.55	61.38
1952	2.03	3.61	4.00	5.13	85.23	0.7324	81.56	59.94
1953	2.50	4.59	4.23	5.63	83.05	0.6974	79.20	56.86
1954	1.52	3.48	3.48	5.21	86.30	0.7502	83.49	63.79
1955	1.61	3.17	3.85	5.46	85.91	0.7438	82.01	54.48
1956	1.43	3.41	3.79	5.76	85.62	0.7392	79.73	56.63
1957	1.76	4.00	4.13	6.15	83.96	0.7123	78.89	55.38
1958	1.60	4.03	4.57	6.45	83.35	0.7029	79.38	55.01

(continued)

Table 1 *(continued)*

Year	P0–P20 (1)	P20–P40 (2)	P40–P60 (3)	P60–P80 (4)	P80–P100 (5)	Herfindahl index (6)	Top 10% P90–P100 (7)	Top 1% P99–P100 (8)
1959	1.89	4.55	4.52	6.97	82.07	0.6829	76.15	57.23
1960	2.00	5.48	5.04	7.03	80.46	0.6582	75.64	55.30
1962	2.37	5.53	6.18	7.12	78.81	0.6335	73.04	47.43
1964	2.17	5.24	6.12	6.87	79.59	0.6452	73.52	47.39
1966	2.45	4.61	6.61	8.85	77.48	0.6153	71.46	46.58
1967	2.25	4.66	6.52	7.56	79.00	0.6368	72.36	46.80
1969	2.33	4.70	6.22	10.16	76.59	0.6035	70.59	44.33
1970	2.38	6.22	6.71	8.44	76.25	0.5975	70.21	42.15
1971	2.62	5.71	4.96	9.25	77.45	0.6148	70.02	42.82
1972	2.38	5.83	7.71	8.21	75.87	0.5923	68.95	41.45
1973	2.50	4.76	7.02	8.36	77.36	0.6133	70.11	41.03
1974	2.51	5.10	6.95	8.48	76.96	0.6076	71.64	41.14
1975	2.85	4.80	7.16	9.17	76.02	0.5945	67.75	40.70
1976	2.24	4.77	7.85	9.31	75.82	0.5925	67.79	40.18
1977	2.00	5.05	7.36	10.89	74.70	0.5783	67.96	40.10
1978	2.43	4.96	7.43	9.97	75.20	0.5841	66.77	39.35
1979	2.23	4.28	7.47	9.81	76.21	0.5984	68.13	40.81
1980	2.29	4.21	6.80	9.93	76.77	0.6061	67.97	39.49
1981	2.91	4.89	7.85	11.23	73.12	0.5567	63.69	35.57
1982	3.28	4.97	7.87	11.82	72.06	0.5430	63.30	35.55
1983	3.14	5.21	8.26	12.03	71.36	0.5343	62.05	35.80
1984	3.21	5.05	9.47	11.35	70.93	0.5285	60.90	32.97
1985	3.53	5.07	9.90	12.32	69.18	0.5074	59.85	34.51
1986	3.42	4.36	9.55	11.68	70.99	0.5298	60.97	35.37
1987	3.60	5.45	9.96	14.19	66.79	0.4805	55.94	28.40
1988	2.86	5.74	8.58	12.37	70.45	0.5230	60.99	35.45
1989	2.97	5.29	8.20	12.37	71.17	0.5322	60.66	33.71
1990	3.36	5.61	7.92	12.57	70.55	0.5240	60.18	34.21
1991	3.62	5.94	8.39	13.12	68.94	0.5044	57.88	31.47
1992	3.66	5.75	8.88	12.49	69.23	0.5075	57.68	31.82
1993	3.80	6.28	8.89	13.96	67.07	0.4827	55.67	29.54
1994	4.27	7.11	8.90	12.99	66.73	0.4770	56.98	30.34
1995	4.01	5.99	7.96	11.86	70.19	0.5182	58.52	31.48
1996	3.43	5.65	7.36	12.34	71.23	0.5324	60.82	32.70
1997	3.04	4.75	6.97	11.14	74.09	0.5694	63.12	32.34
1998	3.00	4.52	6.22	11.54	74.73	0.5785	63.18	34.55
1999	2.96	4.33	5.98	12.63	74.09	0.5713	62.82	34.30
2000	3.05	4.28	5.63	11.77	75.27	0.5864	69.47	39.86

Note: The columns provide quintile shares that are summarized in the Herfindahl index. Columns (7) and (8) provide the share for the top 10 percent and top 1 percent, respectively.

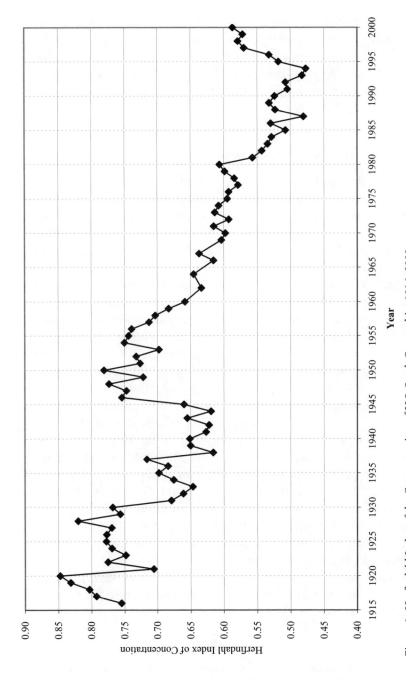

Figure 2. Herfindahl Index of the Concentration of U.S. Stock Ownership, 1916–2000

Note: The figure plots the Herfindahl index of corporate ownership that is constructed on the basis of the dividend shares of income quintiles.

is very dispersed across income groups, while a value of 1 indicates that stock ownership is very concentrated among a particular income group. Column (6) of Table 1 reports the Herfindahl index from 1916 to 2000, and Figure 2 plots the index over this time period. This index provides a summary measure of the change in stock ownership concentration over the past century.

4.3. The Dynamics of Ownership Concentration

Figure 2 shows that stock ownership experienced dramatic deconcentration over the past century, going from an index of 0.85 in the late 1910s to less than 0.50 in the 1990s. This deconcentration did not take place as a one-time phenomenon, nor was it a simple monotonic decline over the century. One can demarcate the 20th century into five periods with distinct changes in ownership patterns.

First, the WWI and post-WWI period (1916–1927) featured a concentration and then sudden diffusion of stock ownership. Stock ownership started out as very concentrated at the beginning of the century, with an index of 0.75 in 1916. Ownership became even more concentrated during WWI, with the index rising steadily to its peak of 0.85 in 1920. The year 1921 saw a precipitous decline of the index to 0.70, and this sudden great dispersion of stock ownership is consistent with the findings of Means (1930). Second, the period from 1928 to 1944 featured a marked diffusion of stock ownership. After 1921, concentration remained relatively steady at about 0.77 for several years, before dropping to less than 0.70 in 1929. In the aftermath of the Depression, the index fell to 0.62 by 1944. Third, the post-WWII period featured a concentration of stock ownership, with the concentration index jumping from 0.62 to 0.75 in a relatively short period.[20] Fourth, the 1950s to early 1990s constitute an extended period of ownership diffusion. Gradual diffusion began in the 1950s and then accelerated through the 1980s and early 1990s. More precisely, the index declined from 0.75 in 1946 to 0.60 in 1980. The 1980s and early 1990s saw a sharp deconcentration of stock ownership from 0.60 to 0.48. Finally, the late 1990s featured a marked reconcentration of stock ownership. The index of concentration of corporate ownership increased sharply back to 0.59 in the late 1990s.

---

[20] It is possible that this may be due to the dramatic increase in the fraction of households filing tax returns during the WWII era. The empirical analysis below controls for this, and also tests the robustness of the results to excluding the period up to 1945.

4.4. Alternative Measures Using Estate Tax Returns

To test how closely the dividend series approximates actual stockholding behavior, it is possible to compare it to an "equity series" constructed using estate tax returns. Estate tax returns data report the *actual amount of equity* held by the decedent filing estate tax return. However, there is a major caveat to using estate tax returns data. Due to large tax exemption levels, less than 5 percent of the overall U.S. decedent population is required to file estate tax returns.[21] Therefore, the construction of equity series using estate tax returns data is confined to the top 1 percent, top 0.1 percent, and top 0.01 percent income fractiles. This is the reason why individual income tax returns data, which covers the *whole* population, is chosen instead of estate tax returns data to construct the time series of ownership concentration.

The equity series for these fractiles is constructed using the estate tax returns data compiled by Kopczuk and Saez (2004).[22] The amount of equity reported by an income fractile is divided by the total amount of equity in the economy (as estimated by Kopczuk and Saez, 2004) in order to calculate the "equity share" for that income fractile. Figure 3 shows that for most of the 20th century the Herfindahl index of concentration based on dividend shares corresponds closely to the equity series based on estate tax returns. This provides some support for the claim that changes in dividend shares approximate changes in shares of stock ownership; however, there are two main caveats.

First, further comparison of ownership shares for the same fractiles reveals that the dividend series shows smaller fluctuations than the equity series, and the share of stocks implied by the dividend series is systematically smaller than the actual share of stocks owned. This evidence suggests that the very rich may prefer to hold stocks that do not pay out dividends. Such stockholding preference may explain why the dividend series is systematically lower than the equity series. However, if this stockholding preference of wealthy individuals does not change over time, then even though the dividend series will underestimate the shares of total stocks accruing to the high-income group, the *changes* in dividend shares will still reflect changes in the concentration of stock ownership.

---

[21] For example, in 2000, the estate tax filing threshold was $675,000, and only 4.4 percent of the overall U.S. decedent population was required to file estate tax returns.

[22] Kopczuk and Saez (2004) use the estate multiplier method first developed by Mallet (1908) to estimate top wealth shares of the living population over the past century. Their wealth composition series is used here to construct shares of corporate stocks held by different income groups.

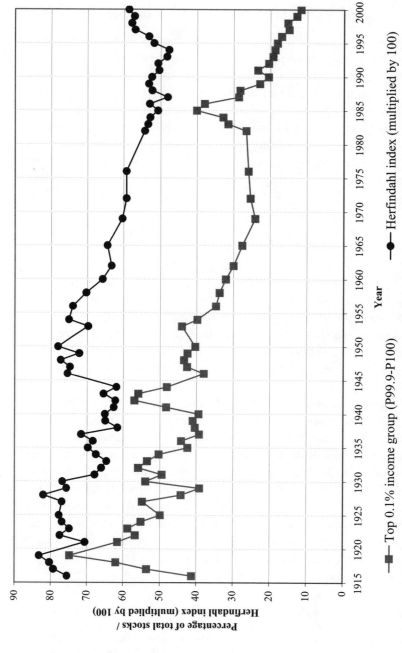

Figure 3. A Comparison of the Estate Tax Equity Series with the Herfindahl Index of Ownership Concentration, 1916–2000

Note: The figure compares the Herfindahl index of corporate ownership that is constructed on the basis of the dividend shares of income quintiles with the equity series for the top 0.1 percent group based on estate tax return data.

366

Second, the index based on dividend shares and the equity series appear to diverge after about 1975. This does not necessarily indicate that the dividend series becomes a worse measure after this time; indeed, it is possible that the problem lies with the estate tax measure. Equity held at death may not accurately reflect equity ownership during one's life – for example, because of the tax incentives to donate appreciated stock late in life. Such issues may have been particularly important when stocks experienced large capital gains in the 1990s. Nonetheless, the empirical analysis in Section 5 below tests for the robustness of the results when the final 25 years of the sample period are omitted. Despite the divergence between the dividend and equity series over that period, the results are highly consistent with those from the entire sample period.

4.5. Comparisons with Measures Employed in Studies of Corporate Governance

While Berle and Means (1932) studied ownership diffusion through the use of both tax return data and more granular work on the shareholders of large public firms, the literature since then has exclusively employed hand-collected data on the shareholders of the largest firms in order to study corporate governance (e.g., Becht and Delong, 2005; Franks, Mayer, and Rossi, 2003; La Porta et al., 1998). Such an approach has some obvious advantages relative to the use of tax returns. Specifically, such approaches emphasize the experience of large public firms, where external financing is most important, and also allow for identification of complex shareholding arrangements. As such, such efforts may capture the central issue underlying agency theory – the ability and incentives of shareholders to monitor managers – more precisely than can tax return data.

Nonetheless, the relative absence of studies using tax return data is surprising. Even though tax return data cannot provide detailed measures of ownership patterns for individual firms, the data can be used to shed light on wider issues of corporate governance, such as the role of investor protections and other factors related to agency costs in shaping widespread stock ownership. In addition, tax return data are particularly well suited to analyzing the relationship between aggregate patterns of corporate ownership and such factors as tax progressivity. Tax return data allow for analysis of the economy as a whole, a depiction of the levels of participation across separate income classes, and can provide a summary measure of concentration across time and countries.

5. Empirical Specification and Results

5.1. The Empirical Specification

The aim of the empirical analysis is to investigate the effects of changes over time in the progressivity of personal income tax rates on changes in the concentration index described in Section 4 above. The analysis seeks to capture changes in progressivity by estimating the effects of changes in the top statutory personal tax rate, while controlling for changes in personal income tax rates at lower levels of income. Specifically, these controls are the marginal rates applicable at incomes of $50,000, $100,000, $250,000, and $500,000 (all in 1999 dollars), as computed by Sialm (2003). Including these controls also (at least to some extent) holds the average tax rate constant, thus isolating the portfolio effects analyzed in Section 3 from the wealth effects of tax changes.

There are, of course, many factors other than personal tax rates that may influence patterns of stock ownership. The distribution of ownership could, for instance, be affected by a growth in stock market participation due to increased financial sophistication among those with lower incomes. The literature on stock market participation has identified a number of determinants of the propensity to own corporate equity. For example, Vissing-Jorgensen (2002) finds that (nonfinancial) income positively affects the likelihood of participation. The effects of income are controlled for here by including changes in real GDP per capita (obtained from the National Income and Product Accounts produced by the Bureau of Economic Analysis). In addition, Griffin, Nardari, and Stulz (2004) find that participation tends to increase in response to strong stock market performance. Thus, changes in the price-earnings (P/E) ratio (obtained from an updated version of the dataset in Shiller, 1989)[23] are included as an additional control.

A number of other relevant controls are suggested by the model in Section 3. The dividend yield was held fixed in the analysis there, but it is possible that firms may respond to tax changes by adjusting their payout policies. Thus, the dividend yield – also calculated using the updated version of Shiller's (1989) dataset and defined as D/P (the aggregate measure of dividends, divided by the aggregate stock price measure, for a given year) – is included as a control variable.[24] The corporate tax rate is also held fixed in the model,

---

[23] This is available at: http://www.econ.yale.edu/s̃hiller/data.htm; see also Shiller (2003).

[24] Stock repurchases are not included in the model. However, estimating the model over the 1929–1975 period, and hence excluding the years since the early 1980s when repurchases have become important, leads to consistent results (see below). Both P/E and D/P are

but an exogenous increase in this rate would increase the corporate tax preference for debt and lead to an equilibrium where a smaller fraction of investors hold equity. Thus, the top statutory corporate tax rate is included as a control.[25] The capital gains tax rate is normalized to 0 in the model in Section 3, but increases in this rate would reduce the personal tax preference for equity. Thus, two measures of the capital gains tax rate – the nominal statutory rate and the effective statutory rate (which takes into account interactions with other elements of the tax code, such as the phaseout of itemized deductions) – are included as controls.[26]

The Herfindahl index constructed in Section 4 classifies taxpayers into income fractiles based on the distribution of income across taxpayers, rather than across the entire population (as the incomes of nonfilers are unobservable when using tax return data). This is unlikely to be a significant issue for the period since 1945 (over which the fraction of households filing returns has been large and relatively stable). However, relatively few households filed income tax returns in the period before WWII, so the measure of stock ownership concentration may be affected by changes in the composition of the population of taxpayers, especially around WWII, when the fraction of filers rose dramatically. This issue is addressed in two ways. First, a control is included for the fraction of households filing an income tax return, as calculated by Piketty and Saez (2003). Second, a test for robustness is carried out by omitting all years up to 1945 from the sample period.

The distribution of equity ownership may also be affected by general changes in wealth and income distribution. Because of a substantial number of missing observations in the measures of wealth distribution constructed by Kopczuk and Saez (2004) using estate tax return data, the measures of top income shares constructed by Piketty and Saez (2003) are used as controls for distribution. These series represent the shares of income received by the top 1 percent, 0.1 percent, and 0.01 percent of the income distribution, where income is defined to include capital gains.[27]

---

expressed as ratios, and it is possible that their interpretation may be confounded by unrelated changes in the denominator. However, using the unscaled stock price, dividend and earnings series instead of these ratios leads to generally consistent results.

[25] These rates are obtained from U.S. Department of the Treasury (2003, Table 1), and represent the statutory tax rate on the top bracket of corporate income. Note that in some years, higher corporate tax rates may have applied inframarginally.

[26] These rates are from Burman (1999, Tables 2–4, pp. 26–27), and apply to long-term gains. The rates used for 1934–37 are based on the 70 percent exclusion for very long-term capital gains.

[27] The set of controls described above is not, of course, exhaustive. For example, Hong, Kubik, and Stein (2004) identify social interactions as an important factor in stock market participation decisions. Such variables, however, are difficult to measure at the aggregate

The empirical specification used to investigate the effects of changes in the top statutory personal tax rate on changes in stock ownership distribution can be represented as follows:[28]

$$\Delta C_t = \beta_0 + \beta_1(\Delta TOPTAX_t) + \Delta T_t \beta_2 + \Delta Z_t \beta_3 + \mu_t \qquad (7)$$

where:

- $\Delta C_t = (C_t - C_{t-1})$ is the first-differenced stock ownership concentration index (i.e., the change in the concentration index from year $(t-1)$ to year t).
- $\Delta TOPTAX_t$ is the first-differenced top statutory personal tax rate (i.e., the change in the rate from year $(t-1)$ to year t)
- ΔT_t is a vector of changes in other personal tax rates (applicable to incomes of \$50,000, \$100,000, \$250,000, and \$500,000, all in 1999 dollars)
- ΔZ_t is a vector of changes in the following control variables: real GDP per capita, the P/E ratio, the dividend yield (D/P), the corporate tax rate, the nominal and effective capital gains tax rates, the fraction of households filing income tax returns, and the income shares of the top 1 percent, 0.1 percent, and 0.01 percent of the population
- μ_t is the error term (potentially subject to serial correlation and heteroskedasticity).

All variables are first-differenced in this specification, to avoid potential problems associated with nonstationarity. In particular, unit root tests (such as the modified Dickey-Fuller test proposed by Elliott, Rothenberg, and Stock, 1996) fail to reject nonstationarity for the levels of the variables in Equation (7). However, these tests reject the hypothesis of a unit root for each of the first-differenced variables. In addition (as discussed in Section 4 above), first-differencing minimizes the measurement problems that may arise from the use of dividends as a proxy for stock ownership.

A more detailed exploration of the changes in the patterns of stock ownership by different income categories involves analyzing the effects of the top tax rate on the ownership shares of particular subsets of the income distribution (in particular, the shares of each quintile of the income distribution, as reported in Table 1). A secondary aim of this analysis is to test the hypothesis

---

level. Other potentially important factors, such as the growth of financial sophistication or the gradual diffusion of information about financial and tax innovations (e.g., tax-favored savings vehicles), are likely to be reflected in an overall time trend. This would primarily affect the level of concentration, rather than the changes that are examined here.

[28] An alternative empirical specification that uses as its independent variable the difference between the top tax rate and the other tax rates leads to generally consistent results.

that higher rates of stock market participation are induced by strong market performance (e.g., Griffin, Nardari, and Stulz, 2004). To this end, the specification includes (in addition to the top tax rate and the various controls discussed above) both contemporaneous and lagged changes in the P/E ratio:

$$\Delta s_{it} = \beta_0 + \beta_1(\Delta\,TOPTAX_t) + \Delta\,T_t\beta_2 + \Delta\,Z_t\beta_3 + \beta_4(\Delta PE_{t-1}) + \mu_{it}$$
(8)

where

$\Delta s_{it} = (s_{it} - s_{i,t-1})$ is the first-differenced share of corporate equity held by individuals in quintile i of the income distribution, where $i = 1, 2, \ldots, 5$. The top quintile includes individuals between the 80th and 100th percentiles; the next includes individuals between the 60th and 80th percentiles; and the remaining quintiles are defined analogously:

$\Delta\,T_t$ and $\Delta\,Z_t$ are defined as in Equation (7).

ΔPE_{t-1} is the lagged first-differenced P/E ratio.

μ_{it} is the error term (potentially subject to serial correlation and heteroskedasticity).

While data on the concentration index C_t is available from 1916, GDP data is only available from 1929.[29] In addition, there are some missing observations for C_t in the 1960s. In total, there are 68 observations over the period 1929–2000 for which all the variables have non-missing data; summary statistics calculated for this sample are reported in Table 2. However, all the regressions reported below use first differences rather than levels. First-differencing eliminates the first year of the sample, along with some additional years in the 1960s around the dates for which C_t is missing. This results in a sample of 63 years over the period 1930–2000 for which the specifications above can be estimated.

5.2. Results

The basic strategy for estimating Equation (7) and Equation (8) involves using OLS on the first-differenced variables, as reported in Tables 3 and 5.

---

[29] While this restriction reduces the sample size, it has some offsetting advantages. First, it eliminates the early period, when the reported data are arguably least reliable. Second, it excludes the episode of the WWI surtax that inspired the tax-based explanation of stock ownership dispersion developed by Means (1930); this enables a purely "out-of-sample" test of Means' hypothesis.

Table 2. *Summary Statistics*

	Mean	Standard Deviation	Number of Observations
Stock ownership concentration index	0.6266	0.0822	68
Top statutory personal tax rate	0.6595	0.2205	68
Personal tax rate at income = $500,000 (in 1999 dollars)	0.4946	0.1806	68
Personal tax rate at income = $250,000 (in 1999 dollars)	0.4003	0.1568	68
Personal tax rate at income = $100,000 (in 1999 dollars)	0.2451	0.1047	68
Personal tax rate at income = $50,000 (in 1999 dollars)	0.1618	0.0749	68
Share of corporate equity held by the top quintile	77.9846	5.8116	68
Share of corporate equity held by the second-highest quintile	8.2382	3.1612	68
Share of corporate equity held by the third-highest quintile	5.9779	1.9681	68
Share of corporate equity held by the fourth-highest quintile	4.5750	0.9998	68
Share of corporate equity held by the lowest quintile	3.1446	1.3027	68
Real GDP per capita (in thousands of 2000 dollars)	17.6321	8.4285	68
Price-earnings ratio	14.9237	5.4945	68
Dividend yield (multiplied by 100)	4.4013	1.4500	68
Corporate tax rate	0.3864	0.1266	68
Capital gains tax rate	0.2433	0.0593	68
Effective capital gains tax rate	0.2588	0.0885	68
Fraction of households filing a tax return	0.7596	0.3153	68
Income share of top 1%	13.1468	3.3396	68
Income share of top 0.1%	4.9491	1.9638	68
Income share of top 0.01%	1.8693	0.9452	68

Note: The variables are as defined in the text. Note that these summary statistics are for the 68 observations over the period 1929–2000 that are used in the regression analysis reported in Tables 3–5.

The procedure proposed by Newey and West (1987) is used to estimate standard errors that are robust to heteroskedasticity and to autocorrelation of unknown form. An alternative maximum-likelihood approach that assumes first-order autocorrelation replicates this analysis in Table 4. Within each table, a base specification is provided for the whole sample period, along

with analyses of subperiods to investigate the relevance of potentially confounding measurement issues.

The OLS results from the specification in Equation (7) are presented
in column 1 of Table 3.[30] These results indicate that increases in the top
personal tax rate have a significant negative effect on C_t, consistent with the
hypothesis from Section 3. The estimated effect of the top tax rate on stock
ownership concentration is of substantial magnitude. The coefficient on the
top tax rate in column 1 of Table 3 is approximately -0.16, so that an increase
in the top personal tax rate from its level at the end of the sample period (39.6
percent) to the highest rate observed over that period (94 percent) would
result in a fall of about 1 standard deviation in the concentration index. Of
course, this would represent a very large change in tax policy, but it should
be remembered that there is a range of 70 percentage points (24 percent to
94 percent) for the top tax rate in the sample used in the regression analysis
(and a range of 87 percentage points for the entire 1916–2000 period). Thus,
while the estimates suggest a large role for nontax factors, they also indicate
that tax policy plays an important role in determining stock ownership
concentration.

An alternative approach to estimating the model in Equation (7) involves
making more specific assumptions about the behavior of the disturbance
term, in particular that μ_t is characterized by an AR(1) process:[31]

$$\mu_t = \rho\mu_{t-1} + \varepsilon_t, \tag{9}$$

where ρ is the first-order autocorrelation parameter and the error term is
$\varepsilon_t \sim N(0, \sigma^2)$. Given the normality of ε_t, it is possible to estimate ρ and the
coefficients of Equation (7) simultaneously using maximum-likelihood esti-
mation. These estimates are presented in column 1 of Table 4. The standard
errors are calculated from the Hessian of the log-likelihood function. White's
(1980) correction is used, so the standard errors are robust to symmetric
nonnormality of the error term ε_t and to heteroskedasticity of unknown
form. The effect of the top statutory personal rate on stock ownership is

---

[30] The reported results use an autocorrelation structure with one lag, but generally consistent
results are obtained using higher lags.

[31] Note that Equation (9) applies to the residuals of the specification in Equation (7), where
the variables are first-differenced. If the model were to be specified in terms of levels,
Equation (9) entails that the residual in the levels equation would essentially follow a
random walk, modified by the autocorrelation process. The residual in year t would be a
weighted sum of the contemporaneous ε_t and all preceding ε's. This would be consistent
with the nonstationarity of the Herfindahl index in levels (as suggested by the unit root
tests discussed above).

Table 3. *Taxes and Stock Ownership Concentration: OLS Results with Newey-West Standard Errors*

Dependent Variable	Change in Stock Ownership Concentration Index		
	(1)	(2)	(3)
Constant	−0.0013	−0.0011	0.0016
	(0.0043)	(0.0045)	(0.0058)
Change in top statutory personal tax rate	−0.1617**	−0.1751	−0.2103**
	(0.0711)	(0.3620)	(0.0877)
Change in real GDP per capita	−0.0064	−0.0066	−0.0091
	(0.0090)	(0.0074)	(0.0095)
Change in price-earnings ratio	−0.0016	−0.0019*	−0.0022
	(0.0014)	(0.0011)	(0.0027)
Change in dividend yield	−0.0128	−0.0032	−0.0194
	(0.0082)	(0.0074)	(0.0136)
Change in corporate tax rate	0.0794	0.2056	0.2054
	(0.2437)	(0.3445)	(0.3509)
Change in capital gains tax rate	0.4070	−0.0334	1.1346*
	(0.2890)	(0.3870)	(0.5975)
Change in effective capital gains tax rate	−0.2221**	−0.0504	−0.5693
	(0.1088)	(0.1517)	(0.4582)
Change in fraction of filers	0.2088		0.2546
	(0.1821)		(0.1607)
Controls for changes in other personal tax rates and in top income shares?	Yes	Yes	Yes
Sample period	1929–2000	1946–2000	1929–1975
Number of observations	63	47	38
F-statistic (*p*-value in parentheses)	2.90***	4.57***	4.65***
	(0.0027)	(0.0002)	(0.0006)

Note: Newey-West standard errors, using one lag in the autocorrelation structure, are reported in parentheses.

* denotes significance at the 10 percent level, ** denotes significance at the 5 percent level, and *** denotes significance at the 1 percent level.

very similar in magnitude to that estimated in Table 3 using OLS and is unchanged in significance. The estimate of ρ indicates a significant degree of negative autocorrelation (the sign is not surprising, as the data is first-differenced). The basic results are also robust to alternative specifications of the behavior of the disturbance term – for instance, to adding a second-order autocorrelation term or a moving average term to Equation (9). Thus, the findings from this maximum-likelihood approach are highly consistent with the OLS results in Table 3.

Among the other control variables, it is worth noting that the P/E ratio has a negative effect in both Table 3 and Table 4 and is significant in the latter. This may provide some support for the notion that strong stock market performance induces higher levels of participation, thereby dispersing stock ownership.[32] The main effect emphasized above is robust to the inclusion of capital gains tax rates and a control for the response of firms through dividend policy changes. These results rely on changes in statutory tax rates as a source of exogenous variation, so it does not appear likely that the measured tax rates are endogenous with respect to the amounts of income reported. Reverse causality (from ownership concentration, and more generally from changes in the distribution of wealth, to tax rate changes) cannot be completely ruled out. This would require, however, that decreased levels of ownership concentration lead to higher tax rates on the wealthy. While it is possible that such a mechanism is operative, it seems much more reasonable that political pressure for high top tax rates is likely to be greater when ownership is more concentrated.

Given the reliance on tax return data, it is important to consider the potentially confounding nature of changes in reporting behavior. The fraction of the population filing income tax returns has a positive effect, which is significant in Table 4. It would appear that increases in this fraction have a compositional effect, introducing into the observed population of taxpayers new households that hold little if any equity. This makes equity ownership appear to become more concentrated, as happens in the data around WWII (see Table 1). While the basic results control for changes in the fraction of filers, an alternative test of robustness is to exclude the period up to 1945, when the fraction of filers was much smaller than in subsequent years. In addition, this test addresses the concern that the negative relationship between tax progressivity and ownership concentration may be driven by factors peculiar to the 1930s. The results for the 1946–2000 period are reported in column 2 of Table 3 (using OLS) and column 2 of Table 4 (using maximum likelihood estimates (MLE)). In Table 3, the coefficient of the top tax rate in column 2 is virtually identical in magnitude to that in column 1; however (perhaps due to reduced sample size), the standard error is much larger, and the effect is insignificant. In Table 4, on the other hand, the effect in column

---

[32] Of course, the result may also reflect reverse causality, with higher levels of participation leading buyers to bid up the price of stocks. Adding the lagged change in the price-earnings ratio to the model (in order to capture lags in the participation decision) does not significantly change any of the results, and the lagged term itself is insignificant. The effect of the price-earnings ratio is discussed in more detail below in the context of the results from Equation (8).

Table 4. *Taxes and Stock Ownership Concentration: Maximum-Likelihood AR(1) Results*

Dependent Variable	Change in Stock Ownership Concentration Index		
	(1)	(2)	(3)
Constant	−0.0006	−0.0061	0.0006
	(0.0028)	(0.0056)	(0.0033)
Change in top statutory personal tax rate	−0.1385**	−0.6206**	−0.1793***
	(0.0614)	(0.2905)	(0.0626)
Change in real GDP per capita	−0.0091	0.0027	(0.0119)
	(0.0069)	(0.0065)	(0.0062)
Change in price-earnings ratio	−0.0017**	−0.0024***	−0.0022
	(0.0008)	(0.0008)	(0.0014)
Change in dividend yield	−0.0104*	−0.0062	−0.0160*
	(0.0062)	(0.0055)	0.0082
Change in corporate tax rate	−0.1116	0.4984	0.0898
	(0.2061)	(0.3033)	(0.1696)
Change in capital gains tax rate	0.2157	0.0069	0.6536**
	(0.2546)	(0.2465)	(0.3252)
Change in effective capital gains tax rate	−0.1146	−0.1929	−0.2386
	(0.1039)	(0.1577)	(0.2388)
Change in fraction of filers	0.2896**		0.3959***
	(0.1292)		(0.0900)
ρ (first-order autocorrelation parameter)	−0.4270**	0.5330***	−0.6517***
	(0.2054)	(0.2024)	(0.1643)
Controls for changes in other personal tax rates and in top income shares?	Yes	Yes	Yes
Sample period	1929–2000	1946–2000	1929–1975
Number of observations	63	47	38
Wald statistic (*p*-values in parentheses)	63.91***	304.28***	258.27***
	(0.0000)	(0.0000)	(0.0000)

Note: Robust standard errors are reported in parentheses. * denotes significance at the 10 percent level, ** denotes significance at the 5 percent level, and *** denotes significance at the 1 percent level.

2 is significant.[33] The robustness of these results to controls for filing as well as this additional analysis suggest that the basic results over the 1929–2000 period are not driven by the increase in the fraction of the population filing tax returns during WWII nor by conditions specific to the 1930s.

---

[33] The magnitude is substantially larger than that in column 1, but the small sample size makes it difficult to conclude that the effect is necessarily larger over this period.

It was noted in Section 4 that the stock ownership concentration index closely tracks a measure of equity ownership based on estate tax return data until about 1975; however, the two measures diverge after that point. To test whether the results are driven by possible mismeasurement of ownership over the period after 1975, these years are omitted from the sample period. As discussed above, this exclusion also addresses several additional, possibly confounding factors. The growth of share repurchases since the early 1980s (see, e.g., Dittmar, 2000) and the growth of tax-favored investment accounts over the same period may affect the results by reducing the tax burden on equity. In addition, the concentration index may be affected by the rapid growth of Subchapter S corporations and mutual funds since the 1980s. The results for the 1929–1975 period are reported in column 3 of Table 3 (using OLS) and column 3 of Table 4 (using MLE). The results are highly robust, with the effect of the top tax rate being negative and significant, and indeed are stronger than over the entire 1929–2000 period. Restricting attention to a period when direct ownership of equity was clearly dominant (see footnote 15), when mutual funds were small and when Subchapter S activity was unimportant, only strengthens the results.

The results discussed so far show that taxes have a significant impact on the summary measure of stock ownership concentration. However, this does not in itself shed much light on which specific income groups change their holdings of corporate equity in response to tax changes. Addressing this question involves estimating Equation (8), the results from which (using OLS with Newey-West standard errors) are shown in Table 5. The analysis focuses on quintiles of the income distribution, and the results reported in columns 1–5 are ordered from the top to the bottom of the income distribution. The results here are highly consistent with a tax-based explanation. For the top quintile, there is a negative and significant effect of the top tax rate on the share of equity ownership. In contrast, this effect is positive for all the other quintiles and is significant for the second and third quintiles. The effect is positive but insignificant for the fourth quintile. Unsurprisingly, the ownership share of the lowest quintile is extremely noisy, and the regressors are jointly insignificant.

The results from Equation (8) can also be used to test the hypothesis that stronger stock market performance leads (possibly with some lag) to increased rates of participation and hence to greater dispersion of ownership. The specification in Equation (8) includes changes in both the current and lagged P/E ratios as measures of stock market performance. Generally, the effects are insignificant and vary in sign. It is worth noting that the effects of the contemporaneous P/E ratio on the shares of the top and second

Table 5. *Taxes and Stock Ownership by Income Quintiles (OLS Results with Newey-West Standard Errors)*

Dependent Variable	(1) Share of Corporate Equity Held by Top Quintile	(2) Share of Corporate Equity Held by 2nd Quintile	(3) Share of Corporate Equity Held by 3rd Quintile	(4) Share of Corporate Equity Held by 4th Quintile	(5) Share of Corporate Equity Held by Lowest Quintile
Constant	−0.0598	0.0151	−0.0061	0.0403	0.0014
	(0.2899)	(0.1536)	(0.0907)	(0.1249)	(0.0752)
Top statutory	−10.4581**	6.3099**	4.5086***	2.3652	0.2615
personal tax rate	(4.9523)	(2.8656)	(1.2802)	(1.6426)	(2.8190)
Change in real	−0.4264	0.1136	0.1800	−0.0094	0.0714
GDP per capita	(0.6072)	(0.2947)	(0.1928)	(0.2214)	(0.1437)
Change in	−0.1330	0.0702	0.0215	0.0322	−0.0185
price-earnings ratio	(0.0859)	(0.0440)	(0.0344)	(0.0280)	(0.0376)
Lagged change in	−0.0412	0.0186	−0.0007	0.0427	−0.0130
price-earnings ratio	(0.0673)	(0.0400)	(0.0231)	(0.0289)	(0.0197)
Change in	−0.9022	0.0872	0.1582	0.2679	0.1890
dividend yield	(0.5447)	(0.2771)	(0.1585)	(0.2031)	(0.1875)
Change in	0.8510	2.0745	−4.6501	−7.9491	10.4458
corporate tax rate	(17.3182)	(9.0101)	(5.2537)	(7.0603)	(8.8345)
Change in capital	25.8286	−0.2680	−14.9347**	−6.8450	−7.2466
gains tax rate	(21.6814)	(9.2005)	(6.9027)	(5.5332)	(9.8933)
Change in	−13.8747*	0.2997	7.8035	5.5314**	1.8581
effective capital gains tax rate	(7.9450)	(4.0679)	(5.3334)	(2.4007)	(3.8999)
Change in	13.5533	−4.5488	−1.9463	−0.6531	−4.2661
fraction of filers	(12.0902)	(6.3079)	(2.4370)	(4.4515)	(3.7229)
Controls for changes in other personal tax rates and in top income shares?	Yes	Yes	Yes	Yes	Yes
Sample period	1929–2000	1929–2000	1929–2000	1929–2000	1929–2000
Number of observations	63	63	63	63	63
F-statistic (p-value in parentheses)	2.79*** (0.0033)	2.15** (0.0217)	4.96*** (0.0000)	2.70*** (0.0044)	1.38 (0.1925)

Note: Newey-West standard errors, using one lag in the autocorrelation structure, are reported in parentheses.
* denotes significance at the 10 percent level, ** denotes significance at the 5 percent level, and *** denotes significance at the 1 percent level.

quintiles are negative and positive, respectively, and are close to borderline significance. In addition, the positive effect of the lagged change in the P/E ratio on the ownership share of the fourth quintile is of borderline significance. Combined with the results for the P/E ratio in Table 4, this suggests a limited role for market performance and valuation levels in determining participation.

6. Conclusion

Changes in the progressivity of the U.S. tax system during the 20th century appear to have influenced aggregate stock ownership concentration and equity market participation. These results do not appear to reflect a variety of potentially confounding measurement issues or other economic mechanisms. The logic of Berle and Means (1932), as embodied in an extension of Miller (1977), appears to help explain corporate ownership patterns throughout the century.

The finding that tax progressivity influences ownership concentration also links this chapter to the broader literature on the rationales for progressive taxes. Since Mirrlees (1971), characterizations of optimal income tax schedules that take account of incentive effects on labor supply generally find that the optimal income tax schedule is close to linear. Slemrod et al. (1994) analyze a piecewise linear two-bracket tax structure and find that, under fairly general conditions, the marginal tax rate is lower in the segment of the tax schedule applicable at higher incomes (although the optimal tax structure involves progressivity in terms of average tax rates). Thus, Slemrod (2000, p. 11) concludes: "In sum, simple models of optimal income taxation do not necessarily point to sharply progressive tax structures, even if the objective function puts relatively large weight on the welfare of less well-off individuals." Further analyses could integrate the influence of taxes on ownership concentration and equity market participation into an optimal tax framework.

Because this study only analyzes data from one country, it is not necessarily possible to extrapolate these findings to other contexts. In particular, progressive taxation should not be considered a sufficient condition for corporate ownership diffusion. Rather, tax progressivity is likely to interact with investor protections and other factors that affect agency costs. For instance, a progressive tax structure alone is not likely to lead to diffuse ownership unless investor protections are strong. Further analysis of time-series properties of ownership concentration in other countries, along with cross-country studies, could usefully illuminate such links.

The links between taxation and ownership concentration open up several further lines of inquiry. The analysis above has focused primarily on the aggregate time-series analysis of changes in the summary measure of ownership concentration. It may be possible to shed more light on the dynamics of the portfolio reallocations induced by tax changes by constructing a synthetic panel of income fractiles or by examining specific tax reforms and their effects through other data sources. This would enable a more precise specification of the tax characteristics of each fractile in any given year and reveal how each fractile's ownership patterns change in response to changes in the marginal tax rate that it faces. There are also a number of additional controls – such as measures of financial sophistication and investor protections – that could be incorporated into the analysis, especially if it were extended to a cross-country setting.

References

Auerbach, Alan J. 2002. "Taxation and Corporate Financial Policy." In A. J. Auerbach and M. Feldstein, eds., *Handbook of Public Economics*, vol. 3. (Amsterdam: Elsevier), pp. 1251–1292.

Auerbach, Alan J., and Mervyn A. King. 1983. "Taxation, Portfolio Choice, and Debt-Equity Ratios: A General Equilibrium Model." *Quarterly Journal of Economics* 98(4): 587–610.

Auerbach, Alan J., Leonard E. Burman, and Jonathan M. Siegel. 2000. "Capital Gains Taxation and Tax Avoidance: New Evidence from Panel Data." In Joel Slemrod, ed., *Does Atlas Shrug? The Economic Consequences of Taxing the Rich.* (Cambridge, MA: Harvard University Press), pp. 355–388.

Becht, Marco, and J. Bradford Delong. 2005. "Why Has There Been So Little Blockholding in the U.S.?" In Randall Morck, ed. *A History of Corporate Governance Around the World.* (Chicago: University of Chicago Press), pp. 613–666.

Berle, Adolph A., Jr., and Gardiner C. Means. 1932. *The Modern Corporation and Private Property.* (New York: Macmillan).

Brav, Alon, John R. Graham, Campbell Harvey, and Roni Michaely. 2005. "Payout Policy in the 21st Century." *Journal of Financial Economics* 77(3): 483–527.

Brown, Jeffrey R., Nellie Liang, and Scott Weisbenner. Forthcoming. "Executive Financial Incentives and Payout Policy: Firm Responses to the 2003 Dividend Tax Cut." *Journal of Finance.*

Brownlee, W. Elliot. 1996. *Federal Taxation in America: A Short History* (New York: Cambridge University Press).

Burman, Leonard E. 1999. *The Labyrinth of Capital Gains Tax Policy: A Guide for the Perplexed.* (Washington, DC: Brookings Institution Press).

Chetty, Raj, and Emmanuel Saez. 2005. "Dividend Taxes and Corporate Behavior: Evidence from the 2003 Dividend Tax Cut." *Quarterly Journal of Economics* 120(3): 791–833.

Curcuru, Stephanie, John Heaton, Deborah Lucas, and Damien Moore. 2005. "Heterogeneity and Portfolio Choice: Theory and Evidence." In Yacine Ait-Sahalia and Lars Hansen, eds., *Handbook of Financial Econometrics*. Handbooks in Finance. (New York: Elsevier/North-Holland), pp. 10–18.

Dammon, Robert M., Chester S. Spatt, and Harold H. Zhang. 2004. "Optimal Asset Location and Allocation with Taxable and Tax-Deferred Investing." *Journal of Finance* 59(3): 999–1037.

Desai, Mihir A., I. J. Alexander Dyck, and Luigi Zingales. 2004. "Theft and Taxes." NBER Working Paper 10978. (Cambridge, MA: National Bureau of Economic Research). (Forthcoming in *Journal of Financial Economics*).

Desai, Mihir A., and Dhammika Dharmapala. 2005. "Corporate Tax Avoidance and Firm Value." NBER Working Paper 11241. (Cambridge, MA: National Bureau of Economic Research).

Desai, Mihir A., and Dhammika Dharmapala. 2006. "Corporate Tax Avoidance and High Powered Incentives." *Journal of Financial Economics* 79(1): 145–179.

Dittmar, Amy K. 2000. "Why Do Firms Repurchase Stock?" *Journal of Business* 73(3): 331–355.

Elliott, Graham, Thomas Rothenberg, and James H. Stock. 1996. "Efficient Tests for an Autoregressive Unit Root." *Econometrica* 64(4): 813–836.

Fama, Eugene F., and Kenneth R. French. 2001. "Disappearing Dividends: Changing Firm Characteristics or Lower Propensity to Pay?" *Journal of Financial Economics* 60(1): 3–43.

Franks, Julian R., Colin Mayer, and Stefano Rossi. 2003. "Ownership: Evolution and Regulation." ECGI Financial Working Paper 009/2003. (Brussels: European Corporate Governance Institute).

Griffin, John M., Federico Nardari, and Rene M. Stulz. 2004. "Stock Market Trading and Market Conditions." NBER Working Paper 10719. (Cambridge, MA: National Bureau of Economic Research). Forthcoming in *Review of Financial Studies*.

Haliassos, Michael, and Carol Bertaut. 1995. "Why Do So Few Hold Stocks?" *Economic Journal* 105(432): 1110–1129.

Hong, Harrison, Jeffrey D. Kubik, and Jeremy C. Stein. 2004. "Social Interaction and Stock-Market Participation." *Journal of Finance* 59(1): 137–163.

Kakwani, Nanak C. 1977. "Applications of Lorenz Curves in Economic Analysis." *Econometrica* 45(3): 719–727.

Kopczuk, Wojciech, and Emmanuel Saez. 2004. "Top Wealth Shares in the United States, 1916–2000: Evidence from Estate Tax Returns." *National Tax Journal* 57(2, part 2): 445–487.

Kuznets, Simon. 1953. *Shares of Upper Income Groups in Income and Savings*. (New York: National Bureau of Economic Research).

La Porta, Rafael, Florencio Lopez-de-Silanes, Andrei Shleifer, and Robert W. Vishny. 1998. "Law and Finance." *Journal of Political Economy* 106(6): 1113–1155.

Lintner, John. 1956. "Distribution of Incomes of Corporations Among Dividends, Retained Earnings, and Taxes." *American Economic Review* 46(2): 97–113.

Luttrell, Kelly. 2005. "S Corporate Returns 2002." *SOI Bulletin*, Publication 1136 (Spring): 59–113.

Mallet, Bernard. 1908. "A Method of Estimating Capital Wealth from Estate Duty Statistics." *Journal of the Royal Statistical Society* 71(1): 65–101.

Means, Gardiner C. 1930. "The Diffusion of Stock Ownership in the United States." *Quarterly Journal of Economics* 44(4): 561–600.

Miller, Merton H. 1977. "Debt and Taxes." *Journal of Finance* 32(2): 261–275.

Mirrlees, James A. 1971. "An Exploration in the Theory of Optimum Income Taxation." *Review of Economic Studies* 38(114): 175–208.

Morck, Randall. 2004. "How to Eliminate Pyramidal Business Groups – The Double Taxation of Inter-Corporate Dividends and Other Incisive Uses of Tax Policy." NBER Working Paper 10944. (Cambridge, MA: National Bureau of Economic Research).

Morck, Randall, and Lloyd Steier. 2005. "The Global History of Corporate Governance – An Introduction." NBER Working Paper 11062. (Cambridge, MA: National Bureau of Economic Research).

Morck, Randall, Michael Percy, Gloria Tian, and Bernard Yeung. 2004. "The Rise and Fall of the Widely Held Firm: A History of Corporate Ownership in Canada." NBER Working Paper 10635. (Cambridge, MA: National Bureau of Economic Research).

Musgrave, Richard A. 1992. "Schumpeter's Crisis of the Tax State: An Essay in Fiscal Sociology." *Journal of Evolutionary Economics* 2(2): 89–113.

Newey, Whitney K., and Kenneth West. 1987. "A Simple Positive Semi-Definite, Heteroskedasticity and Autocorrelation Consistent Covariance Matrix." *Econometrica* 55(3): 703–708.

Perez-Gonzalez, Francisco. 2003. "Large Shareholders and Dividends: Evidence from U.S. Tax Reforms." Working paper. (New York: Columbia University).

Piketty, Thomas, and Emmanuel Saez. 2003. "Income Inequality in the United States, 1913–1998." *Quarterly Journal of Economics* 118(1): 1–39.

Poterba, James. 2001. "Taxation and Portfolio Structure: Issues and Implications." NBER Working Paper 8223. (Cambridge, MA: National Bureau of Economic Research).

Rajan, Raghuram G., and Luigi Zingales. 2003. "The Great Reversals: The Politics of Financial Development in the Twentieth Century." *Journal of Financial Economics* 69: 5–50.

Ratner, Sidney. 1942. *American Taxation: Its History as a Social Force in Democracy.* (New York: Norton).

Roe, Mark J. 1994. *Strong Managers, Weak Owners: The Political Roots of American Corporate Finance.* (Princeton, NJ: Princeton University Press).

Roe, Mark J. 2002. "Corporate Law's Limits." *Journal of Legal Studies* 31(2, part 1): 233–271.

Seligman, Edwin R. A. 1911. *The Income Tax: A Study of the History, Theory and Practice of Income Taxation at Home and Abroad.* (New York: Macmillan).

Shiller, Robert J. 1989. *Market Volatility.* (Cambridge, MA: MIT Press).

Shiller, Robert J. 2003. "From Efficient Markets Theory to Behavioral Finance." *Journal of Economic Perspectives* 17(1): 83–104.

Shoven, John B., and Clemens Sialm. 2004. "Asset Location in Tax-Deferred and Conventional Savings Accounts." *Journal of Public Economics* 88(1/2): 23–38.

Sialm, Clemens. 2003. "Tax Changes and Asset Returns: An Empirical Investigation." Working paper. (Ann Arbor, MI: University of Michigan).

Slemrod, Joel. 2000. "The Economics of Taxing the Rich." In Joel Slemrod, ed., *Does Atlas Shrug? The Economic Consequences of Taxing the Rich.* (Cambridge, MA: Harvard University Press), pp. 3–28.

Slemrod, Joel, Shlomo Yitzhaki, Joram Mayshar, and Michael Lundholm. 1994. "The Optimal Two-Bracket Linear Income Tax." *Journal of Public Economics* 53(2): 269–290.

U.S. Department of the Treasury, Internal Revenue Service. Various years. *Statistics of Income: Estate and Gift Tax Returns.* (Washington, DC: U.S. Department of the Treasury).

U.S. Department of the Treasury, Internal Revenue Service. Various years. *Statistics of Income: Individual Income Tax Returns.* (Washington, DC: U.S. Department of the Treasury).

U.S. Department of the Treasury, Internal Revenue Service. 2003. "Corporation Income Tax Brackets and Rates, 1909–2002." *Statistics of Income Bulletin* (Fall): 284–290.

Vissing-Jorgensen, Annette. 2002. "Towards an Explanation of Household Portfolio Choice Heterogeneity: Nonfinancial Income and Participation Cost Structures." NBER Working Paper 8884. (Cambridge, MA: National Bureau of Economic Research).

Warshow, H. T. 1924. "The Distribution of Corporate Ownership in the United States." *Quarterly Journal of Economics* 39(1): 15–38.

White, Halbert. 1980. "A Heteroskedasticity-Consistent Covariance Matrix Estimator and a Direct Test for Heteroskedasticity." *Econometrica* 48(4): 817–830.

Comments

Jeffrey R. Brown

University of Illinois at Urbana-Champaign and NBER

There is a large literature examining the determinants of corporate governance, both in the United States and abroad. A recent survey of work in this area (Morck and Steier, 2005) explores a wide range of factors influencing governance, including path dependence, legal system origin, wealthy families, politics, financial development, and so forth. Notably absent from this recent literature, however, is the role played by the tax system. This is somewhat puzzling given that the earliest work in this field was motivated in part by the observation that there was a diffusion of ownership during the 1916–1921 period that coincided with sharply progressive tax rate changes (Berle and Means, 1932).

The chapter by Desai, Dharmapala, and Fung steps into this void. The authors explore the role that taxes – specifically the progressivity of the individual income tax system – play in influencing individual ownership concentration and thus, by extension, corporate governance. This very well written chapter nicely summarizes the historical literature and expands our understanding of the topic by using time-series methods to document a correlation between tax rates and individual ownership concentration over most of the past century. As such, this chapter contributes to a deeper understanding of the potential ways in which tax policy can influence corporate governance.

This discussion focuses on three primary issues. First, I examine what questions are, and are not, being asked in this chapter. Second, I explore to what extent the model in this chapter adequately reflects likely behavioral responses by individuals and firms. Third, I will provide some suggestions for further extensions to what is already fairly compelling empirical work.

1. What Questions Are (and Are Not) Being Asked?

The authors' main hypothesis, that tax system progressivity influences corporate governance, can be viewed as a simple two-step process. First, they posit that increased progressivity of the tax system will lead to less concentrated individual ownership. Second, they posit that the less concentrated ownership has direct implications for the efficacy of corporate governance. The first step in this hypothesis is tested in this chapter using time-series data of tax rates and ownership concentration (as proxied by the distribution of dividend income across the tax-filing population). I will discuss both the model and the empirical estimation of this step below.

The second step in their hypothesis, that individual ownership concentration influences corporate governance, is not directly examined in this chapter. This is entirely appropriate, given that the data used in this chapter are not well suited to this task. However, it is worth noting that the implicit assumption in the chapter that aggregate individual ownership is a good proxy for the effect of ownership concentration on corporate governance may miss two potentially important considerations. First, not all individual ownership is created equal for purposes of corporate governance. Imagine two different worlds that have equal levels of individual ownership concentration. In world A, however, all individual ownership is done directly through small brokerages. In world B, all individuals own stock through ownership of mutual funds, and these mutual fund managers vote the shares. Even though the level of individual ownership concentration is identical, it is reasonable to assume that these two worlds might have very different corporate governance outcomes, at least to the extent that concentrated voting rights alter those outcomes. Yet it is not possible to distinguish between these two scenarios using aggregate ownership data.

Second, little consideration is given to the role of institutional ownership, which has also presumably undergone significant change over the past century. To the extent that institutions, such as pension funds, serve as effective "monitors" of managerial behavior, it is the evolution of overall ownership patterns – not just individual ownership patterns – that matter.

2. Modeling Tax Progressivity and Ownership Concentration

In discussing the first step of the authors' hypothesis – that tax progressivity influences ownership concentration – the authors present a model that is an extension of the Miller equilibrium. In this model, there is a continuum of investors who are distinguished by their income and thus their marginal tax rates. The investors allocate their portfolio between corporate bonds and equities. This leads to a standard "tax clientele" model in which investors with low income (and thus low marginal tax rates) hold taxable bonds while high-income (and thus high high-marginal tax rate) individuals hold tax-preferred equity.

The authors then compare two equilibria with different degrees of tax progressivity and show that, in equilibrium, increased progressivity leads to more individuals owning equity and thus more diffuse individual ownership. While the authors do not analyze the comparative statics of the model, the empirical implication of this comparison is that we should observe an inverse relation between tax progressivity and ownership concentration.

The advantage of this model is that it makes the theoretical relation between tax progressivity and ownership concentration clear and intuitive. Two limitations should be noted, however. First, on the investor side, the model does not allow investors to have both taxable and tax-preferred savings vehicles available to them. Rather than holding fewer stocks, higher-income individuals may simply shift their dividend-paying stocks into 401(k) plans. As a result, overall ownership concentration may not change, but rather investors may simply shift around the location of the assets that they already hold (e.g., see Dammon, Spatt, and Zhang, 2004). On the firm side, the model assumes a fixed distribution of dividend yields and thus rules out any dividend supply response. Yet recent research suggests that firms do adjust their dividend payout behavior in response to tax changes and that such a response is at least partially determined by the investor clientele of the firm. (Brown, Liang, and Weisbenner, forthcoming; Chetty and Saez, 2005).

3. The Empirical Results

The primary empirical result of the chapter is that various measures of tax progressivity (e.g., the top marginal rate) are negatively correlated with measures of ownership concentration (e.g., Herfindahl index). This result is interpreted as providing evidence consistent with the model's prediction that tax progressivity will lead to less concentrated ownership.

One potential limitation of the baseline specification is that the authors define the earnings quintiles based on the population of tax filers, rather than the population as a whole. While this is a reasonable approach in recent decades, during the pre-WWII era the income tax applied to a very narrow segment of the U.S. population. As noted by Piketty and Saez (2003), before 1944, due to high exemption levels, it is only possible to obtain adequate tax information on the top decile of the income distribution. Thus, the bottom decile of taxpayers in 1935 might actually represent the 90th percentile of the overall income distribution. To compare this group to the bottom decile of taxpayers in the 1990s, which reaches far down the population income distribution, is unsatisfactory. The authors do include a linear control for the fraction of households filing income tax returns, although it is not clear that this alone is sufficient to address this concern. Fortunately, in another specification, the authors limit the sample to the 1946–2000 period, which is less subject to this concern. While the OLS results lose significance, presumably due to the smaller sample size, the magnitude of the coefficient is nearly identical to that found in the full 1929–2000 sample. This specification is arguably the most important one that the authors provide, as it suggests that the results are robust not only to the change in the tax filing population, but also to alternative explanations that were unique to the macroeconomic conditions during the Great Depression.

A second issue is that the Herfindahl concentration index can sometimes behave in "unusual" ways. For example, Figure 1 shows four different distributions of stock ownership across income quintiles that all share a common Herfindahl index of 0.4. Yet one might plausibly imagine that each of these four distributions has different implications for corporate control and monitoring. To the authors' credit, they also examine an alternative measure of concentration – namely, the share of equity held by each quintile – and find results that are again consistent with their main hypothesis. In future work, it would be useful to explore an even broader range of dependent variables, such as the share of the population owning stock or the share of overall market capitalization that is owned by each income quintile.

Summary

Desai, Dharmapala, and Fung have taken the very useful first step toward reexamining the link between the tax system and corporate governance. This area offers some exciting possibilities for future research, particularly if one moves beyond time-series analysis and utilizes the rich variation in clienteles across firms over time. A richer examination will consider not only how taxes influence individual ownership decisions, but also how the tax system influences institutional ownership.

References

Berle, Adolph A., Jr., and Gardiner C. Means. 1932. *The Modern Corporation and Private Property*. (New York: Macmillan).

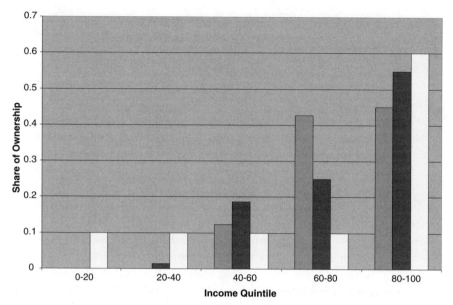

Figure 1. Three Distributions with Herfindahl $(C_t) = 0.4$

Brown, Jeffrey R., Nellie Liang, and Scott Weisbenner. Forthcoming. "Executive Financial Incentives and Payout Policy: Firm Responses to the 2003 Dividend Tax Cut." *Journal of Finance*.

Chetty, Raj, and Emmanuel Saez. 2005. "Dividend Taxes and Corporate Behavior: Evidence from the 2003 Dividend Tax Cut." *Quarterly Journal of Economics* 120(3): 791–833.

Dammon, Robert M., Chester S. Spatt, and Harold H. Zhang. 2004. "Optimal Asset Location and Allocation with Taxable and Tax-Deferred Investing." *Journal of Finance* 59(3): 999–1037.

Morck, Randall, and Lloyd Steier. 2005. "The Global History of Corporate Governance – An Introduction." NBER Working Paper 11062. (Cambridge, MA: National Bureau of Economic Research).

Piketty, Thomas, and Emmanuel Saez. 2003. "Income Inequality in the United States, 1913–1998." *Quarterly Journal of Economics* 118(1): 1–39.

Comments

Jeff Strnad

Stanford University

Desai, Dharmapala, and Fung's chapter is an important effort. Although many scholars have speculated about the impact of dividend taxes on corporate ownership patterns and the ensuing consequences for corporate governance and for the ability of investors to diversify, very little work has been done to determine what kind of link is present. As discussed in the chapter, any such effort faces significant empirical challenges. In this comment, I focus separately on empirical and normative issues.

1. Empirical Issues

I discuss three empirical issues: the use of the dividend proxy for stock ownership, the choice of control variables, and reverse causality.

Because the individual tax return data employed by the authors does not include data on stock ownership and because that data is not readily available elsewhere, the authors use dividend income reported on the tax returns as a proxy for stock ownership. The authors mention several problems with this proxy, one of which is the sharp drop-off between 1978 and 1999 in the propensity of firms to pay dividends. Fama and French (2001) document this drop-off and show that only part of it is due to a shift in market composition toward firms that tend not to pay dividends, concluding that at least half of it is due to a lower propensity to pay, holding firm characteristics (such as profitability, size, and investment opportunities) constant. During the same time period, aggregate share repurchases soared from around 3–5 percent of aggregate earnings to over 30 percent. As noted by DeAngelo, DeAngelo, and Skinner (2004), aggregate dividends did not fall during the time period but increased by about 225 percent in nominal terms. The drop in propensity to pay resulted in the concentration of dividend payments among a smaller set of firms. At the same time, one of the greatest bull markets in U.S. history

created huge returns in the form of capital gains, shifting the composition
of stock returns sharply away from dividends on a proportionate basis.
The nominal increase in the S&P 500 index from 1978 through 1999 was
about 1,650 percent, swamping the nominal aggregate increase in dividend
payments. Clearly, a fixed amount of dividend income in 1999 would tend
to proxy for much more stock ownership in 1999 than 20 years earlier for
an investor holding a diversified portfolio.

The inadequacy of dividend income to proxy for the *absolute* level of
stock ownership would not be a problem for the chapter if dividends were a
good measure of the *relative* stock ownership of parties in different income
tax brackets. The reason is straightforward: The chapter's hypothesis is that
increasing tax progressivity results in a greater diffusion of stock ownership
across income classes, and, as a result, the chapter can and does limit its
focus to *relative* stock ownership. To illustrate the "basic intuition" behind
this hypothesis, the chapter uses a Miller equilibrium model. The model has
two assets: debt, and equity that uniformly pays a fixed dividend rate. In
a Miller equilibrium, a single investor type is marginal across all assets in
the economy. In the chapter's version of the model, an increase in marginal
rates for high-income individuals results in a new, lower-income investor
type being marginal and, consequently, an economy-wide shift from debt
to equity. This shift results from the fact that investor types with marginal
rates in between the rates for the old marginal investor type and for the new
one now wish to hold only equity, while in the previous equilibrium they
preferred to hold only debt. The new equilibrium requires a supply response
by firms: issuing equity and retiring debt.

The authors admit that the model is "highly simplified," but confidently
assert that the impact of tax progressivity in the model "is likely to be quite
robust across a variety of settings in which investors form tax clienteles for
different types of assets." Among other limitations, the chapter notes that
the model does not "allow firms to respond to tax changes by adjusting their
dividend yield." Two other limitations, present in the model but clearly
absent in the real world, are important. First, the model includes only two
assets, and the equity asset has a uniform dividend yield. However, dividend yield varies sharply across equities. Some equities are very similar to
bonds, with fixed payouts that represent a high percentage rate relative to
value and no residual claim on earnings. Examples include many preferred
stocks and common stocks from industry groups, such as utilities, where
most earnings are paid out and regulation limits both upside and downside
outcomes. Other dividend-paying stocks have much lower payouts as percentage of earnings or value. Furthermore, Graham and Kumar (2006), as

well as other empirical studies, identify actual dividend clienteles motivated by both tax and non-tax goals. Second, Miller equilibria have the peculiar feature that there is a single investor type who is marginal across all assets. As elucidated by Dybvig and Ross (1986), this equilibrium is in some sense an "intermediate" outcome. If there are no legal or capital market restrictions on arbitrage, investors will be able to eliminate all of their tax liability, and in equilibrium all investors will be a single type: tax free at the margin. At the other extreme from this "black hole" result, given sufficient legal or capital market restrictions, the equilibrium will be fragmented. No investor will be marginal across all assets, although there will be some who are marginal across certain subsets of assets. Miller equilibria are "intermediate" in the sense that there are enough restrictions on arbitrage to prevent the black-hole outcome but not so many that the equilibrium becomes fragmented. The real-world evidence is consistent with a fragmented equilibrium because it indicates that different assets are priced by investors with very different tax characteristics.[1]

Once heterogeneity in dividend yields and the possibility that firms may respond to tax changes by altering payout policy are admitted to the picture, it is easy to envision a fragmented equilibrium where increased tax progressivity does not result in much, if any, greater actual diffusion of ownership, but where diffusion appears to increase substantially if one measures it using a dividend proxy, as in the chapter. Suppose, for example, that a certain set of investors is marginal across all types of stock while two other groups hold only high-dividend or low-dividend stocks respectively. An increase in marginal rates restricted to high-income individuals would tend to expand the group who held only low-dividend stocks and reduce the group who held only low dividend stocks. After the tax increase, the marginal investor group which holds both types of stocks might be composed of individuals who previously held only high-dividend stocks. But stock ownership and its diffusion would not have to change very much or at all. In equilibrium, there would need to be more low-dividend stock (and less high-dividend stock) due to the shift in the identity of the marginal investor. A shift by a sufficient number of firms from dividends to other forms of distribution would satisfy this equilibrium from the supply side without the necessity of creating

[1] A good example is the comparison between the pricing of taxable versus tax exempt bonds. Tax exempt state and local bond instruments have had significantly lower yields than equivalent taxable securities, suggesting that high-income, high-marginal rate investors are marginal for these securities. On the other hand, Green and Odegaard (1997) present strong evidence that, since 1986, U.S Treasury bonds have been priced as if the marginal investor is tax exempt.

new and more diffuse equity ownership. The dramatic increases in repurchases, the strong drop in the propensity to pay dividends (holding firm
characteristics constant), and the shift in the composition of returns toward
capital gains during the last quarter of the previous century suggest that such
an equilibrium response is possible.[2] Furthermore, note that the dividend
proxy developed in the chapter would create a false signal of greater diffusion
under this hypothetical. Ownership of high-dividend stocks would be more
concentrated among stock owners not in the highest income brackets after
the tax changes, even though there is no change in overall stock ownership in
the population. In sum, theory does not provide a strong basis for asserting
that a substantial tax progressivity effect on ownership concentration exists.
Neither does it inspire confidence in the dividend proxy as a measure of
ownership concentration.

In the face of the potentially problematic nature of the dividend proxy,
the chapter attempts to draw comfort from estate tax data used by previous
researchers, such as Kopczuk and Saez (2004), to estimate the wealth shares
of top wealth groups in the United States. Estate tax returns indicate wealth
holdings at the time of death for various wealth cohorts. Using the "estate
multiplier," essentially dividing by the probability of death, permits those
researchers to estimate the wealth holdings of the corresponding cohort
that is still alive. The chapter argues that its own Herfindahl index of equity
concentration based on dividend shares corresponds closely to the equity
series in Kopczuk and Saez, based on estate tax returns, but admits that
co-movement is restricted to the 1915–1975 period. During 1975–2000, the
two series quite distinctly move in opposite directions. See Figure 3 of the
chapter. The chapter suggests an explanation for this divergence. Gifts of
appreciated property, such as stock with substantial capital gains, result in
significant income tax benefits. A donated dollar of such gains creates a

---

[2] Bond, Devereux, and Klemm (2007) in this volume as well as the "catering theory" literature
also support the plausibility of such a response by firms. Prior to 1982, firms faced legal
barriers to large repurchases. Much of the sample period in the chapter is pre-1982. Thus,
it is worth noting that a strong firm response to shifts in investor demand for dividends
does not depend on the ability to use repurchases and can exist in a "Lintner" type of world
where the market punishes firms that reduce or eliminate dividends. In that world and
without the ability to make substantial repurchases, firms can reduce the rate at which they
initiate or increase dividends to accommodate a drop in demand for dividends. That these
policies are available is clear. Fama and French (2001) show that a reduction in dividend
initiations by firms that have never paid dividends (holding other firm characteristics fixed)
was a significant part of the reduction in propensity to pay that they observed for 1978–
1999. Julio and Ikenberry (2004) document a dramatic drop in the frequency of dividend
increases during roughly the same period.

dollar of charitable deduction that reduces ordinary income, which is subject to high tax rates. The gains themselves escape taxation entirely. The best strategy for the elderly taxpayer is to give away appreciated property while holding onto property without gains for future consumption and other purposes. The 1975–2000 period includes the 1982–2000 bull market, with resulting large, across-the-board gains on equities, making it especially attractive to dispose of them before death. But removing years, including the 1982–2000 bull market, as the chapter does by limiting one of its regressions to 1929–1975, does not address all of the potential problems with using the estate tax data as confirmation of the ownership index constructed by the authors. For instance, there is at least one long bull market during a subperiod of 1929–1975 (1949–1966), and there are motivations other than maximizing the tax benefits from charitable giving for high-wealth individuals to reduce equity holdings as they age. It also is possible to imagine market conditions where there are tax or life-cycle incentives to increase equity ownership as one ages. Although the "estate multiplier" might permit a decent estimate of cohort wealth holdings by extrapolating from the holdings of (typically) elderly decedents, the asset allocation of these decedents may be very different from the allocation of the entire cohort at any given time, and the magnitude and direction of the differences might fluctuate significantly depending on legal and market conditions. There is no reason to expect that estate tax data will yield a very accurate picture of the equity holdings of high-wealth individuals. It is not a good vehicle "[t]o test how closely the dividend series approximates actual stockholding behavior," the goal enunciated in the chapter.

A second set of problems with the empirical results involves the choice and interpretation of the control variables. Out of concern for the possibility that "firms may respond to tax changes by adjusting their payout policies," the chapter includes the change in dividend yield, "D/P," as a control variable in its regressions. The dependent variable in the regressions is the change in the ownership concentration index, and the independent variables include the changes in various tax rates. Dividend yield will be effective at reflecting payout responses to tax changes if and only if dividend yield is sensitive to shifts in the demand for dividends. Because different ownership concentrations imply different levels of demand for dividends, it is hard to exclude the possibility that changes in dividend yield also would be responsive to changes in ownership concentration itself, whether those ownership concentration changes arise from tax changes or from other sources. Thus, if the change in D/P is a good measure of payment propensity responses to tax changes, it is likely to be a fully endogenous variable because it probably will respond to changes in the dependent variable, ownership concentration. In that case, single-equation estimates (with the change in dividend yield as an independent variable), as in the chapter, would be biased and inconsistent. Alternatively, if the single-equation approach is appropriate because the dividend yield variable is exogenous, it will be so precisely because that variable is not very good at capturing the payment propensity response to tax changes, including the portion of the impact of the tax changes that arises indirectly through induced changes in ownership concentration. Failure to control for shifts in payment propensities in response to tax changes would be a serious problem because, as discussed earlier, the theoretical case for a tax progressivity effect is not very strong once these shifts become salient.

It also is questionable whether the change in D/P is an appropriate choice to control for changes in payment propensity induced by tax changes in any event. One problem is that changes in D/P conflate dividend and price changes. The chapter finds that the coefficient of changes in D/P has the expected sign but is insignificant (even at 10 percent levels) in all of the regressions where stock ownership concentration is the dependent variable. The lack of significance is not surprising, even assuming the truth of the hypothesis (implicit in the chapter's version of the Miller model) that the proportion of stock held by the wealthy would fall in response to an increase in dividend intensity. If D/P goes up due to an increase in D, the hypothesis suggests a shift out of equities by high-income individuals. However, a higher D/P also may result from a decrease in P. In this case, there may be no effect, or even a positive effect, on stock ownership by such individuals. For instance, a high D/P ratio may correlate with high interest rate environments where expected future capital gains are high relative to the present dividend yield. As a result, wealthy individuals might want to shift their asset allocation toward equities.[3] Although the chapter claims that the main results are similar (on the basis of unreported estimations) when the regressions include

---

[3] The general difficulty with using ratios such as D/P as control variables is that price reflects future expectations, making inferences from regression results difficult. This difficulty affects another control variable strategy in the chapter, the use of changes in P/E ratios to measure whether market performance and valuation levels impact participation by individuals with lower wealth. It is well known that P/E ratios do not necessarily indicate whether particular securities are bargains or are overpriced. A high P/E ratio, for instance, would result if the market expects earnings to grow rapidly in the near term, an expectation that is reasonable under many circumstances, such as the situation where the economy is at a cyclical macroeconomic bottom. In this case, the corresponding securities may be fairly priced rather than "overvalued." Again, the source of the ambiguity is that the "P" portion of the ratio reflects expectations while the other portion is a current, short-term cash flow or performance indicator.

changes in D instead of D/P, the chapter does not discuss or explain the adequacy of either of these variables by themselves to capture potential payment propensity responses to tax changes.

Another problem with the control variable strategy in the chapter is the failure to include variables that would capture alternative payout methods, such as repurchases. Including such variables would help to distinguish between environments where dividend taxes induce a shift in the form of payouts from environments where they do not. One would expect quite different impacts on the pattern of share ownership in such different environments. The chapter attempts to address this problem by running an estimation restricted to 1929–1975, excluding the 1982–2000 period, when repurchases were extensive. But, as mentioned earlier, repurchases are not the only way to adjust payouts. For instance, in a Lintner framework, which presumes a market penalty for dividend cuts, firms may delay dividend increases or engage in other timing measures to adjust payouts. Even if one does not think these alternatives are significant, it would have been interesting to see whether the regime shift due the post-1982 availability and heavy use of large repurchases affected the connection between ownership changes and tax rates. What would the results look like for a regression restricted to the 1982–2000 period or for a regression over the full period that includes repurchase variables or a post-1982 dummy?

A third difficulty, reverse causality, is discussed directly in the chapter. Because the model in the chapter takes dividend tax rates as exogenous, any association between changes in tax rates and the pattern of ownership is considered evidence that the tax rate changes have altered ownership patterns. However, the reverse causal story is hard to rule out *a priori*. As ownership becomes more concentrated, there will be more shareholders who would experience large individual benefits in absolute terms from lower-dividend taxes. Political coordination among a smaller number of interested parties with larger stakes will be easier in a Downsian sense. One might expect that a reduction in dividend tax rates would be more likely as a result. The chapter dismisses this possibility, stating that "it seems much more reasonable that political pressure for high top tax rates is likely to be greater when ownership is more concentrated." However, it is evident that the political forces that shape the tax laws are not limited to broad constituencies concerned about distribution, and, outside of the first part of the 20th century, it is not clear that there is much public concern about ownership concentration independent of distribution. More concretely, changes such as the dramatic dividend tax cut in 2003 are not easy to understand from a distributional or ownership concentration perspective. Ownership concentration (measured using the index developed in the chapter) increased

significantly during the decade preceding the 2003 cut. On the distributional side, it arguably would have been much more politically expedient
for the administration and Congress in 2003 to reduce rates for individuals
with high incomes instead of cutting dividend taxes. If the concern was the
2004 election, general rate changes probably would have had more immediate economic and political impact per dollar of revenue lost than reducing
taxes on dividends, while at the same time involving similar distributive
outcomes.

2. Normative Issues

The chapter is primarily positive, attempting to show a connection between
dividend tax rates and equity ownership patterns. At the same time, however, the chapter has its eye on potential normative implications. Three
such implications mentioned explicitly or implicitly in the chapter are of
particular interest: broader ownership increases diversification possibilities for individuals not in the top wealth cohort; ownership dispersion
is an "important element" or a "critical dimension" with respect to the
economy's "corporate governance environment"; and the "ownership society" idea – broader shareholding expands the group of individuals whose
political inclinations and psychological habits will be affected by owning
property.

Focusing on distribution, it is not clear why wide participation in stock
ownership is important in itself or why, as the chapter suggests, it would
be interesting "to integrate the influence of taxes on ownership concentration and equity market participation into an optimal tax framework."
Would a society where consumption opportunities are close to being equal
but where stock ownership is concentrated be objectionable? It may be that
broad stock ownership induces many individuals to vote more like "owners,"
but the distributional impact and normative desirability of such an effect are
not clear. In an optimal tax framework, ownership concentration variables
might have an instrumental role, indicating the impact of portfolio composition on consumption and risk for various income or wealth classes, but it
is hard to see any normative role for the level of ownership concentration
as a social objective in and of itself.

From an efficiency standpoint, increasing portfolio diversification in the
face of transaction cost or cognitive barriers might be desirable. On the
other hand, there may be big advantages to allowing large concentrated
holdings. A large long-term holder has increased incentives to monitor the
firm, while diffusion of ownership tends to weaken corporate governance

by exacerbating free-rider problems associated with monitoring. More generally, if it is easier (in a tax cost sense) to hold large positions, potential speculative profits will be higher relative to the (largely fixed) costs of gathering information, increasing the ability of entities and individuals to supply capital market discipline.

It appears, then, that it would be desirable to combine concentrated holdings with diversified returns. There are easy ways to accomplish that result, at least in theory. Consider a cash flow consumption tax on corporate earnings at the shareholder level with a 95 percent flat rate. Because this tax involves a deduction at the time of investment, large holdings would be facilitated. The government would be a nonvoting, passive co-investor fronting 95 percent of the money. At the same time, the government would receive 95 percent of all corporate earnings and could distribute these earnings widely among the populace.

In contrast, increasing dividend taxes to spur broad ownership does not appear to be a very good policy. If broad ownership drives out big holders, monitoring and capital market discipline probably will suffer. In addition, it is not clear that it is efficient to have millions of individuals go through all the costs of planning and maintaining a diversified stock portfolio.

There is another important aspect to consider. A motivated large holder can use financial engineering to combine voting power with a variety of financial positions and, at the same time, make dividend taxes largely a matter of choice. Although the exact positions required under the tax laws would be more complex, it is easy to understand how such engineering would work by considering the simple put-call parity relation: stock + put = call + bond. Suppose that an investor wished to accumulate a large position in a particular company while speculating on the upside and avoiding taxes on dividends. The investor could buy the company's stock, buy puts, and borrow. From a financial perspective, this position is equivalent to a call, thereby providing speculation on the upside. The investor would be able to vote the stock. Dividends are canceled out by investment interest both on the real side and on the tax side.[4] Using other combinations of the put-call parity relation creates other possibilities, such as: (1) obtaining voting shares without any financial risk or dividend taxes; or (2) obtaining voting shares with dividends but eliminating any other financial risk. In sum, given the current scope of financial engineering possibilities, dividend taxes arguably

---

[4] Under the current Internal Revenue Code, cancelation on the tax side would require a special election.

are irrelevant for large investors and entities that are the prime candidates to provide monitoring and capital market discipline.[5]

3. Concluding Thoughts

The chapter provides a good start for the important task of unpacking the connection between dividend taxation and corporate ownership patterns. As the chapter suggests, and as is elaborated further in this comment, anyone undertaking this task faces formidable empirical obstacles.

The chapter is broadly positive, but in any such effort, the question of normative significance lurks in the background. The pattern of corporate ownership may have important efficiency consequences, but it is not clear that manipulating the pattern of corporate ownership via dividend taxes is a good way to address normative goals involving diversification, corporate governance, or distribution. Finally, given the current scope of financial engineering possibilities, it is unlikely that dividend taxes have much impact on large players capable of serving a monitoring or capital market discipline role.

References

Bond, Stephen R., Michael P. Devereux, and Alexander Klemm. 2007. "Dissecting Dividend Decisions: Some Clues About the Effects of Dividend Taxation from Recent UK Reforms." In Alan J. Auerbach, James R. Hines Jr., and Joel Slemrod, eds., *Taxing Corporate Income in the 21st Century*. (Cambridge: Cambridge University Press), pp. 345–400.

DeAngelo, Harry, Linda DeAngelo, and Douglas J. Skinner. 2004. "Are Dividends Disappearing? Dividend Concentration and the Consolidation of Earnings." *Journal of Financial Economics* 72(3): 425–456.

Dybvig, Philip H., and Stephen A. Ross. 1986. "Tax Clienteles and Asset Pricing." *Journal of Finance* 41(3): 751–762.

---

[5] These large investors would be able to implement effective financial engineering strategies at a low cost per dollar of investment even if investment banking or special trading services are required. Smaller investors, however, would not.

The chapter refers to evidence that the broad mass of taxpayers do not fully exploit financial engineering approaches that might result in lower tax liability. On the corporate governance front, however, big players are key. It is clear that financial engineering is available and commonly employed by such parties. For example, investment banks and other financial service providers offer a variety of financially engineered programs that allow insiders with heavy appreciated stock positions to diversify without triggering capital gains taxes on the underlying positions.

Fama, Eugene F., and Kenneth R. French. 2001. "Disappearing Dividends: Changing Firm Characteristics or Lower Propensity to Pay?" *Journal of Financial Economics* 60(1): 3–43.

Graham, John R., and Alok Kumar. 2006. "Do Dividend Clienteles Exist? Evidence on Dividend Preferences of Retail Investors." *Journal of Finance* 61(3): 1305–1336.

Green, Richard C., and Bernt A. Odegaard. 1997. "Are There Tax Effects in the Relative Pricing of U.S. Government Bonds?" *Journal of Finance* 52(2): 609–633.

Julio, Brandon, and David L. Ikenberry. 2004. "Reappearing Dividends." *Journal of Applied Corporate Finance* 16(4): 89–100.

Kopczuk, Wojciech, and Emmanuel Saez. 2004. "Top Wealth Shares in the United States, 1916–2000: Evidence from Estate Tax Returns." *National Tax Journal* 57(2, part 2): 445–487.

Index